Wives and Mothers, Schoolmistresses and Scullery Maids
Working Women in Upper Canada, 1790–1840

Jane Errington argues that the role of Upper Canadian women in the overall economy of the early colonial period has been greatly undervalued by contemporary historians, and illustrates how the work they did, particularly as wives and mothers, played a significant role in the development of the colony.

Errington explores evidence of a distinctive women's culture and shows that the work women did constituted a common experience shared by Upper Canadian women. Most women in Upper Canada not only experienced the uncertainties of marriage and the potential dangers of childbirth but also took part in making sure that the needs of their families were met. How women met their numerous responsibilities differed, however. Age, location, marital status, class, and society's changing expectations of women all had a direct impact on what was expected of them, what they did, and how they did it.

Considering "women's work" within the social and historical context, Errington shows that the complexity of colonial society cannot be understood unless the roles and work of women in Upper Canada are taken into account.

ELIZABETH JANE ERRINGTON is professor of history, Royal Military College of Canada.

Wives and Mothers, Schoolmistresses and Scullery Maids

Working Women in Upper Canada, 1790–1840

ELIZABETH JANE ERRINGTON

McGill-Queen's University Press
Montreal & Kingston • London • Buffalo

© McGill-Queen's University Press 1995
ISBN 0-7735-1309-4 (cloth)
ISBN 0-7735-1310-8 (paper)

Legal deposit fourth quarter 1995
Bibliothèque nationale du Québec

Printed in Canada on acid-free paper

This book has been published with the help of a grant from the Social
Science Federation of Canada, using funds provided by the Social
Sciences and Humanities Research Council of Canada.

McGill-Queen's University Press is grateful to the Canada Council for
supporting its publishing program.

Canadian Cataloguing in Publication Data

Errington, Jane, 1951–
    Wives and mothers, schoolmistresses and scullery maids: working
    women in Upper Canada, 1790–1840
    Includes bibliographical references and index.
    ISBN 0-7735-1309-4 (bound)
    ISBN 0-7735-1310-8 (pbk.)
    1. Women – Ontario – Social conditions. 2. Women – Ontario – History –
    19th century. 3. Women – Employment – Ontario – History – 19th
    century. I. Title.
    HQ1459.O57E77   1995   305.43'009713'09034   C95-900482-3

This book was typeset by Typo Litho Composition Inc.
in 10/12 Palatino.

To ESE, AMT, and CME

Contents

Maps and Illustrations

Preface

At the end of November 1827, Mrs Julianna Fierheller, the "eldest Daughter of the Reverend *John D. Peterson*," died. "Beloved by all those who knew her," George Gurnett, the editor of the *Gore Gazette*, stated, she had left behind "a deeply afflicted Husband, and infant Son, and a long train of mourning Relatives and *Friends*." Gurnett was sensitive to the fact that "the habit of eulogizing, *indiscriminately*, departed friends, for real or supposed virtues" was "all too common at the present day," and he reassured readers that "the present brief notice" was "not exaggerated." This obituary was merely a just tribute to a woman who, though only twenty-three years old, had nonetheless made a significant contribution to her community and whose "excellent and exemplary character as a Daughter, Sister, Wife, Mother, Christian, and Neighbour, will be long cherished."[1]

Julianna Fierheller had undoubtedly never attracted such attention during her lifetime. Indeed, few women in Upper Canada ever did. Although between 1790 and 1840 almost half the population of Upper Canada was female, women's lives, their activities or their work were rarely chronicled in the public press. Only when a woman of influence, such as the wife of the presiding lieutenant-governor, stepped onto the public stage did local newspapers briefly divert their attention from international or local news. It is easy to overlook mention of women even in the short reports from the courts or the notices of Upper Canadians looking for work or advertising their businesses.

It was only in the obituary section of individual newspapers that women's names appeared almost as frequently as men's. But even here, the highly stylized and almost ritualistic acknowledgments of a woman's death presented an incomplete and often distorted picture of her life. A woman deemed worthy of special notice – the wife of a local luminary or politician – was almost always characterized as having been a "virtuous and affectionate wife" and "kind and indulgent mother." She was portrayed as having been "so conspicuous in her social intercourse of life" that she had "never failed of securing, not only the most prominent attachment and respect of those who ranked in the circle of so desirable an acquaintance, but of all who can view with admiration the practice of the noblest virtues of our neighbours."[2] Kindness, simplicity of manners, Christian commitment, intelligence, industry, frugality, goodness, and generosity to the "distressed" – these were the qualities that leading Upper Canadians obviously cherished in their women.

Colonial contemporaries probably read such notices with a certain degree of scepticism, and perhaps some envy. The litany extolling prominent women's lives described a world and lifestyle unknown to "ordinary" women of Upper Canada. Mrs McGill, for example, who had apparently "possessed the benevolent and amiable qualities" of her sex in "an eminent degree," could afford to cultivate the "womanly" virtues.[3] She had obviously lived in a big house and had probably had servants to do her bidding. But Upper Canadians would also have understood that in certain fundamental ways, Mrs McGill's life had been little different from their own. She too had been a daughter, wife, and mother; she had shared many of the delights and inevitable uncertainties that came with marriage; and she had had to cope with the same impediments that confronted all women in the colony. But no one would have denied that the very presence of such a eulogy set such women apart from most others in the colony. Julianna Fierheller and Mrs McGill were clearly more than just wives and mothers. And their deaths had provided colonial leaders with an opportunity to use their lives as object lessons to all Upper Canadians.

For encoded in the eulogy was a message about the "good woman" of Upper Canada. She lived and worked in the private world of her home; her life revolved around her husband and her children. It was only fitting, her admirers implied, that the lifetime work of such a good woman had been not "so much known abroad and in the bustle as [it had been] ... valued in private."[4] According to the obituaries, being "a tender wife, an affectionate parent and a steady and sincere friend" was the most important contribution that a woman could make to her community.[5] Julianna Fierheller, Mrs McGill, and others of their rank were important social and moral symbols of "true" womanhood; to colonial leaders, they represented one of the essential components of the new society that was to be established in Upper Canada.

Historians have often dismissed the ritual obituary as artificial and facile. At the same time, somewhat ironically many seem to have accepted, if only unconsciously, that the image of Upper Canadian womanhood presented in the eulogies was the essential reality of all colonial women's lives. As a result, not only have historians failed to break the code of the obituary but in many instances scholars have failed to realize that there was a code at all. Instead, such obituaries have been allowed to mask the complexity of colonial women's (and I would argue men's) daily and life experiences. And they permit historians to discount the very real contribution that women made to Upper Canadian development.

Women are markedly absent from most accounts of Upper Canadian life and development.[6] This is perhaps not surprising given the priorities and interests of most Canadian historians. Until recently, many scholars have considered the history of Upper Canada only as it relates to the development of the industrial, democratic nation-state of Canada of the late nineteenth and twentieth centuries. Studies of the colony have therefore tended to concentrate on its "great" men and momentous events, on the broad economic and social developments of the pre-Confederation period, or on how the "inevitable" coming of industrialization affected workers', and almost always men's, lives.[7] As colonial women did not vote, take any part in politics, help to build the canals, regularly work on the shop floor, or usually engage in other "productive" activities, some scholars seem to have concluded that by default they must have lived in quite a "separate" world from men. Indeed, at times, the reader is often left to wonder if there were really any women in the colony at all.[8]

A related, although I would argue, more significant factor in our lack of consideration of the lives of Upper Canadian women is the unspoken belief of some that, then as now, what has traditionally been considered "women's work" had little or no redeeming social or economic value. Women were, after all, dependent on their husbands for their homes, their positions in society, and in some cases, their very survival. Their absence from many modern histories of the period confirms the view that being a wife, a mother, a neighbour, and a Christian did not materially aid the development of the colony. Moreover, it is implicitly asserted that women were merely fulfilling their biological destiny when they became wives and mothers. Their labour in this realm was therefore not really work but rather, a "natural" activity that required no special skill and (many seem to presume) took little effort.

The following study explicitly challenges such assumptions. It attempts to break the code of the ritualized eulogies and to begin a discussion about the lives of women in Upper Canada between 1790 and 1840 by examining the work they performed. It presumes that in order to do this, we must first consider Upper Canada in its own terms and as those who lived there viewed it. Further, this study accepts that the virtues and the work that colonial eulogies extolled were valued in the pre-industrial society of Upper Canada. Residents knew that being a wife, a mother, and a good neighbour was important work. The following discussion also recognizes that women's lives and the work they performed included a wide range of activities that varied, often considerably, depending on their financial, social, and marital status.

To do this, we must first make invisible women visible.[9] We must accept that by their very presence the female half of the population helped to give shape and substance to their communities. Perhaps most importantly, we must try to hear the voices of the women themselves, which sometimes in harmony, but often in counterpoint, echoed the complexity of life and experience shared by all in the colony.[10]

A few historians have already begun this task. Recent biographies of Elizabeth Simcoe, Anne Powell, Catharine Parr Traill, and Susanna Moodie have added immeasurably to our understanding of the experiences of a few of the "important" women of the colony.[11] Such work is to be encouraged and must continue. But what has sometimes been termed "compensatory" history can and does create its own problems. Like the histories of "great" men, stories of prominent women often present a distorted view of their subjects and where they lived. Not only were such women usually exceptional but many biographers have, inadvertently or by design, concentrated on aspects of their lives that set them apart from their colonial sisters. Only a few have attempted to write a biography that reflects the totality of these women's experiences and tries to place them in their own time and place.[12]

The preference for writing about prominent women arises in part because of the "problem of sources." Most women in Upper Canada did not have either the ability or the time to keep a journal or maintain an extensive correspondence. Those manuscript records that have survived tend to have been written by relatively affluent, exceptional individuals, or, like those of Traill and Moodie, were from the beginning written for publication. The sources traditionally relied on by social and economic historians – land records, tax rolls, census data, and the like – also do not appear to chronicle women's lives. Most women did not own land, pay taxes, or run successful businesses. In short, Upper Canadian women seem to have no voice.

The *apparent* problem of sources is compounded by the historical profession's rather traditional definition of "work."[13] The writing about women's work in Canada and elsewhere has been driven to a large degree by contemporary concerns of and about women in the modern workforce. Not surprisingly, scholars have concentrated on women's experiences in what is often termed "productive" labour, or that work for which women, and of course men, received a wage or other tangible goods. But as Angela John points out, such terms of reference hide more than they illuminate. "Many of the categories used to define and describe employment ... are inadequate, inappropriate and sometimes misleading when applied to women's experiences." Women in Upper Canada, like their sisters in Great Britain and the United States, "frequently slipped in and out of" what is usually accepted as "productive" work and their wage work was often invisible.[14] Certainly, there were women in the colony in the first half of the nineteenth century who, at some time in their lives, went "out to work" for wages, produced goods for the marketplace, or ran shops and small businesses. Their numbers are, however, relatively small (although they were undoubtedly greater than has been previously assumed). More to the point, such women and such work cannot be said to be representative of the majority of Upper Canadian women or to reflect the totality of women's labouring activities.

Assessing women's work using a definition that presumes payment of services and well-defined, formal tasks only perpetuates stereotypes of colonial women. More important, it also devalues the real work that women in Upper Canada (and I would argue, women of other times and in other places) performed. As Louise Tilly and Joan Scott, Mary Ryan, and a growing number of British and American historians have so ably chronicled, in pre-industrial communities like Upper Canada, women, work, and family must be seen as inseparable categories.[15] Narrow categories of "productive" and "reproductive" labour must be replaced by new definitions of work that take into account not only paid and unpaid labour but also the impact that place and conditions of work, its purpose, and the expectations of those involved had on a worker's activities. In short, the eulogies of prominent colonial women must be taken as both a reflection of colonial leaders' aspirations for the colony and at least a partial statement about what women actually did.

This study of the nature of women's work in Upper Canada is a preliminary probe into what at least some colonial women considered their work to be, by describing and analysing what they did.

Part One considers the all-important women's world of "reproduction." Marriage and motherhood were the two central events in most
colonial women's emotional and physical lives: they defined whom
she was, where she lived, and what she did. Marriage and motherhood also provided the context within which and from which almost
all of women's other work was performed. For, as Parts Two and
Three illustrate, much of women's domestic work – keeping her
house and family clean, ensuring that the members of the household
were fed and clothed, and fulfilling the various responsibilities of
companion/consort for their husbands, was physically done in and
around the home.

But as the following tries to make clear, what was involved in ac-
complishing this work depended on where a woman lived, and the
financial resources and composition of her household. It would also
be a mistake to suggest that women in Upper Canada worked alone
or were isolated within the confines of their individual households or
businesses. As women themselves realized, they needed the help of
other women to successfully fulfil their roles as wives and mothers.
Parts Two and Three therefore consider the lives and work of women
alone, and in community with others within two broadly defined
types of households – the farm/artisan household, and that of the
"big" house of more affluent Upper Canadians.

Of course, not all women either lived on the farm or worked in the
big house. As Part Four illustrates, despite the rhetoric of domesticity
and the assumption that women should work in the home, a number
of women, particularly those in towns and villages, either were
obliged because of family responsibilities or chose to start their own
small businesses. But, as emphasized throughout this volume, these
women too were part of an often complex community of women. The
lives of female merchants and proprietors often intersected with
those of women who lived in the big house and on a nearby farm.
Moreover, such women shared many of the concerns and experiences
that preoccupied non-income earning women.

I realize that the categories of work set out in the following discussion are themselves artificial and in some ways oversimplify the story
of women's work. The various groupings of women who are identified here primarily by their roles or by "occupation" inevitably have
within them wide variations as to lifestyle and expectations. Moreover, women in Upper Canada simultaneously assumed a number of
the roles and were involved in more than one household. It must also
be noted that certain groups of women are notably absent from this
discussion. Although working in the colony, and at times part of the
community of women, Native and Afro-Canadian women have not

been considered here at all. And no attempt has been made to consider the lives of those women who were attached to the local garrisons. The specific impact that race, ethnicity, religious belief and affiliation had on women's work and their own expectations has also received only cursory attention.[16] In short, although this study considers some of the fundamental factors that shaped many women's lives and work in Upper Canada, it is by no means complete. Our understanding of colonial women's lives and the complex, often interdependent world of women's work is only just beginning.

I BEGAN this project a number of years ago with the assumption that I would be able to complete a *general* history of women in Upper Canada in three or four years. I was soon overwhelmed, however, by the complexity of women's lives and a wealth of sources. The question of colonial women's changing legal status and the often sharp dichotomy between the law and the manner in which women and men actually conducted their lives has become a study unto itself. So too is trying to understand and appreciate the varied experiences of women as immigrants. Even after I had narrowed down my original topic to what seemed a more manageable study of women's work in the colony, I was confronted with the realization that there was far more to be explored than could possibly be accomplished within one volume.

What began as an intriguing academic endeavour quickly became a very personal pursuit. As I worked through the documents and then tried to recreate the world of work of Upper Canadian women, I was continually struck by how much has *not* changed. Certainly, life in the late twentieth century is better for many women than that at the beginning of the nineteenth. Scientific "breakthroughs" have given many women choice as to whether or when they will become mothers. Better nutrition and medical intervention have significantly increased our life expectancy and that of our children and husbands. Today, it is hard to ignore women in the public workplace. We vote; we own land and run businesses; and, increasingly, we voice our concerns about our own circumstances and those of others. But what I found startling is how much of the rhetoric of the nineteenth century continues to resonate in the contemporary world. Although it is now expected that women will go "out to work" and find fulfilment in business, it is still largely women's work to keep their homes clean, to care for children, and to look after their husbands. "Progress" has not resolved the dilemma faced by battered wives and it has not assured many women equality in their places of work or their homes. Indeed, my continuing fascination with this topic arises in large part because many of the difficulties confronting women today had their roots in our colonial past. Even more intriguing is that so much of what "my" women of Upper Canada did and so many of the concerns they expressed continue to be echoed a century later by my female friends and even by myself. In the end, this study has reaffirmed my own sense of womanhood and of the connections that bind women together. Perhaps most importantly, it has made me doubly aware of how important women friends, colleagues, and family members are in my life.

This project would not have been possible without the support of many individuals and organizations. I would like to acknowledge the support that the Social Science and Humanities Research Council of Canada gave to this project, in the form of a strategic grant for women and work, and the financial assistance that I received from my university, the Royal Military College of Canada (RMC). The publication of this book was made possible by a grant from the Social Science Federation of Canada.

More important on a personal level was the encouragement and help I received from colleagues and friends. The librarians and archivists at Queen's University, RMC, and the Ontario Archives uncomplainingly gave me their time and expertise. My colleagues at RMC and particularly members of the History Department willingly listened to my periodic frustrations and actively encouraged my work. A number of students patiently went through boxes of microfilm, checked footnotes, tracked down references, and generally provided their time and considerable enthusiasm to the project. Thank you Laura Haycock, Jessica Hamilton, Greg Kennedy, Emily Christie, Michelle Lyons, Megan Armstrong, Anne MacPherson, and Andrew Kirk. I would also like to thank Karen Brown and Cynthia Gentles for helping with the seemingly neverending task of putting material on to disk and checking that which I already had there. And the painstaking work of copyeditor Victoria Grant has materially improved the final product.

Once the writing began, others helped me to formulate my ideas and sharpen my conclusions, realizing always, of course, that any shortcomings of this work are mine alone. To George Rawlyk, a longtime friend and colleague, my heartfelt thanks for comments on an earlier draft of the manuscript and his quiet encouragement. Donald Akenson's support as friend and editor has been invaluable. Roberta Hamilton contributed to the completion of this book in more ways than I think even she realized. Her perceptive suggestions on an earlier version of the manuscript added immeasurably to my understanding of my subject. More important, however, she is a treasured friend whose support and enthusiasm was and continues to be invigorating and comforting.

My thanks also go to other members of my own community of women and men friends who listened to my woes and delighted in the small triumphs. These include the farm folk and particularly Kate Benidickson, the Banfield family – Mary Alice Paul, Emma, and Lucy – and Nancy MacMahon and James De Jonge. Members of the Ontario Women's History Network helped me to maintain my connections to women's scholarship and friendship. And although most I have never met, I am indebted to all those women scholars, many of whom are cited in the following pages, who have written so eloquently about the experiences of other women.

My biggest debt, however, is to members of my own family. This book is dedicated to the three women who inadvertently provided the inspiration for this book and who, during their lifetime and even now, continue to have a significant influence on who I am and how I approach the world – my grandmothers, Agnes Myles Tusting and Clela Margaret Ellis and especially my mother, Elizabeth Stewart Errington. I was fortunate in that not only did I know them as my mother and my grandmothers, but in my adulthood, each, in her own way became a valued friend, supporter, and mentor. These three very different but equally remarkable women showed me, through their actions and their words, the importance of friends and family. They taught me that alone, but also in concert, individuals and particularly women can have a remarkable impact on those around them. Collectively, they bequeathed me their strength and, I hope, their tolerance. Each of these women was, like women in Upper Canada, a wife, mother, sister, and friend, and I continue to be astounded and delighted by their ingenuity and ability in coping with all that this entailed. As a daughter and friend, I miss their strength, their generosity, their humour, and their support. In a small way, I reaffirm my connection to these three women by reclaiming my first name, which was also my mother's. And I only wish that she, who was so interested throughout the early stages of the writing of this book, could now see the final product.

I would like to conclude with a very special thanks to another, equally important member of my family. My father, William Errington, also values family and friendship. And it is because of his ongoing encouragement and support that this book is finally finished.

Wives and Mothers, Schoolmistresses and Scullery Maids

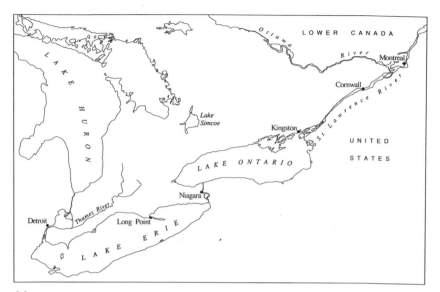

Map 1
Upper Canada, 1794
(Victor Dohar)

1 Prologue: The Howling Wilderness and Fruitful Fields

In the spring of 1792, Elizabeth Simcoe, wife of the newly appointed lieutenant-governor of Upper Canada, anticipated her journey from Quebec to the upper province with considerable eagerness. "I quite enjoy the thoughts of the long journey we have before us and the perpetual change of scene it will afford," she wrote in her diary in March.[1] Elizabeth was somewhat concerned, however, that her winter at Quebec had "been a very bad prelude to going into the Upper Country." Friends had warned her that Upper Canada was a lonely wilderness, without amenities or any "society." Elizabeth was not deterred, although she did acknowledge that "I should have been fitter a great deal for solitude and enjoy it more coming from Black Down [her home in Devon] than after spending six months in the midst of Balls, Concerts, assemblies and Card Parties every night."[2]

She need not have worried. Although in 1792, Upper Canada had only between 5,000 and 6,000 European residents, in the garrison communities of Kingston, Niagara, and Detroit loyalists, merchants, and a few hundred settlers from the United States had already established what to Elizabeth seemed "a pleasant society within a certain circle."[3] Throughout her four years in the colony, Elizabeth's time was taken up with entertaining guests, attending balls and formal dinners, giving and going to tea and card parties, and generally looking after all those official duties incumbent upon the wife of the lieutenant-governor. In fact, it was not until June 1793, after she had been in the colony for a year, that she and her husband managed to dine

Illustration 1
Portrait of Elizabeth Posthuma Simcoe
from a watercolor by friend Mary Anne Burgess
Picture Collection, MTL (T30840)

alone "for the *first time* since we left Quebec ... We enjoyed the half holiday amazingly," she recorded in her diary.[4]

Upper Canada provided Elizabeth Simcoe with a unique opportunity for adventure. She and her growing family lived and entertained foreign dignitaries in tents.[5] Elizabeth delighted in taking her meals outdoors and welcomed all opportunities to explore the colony on horseback, on foot, and by canoe. She was always careful to maintain the trappings of gentility suitable to her position and her husband's position, however. She also took advantage of the privileges of rank. As wife of the lieutenant-governor, she had servants or British soldiers from the garrison to cook, clean, and look after many of the mundane necessities of housekeeping. The Simcoe entourage included a nurse to cope with the children and a maid for Elizabeth.

Moreover, she was aware from the outset that her residence in Upper Canada was but a brief interlude. At the end of her husband's tenure of office, she would return to her family home in Devon and to the life of an English country gentlewoman.

The vast majority of American and European women who came to Upper Canada after 1784 could not share the lifestyle or the experiences so enjoyed by Elizabeth Simcoe. Loyalist women and men were refugees who had been forced to abandon their homes, their cherished possessions, and in some cases, members of their family when they had fled north to the "complete wilderness" of Upper Canada.[6] Most women had little choice but to accompany their husbands or fathers in their quest for security and opportunity on the British frontier. Families usually arrived in the colony lacking money and carrying only a few possessions. Initially, they had no home to go to and no servants to help ease the transition. And most Upper Canadians knew that there was no going back. What one traveller described as "a country yet to be formed" was their new home.[7]

When Samuel Ryerse, a loyalist, decided in early 1794 to leave New York City for the wilds of Upper Canada, his wife, Margaret, at first resisted.[8] The family had just returned to the United States after four unsatisfactory years as refugees in New Brunswick and Mrs Ryerse preferred enduring "the raucous bitter feelings" against former loyalists that were so upsetting her husband to the upheaval of yet another move. It was only the unhealthy conditions of the city, which had claimed the lives of seven of her eight children, that finally convinced Margaret to "consent" to her husband's proposal.[9]

The Ryerse family arrived in Niagara later that year. After a brief time in the colonial capital, Margaret and her eighteen-month-old son moved up-country and stayed with the Troyers, a "kind, good [German] family" in their "miserable log House or rather Hut" while Samuel and his older son searched for suitable land and began to build the family a home. Mrs Ryerse waited three weeks for their return. Then, frantic with worry, she gathered her son and began to search for them. "After a weary day's paddle along the coast, they [Mrs Ryerse and Mike Troyer] saw a blue smoak curling above the trees" and Samuel lying in a rough lean-to recovering from the fever. It was only after "a party of pedestrians," themselves "on the lookout for Land" passed by that "the wished for log house" was built. Amelia Ryerse Harris, born a few years later, recounted that "on Removing from the Shanty ... my mother felt as if [it was] a Palace. They bought a cow from Mrs Troyer and collected their goods and when cold weather set in, they were tolerably comfortable."[10]

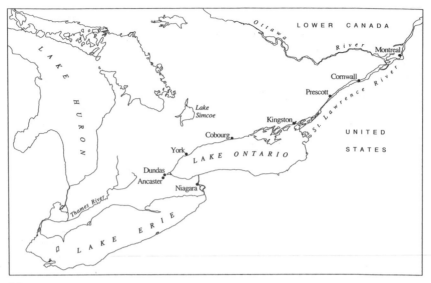

Map 2
Upper Canada, 1815
(Victor Dohar)

It was many years before the Ryerses and the thousands of other pioneering families in Upper Canada had the time, the inclination, or the financial resources to hire a personal or children's maid or to entertain formally. In the beginning, most were preoccupied with the need to build homes and begin the back-breaking work of providing for their families. Gradually, settlement increased and the demands imposed by the frontier on the earliest European arrivals dissipated. By 1840, Upper Canada had a population of about 425,000.[11] While new lands were being opened up in the interior, plots of land once covered by trees and rocks had been transformed "into fruitful country."[12] The older commercial centres of Upper Canada were almost unrecognizable and well-travelled roads linked them to dozens of new towns and villages that had sprung up "as if by enchantment."[13]

Even in 1840, however, few women enjoyed the lifestyle or opportunities that had been available to Elizabeth Simcoe. Most women continued to live on the land. And as the colony had matured, the differences among various socio-economic groups, and therefore among women's daily lives, had widened. Despite this, Elizabeth Simcoe and Margaret Ryerse would have found the experiences of women living in the colony in 1840 familiar. Like almost all other women, Elizabeth and Margaret were politically and legally subordinate to their

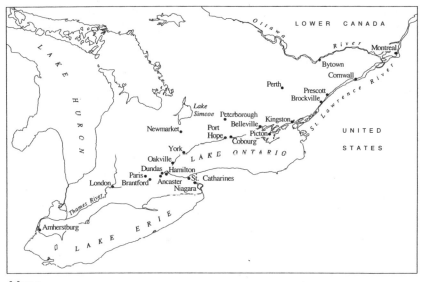

Map 3
Upper Canada, 1835
(Victor Dohar)

husbands, fathers, and other men in the colony. Moreover, throughout the first half of the nineteenth century, most Upper Canadian women were wives and mothers; they shared the uncertainties of motherhood, the responsibilities of running a home, and the work of looking after their families. Not surprisingly, their experience and their sense of whom they were was largely defined by their relationships to their families. It was the intersection of these various factors – their sex, where they lived, the economic and social circumstances of their families and, to some degree, when they arrived in the colony – that gave shape to women's lives, and determined the nature of their work.

BETWEEN 1790 AND 1840, Upper Canada was predominately a rural community and residents' lives were dictated by the need to clear the land and by the seasonal rhythms of planting, tending, harvesting, and marketing their crops.[14] As soon as Mrs and Cpt Ryerse and their two sons moved from their "Indian" style shanty into their log house, Samuel "succeeded in hiring 5 or 6 men for as many months ... to get some land cleared so that they could plant maize, potatoes and garden vegetables for their next year's consumption."[15] During the first few years on the farm, Cpt Ryerse and other settlers cleared as much of their land as possible, perhaps between four and seven acres annually. The rate of clearing then usually decreased as households devoted more of their time to planting and harvesting crops, tending livestock, and maintaining and augmenting outbuildings. Eventually, the most successful farmers such as the Ryerses were managing to produce a surplus that they sold at local markets.[16] Yet, even for the Ryerses, who had sufficient capital and income from the captain's half-pay to hire help and buy certain goods and supplies, farming was never "a life of ease."[17]

Initially, most Upper Canadian farmers coped without the benefit of roads, close neighbours, shops, or even a mill.[18] Amelia Ryerse Harris remembered that a year after her parents arrived in Upper Canada, "Long Point [where they had taken up land] now boasted four inhabitants in 20 miles, all settled on the Lake Shore." Their nearest neighbour, Peter Walker, who lived "at the mouth of Patterson's Creek was three miles distance by water, 6 by Land."[19] Pioneering, and then farming, in Upper Canada was, by necessity, a family affair. To meet the physical conditions of the frontier and the ongoing demands of working the soil, Upper Canadians were forced to rely on "a corporate family economy, a domestic system of production that bound family members together, like a single body, in a common enterprise of subsistence."[20] Work was usually divided by gender and age. Men hunted, worked the fields, and tended to the heavy outdoor chores. Farm women kept the home, raised the children, and provided the food and clothing needed for daily subsistence. As soon as they were old and big enough, children helped their parents. In short, all members of the household, except the very young and the infirm, had to contribute what they could to ensure the survival and wellbeing of their family.

Yet, even in the earliest years, the isolation of the Upper Canadian backwoods was never absolute. Passing travellers, peddlers, and itinerant preachers provided farm households with news, advice, and companionship. When many hands were needed – to raise a barn, chop, husk corn, quilt, or harvest – the Ryerses and other farm families turned to their neighbours, who were often separated by miles of bush, for assistance. The traditional bee, or frolic, provided both a means of corporate labour and an occasion to socialize. As late as 1832, Catharine Parr Traill, an English gentlewoman who had recently arrived with her husband to settle north of Peterborough, commented that the bee continued to be "highly useful and almost indispensable to new settlers in the remote townships, where the price of labour is proportionately high and workmen difficult to be procured."[21]

As historian Mary Ryan noted in her study of Oneida County, "a frontier is by definition temporary, doomed to extinction probably

within the space of a generation."[22] Within a generation of their arrival, many loyalist and American settlers of the 1790s were working
prosperous farms. Many of "the original log houses" or shanties had
been replaced by "good frame buildings," each with a barn, a large
garden, and perhaps a hen house and other outbuildings.[23]

Rural development in Upper Canada was uneven, however. Travelling between Glengarry and Prescott almost thirty years after Elizabeth Simcoe had first made the trip, British traveller John Howison
passed through sixty miles of "half cultivated fields, log houses and
extensive forests." He observed that, in contrast, the Niagara region
was "thickly populated" with "many cleared spots and cultivated
fields."[24] Moreover, as land along the north shore of the St Lawrence
and Lake Ontario, and particularly in the vicinity of Kingston, Niagara, and York was settled, new land was being opened up and the
pioneering cycle was re-enacted. Second- and third-generation Upper
Canadians moved frequently in search of better lands or new opportunities.[25] After the War of 1812, hundreds of British immigrants also
made their way into the expanding Upper Canadian frontier.[26]

When Catharine Parr Traill and her husband Thomas arrived in
Upper Canada in the summer of 1832 to take up land in the Ottona-
bee District, their journey to their new home traced the history of
colonial development. After brief stops at Montreal to disembark
from the ocean-going *The Laurel* at Lachine to enable Catharine to
recuperate from a bout of cholera, and then at the regular stations
on the St Lawrence, the Traills arrived in Cobourg, the jumping-off
point for their trek to the interior. After two days in what Catharine
described as a "neatly built and flourishing village surrounded by
open fields, pleasant farms and fine flourishing orchards," the
Traills set out in a light wagon for Peterborough. Initially, they encountered "very few specimens of the old log house and shanty,"
Catharine reported to her mother. In fact, on the plains north of Cobourg, "there were several settlers ... possessing considerable
farms" and most of the homes were "very good [with] neat fences."
Once they arrived in Peterborough, where Thomas Traill bought
lakefront property in upper Douro, it was evident that the wilderness was not too distant, however. In mid-October, the couple set
out to meet Catharine's brother, Samuel Strickland, who had emigrated to the area some years before. This last leg of their journey
took them into the heart of the frontier. The road "encumbered by
fallen trees and interrupted by cedar swamps" was increasingly difficult for the wagon and horses to navigate. The Traills only reached
their destination after a long, lonely day travelling hesitantly along
a blazed trail. "It was dark ... when we suddenly emerged from the

Illustration 2
Portrait of Catharine Parr Traill
AO (S2154)

depth of the gloomy forest to the shores of a beautiful lake," Catharine wrote. Despite their careful arrangements, there was no one to meet them and "I sat in anxious expectation," she remembered, waiting for her brother to arrive. "We could see no sign of habitation ... no gleam of light from the shore to greet us." Finally, after some considerable confusion, Samuel appeared and took them across the lake to his home.[27]

Catharine Traill and a number of other British emigrants had certain advantages that many new arrivals to the colony did not share. Catharine was "not ... obliged to go at once into the rude shanty" but stayed with the Stricklands until her own log cabin was "habitable" and a small piece of land cleared.[28] When Frances Stewart and her husband and three children arrived from Ireland in 1822, they stayed with the Henrys, a Cobourg family, before proceeding on to their uncleared farm near Douro Township.[29] Englishwoman Mary Gapper, who came to the colony in 1828 with her mother and her brother Anthony to visit two other brothers who lived on relatively well-established farms about ten miles north of York, had almost eighteen months to acclimatize herself to rural conditions before she married Edward O'Brien and moved to a partially cleared farm.[30] When Anne Langton came to Upper Canada with her parents and aunt in 1828, she and her family moved into her brother John's new, two-storey house on a rapidly developing farm near Sturgeon Lake.[31]

Susanna Moodie, Catharine's sister, who had arrived in the colony with her husband Dunbar, her daughter, and a young maid just prior to the Traills, was not quite so fortunate. For a time, she lived in what she at first thought was a cattle-shed or pig-stye, situated "in a rocky upland clearing ... surrounded on all sides by dark forest." When the Moodies moved into a log house some months later, it was infested with mice and for Susanna, was only a marginal improvement over her first home.[32]

British gentlewomen immigrants often commented on the difficulties they experienced living in the "wilderness."[33] Yet even Susanna Moodie's situation was more attractive than that which at least many emigrants had to endure. She had a home to go to. As will be discussed later, she also had distinct economic advantages over most of her neighbours. Relative affluence never completely negated the circumstances of her new home, however. In the end, many gentlewomen immigrants were also farmers' wives. They soon discovered that their lives in rural Upper Canada were not at all what they had been at "home." In a number of important ways, their lives were also quite different than that of those women who had settled in one of Upper Canada's growing towns and villages.

Whether living on an only partially cleared lot or on a well-established, productive property, colonial farm women were actively involved in producing goods and services for their households. They cooked, cleaned, mended, and coped with seemingly endless household chores. They also usually kept a garden and periodically helped in the barn and the fields. Certainly, the lives of such farm women, like almost all women at the time, were also dictated by the cycles of pregnancy, childbirth, and lactation. But, although their daily routines closely resembled those of some of their urban sisters, the comparative isolation of rural life together with meeting the demands of the land meant that in many important respects, their life on the farm was unique.

WHEN ELIZABETH SIMCOE and Margaret Ryerse came to the colony, Upper Canada boasted only three real centres of settlement – Kingston, Niagara, and Detroit. And only Detroit, which was relinquished to the United States in 1794, was a community of any size and sophistication.[34] When Ann Kirby Macaulay, wife of loyalist and merchant

Robert Macaulay, had arrived in the village as a new bride in 1791, the small town situated in the shadow of the local garrison had only "fifty wooden Houses and Merchant Store Houses."[35] It was nonetheless the principal settlement in the eastern half of the colony. Moreover, its location, at the junction of the St Lawrence River and Lake Ontario, ensured that as the major transhipment point for all goods coming into and going out of the province, Kingston was already "a place of considerable trade."[36]

In 1792, Lieutenant-Governor Simcoe chose, however, to make Niagara the provisional capital of the colony and, as a result, the small village in the western portion of the province briefly experienced "a rapid rise" in population and prosperity. By the time Elizabeth Russell arrived in Niagara in 1794 with her brother Peter, who was a member of the new executive council and would, by the end of the century, be the administrator of the colony, it boasted a court house, a jail, a legislative building, and its own newspaper.[37] Within a year, the Russells, together with other prominent residents of the town, had moved out of their log houses into "excellent dwellings" in "the upper end of the town."[38] Niagara's prominence was short-lived, however. Although for the next twenty years, it continued to be the entrepot for thousands of American immigrants searching for land and a regional transhipment depot,[39] its accelerated growth was abruptly arrested when Lieutenant-Governor Simcoe decided to establish the permanent colonial capital in York.

Not surprisingly, "the projected change [from Niagara to York] was by no means relished by the people at large." Many members of the government, like Peter Russell and his sister, had invested considerable capital and effort into building new homes in Niagara. Moreover, the western community was "a much more convenient place to resort to [for] most of them than Toronto." In 1795, York was an isolated backwater with, according to one report, only twelve houses and "Indians [as] its only neighbours."[40] The lieutenant-governor was nevertheless determined. The new town site was surveyed, lots were distributed, and by 1799, the move was complete. In 1806, although George Heriot marvelled at "the advancement" of York, it was still really a frontier town.[41]

Despite their diminutive size, even in the early years, Kingston, Niagara, and York offered local residents economic and social amenities and opportunities unavailable to most Upper Canadians. By 1800, each of the three colonial centres boasted a number of inns and taverns, a weekly market, an Anglican church, at least one school, and a number of general and speciality shops. Although most households maintained a garden and at least some kept some livestock, increasingly townsfolk relied on the local baker, tailor, hatmaker, seamstress, carpenter, and other skilled craftspeople for some or all the goods and services their families required.

Kingston, Niagara, and York dominated the political, economic, and social life of the colony throughout the first half of the century. But by 1800, dozens of new villages were appearing at busy crossroads, at river crossings, and on the shores of Lakes Ontario and Erie. Each new settlement had at least one general store and a tavern; most had a market, and all soon had a church, a school, and a number of small shops and businesses. As Anna Jameson, the wife of the newly appointed vice-chancellor explained in 1837, "where there is a store, a tavern and a church, habitations soon rise around them."[42] Initially, Hamilton, Peterborough, Newmarket, Bytown, and other villages throughout the colony had, like Oakville, "the appearance of a straggling hamlet, containing a few frame and log-houses." In 1837, Oakville had "one brick house (the grocery store, or general shop, which in a new Canadian village is always the best house in the place), a small Methodist church ... and an inn dignified by the name of the 'Oakville House Hotel'." But, as Anna Jameson observed, "from its situation and other local circumstances," Oakville, like many other villages, would soon become a place of some importance.[43]

There is no question that residents of Upper Canada's growing towns and villages benefited from "the greater complexities of a pecuniary civilization."[44] On Sunday, they could attend a local church. During the week, they gathered at one of the local taverns or coffee houses for refreshment, information, and entertainment. Increasingly, some village children spent at least a few days in school; their fathers "went to work" or, more often, retired to their shop or work bench; and their mothers coped with the daily chores of keeping house, visiting neighbours, and perhaps helping their husbands in the shop.

It was, however, in Kingston, York, and to some extent Niagara, that residents enjoyed the benefits of a relatively mature urban life. By the time that Helen MacPherson Macaulay arrived in Kingston in 1832 as the new bride of John, first son of Ann Macaulay, the town's population had grown to approximately 3,000.[45] Helen's mother-in-law Ann Macaulay now lived in a large stone house and kept a number of servants. Although in the 1830s the Macaulays, like many of their neighbours, continued to work an extensive kitchen garden, they relied increasingly on the local market and on grocers and dry goods stores for food for the table. They also patronized millinery, dressmaking, and tailor shops; they attended local theatrical and musical productions; and worshipped weekly at St George's Church.

Helen and her family moved to York, the provincial capital, in 1837. As a growing commercial centre, with a population of about 10,000,[46] York now rivalled Kingston in size and sophistication. For Anna Jameson and Helen Macaulay, this meant they had both the opportunity and, as members of the colonial elite, the obligation to participate in a hectic social life. For the thousands of immigrants who arrived in the city in the 1830s, the capital offered relative comforts and the possibility of employment. In addition to Government House, a jail, and a court house, York had numerous taverns, many seemingly prosperous shops, and a number of churches.[47] While Surveyor-General Macaulay worked at his office, Helen could go out in her carriage to visit friends or to shop. At the end of the decade, their daughter Annie attended one of the growing number of ladies' academies in town.

Even in the 1830s and 1840s, the majority of rural women and their families did not regularly share in these benefits. Distance from a village or town, the poor state of the roads, and the demands of working the land precluded most from regular trips to town, to the shops, and for many, to church. Yet from the beginning of colonial settlement, there were ties and institutions that bound Upper Canada's rural and urban communities closely together. As historian Douglas McCalla has so ably illustrated, "the principal local business institution, and the one component of the business system with which ordinary Upper Canadians routinely came into contact was the town or country retailer."[48] Despite the best intentions and efforts of family members, no individual farm in Upper Canada could be self-sufficient. From very early on in the colony's development, cash-strapped farming families depended on the proprietor of a store in a nearby village for credit to buy the essentials that they could not produce themselves. Soon, some farmers began to transport their surplus produce or their cash crop to market or to an area merchant. Although this frequently necessitated rather lengthy and difficult journeys over ill-marked, rude roads, or by sleigh along rivers and over the ice, farmers sometimes travelled considerable distances to attain the best price for their goods.[49]

Rural Upper Canadians were, in fact, surprisingly mobile. After 1800, many farm families took annual winter off-farm trips to visit family and friends. Trips to the mill, to a camp meeting, or for shopping and marketing were sometimes extended by a night or two at a local inn. Soon, members of some rural households began to gravitate to the nearest village or regional centre to go to school or look for work. As the colony's market economy became more complex and diverse, and intercolonial communication improved, contact between rural and urban communities increased. In the 1820s and 1830s, only those in the very outer fringes of colonial settlement did not have some regular contact with town life.

The growing economic and personal interdependence and the interaction between town and country inevitably had an impact on the lifestyle and expectations of rural residents in particular. Some farm families were able to buy goods in town rather than produce them themselves. Despite this, throughout the first half of the nineteenth century, living on a farm *was* different than living in town. And the life and work of farmers' wives and daughters was for much of the time quite different than if they had been attached to an urban household. Where one lived was not the only factor that shaped colonial women's work, however. Of equal, and some might suggest, greater influence was a woman's economic situation and social status.

AS HISTORIAN PETER RUSSELL has pointed out, since the beginning of colonial development, Upper Canadians had a strong sense of "social hierarchy" and "prestige and stratification."[50] An individual's place in society rested on a combination of factors, including relative wealth, occupation, skills, education, land holding, and self-expectation.[51] For the vast majority of women in Upper Canada, their social and economic status, and therefore the work they engaged in, was directly determined by the work and status of the male heads of their households.

Scholars have often found it difficult both to classify the various social and economic gradations within Upper Canadian society and to determine where an individual or family ranked or fit within each stratum. What for later analysts is often a complex and difficult puzzle was for Upper Canadians self-evident. Residents themselves appear to have had no difficulty in identifying those who made up what Elizabeth Simcoe had considered that "certain circle" of "pleasant society."[52] Women and their farming husbands who settled in the Upper Canadian outback and the wives and daughters of local artisans, mechanics, and labourers were not confused about where they and their neighbours ranked in the social and economic order.

When Margaret Ryerse and her family first came to the colony, there appeared to be little to distinguish them from the thousands of other immigrants who were settling on the frontier. Yet it was soon apparent that the family was privileged. The Ryerses were members of the gentry and, like other relatively wealthy or well-connected loyalist families and households attached to a half-pay officer, the Ryerses were recognized by their neighbours as a family of property and standing. As a prominent loyalist, Captain Ryerse was entitled to a substantial land grant. The family also appears to have had considerable capital and, as a half-pay British officer, Captain Ryerse had a secure income. Moreover, as a result of his personal association with Lieutenant-Governor Simcoe, he also gained considerable political influence. Shortly after he arrived in the colony, he was appointed a district magistrate and he subsequently became a senior officer in the local militia.[53]

Most Upper Canadian farm families did not share such good fortune. Their land holdings were small and their success depended on the family's ability, not only to clear and work the land, but also to find waged employment. The experience of the Troyers, for example, the family with whom Mrs Ryerse initially stayed before joining her husband on their own land, may have been quite common. Though Mr Troyer was locally known as "the doctor" and was undoubtedly respected for his skills, the household's economic circumstances encouraged their daughter Barbara to accept a position as a "help" in the Ryerse household.[54]

As the colony matured, the relative economic and social distinctions between various groups of farm families became increasingly evident. Gentlewomen including Mary Gapper O'Brien, Catharine Parr Traill, Susanna Moodie, and Anne Langton had little choice but to perform much of the work that was demanded of all women in farm households. But they were never completely dependent on the goods and income generated from the farm for their survival. Like a number of post-Napoleonic War immigrants, they brought household goods, including furniture, with them to the outback. Some women, such as Fanny Hutton who joined her schoolteacher, farming husband William in the Belleville area in 1834, continued to receive packages and financial assistance from home for some time.[55] More important, many of these women were attached to gentlemen farmers who regularly received a small but steady income from their half-pay as retired British officers.[56] Some men also attained patronage appointments as officers in the local militia, justices of the peace, magistrates, and land superintendents, which added a small regular stipend and often a portion of fees they collected to the family coffers. Mary O'Brien, Anne Langton and a number of others were therefore able to purchase many household and luxury items; at least periodically, they also had the means to hire women and men to help in their homes and to work in their fields. And inevitably, their neighbours turned to them for advice, for personal and financial support, and for employment.[57]

It is not surprising, therefore, that for the Traills and other British and American immigrants of similar financial circumstances, the transition from pioneering to farming was relatively rapid. At the end of 1832, Catharine Parr Traill described her situation as a "Robinson Crusoe sort of life." Three years later, she was able to report that she and Thomas were quite comfortable living in their log house with its "large and convenient kitchen" and a pretty flower garden.[58] Although in the end, farming did not bring the Moodies, the Traills, or the O'Briens the financial security that they had so desperately sought, these gentle pioneers were never destitute.[59]

Less affluent women and men who came to Upper Canada between 1790 and 1840 to farm had a much more difficult time. With little or no capital, many families had to live in small log houses or shanties for years after their arrival. Relying only on a combination of household and community labour to clear and work their small holdings, some never moved beyond a subsistence level of existence. It was common for small farmers, recent immigrants, squatters, and tenant farmers to hire themselves out to their more prosperous neighbours in order to provide necessities for themselves and their families.[60] Their wives and children not only helped in their own fields but also often joined the ranks of the seasonal wage labour force and worked for others.[61] The account books of Hamnett Pinhey of March Township (near Ottawa), John Thompson of Brantford, Captain William Johnson, and other members of the landed gentry regularly recorded the wages and, in some cases, the activities of these "ordinary" men and women.[62] The journals and correspondence of Mrs Ryerse, Mary O'Brien, Anne Langton, and other gentle farm women provide brief, if at times rather distorted, glimpses of the lives and work of the girls – usually the daughters and wives of neighbours – who helped in their homes.

Visitors to Upper Canada in the 1820s and 1830s frequently commented on the often sharp social and economic differences between rural residents. John Howison scathingly noted that life among the "peasantry" of Upper Canada, was "in a state of primitive rudeness and barbarism." At the same time, he found that in the Niagara region "the farms [were] in a high state of cultivation and their possessors ... comparatively wealthy." Yet even here, residents "were still the same untutored incorrigible beings they probably were" when they had arrived twenty or thirty years earlier. Though there were in Upper Canada respectable residents on the land who showed a "steadiness and spirit of industry," for the most part, Howison concluded that "the better class of people" lived in the centre of settlement.[63]

Certainly, distinctions among Upper Canadians based on wealth, social and political standing, and influence were most readily apparent in the colony's towns and villages. By 1792, two of Upper Canada's wealthiest and most influential merchants, Richard Cartwright of Kingston and Robert Hamilton of Queenston, had already built themselves large stone homes.[64] Other enterprising merchants and senior government officials quickly followed suit. By 1800, Kingston, Niagara, and York each had a number of large and imposing houses that were both symbols and physical testimonies of their residents' social, economic, and political prominence.[65]

When Elizabeth Simcoe arrived in the colony, she assumed the social leadership of what was already a self-styled Upper Canadian aristocracy. Under her direction, the women of the "big" houses, including the wives and sisters of senior government officials, principal merchants, and a few professionals, were expected to conform to certain social rituals and to assume responsibilities that came and were commensurate with their rank. Thus, in addition to running their households, Ann Macaulay and Elizabeth Russell had to participate in a myriad of social functions and engage in philanthropic work. Although the Simcoes presided over this tightly-knit club for only four years, the standards of social conduct, activities, and personal behaviour that they established persisted for the next fifty years.

As the colony matured, the original guard of colonial elite was gradually replaced by new faces and families, and the size and scope of the Upper Canadian upper class inevitably grew and became more complex. Increasingly, social as well as political influence was concentrated in the colonial capital, York. In the 1820s and 1830s, the "best" families of Kingston and Niagara did continue to exercise considerable social and political influence. At the same time, however, local leadership groups began to emerge in each of Upper Canada's smaller communities. The wife of the village shopkeeper, the minister, the schoolteacher, and perhaps the doctor were often recognized by their neighbours as respectable and locally prominent women and they were expected to assume a leadership role within their communities. The scope of these responsibilities varied depending on the size of the community in which they lived and the financial and social circumstances of their husbands. For example, when Irish gentlewoman Harriet Dobbs married Robert Cartwright, the son of Richard Cartwright and a Church of England clergyman in the early 1830s, she immediately joined the ranks of Kingston "society."[66] On the other hand, when Anne Geddes married William Macaulay, second son of Ann Macaulay of Kingston, she never really became a society matron, even though the Macaulays were one of the most prominent families in the colony. Anne was, however, one of the leading ladies in the village of Picton, where her husband had his parish. There was no question that Anne's sister-in-law, Helen MacPherson Macaulay, was not only a member of the Kingston elite (being the daughter-in-law of Ann) but that her marriage to a prominent government official and the family's subsequent move to York elevated her to the heights of colonial "society."

In the 1820s and 1830s, Upper Canadians made quite clear distinctions between those who inhabited the highest ranks of society and those who, though respectable, did not share their elevated position. Moreover, the gradations and complexities that characterized the colonial elite mirrored the growing social and economic differences that were emerging within the rest of the general population. By the 1830s, urban centres in Upper Canada had a significant number of residents who would have considered themselves part of the middling ranks of society. A number of small shopkeepers, independent artisans, skilled craftspeople, hotel- and innkeepers, and some schoolmasters or schoolmistresses who owned their own businesses and small homes were certainly respected and respectable members of their communities. Like most farmers, it is probable that many in this group of urban dwellers had little real disposable income.[67] Yet notices in local newspapers, travellers' accounts, and a few diaries suggest that a number of them often employed one or two general servants. Many urban trades- and craftspeople and small retail families also had sufficient income to support local schools and churches and to donate money to various benevolent institutions. In most cases, women of this middle class, broadly defined, did not work "outside" the home. But within the context of the pre-industrial colonial economy, working "in" the home often included assisting their husbands in family businesses or taking in work to supplement the family income. After 1820, a few single women proprietors and school teachers, such as Mrs Jane Jordan who ran a hotel in York, and the Misses McCord who operated a successful girls' school in the capital in the 1830s, would have considered themselves and have been viewed by their neighbours as "respectable."

Most single or widowed women in Upper Canada were, however, part of that growing group of "working poor" who depended solely on selling their labour to make ends meet. Often unskilled and without the ability to obtain capital or credit, those in what were termed the "lower ranks" of society were usually day labourers, domestic servants, apprentices, or indentured servants. They lived with their employers, or tried to earn sufficient income to pay the rent on a small shanty. As advertisements in local newspapers attest, the working poor included many newly arrived British immigrants who did not have the means to take up land. There were others who, having failed to gain a subsistence from their farms, had been forced to move to the nearest village to look for work. A growing number of those of the "lower" classes were young single women and men, both recent arrivals from Great Britain and daughters and sons of local farmers who were drawn to colonial towns by the promise of economic and social opportunity. Many such young people, like the growing number of widows, orphans, and unemployed adults and children were periodically forced to beg for their food and lodgings or to rely on various private aid societies for support.[68]

A woman's place in the increasingly complex social and economic order of Upper Canada and the work she was expected to undertake were inextricably tied both to the occupation of her husband and to her family's financial resources. Although Anne Langton lived on a working farm, at times her work as housekeeper more closely resembled that of many urban gentlewomen than that of her less affluent rural neighbours. Mary O'Brien's ties to the best families of York enabled her and periodically required her to assume the role of an upper-class matron. The same was true of Anne Macaulay of Picton.

Women's lives and work in Upper Canada differed, sometimes significantly, depending on where they lived, and the economic and social status of their households. For some, time of settlement also made a difference in their lives and work. The first arrivals to the colony had to contend with primitive living conditions that obliged them to do much of their own housework. Thirty years later a woman such as Helen Macaulay could, and was expected to, live in a big house; she had resident household staff and she sent her daughter to school. But, throughout the first fifty years of colonial development colonial women also shared many experiences and worked within common "disabilities." Neither Elizabeth Simcoe in 1792 nor one of Mary O'Brien's "helps" in the 1830s could escape the impact that their gender had on their daily lives.

AS LOUISE TILLY and Joan Scott have chronicled, in the pre-industrial, western world, women, work, and family were "inseparable categories."[69] Regardless of any differences in where they lived or in their status, women in Upper Canada shared, by reason of their sex, certain fundamental responsibilities. As wives, they assumed the primary responsibility for feeding and clothing their families. As wives too they also shared the physical discomfort of pregnancy, the pain and danger of childbirth, and the anxieties that came with raising their children. Certainly, the manner in which these responsibilities of "reproduction" were fulfilled depended to a large degree on the geographic, economic, and social circumstances of the family. Helen Macaulay, for example, could afford to hire servants to keep her home and a nurse to attend to her children. Fanny Hutton relied on her daughters to help with the housework and younger children. Both women, however, performed what was considered by almost all Upper Canadians to be the most important aspect of women's work – duties recognized for centuries as devolving to those individuals biologically capable of reproducing the family.

Yet, in Upper Canada during the early years of the nineteenth century, women's work was gradually beginning to encompass a broader social definition. What has since been described as "the cult of true womanhood," which emerged in the first decade of the century, posited that not only were there biological differences between men and women, but that there were also real and very important emotional, spiritual, and, some suggested, intellectual and moral differences.[70] As a result, although women continued to bear the responsibilities of reproduction, colonial leaders began to assert that women also had a special duty to promote certain social and moral values within their communities.

Men, it was argued, were naturally daring, bold, and had "strength of mind" as well as "strength of body."[71] Women were frail, often irrational, and naturally submissive. Women, for example, were "not formed for great care themselves, but to soften" that of others.[72] Indeed, it was frequently asserted that "it is beautifully ordered by Providence" that woman was man's "stay and solace."[73] Men and women were therefore clearly intended by both God and nature to fulfil different, yet complementary duties within the family and in society at large. It was presumed that the "exterior" world – of politics, of the market, and of business – "which is the most extensive," was the domain of men. "The interior" clearly belonged "to the wife." Indeed, many believed that "women who strayed beyond the home are out of their proper sphere and consequently without grace."[74]

The promotion of the idea of "separate spheres" had originated in Upper Canada's two imperial centres, where growing industrialization and urbanization were fundamentally altering the pre-industrial work patterns of the household and its residents. In Great Britain and the United States at the beginning of the nineteenth century, an emerging middle class was also beginning to assert a lifestyle and social and moral values that placed considerable emphasis on the family and on the need for "good" women to provide "proper moral order in the amoral world of the market."[75] As historians Leonore Davidoff and Catharine Hall have illustrated, the image of the "angel in the house," whose rule over her private domain directly influenced the manners and morals of the nation, was one of the key symbols of British middle-class values.[76] Inevitably, this idealization of womanhood was an intrinsic, if unconscious, part of successive colonial officials' and "gentle" immigrants' cultural baggage. It was also "of central importance to the way in which ... they defined themselves and their status."[77]

That the concepts of femininity embodied in this ideology were sharply at odds with the economic and social reality of most women's lives in Upper Canada, no one would have denied. In 1790, Upper Canada was a wilderness frontier. Its residents were a heterogeneous mixture of peoples "born in different states and nations," speaking "several languages," and holding often widely differing views of the future of the colony.[78] Even in the late 1830s, it was still a pre-industrial society where most residents' lives were governed by traditional patterns of work and family. The cult of true womanhood was nonetheless considered by colonial leaders to be an important part of the "blue print" of what the young colony of Upper Canada should eventually become.[79]

Even before he arrived in Upper Canada, John Simcoe had announced his intention of making Upper Canada's "Establishments, Civil and Military ... the Epitome" of those at home. And, he had written to the colonial secretary Sir Henry Dundas, in order to help stave off the pernicious influence of American republicanism and to bring British order to the colony, "the utmost attention should be paid that British Customs, Manners and Principles ... be promoted and inculcated."[80] An intrinsic part of this new order was the well-regulated family,[81] an institution that depended on the character and the activities of the "good" woman.

Reflecting the principles enshrined in the British Constitution, colonial families, it was believed, had to be strongly hierarchical. At the head of each family unit and the root of all authority was the husband/father. At its centre and the enduring symbol of obedience and willing submission was the wife/mother. Fulfilling such a role *was* truly women's work. For from within the security of the home, the influence of the good woman, the responsive wife, and the gentle mother would radiate throughout society at large.[82]

For the vast majority of colonial women, the incongruity between the emerging gender ideology and their daily lives must have been both striking and disconcerting. Those same colonial newspapers which so assiduously promoted and extolled in articles, short stories, and poetry the "true woman" with a contented husband at her side and children on her knee, also displayed by the contents of their advertisements and notices a world that had nothing to do with domestic harmony and willing subordination. And the surviving diaries and letters of both women and men of the middle and upper levels of Upper Canadian society revealed interpersonal relationships and family situations that were decidedly at odds with the rhetoric of domesticity.

In most Upper Canadian homes, the divisions between the public and private sphere were never clearly delineated. Like their mothers and grandmothers, all colonial women worked hard within their homes; most took an active and essential part in maintaining the family economy, and many worked for wages at a variety of occupations in the public marketplace. Even affluent women such as Elizabeth Russell and Helen Macaulay were rarely able to retreat into the private world of the home.

Yet, particularly in the second generation of Upper Canadian development, this new ideology was becoming an accepted part of the social rhetoric and few, publicly at least, challenged its legitimacy. Moreover, for a growing number of respectable immigrants, the cult of true womanhood was a familiar prescription of conduct and one that defined whom and what they were or hoped to become. As colonial gentlewomen struggled to cope with their day-to-day work, they were always conscious of the disjunction between their lives and the socially "accepted" norms of behaviour.[83] And a number of them, like Susanna Moodie, were often distressed at their inability to conform to what were both personal as well as social expectations. But even the thousands of "ordinary" women in the backwoods and those in town who sold their time and energy to middle- and upper-class households and, by definition, could not meet such expectations, were obliged to function within a culture that increasingly accepted such values and role divisions. As Carroll Smith-Rosenberg has explained, "even those who rejected a life entirely consistent with such ideals could not elude them completely for they existed as parameters with which and against which individuals either conformed or defined the nature of their deviance."[84] In Upper Canada in the 1820s and 1830s, women were increasingly judged on their ability and willingness to meet the new standards. The unwed mother and the deserted wife were often ostracized.

This is not to say that the new social standards for womanhood controlled women's lives completely. The degree to which a woman could or wanted to conform to these cultural norms was determined, in part at least, by her financial status and location. The majority of women in Upper Canada could not because of personal circumstances emulate such standards. Others clearly choose not to do so. Moreover, all colonial residents were aware that, despite the rhetoric of a woman's innate weakness, the actual work performed by women, as wives, sisters, mothers, farmers, craftswomen, mistresses, and maids was essential to the development of the colony as a whole.

"Around the Domestic Hearth": Wives and Mothers and Reproduction in Upper Canada

"There is a holiness about the fireside of a well regulated family,"[1] Anglican cleric John Strachan wrote in 1812. Only within the bosom of the family did an individual find love, strength, consolation, and happiness. "Take away the endearing names of father and mother, son and daughter, brother and sister, and human life becomes a prey to misery and despair. There is nothing left worth possessing; the choicest springs of felicity are dried up, and man is no longer a social being."[2]

In Upper Canada, to marry was both a civic duty and an individual imperative.[3] "Happiness of life," colonial leaders asserted "depend[ed] much on domestic union and friendship."[4] Without the security and haven of love, affection and mutual obligation that the institution of marriage provided, a woman or a man was "a roving restless being ... the sad victim of untamed passions."[5] And without the firm foundation of well-regulated families, it was widely believed, society was open to disorder, to instability, and to anarchy.

It is not surprising, therefore, that in Upper Canada, bachelorhood and spinsterhood were often condemned from the pulpit and ridiculed in the press.[6] Young women and men were encouraged to marry and once formalized, the state made it virtually impossible for a couple to dissolve the union. Moreover, though Upper Canadians generally considered relations between husband and wife a private affair, the relationship was carefully regulated by colonial law, which supported the authority of the husband and, if necessary, enforced the subordination of his wife and children.

The implications of this for Upper Canadian women in the first half of the nineteenth century were profound. Though all women did not marry, or remarry if widowed, the vast majority did. Indeed, as in colonial New England, in Upper Canada "the words wife and woman" were virtually "synonymous."[7] So too were the words "wife" and "mother." Marriage was a defining event in a woman's life. It determined where she lived, her social and economic status, and usually the nature of her work. All married women in Upper Canada were, by definition, mothers, teachers, domestic workers, nurses, and surrogate husbands/fathers. Most wives were also unpaid farm workers or assistants in family businesses. Many wives were obliged, periodically, to find waged work; and although subordinate legally and economically to their husbands, a few pursued independent careers. For the majority of women in Upper Canada, as in other pre-industrial societies, marriage was as much an economic as a social arrangement. And a woman's willingness and ability to take an active part in maintaining the family economy was essential for the family's survival and prosperity.[8]

Yet in Upper Canada, the definition of a good wife and mother was beginning to change in the first half of the nineteenth century. Particularly among the colonial middle and upper classes, it was no longer assumed that marriage was merely a vehicle to ensure the physical well-being of individuals, the growth of the nation, or the orderly transfer of property, although these functions continued to be important. Marriage and the institution of the family now also began to take on broad emotional and ideological dimensions. A woman and man, it was believed, should marry for love and their subsequent relationship should be based on mutual trust and affection.[9] In addition to being an hierarchically constructed unit of authority and production, a family was also expected to be a haven and a place of solace and strength for all its members. "It is at home, at our fireside," John Strachan reminded readers of the *Kingston Gazette*, "that our choicest pleasures are tasted."[10]

The growing acceptance of the idea of "companionate" marriages[11] and the emotional dimensions this superimposed on family life both promoted and reinforced new expectations of the abilities and the work of the "good" woman. After all, as a brief snippet in the *British American Journal* explained, "there is one excellent trait in the female character ... which is admirably adapted to their condition in life." While men sought "pleasure in variety" and found being confined at home "wearisome," women had "a happy knack of making themselves contented at home" which was "their little world."[12] It was in the home that a "good" woman found scope to develop her special talents and attained fulfilment and respect. Though husbands and wives were "equally yoked" and shared the responsibility of ensuring their marriages' success, they had decidedly "different duties to perform."[13] In addition to performing that "series of discreet duties" that women had traditionally assumed on marriage,[14] wives and mothers were also now expected to be the emotional and moral focal points of their families and, through that, of society at large.

Not surprisingly, the dictates of middle-class domesticity so assiduously promoted in the pages of colonial newspapers, in contemporary literature, and from the pulpit, were often sharply at odds with the reality of family life in Upper Canada. Certainly, the ideology of separate spheres misrepresented the complexity of working relations within various colonial families. More important, all marriages were not companionate; and all married women in Upper Canada were not, or could not, be "good" wives and mothers, as defined by the cult of true womanhood. Individual personalities, financial and social circumstances, unforseen events, and the nature of the colonial economy inevitably affected a woman's (or a man's) ability or desire to meet the new social prescriptions.

Ironically, historians and other scholars have often tended to confuse the rhetoric of true womanhood with the reality of married life in Upper Canada. Certainly, some scholars have recognised the importance of the tasks that Upper Canadian women performed, either within the informal economy of the family and the neighbourhood or the formal economy of the marketplace.[15] Most who consider the social and economic development of the colony continue to divide any discussion of colonial workers into two discrete categories – "reproductive" and "productive." Their analyses concentrate, at times, almost exclusively, on the lives and work of those colonists (usually men) who received direct remuneration for their labour.[16] Such categorization implicitly perpetuates the myths of nineteenth-century womanhood and it misrepresents the complexity of colonial society. It also explicitly devalues the contribution that all Upper Canadian women made to the economic and social well-being of their communities. For, by failing to consider the often widely differing relationships within colonial families and what it actually meant to be a wife and mother in Upper Canada, scholars ignore one of the central foundations of women's lives. Marriage and motherhood were considered the most important work that any colonial woman could undertake. As important, a woman's actual relationship with her husband and her day-to-day experiences as a mother were the basic context – the conditions of work if you will – within which and from which she performed the myriad of her other duties.

2 "The Most Important Crisis": Marriage in Upper Canada

Early in June 1836, Mary O'Brien recorded, "last night my damsel confided to me a distress." One of the young carpenters was seeking "her in marriage, as she has supposed till today in jest; [the girl] was now, however, led to believe that there was something serious in it." The maid's distress resulted from a number of factors. She was already "promised by her mother to another young man," and though "it seems she cares but little" for her mother's choice, "she had given consent to the arrangement." In addition, though the maid was attracted to the young carpenter, she did not want to marry yet. Mary sympathized with the girl. She was also pleased that "the superior charms of the carpenter ... had at least set her [the maid] on thinking how she would like the reality" of marriage. Mary O'Brien was not willing, however, to become involved. "Under the circumstances," she wrote, "I thought I could do nothing better than to send her back to her parents as speedily as possible."[1] The young maid's predicament was probably not unusual. The question was not whether to marry, but whom to marry.

It is estimated that 90 per cent of all women in Upper Canada married, usually between the ages of twenty-one and twenty-two.[2] For Mary's maid and other young girls, marriage was a rite of passage. When they became wives, they also became adults and, it was considered, fully productive members of their society. Yet for many colonial women in the first half of the nineteenth century, marriage must also have invoked feelings of profound ambivalence. Though becoming a wife often brought some degree of freedom from one's family, it also meant the loss of personal autonomy to a new husband. It promised companionship; yet women could also not help but be aware that many unions were fraught with tension and sometimes violence. Marriage offered new opportunities for personal development and some limited authority over the lives of others. It brought with it, however, onerous responsibilities. And given that all marriages presumed motherhood, women were aware that marriage could also be dangerous.

"IN THE FATE OF A WOMAN," a letter in the *Farmers' Journal* in 1828 commented "marriage is the most important crisis, it fixes her in a state of all others the most happy or the most wretched."[3] Upper Canadian women such as Mary O'Brien and her maid were well aware of this. Once they had accepted a man's proposal, they would have to leave the security of their childhood home and enter into a largely unknown realm where their happiness, their fate, and, indeed, in some cases their very lives depended on the abilities and personalities of their mate. A woman had to choose her husband wisely.

Upper Canadian girls usually married someone from their own community – the son of a neighbour, a family friend, or a work mate. Their future husbands were most often two or three years older than themselves, though it was not unknown for an older woman to select a younger spouse.[4] Parents had considerable influence over their daughter's choice of a mate. The mother of Mary O'Brien's maid undoubtedly believed that her arrangements would be honoured. And many parents sanctioned a courtship by providing an opportunity for the couple to meet and get to know each other.[5] The courtship was also supervised by neighbours, friends, and sometimes employers. In the end, however, the decision as to whether or not to accept a proposal of marriage usually remained with the girl.

For a woman in Upper Canada, affection for her suitor was one of the most important criteria in her decision to marry. Mary O'Brien's maid, for example, was clearly not attached to her betrothed but was attracted by the O'Briens' young carpenter. Mary Gapper O'Brien herself had only considered Edward O'Brien's proposal in 1830 because she had believed she would "receive ... the possession of a heart capable of entering into all my views & feelings & attached to me with an affection so exactly suited to my humour that I sometimes fancy I myself have dictated it."[6] Not all women, however, had the opportunity to develop such close emotional bonds with their future husbands. Frequently other considerations placed distinct limitations on a woman's decision whether or not to marry, and then whom to marry.

Almost a year after her arrival in Upper Canada, Mary Gapper recorded in her journal, "I have another little anxiety which occupies my thoughts very often … I do not often concern myself with the future, there are many pleasant paths thro life, neither of which perhaps may be mine, but if grace be granted me to tread the straight & onward way, I will, I trust I shall not murmer at the roughs & thorns with which it may be strewn."[7] Mary refused to identify her "little anxiety." Over the next few months, however, she continued to make periodic, though often oblique, references to the decision she was being asked to make. Edward O'Brien had asked her to marry him.

The problem Mary confronted was not whether she loved Edward, but rather where her duty lay. Mary and her widowed mother had come to Upper Canada to visit her brothers. They fully intended to return to England to live with Mary's older sister, Lucy. Mary therefore declined Edward's proposal, though she wrote to Lucy, "I grant it possible … that my happiness might have been increased by a marriage with a person in whom I believe I might have been sure of finding a kind & agreeable companion to whose happiness I could have in return essentially contributed." But as she explained, "circumstanced as I am," this was impossible.[8] "My future life should be determined by what was necessary to the comfort of you and my mother."[9]

Neither Edward nor Mary's family in Upper Canada was willing to let the matter drop, however, and they began to pressure Mary to reconsider her decision.[10] Unbeknown to Mary, Edward tentatively but formally spoke to Mary's mother of the matter. As Mary recorded, this "set him at liberty to speak and act without constraint before all the family circle."[11] Mary's sisters-in-law also presented "repeated arguments in favour of matrimony."[12] Mary clearly resented such interference and she "cautiously avoided" trying "to influence" her mother, for she was aware that her marriage would "separate [her mother] from one or other of her daughters."[13] Nonetheless, Mary too began to try to find a way to reconcile what she considered to be her duty with her desires. "In short," she wrote in a long letter to Lucy in March 1830, "to render new ties compatible with those that are already so dear to me."[14] Mary's dilemma was only resolved when she received a letter from Lucy that decided "my vacillating plans." Lucy had released Mary from all her sororial obligations and wished her joy in marriage.[15]

Delighted, Mary planned to marry almost immediately. Yet she continued to be aware that marriage to Edward would entail certain "sacrifices." Mary had no financial need to marry and indeed, becoming Edward's wife might result in less financial security. She also rather cryptically noted that after her marriage she would have to give up "my independence, my power of motion, my hermitage, my philosophizing life, my general utility & alass some of my more peculiar associations."[16] There were more serious consequences, however. "There is so much in the moment of this decision that was painful for I could not forget friends from whom [marriage will] separate me even at the side of the one to whom it unites me." Mary particularly feared that her marriage would sever or fundamentally alter those special ties of love and affection between herself and Lucy. "Evenst while rejoicing," Mary had "tears of regret" and she implored Lucy never to "deviate from our old plan of perfect truth in all that concerns us" and promised to reciprocate.[17]

Mary's dilemma and her months of soul-searching must have been shared by many other women in Upper Canada. Marriage often meant leaving family and giving up friends, perhaps permanently. When Helen MacPherson accepted John Macaulay's proposal of marriage in 1833, she knew that she might never see her mother and brother in Scotland again.[18] For Helen and Mary, marriage also meant forsaking those special duties to care for aging parents or busy sisters. It was therefore particularly important to them and to other betrothed couples that they have the blessing of their respective families.[19]

Such anxieties and internal conflicts over the decision to marry probably did not plague younger or less affluent women to the same degree. Marriage did not always mean forsaking family and friends. For many, it offered some form of independence and the opportunity to preside over one's own house. It also undoubtedly offered many girls a greater chance of financial security and a means of escape from employment. Yet even the parlour maid with no encumbrances and the apparently carefree gentleman's daughter could be subject to pressures that limited their ability to chose a husband freely.

In Upper Canada, it was considered a woman's duty to marry. An unmarried woman was an object of pity, of scorn, and often, of ridicule.[20] In particular, an older single woman was subjected to considerable pressure from family and friends to find a husband, or to accept what earlier might have been considered an unsuitable suitor. While Mary Gapper had struggled with her conflicting duties, her sisters had not been loath to apply pressure in favour of marriage. Similarly, Anne Powell, wife of the chief justice of Upper Canada, had tried to persuade her reluctant daughter, Mary, to accept the suit of the then attorney general, John MacDonell, in 1811–12. In the end, Anne had relented, believing that "an arranged and loveless marriage was not an option."[21] Parental encouragement was obviously not the only pressure to be brought to bear on an unmarried woman.

Illustration 3
Portrait of Anne Murray Powell, 1834
from a painting by Grove Sheldon Gilbert
John Ross Robertson Collection, MTL (T15180)

A determined suitor could also apply considerable pressure on a
woman of his choice. Mary O'Brien reported in 1833 that her maid
Elineor was "in a queer complexity." The girl had just heard "that one
of the men who left us last week, [had] caused matrimonial banns to
be published between himself & without her having thought seriously on the subject." The girl "has no kind of love for him tho' she
likes him well enough to marry him." Nonetheless, a few days later,
fearing gossip and aware of "the seriousness of her lover's intentions," the girl yielded and agreed to the marriage.[22]

A number of young girls were also subjected to physical as well as
emotional coercion. Though Upper Canadian illegitimacy rates were
apparently quite low, social pressure did force some pregnant girls to
marry the fathers of their children or if they were unfortunate, any el-
igible and willing man.[23] A number of widows too undoubtedly
found themselves in the situation where they desperately needed to
remarry to provide a home for themselves and their children.

Women who were fortunate married for love and affection. For
those who did not have this luxury, the decision to marry was accompanied by ambivalence, anxiety, and sometimes reluctance. Even
those like Mary Gapper who had a real regard for their future hus-

bands and the opportunity to make their choice freely, had doubts. For women could not help but be aware that their decision was crucial to their future. Marriage not only began a personal relationship with their future husbands, but also set the conditions and framework within which they performed much of their other labour.[24]

MANY ARTICULATE Upper Canadians believed that the ideal marriage relationship was one of mutual confidence, affection, and respect. A man and woman should marry for love and a considered appreciation of their perspective mate's character and ability.[25] Ideally, the new husband and wife became friends as well as lovers. "Power on either side" of the relationship had to be "totally banished from the system," one commentator exhorted.[26] Husband and wife should support each other and respect each other's particular abilities and duties.[27] In short, the rhetoric of the time promoted the idea of the companionate marriage. Yet, this new emphasis on the emotional aspects of marriage in no way compromised the hierarchical structure of the family. Throughout the first half of the nineteenth century, Upper Canadian households were openly patriarchal.

In 1826, an article in the *Farmers' Journal*, "The Happy Match," described the "purpose" of a wife. A man chooses his wife, "first because he loved her, and in the second place because he knew she was sensible, economic and industrious ... A man gets a wife to look after his affairs, to assist him in his journey through life, to educate and prepare his children for proper station in life, and not to dissipate his property."[28] The wife's "greatest ambition" should be "his welfare and happiness and that of his children."[29] Her greatest happiness was to be found in a successful marriage.

It was accepted that a man had some responsibility for ensuring that his marriage remained harmonious. In addition to choosing a mate wisely, he had to cultivate "the benevolent affections" of his wife and children.[30] He was advised to nurture the tender plant of his new relationship and to "endeavour to secure the perfect confidence" of his wife.[31] A husband had to be sensitive to his wife's needs, promote her comfort, and openly appreciate her work in the home. And perhaps most important, it was advocated that he spend time with his wife and children beside "the cheerful hearth."[32] The partner who was responsible for providing the "cheerful hearth" and ensuring the welfare and happiness of the family was his wife, however.

> Happy is he, sincerely bless'd!
> The man who by propitious fate
> Is of a virtuous wife possessed!

A careful, kind and loving mate
No cares or fears his quiet can destroy,
Nor shake the solid basis of his joy.[33]

A married woman's first duty was to ensure her husband's well-being. Biblical injunction, legal doctrine, and new social expectations all dictated that a wife was to love, honour, and obey her husband, to look after his temporal and physical needs, and to be a lifelong support and companion. A good wife "acts not for herself only, but she is the agent of many she loves and she is bound to act for their good, not for her own gratification," an article in the *Farmers' Journal* reminded Upper Canadians in 1829.[34] "A husband retains the prerogative of his sex in a marriage," Julia was advised. "His will expects to be pleased, and ours must be sedulous to please." Yet, "the offices of a wife [also] includes the exertions of a friend; a good one must frequently strengthen and support that weakness which a bad one will endeavour to overcome." Indeed, "there are situations where it will not be enough to love, cherish, to obey;" a woman "must teach her husband to be at peace with himself, to be reconciled to the world, to resist misfortune, to conquer adversity."[35] This, to Upper Canadians, was the crux of a happy and productive marriage. Companionship was hierarchically arranged. Husbands were to be served and satisfied. Women were to be submissive and dependent. At the same time, wives had a responsibility to exercise their considerable moral strength in support of their husbands and to influence them into proper actions and attitudes.

Throughout the nineteenth century, Upper Canadian women received considerable and explicit advice from the press and the pulpit on how to secure domestic accord and a well-regulated family.[36] "It is the innate office of the softer sex," "Matrimonial Maxims for Married Ladies" maintained, "to soothe the troubles of the other."[37] At all times, it was asserted, a woman was to be "never out of temper" with her husband or try to manage him. "Sweetness of temper, affection to husband and attention to his interest constitute the duty of a wife," one woman reminded her daughter.[38] A father counselled his daughter, "a difference with your husband ought to be considered as the greatest calamity" and "one that had to be assiduously guarded against."[39] This was despite the fact that men were acknowledged to be "prone to sudden actions and irrational acts." "Even the best man," Mrs Bennington noted in the *Upper Canada Gazette* in 1807, "are sometimes so inconsistent with themselves" and have "some oddities of behaviour, some peculiarities of temper" so as to be subject to "accidental ill humour or whimsical complaints." Do not, she and others warned women, upbraid or berate him. Rather, "study your husband's temper" and "deny yourself the trifling satisfaction of having your will or gaining the better of an argument."[40] A good wife could make a good husband, young wives were told. With tenderness, "a man's manners will soften" and his soul "will be animated by the most tender and lively sensation."[41] Women were to govern "by the power of mildness to which even strength [would] yield."[42] A woman's power, which originated in her moral superiority, as well as her happiness, ultimately rested in her husband's esteem and love. It was in her interests, therefore, to preserve and increase his affection for her.

First and foremost, to be a good wife, a woman had to be a "good" woman. This meant that she had to be a devout Christian.[43] Young women were advised to "labour under the grace of God," to study the Scriptures and to apply them in their daily activities.[44] A good wife also had to be "amiable," with "goodness of heart and purity of manners" so as to be able to "impart a moral excellence to all around her."[45] Only "a virtuous and discreet wife" could ensure that her home was "a temple pure and uncontaminated," a haven from the tumults and immorality of the world.[46]

Upper Canadians seemed to be preoccupied with the question of female "purity," a term that included female chastity. Direct and explicit references in local newspapers to the destructive effects of a woman's sexuality were rare. However, the passionate temptress was a familiar image in the Upper Canadian press. Moreover, it was presumed that women could "bewitch" and enslave men with their charms.[47] Short stories in the local press confirmed that an unscrupulous woman could lead an unsuspecting man astray. Didactic tales graphically illustrated that young girls without innocence were brought to despondency and despair. That some, perhaps many, women in Upper Canada did sell their sexuality to earn a living is beyond question. This was never openly acknowledged, however.

Reports from the courts in community newspapers did sometimes include brief mention of women charged and convicted of keeping a house of ill fame, being drunk and disorderly, or keeping a disorderly house.[48] In 1829, the editor of the *Colonial Advocate* added a brief commentary to his report of the case of Margaret Tripp, a prostitute who had committed suicide while in prison. The cause of her despair, the editor judged, was her "great distress of mind" at "having lost [her] station and character in society." Mothers were warned to take heed of this object lesson and to guard the virtue of their children carefully.[49]

Local newspapers did frequently include "cautions" to young girls to be wary of "irrational love" and romance.[50] It was asserted that girls should also deny themselves the dubious pleasure of flirting. An article on the "Deportment of Females" in the *Brockville Gazette* in

1832 found "the present familiarity among the sexes ... both shocking to delicacy and to the interests of women."[51] Young women were advised that although beauty might bring admirers and wit might solicit attention, neither could ensure happiness or fulfilment. In fact, a brief commentary explained, "beauty has frequently outdone its possessor."[52] Rather than trying, perhaps desperately, to attract men with their physical charms, colonial leaders told women to cultivate modesty, humility, and chastity. An article in the Methodist *Christian Guardian* went even further. "Beauty, address, form, courtesy, softness, delicacy, ease may characterize you as women that are amiable, but it is only wisdom and knowledge that can render you happy at home, useful in society, calm in a dying hour, and forever blessed in a better world," it asserted.[53]

A well-bred woman and wife was always "well informed in every species of general knowledge." She continuously cultivated "rational ideas about religion and general world affairs" and was able "to converse well."[54] Women were warned, however, to occupy themselves "only with household affairs."[55] Though a wife should always exhibit a knowledgeable interest in her husband's concerns, she must avoid idle curiosity and speculation about her husband's business, and refrain from giving advice until asked.

Husbands were reminded, nevertheless, that within marriage often "the best domestic economy is that where the wife has most authority."[56] Indeed, some asserted that when it came to household matters "the lady is frequently more accurate than the gentleman and much better qualified to decide upon many arrangements of economy and comfort." Thus a wife should not only be consulted about all decisions relating to the family, but sometimes her views should be deferred to.[57]

Such attitudes illustrate the contradictory expectations that Upper Canadian wives confronted. There is no question that the husband was the "master" of the house and his wife was expected to heed him. He bore the ultimate responsibility for the welfare of the family. A wife's contribution to family decisions, therefore, had clear bounds. When a woman was "insensible to the voice of her chief, when she tries to usurp his prerogative and to command alone," the inevitable consequences were "misery, scandal and disorder."[58] The clever, virtuous, and good-hearted wife could ensure peace and harmony in her home; a silly, inattentive, and selfish wife brought only discord and dishonour to herself and her family. The primary responsibility, in the end, rested with the wife.

BEFORE HER MARRIAGE, Mary Gapper O'Brien was certain that when Edward talked "with the utmost simplicity" of her happiness being increased if she married him, he was sincere. "He has always been accustomed to sacrifice his own interest & pleasure to those he loves & he could so willingly devote his life to me," she wrote three months before her marriage.[59] Mary's diary of the first years of their marriage suggests that she was not disappointed. Like many middle-class couples in Upper Canada, Mary and Edward enjoyed a companionate relationship. So too, it seems, did Helen and John Macaulay and John's brother, William Macaulay and his wife Anne, of Picton, William and Fanny Hutton of Belleville, and a number of other colonial couples. Many Upper Canadian gentlewomen considered their wedding anniversary an occasion for celebration.[60] Though marital disagreements must have erupted periodically, these women appear to have had a "sincere regard" for their husbands; and correspondence between a number of couples indicates that wives and husbands consciously attempted to accommodate the wishes and needs of their partners.[61] William Macaulay's explanation to his mother as to why he intended to take his wife to Britain to recuperate from a lengthy illness provides some insight into their relationship. William acknowledged that they could not afford the trip. But, he wrote, "Ann has been a faithful & good wife & I am persuaded that such a voyage, if safely returned from will lengthen her life for some years." William believed he had a duty to further his wife's well-being. He obviously also cared for Anne deeply.[62]

For many couples, the mutual obligations that existed between husband and wife also extended to other members of their new families. Though on her marriage Helen MacPherson Macaulay was obliged to leave her mother to the care of her brother in Scotland, when she arrived in Upper Canada she became an integral member of her husband's family. Marriage to John also meant becoming the sister-in-law of Anne Macaulay of Picton and the daughter-in-law of Ann Macaulay of Kingston. After congratulating her brother-in-law on his marriage, Anne Macaulay stated that it was wonderful to have another sister. And she continued, "your mother will be much more comfortable and happy in having a daughter near her." Then, in what was a rare glimpse of family dynamics, she noted, "you are about to give her another daughter, but I must with due respect to you & yours that is to say for myself, that she cannot have one that will surpass me in love & respect for her."[63] Ann Macaulay Senior was truly fortunate in the respect and attention her daughters-in-law displayed towards her. Her children attended her when she was ill, supported her in financial and domestic concerns, and generally cemented ties of kin, which strengthened until Ann's death in 1850. In return, Ann willingly took John's children for extended periods of time, provided support for her family, and offered often unsolicited advice.[64]

Helen's role as wife to John and daughter to his mother was complemented by her growing attachment to her new sister-in-law, Anne. Helen relied on Anne's assistance during three difficult deliveries and a number of family illnesses. The two women visited each other frequently and their correspondence illustrates a friendship that both of them valued. At the same time, Helen frequently visited one of her own brothers then living in Montreal. Moreover, living in Kingston or York provided her with the opportunity to resume close contact with her married sister who was living in Niagara. Helen Macaulay and Mrs Hamilton regularly exchanged visits; the sisters helped each other through childbirth and other family crises.[65] The fact that her sister was already living in the colony may have made Helen's decision to marry John somewhat easier.

John Macaulay sometimes chaffed at the frequent absence of his wife.[66] At times, he also found coping with his wife's family rather difficult. Marriage for the Macaulays, as for other Upper Canadian couples, brought mutual responsibilities, however. Thus, while his sister-in-law and her children were staying with the Macaulays in York in 1839 while they were recovering from the fever, he managed with apparent good grace. After the visitors had left, John wrote to his mother that "we are by ourselves once more after having had a houseful for some time past. I do not like such a crowd but it was of course unavoidable."[67]

The importance of immediate and marriage-related kin was not limited to Upper Canada's middle class. For all Upper Canadians, family, including second cousins, was their basic social and economic unit. Both native-born Upper Canadians and newly arrived immigrants depended on relatives for personal and economic support and encouragement. Wives took their responsibilities to both their new and old families seriously. They also relied on relatives, and in particular those who were female, for assistance in meeting the physical and emotional needs of their own immediate families.

However, some Upper Canadian women could not draw on extended family networks for support in fulfilling their duties as wives and mothers. Many did not share a relationship of mutual respect and support with their husbands. Indeed, in a number of households, marriage was a relationship to be endured, not enjoyed.

IN NOVEMBER 1830, Mary O'Brien recorded that "an unhappy young woman, the wife of a neighbour," had "called this morning to ask advice from Edward ... Her husband had used her so ill as to drive her away from him about two years since & he had just now taken another wife & not content with that on her returning to the neighbourhood, seeks her out to abuse her threatening her life." Edward apparently had "had his eye on the culprit" for some time and he urged the young woman to prosecute her husband "for the public good." What was surprising, Mary O'Brien reported, was that the unfortunate wife "seems nothing loath &, indeed for the public good it is very necessary, as the crime is fearfully common."[68]

For many women in Upper Canada, marriage was not the sanctuary so glibly represented in the public press, nor the satisfying personal relationship shared by such as the O'Briens or the Macaulays. As Suzanne Lebsock discovered about the women of Petersburg, South Carolina at about the same time, for all women in Upper Canada, "marriage ... was only as companionate as the husband allowed it to be." There was little "to stop [a husband] from lapsing into authoritarian behaviour – very little that is, except the genuine respect for his wife's feelings and judgement."[69] For many colonial women of all classes, marriage was an exercise in raw power. Marital discord resulted in heated arguments and marital breakdown. A number of women were subject to physical and emotional abuse and some died as a result.

The potential for unhappiness, abuse, and marriage breakdown was institutionalized in Upper Canadian law. On her marriage, a woman became a *femme covert*.[70] Unless she entered into a prenuptial agreement with her husband or maintained a separate estate under the control of an independent trustee, she relinquished both herself and her property to her husband. In the first half of the nineteenth century, it was rare for women in Upper Canada to maintain their own estates.[71] Almost all women became "one with their husbands," and were required to honour and obey their spouses. In return they were entitled to their keep.

The legal restrictions placed on a wife's actions and basic rights were reenforced by social custom. Set beside the image presented in local newspapers of the good wife – caring, quiet, and submissive – was that of the shrew and the gossip. Amusing but pointed anecdotes told stories of henpecked husbands, of men who were impoverished by the extravagance of their wives, or husbands who were betrayed by them. In such instances, it was maintained that "a man had a right to chastise his wife moderately."[72] One newspaper article explicitly suggested that there were women (and it particularly identified uneducated Irish women) who "do not dislike their husband for beating them occasionally."[73] Society decreed that it was only when "such acts put her life in jeopardy" that a woman could defend herself or might be justified in taking the ultimate action – leaving her husband.[74] Most women, it was widely believed, deserved whatever treatment their husbands chose to bestow upon them. And when a wife was injured or died at the hands of her husband, the courts and Upper Canadians generally looked away.[75]

In 1839, for example, Anne Macaulay wrote to her sister-in-law Helen of the shocking circumstances of a young woman who had been shot "thro the head" by her husband. Though neighbours and the courts declared that the wife's death was an accident, Anne noted that the husband did not have a good character.[76]

In some circumstances, the community felt compelled to investigate a wife's death. In August 1830, Jack Evans was charged with murdering his wife. Evidence was introduced that Mrs Evans had been beaten by her husband for a number of years. On the night of her death, a neighbour "had heard screams and loud shrieks which appeared to be those of the deceased." Shortly thereafter, Jack Evans, who was drunk, set fire to his house. After some deliberation, the court found Jack Evans not guilty of the charges. His wife had died, it was determined, as a result of having been intoxicated and therefore being unable to flee their burning home.[77] A similar verdict had been reached a year earlier in the case of Thomas Bailey, who had been charged with beating and wounding his wife. The jury had acquitted him after finding that there was clear evidence that both of them were drunk.[78]

Although the courts considered that both Thomas Bailey and Jack Evans were rather unsavoury characters, they found no fault with the men's treatment of their wives. What is striking to the contemporary observer is that neither the juries nor the magistrates even commented on the unchallenged evidence of previous battery. Instead they chose to identify mitigating factors that helped to explain each tragedy; moreover, they implied that Mrs Evans, Mrs Bailey, and other women in their situations were actively culpable in their own deaths.

There were a few instances when the husband's guilt seemed to be beyond dispute. In 1834, the *Colonial Advocate* reported that Robert Richardson had killed his wife "by beating her about the head and body with the butt end of a gun." The report continued, "After killing his wife, he laid the corpse upon the bed and put a suckling infant upon her arm." The circumstances were particularly tragic because Mrs Richardson had previously fled from her home and taken sanctuary with a neighbour because "she was afraid her husband would murder her." Richardson had pursued her relentlessly, however. And after a few days, he had finally managed to detain and kill her when she had returned home briefly to retrieve her bedding. The *Advocate* reported that Richardson, like so many battering men, "was much addicted to intoxication." There was no question in the editor's mind, however, that Richardson was guilty. In fact, he convicted himself, for after killing his wife, Richardson shot himself.[79]

Most wife-murderers did not resolve the matter so expeditiously. In 1832, Henry Sovereign was charged with killing his wife and six of their eleven children. Local newspapers provided graphic descriptions of Sovereign's "unnatural and inhuman cruelty."[80] He had apparently stabbed, beaten, and in some instances mangled his victims and left their bodies strewn about the Sovereign home. Sovereign had been discovered with a bloody knife in his pocket and a bludgeon concealed in his bed. The prima facie evidence at the scene of the crime was convincing. Sovereign was convicted and publicly executed.[81]

Between 1820 and 1840 at least five men were convicted of murdering their wives. In each instance, the newspapers reported that it was common knowledge that the husband had been "in the habit of treating his wife cruelly."[82] However, members of the court never commented on a couple's history or suggested that a battered wife might still be alive if neighbours or the law had intervened earlier. On the contrary, it was implied that these men's wives should have known better than to attach themselves to intemperate men; other women were explicitly warned to avoid a similar fate.[83]

The evidence seems to suggest that such spectacular tragedies were rare in Upper Canada. Wife abuse was not. Upper Canadians assumed that some men abused their wives. Though the practice was never officially applauded, it was usually ignored and unreported.[84] Marriage was, in this instance, a private affair. Many accepted that like the courts, neighbours and family had no business intervening between husband and wife.[85] It is not surprising, therefore, that even when Upper Canadians were aware of an abusive relationship, many carefully avoided becoming involved.

In 1805, for example, it was known among some of the best families of York that Mrs Wyatt, "a lively good-humoured pretty little girl" of seventeen, was abused by her husband, the new attorney general. "Confinement to the bed-post, locking up in the cellar, bruised Arms & broken head were the portion of the little pretty woman from her brutal and deluded husband," Elizabeth Russell noted in her diary.[86] Neither Elizabeth nor anyone else of her social circle considered it their affair to intervene.

Similarly, Fanny Waite, a recently arrived Irish immigrant, came to her brother, Isaac Wilson, in 1828, seeking both financial help and emotional support.[87] Fanny was married to a man who appears to have been both bad-tempered and a spendthrift. With six children and no independent financial means, there was little Fanny could do to escape her "misery and distress." It was her intention, she told her brother, "to leave Waite altogether as soon as she could get a situation." Though three of her children had already left home, Fanny realized that it would still be difficult to find employment. More to the point, she did not expect that her husband would let her go. In the interim, Isaac Wilson recounted to his brother at home that their sister's situation was desperate. "If it was not for the charity of their neighbours they would be starving to death as the most of their living was bread and water, sometimes potatoes, but no salt to them. All the bed they had was some straw in one corner of the house swarming with fleas and bugs and they had nothing to cover them with. She had not had her clothes off all winter last. She said they had about six or seven acres of wheat but there were so many debts to pay there would be very little left for themselves. She said that instead of preparing ground for next years wheat he had been busy for 3 or 4 weeks making a fine gate."[88] Isaac loaned the couple £5. It was not until 1832, when money from a legacy finally arrived in Upper Canada that Isaac was able to provide more substantial material aid. He refused to relinquish Fanny's inheritance to her husband, however. Isaac again advanced the couple money two years later, this time £100 to defray the cost of building a house.[89]

There is no record if this financial aid relieved the Waites' situation. What is startling is that Isaac Wilson, though willing to listen to his sister and sometimes to provide her with financial support, apparently never intervened with her husband on her behalf. He certainly never appears to have suggested that Fanny leave her marriage. In the first half of the nineteenth century, it was up to the couple themselves to resolve their differences. In practice, it was left to the wife either to live within an unhappy marriage or to extricate herself as best she could.

The remedies available to women caught in an unhappy and perhaps abusive marriage were very limited. Family and society pressures dictated that once married, only death could legitimately separate husband and wife. Society told women to accept their fate and attempt by their example to change their husbands' actions and nature. Increasingly, women were advised to avoid attaching themselves to men who showed a tendency to intemperance and violence.[90] None of these suggestions resolved the dilemma faced by a woman living with an abusive husband.

For Mrs Wyatt and other elite women, leaving their husbands and seeking a divorce was out of the question. Divorce, which required an act of Parliament, was almost impossible to obtain. More to the point, the resulting publicity could destroy the woman's reputation. Not only would Mrs Wyatt have been ostracized by society, which had refused to acknowledge her plight in the first place, but it is likely that her family would have rejected her. This was what happened when Anne Powell's granddaughter, Elizabeth, abandoned her husband, John Stuart, and their three children in 1840 "after five years of marital unhappiness."[91] Elizabeth's family immediately refused to have any further contact with her. Elizabeth's notoriety also barred her from polite society.

Much more appropriate were the actions of Anna Jameson in 1837. After some years of unhappiness, Anna and her husband Robert, the newly appointed vice-chancellor of the province, apparently "reached an accommodation." Robert Jameson had come to Upper Canada alone in 1833 to become attorney-general. Anna arrived three years later, after the announcement of his new appointment, to establish his household and to give "the appearance of conventional normalcy."[92] She left shortly after her husband assumed his new position with a formal separation agreement that gave her an allowance and her independence.

Such an amicable resolution of marital differences was quite rare in Upper Canada. Only a few formal separation notices were published in local newspapers throughout the first fifty years of settlement. The notice of Jane and John Milton of Kingston, which appeared in 1817, was quite exceptional. After informing the public that the couple had "mutually agreed to part," the notice then outlined the division of the family properties. Jane received a portion of the livestock and farm implements and the right to remain in the marital home. (This implicitly acknowledged her ability and willingness to run the farm.) In addition, the two agreed "not to molest each other."[93] A few other separation notices published in subsequent years also made reference to a property settlement and provisions for the wife's support and maintenance.[94] Most, however, were merely a statement of the couple's determination to part and the husband's caution to the public that as a result, he would no longer pay his wife's debts.[95]

Given that many estranged couples probably had little property to divide, it is not surprising that formal separation agreements were rare. What is striking is that some couples actually went to the trouble and expense of formally working out and publicizing an agreement. The negotiations preceding such notices were undoubtedly protracted and painful, as a notice in 1838 from William Lougheed of Toronto Township suggests: "Whereas my wife, Hannah Lougheed has by diverse disputes and controversies with myself and others, acted very litigiously – I have, for the purpose of putting an end to the like in the future, left all differences between us to the arbitration of three magistrates of the Home District, and have entered into a joint bond with her to abide by their award, under the penal sum of two hundred pounds." He concluded his notice by saying, "I hereby caution the Public, Lawyers, Magistrates, merchants and all others, that I will not hold myself accountable for any debt she may contract in future."[96] Most women and men were neither inclined nor able to resort to such measures to resolve their marital difficulties. The action of choice, or the only option available to them, was to leave the marriage without any "forewarning."[97]

BETWEEN 1793 AND 1840, hundreds of notices or "cautions" appeared in local newspapers from aggrieved husbands.[98] "Whereas my wife Ezza Mark has left my bed and board without any just provocation on my part, I hereby give notice that I will not be accountable for any debts she contracts from this date, nor will I allow any of my debtors any money they pay her on my account & I also hereby caution all persons from harbouring her under their roof."[99] The husband's statement that the public was not to "trust" his wayward wife or to harbour, protect, give, or lend her anything had the force of law. By inserting such a notice, a husband absolved himself of any further financial or personal responsibility for his wife. Some men may have used this formula to control what they believed were their wives' "impecunious" behaviour. William Durham, for example, made no mention of desertion when he cautioned the public that his wife "seems determined to run me in Debt."[100]

In most instances, however, the situation seemed clear. The man's wife had "absconded" or "eloped" or "left" the home, usually without "any cause or just provocation." None of the desertion notices ever suggested that a wife might have cause to leave her husband. It was always the husband who was the aggrieved partner. It was the husband who had been provoked beyond endurance. The circumstances, it was presumed, left him no choice but to deny his wife. Newspaper editors appear to have had standard forms for such a situation. Many husbands used the occasion, however, to air specific grievances against their wives, to justify their actions or perhaps hoping to gain the public's sympathy.

Some deserted husbands such as George Crammer made reference to their wives' "impudent manner"; others such as Samuel Barick complained that his spouse's behaviour "render[ed] her unworthy of being my wife."[101] William Baird, for example, had been "under the disagreeable necessity of turning [his wife Mary] away" as a result of her "guilty conduct."[102] According to John B. Doute, he had "turned his wife [Rosaena] away" as she was "in the constant habit of getting intoxicated and neglecting her work."[103] A few men, perhaps in an attempt to humiliate their wives and their lovers, actually named the men with whom their wives were now living.[104]

In a few instances, a husband claimed that his wife had been "instigated by the devil" or "evil disposed persons."[105] "Her vile parents," John Anderson wrote in 1798 paid "no regard to [his wife Nancy's] marriage ... but violate[d] the laws of God and man."[106] Abraham Matice's complaint of his wife Sara was that she refused to live on their farm, knowing full well that they could not afford to live in town.[107]

A number of deserted men charged that their wives had not only left, but had "stolen" household items, money, or promissory notes. As a result, their husbands informed the public, these women were to be considered thieves as well as social outcasts. When Jemina Lyon and her children left her husband in 1828, for example, Ruben cautioned the public that notes given him by Samuel Dunham had been "unlawfully taken" and payment would "be stymied."[108] Lewis Stanley charged his wife Sara with stealing two notes and a bond for two hundred acres of land.[109] John Shellagh cautioned the public that not only had his wife Mary Angelic "eloped from my bed and board," but "she had stripped my house of everything valuable & carried them off in the absence of myself & my son while at work in the field, for which she can assign no reason, except of my checking of her (by speaking) for frequently getting beastly drunk, striving to barter her daughter (under 16 years of age) to a half Indian for three gallons of rum; & for her bad example to her two younger daughters, one 14 the other near 5 years old."[110]

A husband owned not only all family property, but was also responsible for and had the right to custody of his children.[111] Mary O'Brien recorded meeting a woman who had "*stolen* her three children from her husband," who was a half-pay officer "whose ill-conduct was no longer to be borne."[112] In 1830, Jonathon Hale, in an attempt to forestall his wife from retrieving his children, informed the public that any person or persons attempting to "induce" or "entice" his children "from their lawful home" or "detaining them" will be "prosecuted and subject to damages as the law directs."[113] Three years earlier, Sylvester Glynn had been somewhat more accommodating. He had offered in 1827 that "if the children will return, they shall be comfortably provided for."[114]

There were a number of fathers, however, who did not want to be responsible for their children when their wives left.[115] And ironically, in those circumstances when children, perhaps in desperation, were left behind, some husbands seized this as evidence of their spouse's perfidity. "Look at a good woman's conduct," an indignant George Lee stated in 1830, "who has left a family of small children, her husband & left her house by the advice of some person or persons who are neither the friends to her or her family."[116] According to Patrick McDallogh in 1826, his wife Brigid, "has again walked away with herself and left me five small children and her poor blind mother, and left nobody else to take care of the house and home etc and I hear she has taken up with Tim Ghighn, the lame fiddler the same that was put in the stocks last Easter, for stealing Barney Doody's gamecock."[117]

It appears that, despite their public notices, some husbands hoped that their wives would return. Ira Meed, for example, concluded his caution in 1828 that "if she [Marie] will return to her duty, she will be cheerfully received & kindly treated."[118] John Kelley notified his wife, Desire, a year later that "my door is open to receive her, should she see fit to return."[119] Henry Bertram stated that he placed his caution only after having for two years requested that his wife, Hepsebah, return.[120] At least one woman, Mary Armstrong, returned to her husband, and probably many more did so as well. Mary Armstrong, however, did not remain and in 1831, her husband John cautioned "with regret" that "again" he would pay no more debts, "she having left my bed and board a second time without just provocation."[121] It is clear that most deserted husbands did not expect their wives to return, and a few were obviously delighted that their spouses had finally left. Clark Molton was explicit. "Thank God my wife Susan has left my bed and board without provocation," he announced in 1833.[122] Charles Eddy Jr of Burford took only a few days to notify the public of his wife Sarah's desertion.[123]

It is impossible to determine with any level of certainty the total instance of marriage breakdown in Upper Canada between 1790 and 1840. Not only do we have no complete record of the number of marriages during this period, but apart from the notices published in local newspapers, there is no official record of separations. Moreover, it is likely that a number of husbands, perhaps knowing that their wives had left the area, or hoping to avoid acknowledging publicly that they could not control their wives, never officially published a "caution to the public." Others clearly waited years to notify the public of their marriage breakdown.[124] In some instances, it was only when a man "heard of [his wife's] return to this province" or her actions threatened to embarrass him or run him into debt that a notice was quickly printed.[125]

The extant desertion notices do make clear, however, that if not a common occurrence, marriage breakdown was not particularly unusual.[126] Moreover, whether children or property were taken or left, whether a wife had a lover or merely left with apparently no cause, it was in all instances the husband who was considered the wronged partner. Even wives who fled abusive, physically dangerous relationships could do little to defend their actions. In Upper Canada, deserting wives had no rights. They had no power to force their husbands to provide maintenance for their children. Many had no way to support themselves.

A number of wives received help from their own families. In 1814 or 1815, Esther Hawley Ham was, in fact, encouraged by her parents to leave her husband. Some months before, she had returned to her parents' home to recuperate after a difficult childbirth. When her husband violently demanded she return to the marital home, Esther's parents became concerned. Learning subsequently of their son-in-law's continued abuse of Esther, her parents "marched down to their daughter's farm" to retrieve her.[127] All attempts to resolve this marital dispute were unsuccessful. And almost ten years later, when Esther's father took his son-in-law to court to gain maintenance for his daughter, the presiding judge was not receptive. Despite evidence of Ham's abuse of his wife, Chief Justice Campbell stated that "the law was decidedly hostile to the practice of wives running away from their husbands." Moreover, the chief justice was very critical of Esther's parents for having become involved in the dispute and encouraging their daughter's transgressions. In the end, though the judgment was in favour of the Hawleys, the settlement was tiny. The jury, taking the advice of the chief justice, awarded Esther one month's maintenance, £2.10, not the £1,000 requested.[128]

Although the courts rarely supported a wife's pleas for assistance and society considered marital disputes a "private" affair, fragmentary evidence suggests that the actions of Esther Ham's parents were not unusual. And as Mary O'Brien's journal and the Richardson tragedy, cited earlier, indicate, battered and abused wives also did find some support from neighbours and friends.[129]

Women without family or friends in the area, or who perhaps feared that their husbands would pursue them, often moved out of the community to try to start a new life. Undoubtedly, many of those with children claimed to be widows, thus hoping to gain sympathy and social acceptability. There were also a few who remarried, knowing that their previous husbands were still alive. Peter Lepard was incensed in 1811 to discover that his new wife Jane already had a husband. "This is to notify all persons that a Woman came from Albany to East Gwilliamsbury who said she was the Widow of two Husbands and called herself Jane Muckieroy or Jane Thomas, but her maiden name was Jane Finch. She deceived me & I married her. Afterwards she told me that one of her husbands was alive, and I found out that she was un-wholesome." As a result Peter Lepard emphatically stated "therefore I do not consider her as my wife, and forewarn all persons from credit-ing or harbouring her on my account as I will pay none of her con-tracts."[130] John Beers of Saltfleet too was indignant in 1832. "The publick is hereby cautioned against a pox-marked Irish Woman, about 5 feet in height, by the names of MARGARET MACDONALD, alias HA-ZELIP, alias JOHNSON, alias SPENCER, alias SMITH, alias BEERS which name she has severally borne, having been the wife of all one of whom [Johnson] is a man of colour. I was married to her on the 26th of De-cember 1831, without knowing of her former husbands, and she hav-ing since absconded without my consent, I due hereby forbid all persons harbouring or trusting her on my account."[131] It is likely that other bigamous women were not discovered.

A number of women remained in their communities, however, and attempted to gain some recompense from their husbands directly. Challenging the law on married women's property, a few claimed that they had retained control of their property after their marriages. In 1799, Magdeline Utter, for example, replied to her husband's stan-dard separation notice that he would "not be responsible for her debts" by stating publicly that the economic situation in their house-hold was quite at variance with the "norm." "As the poor man had never paid any occasion or even any expense on my account, on the contrary, as he has expended considerable of my property for his debts and [I] am still dunned on his account, this is to give the public notice that I shall pay no debts of his contracting after this date."[132] Twenty-six years later, Mary Buckley of Kingston was prompted to insert a similar caution to the public against her hus-band, Barnard.[133]

Some wives attempted to assert their legal rights to maintenance in other ways. Anticipating her husband's separation notice, Charlotte Reid of Kingston warned the townspeople in 1819 not to purchase any property from her husband, Dr Reid, as she refused to relinquish her dower right.[134] Elizabeth Dieurran, also of Kingston, cautioned the public in 1814 from buying any property from her husband John, who had left her, "for there is no property which he can produce but that formerly belonged to me before marriage."[135] It is not known if any of these and other claims of separate property rights aired in the local newspapers were successful. What is significant is that a few women actually tried.

MOST MARRIED WOMEN did not, for a variety of reasons, assert such claims, and had no choice but to acknowledge their husbands' "right by law" to forbid anyone "trusting them."[136] Some were unwilling, however, to accept quietly their husbands' versions of their actions or motivations. Not only were they determined "to set the record straight" by replying to their husbands' notices that they "were not to be trusted," a number also probably hoped to expose their spouses to ridicule and public contempt.

Nancy Durham replied to her husband's accusation in 1799 that she "*prefers other men*" by stating emphatically that "in the sense you mean, the assertion is *false* and *scandalous*." She continued, "in another sense it is true." "There are but few men who less deserve any affection and none excepting yourself." Her husband, John, she charged, had tricked her into marriage and then left her for three years, during which time he had become a fugitive from justice. "I have never refused to do my duty," she asserted, "and share the disgrace you have incurred." And rather pathetically she concluded, "it is my fate to be tied in marriage to the basest of men."[137] Nancy Durham was obviously not alone in her plight. Sarah Peter rejoined "that nothing but fear for her life induced her to leave" her husband in 1829. Moreover, she stated, "the bed belongs to her."[138]

In a very long reply to her husband in 1824, Elizabeth Sheltenburgh told the story of how her husband John had refused to make a home for her or to provide support and was most often away altogether. "It is plain from your conduct," she wrote to the *Niagara Gleaner*, "that your sole object with me is to gratify a brutal passion without any trouble or cost to yourself." John, she charged, continued to come to her bed, despite his public renunciation. "You forbid the world to trust me," she declared, "and yet, wretched man, you can trust yourself asleep and unprotected in my very arms. Oh duplicity! Thou art personified and thy name is John Sheltenburgh."[139] In January 1820, Hannah Snider considered it a duty, not only to herself but also to her children to set the record straight concerning her marriage. She had not left her husband. Rather, he "himself withdrew from me and his children," leaving them "without the means of support or bedding at that inclement season of the year." She considered, "it necessary to state that his conduct has been for many years past, marked with the utmost severity and a total want of feeling either to myself or his children." Moreover, he had not furnished food or clothing since the previous October "although the children is an infant at the breast."[140]

One very suggestive marital dispute erupted in 1819 between Catherine and William Woodward of Kingston. In a reply to her husband's standard notice, Catherine stated that it was not she but William who had "turned me off without provocation." To make matters worse, he had "traded upon her money" and had made a fortune, and had then abandoned her for another woman.[141] In the next issue of the *Kingston Chronicle* William told his side of the story. During the nine years of the marriage, he wrote, he had "by industry and perseverance" improved and added to his property and the marriage had been satisfactory. It was when his daughter by a previous marriage had arrived from the United States that tension and acrimony had developed. His wife, he charged, had used his daughter "in a shameful and unnatural manner." The subsequent two and a half years of constant abuse had forced him to propose a separation, to which Catherine had agreed. It was only after this, he carefully explained, that at his daughter's prompting, he had begun to help and support his sister's daughter, whose husband had left her. He had provided his niece with "asylum in his house for the winter" and in return, his daughter was receiving help in the management of the household affairs. It was "from this circumstance" he concluded, that his wife "thought fit to publish her ridiculous statement, and to endeavour to injure me in the opinion of my friends and traduce the character of an innocent woman. I therefore consider it a duty I owe to myself to caution any person from trusting the said Catherine."[142]

Whether Elizabeth Sheltenburgh and other Upper Canadian women managed to embarrass their husbands or gain public sympathy is unclear. Certainly, William Woodward seemed concerned about his public image. At least a few others were as well. A curious report issued by six "good citizens" of Brockville appeared in that community's local newspaper in 1831. "We the undersigned having been appointed to investigate the conduct of Mr Ira Marcial, in relation to his treatment of his wife, in justice to that gentlemen beg leave to state to his friends and the public that after a minute investigation and examining many respectable witnesses, we are one and all candidly acquit Mr Ira Marcial of any indiscreet conduct towards his wife." Indeed, the investigators found that "on the contrary, she has been guilty of such misdemeanours as are unworthy of a wife and a virtuous women."[143]

We do not know if the good residents of Brockville were convinced by the citizens' report. One also wonders what happened to Mrs Marcial after this announcement was published. The tone of the notice suggests that relations between husband and wife had been strained for some time. Did this investigation lead to reconciliation? Or, as would seem more likely, had Mrs Marcial already left her husband?

The rights and wrongs of these and other marital disputes that appeared in the local newspapers are beyond the ability of this historian to determine conclusively. What is clear is that in early Upper Canada, marriage and the position of women in the home was often not what community leaders attempted to depict. Many marriages were fraught with tension, dissatisfaction, anger and violence and usually women were the target. Many relationships were not permanent or long-term. And regardless of the circumstances, it was almost always the women who were blamed. Given the social norms and the lack of legal protection available to women in Upper Canada, it is surprising that any wife would dare to assert her independence and publicly claim financial rights. Most were obliged to cope as best they could within the marriage or to rely on family and friends for support if their marriage became intolerable.

A BRIEF ARTICLE in the *Colonial Advocate* in 1829 does suggest that the public rhetoric of domesticity was beginning to have some impact on Upper Canadians' expectations of relations between husbands and wives. "From long observation," the editors wrote, "we have found that in ninety-nine cases in a hundred, where a wife has been advertised, the husband is a worthless sot and the wife a heart-broken and excellent woman." The editors then claimed that "our invariable rule is to reject such notes, and we believe that other printers, if they reflected on the subject as we have done, would follow our example. The value received from an advertisement of this description, should not be set in competition with the wounded feelings of an innocent female and her helpless children, thereby inflicted."[144] Such explicit support for an unhappy and perhaps battered wife was rare. It would be another two or three generations before the law and cultural values and social mores took the plight of abused married women seriously.[145]

In Upper Canada between 1790 and 1840, marital relationships varied enormously. Some women enjoyed a companionate relationship that offered security, affection, and trust. The O'Briens, the Macaulays, the Huttons, and other couples appear to have worked together through disagreements, during illness, and throughout financial disasters. In such instances, marriage marked both the beginning of a new family and the strengthening of the old. It provided both women and men with a sense of personal security from which to embark on other endeavours.

Many other women in Upper Canada were not so fortunate. Personality clashes and financial difficulties strained some marriages to the breaking point. The abuse of alcohol encouraged wife battery. So too did the social and legal institutionalization of patriarchy that provided women with little guarantee of personal safety if they stayed within the relationship and blamed them if their marriage failed, no matter who left.

Whether a marriage was "happy" or characterized by overt violence and abuse, it was a defining event in most women's lives; it was also the one institution within which most women in Upper Canada had to live and work. Publicly, being a wife and sustaining the marriage *was* women's work. Privately, and for individual women, the nature of their marriage relationships established the basic conditions within which almost *all* work was accomplished. The state of a woman's marriage and her relations with her husband had a direct impact on her ability to carry out her other work. It certainly had an immediate impact on how she fulfilled the responsibility of being a mother.

3 "A Fountain of Life to Her Children": Mothering in Upper Canada

In Upper Canada, being a mother was perhaps the most important role assumed by any woman. Only women, of course, could bear and suckle children. It was also believed that only women could effectively care for and ensure the physical well-being of their children. For it was traditionally in the home, at their mother's side, that children first learned their letters, respect for authority, and the value of hard work. In the premodern world, it was recognized that mothers therefore made a crucial economic contribution both to their families and to society at large. Children were a valuable asset and were also a vital source of labour. The injunction to be fruitful and multiply was very much a woman's duty and how well she performed this work had a direct impact of the welfare of her family.[1]

Yet as the nineteenth century unfolded, though the economic importance of mothering persisted, the idea of motherhood began to assume moral and emotional dimensions. Certainly colonial leaders stressed that *both* parents bore the responsibility of ensuring that their children were productive members of society. It was mothers, however, who were expected to assume the primary responsibility for their children's moral, religious, and personal development. There was no picture "more charming" to Upper Canadians "than that of an intelligent, virtuous mother assiduously instructing her infant offspring and using her daily endeavours both to inform their minds and fashion their hearts aright."[2] The value of a woman "who makes her husband and children happy, who reclaims one from vice and trains the other up in virtue" was, it was argued, incalculable. "In no relation [did] woman exercise so deep an influence [on society], both immediately and prospectively as in that of mother."[3] In the nursery, children learned "the principles of virtue and integrity"; early lessons in the home were "deeply engraven on the heart" and provided the foundations of "their earthly career."[4] The work of a good mother, many Upper Canadians believed, was invaluable.

For the thousands of women in Upper Canada who actually became mothers, "reproduction was the axis" of their lives.[5] Motherhood, at least as defined by the social prescriptions of the cult of true womanhood, was not. Indeed, colonial women's experiences as mothers usually bore little resemblance to the images glorified in the colonial press. For women in Upper Canada, motherhood was not an option but one of the inevitable consequences of marriage or, if unlucky, of being sexually active. Becoming a mother was a dangerous and potentially lethal process. Being a mother required considerable physical effort and skill and often took an immense emotional toll. It is not surprising that not all women welcomed the condition. For a single woman, becoming a mother could be disastrous. For a woman with an already large family, another pregnancy might threaten financial destitution or herald more work and worry than she could cope with. There was little most women could do to avoid it, however.

This is not to suggest that women in the colony were not mindful of or influenced by the new social expectations of motherhood. But the public responsibilities and liabilities of motherhood were the consequence of an intensely personal event. For support and advice about how best to manage, women turned, not to prescriptive literature or in most cases even to their mates but rather to other women – their mothers, daughters, sisters, women friends, and neighbours. Motherhood was one aspect of a woman's life which she shared almost exclusively with other women.

UPPER CANADIANS made little explicit reference, either publicly in the press, or privately in diaries and letters, as to *how* women became mothers. There was never any question, however, about *who* should become a mother. In Upper Canada, motherhood was a cultural institution. It was presumed, and sometimes explicitly stated, that marriage was an absolute prerequisite for motherhood. One of the primary purposes of marriage, after all, was to have children. Pregnancy and childbirth were visible symbols of a married couple's love and the fruition of their union. Pregnancy and childbirth without the benefit of marriage were evidence of a woman's depravity and immorality.

In 1817, Anne Powell found herself in a rather awkward and embarrassing situation. A young servant girl of "respectability" in whom Anne had shown particular interest was suddenly taken to her bed. Three months earlier, Anne had expressed some concern that the maid had seemed ill and might have "dropsy or something worse." She had not pursued the matter further at that time, however, and the "something worse" was unfortunately now evident. Though the servant girl protested her innocence, Anne's son, a doctor, confirmed the girl's condition. After thirteen hours of "dreadful sufferings" and with a newborn baby at her side, it was impossible for the maid to continue the pretence. Out of "Christian charity," Anne Powell gave the new mother and child her own "warm chamber in preference to the drafty servants' room." Anne was nonetheless scandalized by the affair. "This is a quite a history of a proof of moral depravity," she wrote "of which I have before heard but never until now witnessed it."[6] And Christian charity notwithstanding, a day after giving birth, the girl was dismissed.

The plight of Anne Powell's unnamed maid was not particularly unusual in Upper Canada. Neither was Anne's reaction. For a woman to engage in sexual activity outside marriage was roundly condemned by certain segments of Upper Canadian society. Yet all realized that a woman's biology and her emotional nature could, if uncontrolled, lead to such transgressions. Women, it was believed, were dominated by their reproductive organs.[7] The very characteristics that enabled them to bear children also made them emotionally and psychologically unstable. A woman's sexuality was also potentially dangerous – to herself, to men, and to society at large. Good women denied their "baser" instincts. Even when pictured with a child at the breast, "good" mothers, who were, of course, first "good" wives, were portrayed as essentially asexual.[8]

The pregnancy or motherhood of a single woman was an undeniable sign of a girl's immorality. Indeed, such a situation was almost considered "unnatural." Upper Canadians acknowledged that in exceptional circumstances, a man might bear some of the responsibility if a single girl became pregnant. It was conceivable that the best of young girls *could* be ravished by a persuasive man who took advantage of her passionate nature.[9] Even then, however, it was almost always the unfortunate girl rather than the offending man who bore the blame. Reports from the courts and a few apparently autobiographical accounts in the press indicate that it was the girl and not her errant paramour who was obliged to accept the consequences of extramarital sexual intercourse.

"In this small community," one matron in York wrote at the turn of the century, "unmarried men make up the majority; and it must awaken pity in every mind, not rendered callous by vice," she noted, "to witness the dissipation which reigns."[10] All too often, she observed, young girls were abused or raped by older men. Theft and violence against women were rife, and illegitimacy was a common occurrence. As the matron so correctly stated, men were rarely punished for their actions. Rather, it was the single and now pregnant young woman who was "invariably avoided by the wise and the good [and who] we see ... unpossessed of rank and respect."[11]

The illegitimacy rate in Upper Canada is unknown for this period.[12] And certainly, not all unmarried mothers were shunned by their communities. In 1842, one traveller to the colony was puzzled by the attitude of a woman who informed him that her daughter Betty had been born two years before she had married. The woman was in no way ashamed of this and it did not appear to have harmed her prospects of marriage. Indeed, she informed the visitor, the attitudes of females "of the old country" on this matter were "ridiculous."[13]

It is clear, however, that motherhood was a disaster for a number of single women. Given the attitude of many colonial employers and leading citizens, at least some single pregnant women attempted to hide their condition and, if possible, birth the child away from home or their place of work.[14] Like Anne Powell's maid, a few were successful, at least for a time. In 1838, Ann Macaulay was shocked when her maid "Mary had a child by Michael." As Ann reported to her son John, "It happened she was not long ill as it was born in the porch, they took her over the way where they got a room for her. I had not the least suspicion of her being in such a state." Mary, like Anne Powell's maid, was summarily dismissed.[15]

The options that were open to Mary and other unwed mothers in Upper Canada were limited. Many women probably married their lovers, either before or after the child was born. If the father of the child was reluctant, a few women tried to force him at least to acknowledge responsibility for his actions. Mary Bowen, a single girl who was apparently pregnant, publicized her plight in the local newspaper. Thomas Harris, who now intended to marry another girl, was guilty of the breech of promise of marriage, she stated in the *Kingston Chronicle*. "By his false insinuations" he has "caused me to go astray from the path of my duty to myself and my God and by that means has involved me in trouble and shame and caused the displeasure of my parent and my God to fall on me by depriving me of my home and communion which I formerly held with my brethren and my God."[16]

More frequently, girls turned to their parents, who pursued the matter on their behalf. One father, Mr Thompson, sued John Brown in 1824 for loss of his daughter's services, "she having born a child" which she claimed was the plaintiff's. The judgment was upheld, despite evidence that this was not the first time Maria Thompson had "fallen." She had been observed, one witness stated, with another man "as closely connected as man and wife."[17] In the same assizes, a Mr Fuller was unsuccessful in his suit against Mr Secord. Though there was no question that Secord was the father of the child, the court found that the Fullers had willingly permitted him to bed their daughter.[18]

However, it was the exceptional woman or family who was willing to pursue such matters publicly. Most chose to try to cope with the situation privately. One way of hiding a girl's transgressions was to dispose of the actual evidence.

It is unknown how prevalent infanticide was in Upper Canada. That at least some women in Upper Canada actually killed their newborns is without question.[19] From time to time, local newspapers reported that an infant had been found abandoned or a baby's body had been retrieved from a well or river. When possible, colonial authorities punished the mother and any other accomplices. In 1834, Mr Harvey Wood (the putative father), Hiram Wood (the grandfather), Julia Harvey, and Mary Stillman (the mother) were all convicted of causing the death of an infant "by exposure to cold, the want of proper nursing, nourishment and care, and through neglect and violence."[20] That same year, "the wife of a respectable farmer" was committed to jail for advising and assisting her daughter "in the destruction of an illegitimate newborn infant." The daughter had fled.[21]

The courts frequently found it difficult, however, to refute the mother's assertion that the child had died naturally.[22] In other cases, though a child's body provided evidence of a crime, the mother was never discovered. Then the newspapers were left to report rumours – that an abandoned or abused newborn belonged to "respectable" parents or to a woman of high rank.[23] In 1834, for example, the *Hallowell Free Press* recounted that the parents of a newborn infant found abandoned outside a family's door were from the "highest" ranks of society.[24]

Infanticide, it seems, was committed by women and men of all classes of colonial society. Regardless of the perpetrator, it was considered one of the most heinous crimes. Only an "unnatural" woman who had embraced the depths of depravity could kill her child or abandon it to the elements.[25] In 1831, one York newspaper, the *Cana-*

dian Freeman, feared that such atrocious acts were increasing. After reporting the discovery of a murdered newborn child in a box in a well, the editor continued, "The crime of infanticide is becoming of frequent occurrence in this town ... This is the third infant that has been butchered no doubt by the unnatural monsters who gave them birth ... within the last 4 or 5 years." Such "wickedness" was harming the "character of our community," and he called on the government to take measures "to check such atrocious" acts and clean up "such foul and indelible stains."[26] Infanticide violated both the law and community standards. It was an affront to those images of womanhood that community leaders were carefully nurturing. And it was the community, not the degenerate woman, that deserved protection and aid.

Few Upper Canadians would have consciously associated unwed mothers with their public image of motherhood. Rather, their veneration of motherhood was an integral part of the conception of the good woman. Motherhood in Upper Canada was a cultural institution that depended upon and also reinforced the importance of marriage and family. Certainly, the manner in which individual women responded to motherhood was determined at least in some part by their marital status. It also depended on many other factors, including the family's financial circumstances and a woman's previous experience as an expectant mother. For some married women, motherhood was eagerly anticipated; for others, it was dreaded.

"AT 4 O'CLOCK this evening, Mrs Johnson safely delivered of a son – I call *George* after the dear boy I lost." Two years later, Captain William Johnson of Georgina again recorded in his diary, "Today my dear Margaret was born."[27] With no reference to the health of mother or daughter, the next day he simply wrote, "Paid Mrs Elwes for her attendance $5.00." These simple notations are easily overlooked among Captain Johnson's daily and at times voluminous record of the weather and the work accomplished on the farm. They certainly display little of the apprehension or the joy that his wife's confinements must have fostered in the Johnson household, since even in the busiest and most harried of households, the birth of a child was a momentous event. Only women, however, experienced the discomfort of pregnancy and the pain and danger of childbirth.

Married women in Upper Canada expected to become pregnant shortly after their wedding, and then again at approximately two to three year intervals thereafter until they reached menopause. Though the average number of children in any one family is unknown for the first half of the nineteenth century, large families with as many as nine or a dozen children were apparently not unusual.[28]

Upper Canadian women, like their Anglo-American sisters, first suspected that they were pregnant when their menstrual cycle was interrupted and they began to experience some physical discomfort. The quickening of the fetus confirmed the pregnancy.[29] For the next four or five months, women coped with the tiredness, physical awkwardness, and sometimes active illness as best they could.[30] Certainly they received little public advice on the matter.

In 1812, one newspaper article did advise mothers to make sure that their daughters were healthy and strong. "Daughters are to be the mothers of the next generation," they were reminded. "A pale, weakly, softly mother" could not produce "a race of heroes and statesmen, men of vigorous minds and strong constitutions."[31] Some time later, a brief article on "Medical Remarks on Marriage" warned girls not to marry and have children until "their constitution is confirmed." If they did not wait, their "health and future comfort are sacrificed either to the inconsiderate vehemence of a girlish passion, or to the baser gratification of one desirous to unite itself with youth." The "Physician" recommended that a girl be twenty-four or twenty-five years old "before subjecting herself to the cares and fatigues which the duties of married life necessarily impose." He also warned women "about to become mothers" to avoid "visiting, late hours, dancing & other dissipations."[32]

At least until 1840, Upper Canadians publicly expressed little concern about the problems a woman might have during pregnancy.[33] It seems to have been presumed that women instinctively understood such matters. Certainly, pregnant women relied on their common sense to cope with the inevitable side effects of their condition. They also sought the advice of family, women friends, and perhaps a local granny or midwife.[34] Within the constraints of their individual circumstances, most pregnant women tried to take care of themselves. For example, when she was pregnant, Mary O'Brien was conscious of the need to take moderate exercise and to avoid heavy physical work whenever possible. This did not prevent her from experiencing increasing tiredness and lethargy as each pregnancy progressed. And as she complained to her sister during her first pregnancy, she had to continue with her "multitudinous bustling employments ... at moments snatched from sickness."[35] Only affluent women had the opportunity afforded by their financial means and the availability of professional help "to retire" almost completely during the last part of their pregnancy. Most Upper Canadian women had little choice but to continue to work until just before the child was born. And although many could rely on older daughters or other adult women in the household or neighbourhood to relieve them of at least some of their daily work, this did not assure a healthy or safe pregnancy.

In January 1829, Mary Gapper recorded in her diary that "Mary [Southby, her sister-in-law] is poorly tonight & has been putting us on the qui vive, but if with reason, she must have strangely miscalculated." Mary Southby had gone into labour, and the next day, "in defiance of all our precautions & ... after a few minutes of intense anxiety for her safety" gave birth to a stillborn son. Mary Southby had not miscalculated; the child was three or four months premature.[36] Though it appeared that she would recuperate rapidly, ten days after the birth, the family's "anxiety was heightened to alarm."[37] It was another two weeks before Mary was on the way to full recovery. She did not have long to regain her health, however. Three months after the first miscarriage, Mary Southby discovered that she was pregnant again. By the beginning of the second trimester, she was "weak, & unfit for any exertion." The family consulted a doctor in York but he predicted that "without great care we should have a repetition of the last event." Mary Southby miscarried that October at seven months, and this time it took her a month to "resume the reins."[38]

During her fourth pregnancy (the Southbys did have a young daughter) Mary Southby took particular care of herself. In March 1830, her sister-in-law noted that though "Mary has given me a new source of anxiety ... which may endure until perhaps Sept," there was room for hope. Mary was in much better physical health than during her previous pregnancies.[39] And so as not to be "as ill as on the two preceding occasions," she took regular moderate exercise, refused "to ride beyond a walk," and again consulted a doctor.[40] All Mary Southby's precautions and the careful attendance of her family were in vain, however. On 10 July 1830, just five months into her pregnancy Mary Southby was "obliged to go to bed." Despite taking opium as prescribed by Doctor Daly, "before ten o'clock" the next day, Mary O'Brien recorded that "our disappointment was consum(m)ated and our anxieties almost dissipated; she had suffered more acutely than I had ever before seen her do but the moment which terminated her pain seemed also to restore her to health & almost her usual strength & spirits." Not only was the baby premature, but it had, according to the doctor been dead eight or nine days before Mary had gone into labour.[41] The only difference between this latest pregnancy and the previous two was that Mary recovered more rapidly.[42]

For Mary O'Brien, who in mid-1830 was herself already pregnant with her first child, her sister-in-law's persistent illnesses during her pregnancies and her inability to carry a child to term were salutary reminders of what she too might experience. Indeed, the possible complications of pregnancy were never far from Mary's mind. During the sixth month of her first pregnancy, Mary wrote to her niece, Cara, that she was physically well, though quite thin. More important, she confided, "my own feelings do not fail to remind me almost every moment of the awful crisis to which I am fast approaching."[43] Two and a half months later, Mary continued to anticipate the birth of her first child "with desire & with trembling." "My death," she wrote to her sister, "I cannot reasonably perhaps anticipate as a probable event yet it cannot be more than usually present in my mind." If it was the will of God to take her and her child, then Mary accepted it. She had one dread – that "my faith should be found wanting."[44]

Such concerns for the future did not stop Mary from preparing for her baby. Clothes had to be made and a cradle prepared. Even this, however, evoked bittersweet apprehensions. In January 1831 she recorded that her mother "has done all my baby work for me – my preparations have truly not been very extensive." Mary explained that "I have not been very zealous of admit(t)ing assistance since the dear object of all these labours may perhaps be destined to depend on others for future protection & if I am permitted to be its nurse there will soon be enough care as well as affection expended on it to bind it to me."[45]

Mary O'Brien's children did not have "to depend on others for future protection." Moreover, her subsequent pregnancies appear to have been without serious incident. It is likely, however, that throughout each one, Mary experienced similar anxieties about her own health and that of her child. Such trepidation was undoubtedly shared by most women, who knew from their own experience or that of a neighbour or friend, how debilitating and dangerous pregnancy could be.

THE DISCOMFORT and potential dangers of pregnancy were only the beginning of a woman's sometimes perilous experience of motherhood. The actual circumstances of Mary O'Brien's first confinement are unknown. She apparently stayed with one of her sisters-in-law and was attended by family members. She returned home a month after her son's birth.[46]

In her second confinement, sixteen months later, Mary was at home. Although all the family, including Mary's two sisters-in-law had planned to be in attendance, labour started earlier than anticipated. As Mary recorded, "[I awoke] to strange and ominous sensations. Edward set to work to get the stove up and I lay as quiet as I could on the sofa ... After dinner I went into Mama's room to get out of their way and from thence I did not very immediately return, for a few minutes made me the mother of another son. The nurse had not arrived but Mamma was so completely taken by surprise that she had not time to be alarmed & with Edward's assistance & Flora's [the maid] ministrations, she did all that was requisite for me & the baby."[47] During her next two confinements, in 1835 and again in August 1836, Mary was supported by the family and had a doctor present. In the summer of 1837, though Edward was away on business, Mary was attended by both a doctor and nurse.[48]

Susanna Moodie's third confinement in the mid-1830s, was considerably different. When Susanna, then living on a farm, came to term, she was for all intents and purposes alone. Her good servant, Mary, had suddenly returned to her father; her husband was ill with the fever, her younger daughter Addie was "sick almost to death of the summer complaint and the eldest [daughter] still too young to care for herself." Only after considerable searching and "offering enormous wages" did Susanna succeed in getting a nurse "to attend her through her confinement." But then the nurse "was attacked by the same fever." "In the midst of this confusion and with my precious little Addie lying insensible on a pillow at the foot of my bed – expected every moment to breathe her last – on the night of the 26th of August, the boy I so ardently coveted was born." Rather than a happy event, Susanna Moodie remembered that time "as a melancholy season, one of severe mental and bodily suffering. Those who have drawn such agreeable pictures of a residence in the backwoods never dwell upon the periods of sickness, when, far from medical advice and often, as in my case, deprived of assistance of friends by adverse circumstances, you are left to languish, unattended, upon the couch of pain."[49]

The circumstances of Susanna Moodie's confinement, it must be stressed, were very unusual. Childbirth in Upper Canada was most often a communal affair. Husbands and fathers were banished from the room and throughout the first half of the nineteenth century, expectant mothers in Upper Canada were usually attended by women relatives and neighbours. Although after 1815, a growing number of relatively affluent women appear to have been increasingly willing to consult a doctor and to have one in attendance, most households relied on a local midwife or granny – an older woman who had children of her own and had acquired some expertise, having attended a number of births, for professional advice and assistance.[50]

It was not always possible to get even a "trained" midwife in rural Upper Canada. In February 1830, Mary O'Brien and her sister-in-law Fanny were called to attend "a poor Yorkshire woman who was apparently in immediate want of the assistance of a Granny."[51]

Though neither Fanny nor Mary had any experience, they were the only help available and as neighbours and as women, they felt obliged to offer whatever support they could. Over the next seven years, Mary assisted at least four other neighbourhood women during childbirth.[52] When Frances Stewart gave birth to Charles Edward in 1832, "a suitable nurse could not be heard of." Frances was forced to turn to a local doctor's sister, who was "a good and true friend" for assistance.[53]

Experienced and, in some cases, trained midwives were increasingly available in Upper Canada's growing towns and villages, and at least a few of them advertised their expertise in local newspapers. In 1829, Mrs Sarah Tebutt who had, according to her advertisement in the *Colonial Advocate*, practised midwifery for several years in England before she had arrived in the colony, set up a practice in York.[54] Four years later, Mrs Smith offered "testimonials" of experience gained in Edinburgh to the ladies of Kingston.[55] At least one midwife, Mrs Margaret McCaul, relied upon her reputation gained while living in York to attract clients after she moved to Brockville.[56] It is likely that many and perhaps most midwives could not afford or did not need to place notices in local newspapers to gain clients. Even in the colony's largest communities, midwives relied on word of mouth, their own reputation, and recommendations from other women within the immediate community to gain employment.

It is somewhat ironic that as the number of professional midwives in Upper Canada appears to have increased, so did the number of male doctors eager to attend birthing women. In the 1820s and 1830s, it was not unusual for middle- and upper-class women such as Mary Southby or Mary O'Brien to take the advice of a doctor during their pregnancies and to have one on hand to oversee and, if necessary, to intervene during the birth.[57] Some affluent women who had had difficulties in previous pregnancies sought all the professional help they could get and could afford during their pregnancies and the births of their children. Helen Macaulay, for example, had a doctor, a midwife, and a nurse in attendance for at least two of her three pregnancies.

Little is known of the circumstances of Helen Macaulay's first pregnancy and the birth of her daughter Annie in 1835. What is evident from the family correspondence is that subsequent pregnancies were difficult. In the seventh or eight month of what was probably her second pregnancy, Helen was "confined to bed." John, clearly concerned about his wife's health, engaged a professional nurse and arranged for a doctor to visit regularly.[58] As he reported to his mother, John hoped that with "the greatest care ... all might yet end well."[59] Helen Macaulay was fortunate. Two weeks later, after a long and difficult labour, Helen gave birth to a daughter. Helen and her new daughter, little Helen, continued to be supervised by Dr King. John wrote to his mother that, given the circumstances (the child had been in the breech position, in addition to being a month premature), Helen "is doing remarkably well" and he hoped "in a fortnight or so" she would be able to "get into the labour again."[60] But Helen developed a high fever and took "severe pains" at the end of December and her subsequent recuperation took some considerable time. In March 1839, John, grateful that his wife had survived at all, reported that Helen was still only "pretty well."[61]

Helen's experience during her next pregnancy was even more frightening. In probably her fifth or sixth month, Helen, tired and often ill, moved her bed to the dining room to avoid climbing stairs. "I feel much more knacked by my situation more so than either of the former occasions," she wrote to her mother-in-law. Given her past experience and her present health, John "doubted whether she [would] reach her anticipated time in May."[62]

The presence of Dr Telfer and Mrs Hayden (perhaps a nurse midwife) was obviously considered essential when on 10 April 1840, Helen gave birth to triplets, at least two months prematurely. After the birth, though mother and daughters appeared to be thriving, Helen was understandably exhausted. Dr Telfer was kept on call and John engaged a young healthy English woman "to act as wet nurse."[63] The youngest and smallest of the triplets died two days later. The other two died within the week. John kept the news of the infants' deteriorating condition from his wife and attended to much of the nursing himself.[64] As his sister-in-law, Anne, described the situation to his mother, "poor John never went to bed until four in the morning and held the little darling himself a great part of the time." In a subsequent letter, she described how "poor John was really quite knocked up on friday and saturday nights. I do not think he ever had so severe a trial in his life as witnessing the agony of his darling babe."[65]

Helen apparently "escaped the fever," though her recovery was understandably complicated by the deaths of the three newborns.[66] Within a month of her confinement, Helen was up and out in the family carriage; she continued to be very thin, however. Helen did not fully recover until after the couple had travelled to Sarasoga Springs, New York in the fall and Helen had taken further medical advice and treatment.[67]

Helen Macaulay's and Mary Southby's experiences were tragic; however, when compared to the situations in which other women found themselves, the two women were fortunate. Though they lost their newborns, Mary and Helen survived. Many women in Upper

Canada did not. Mortality rates during childbirth are unknown for this period. Obituaries in the local press suggest, however, that such tragedies were relatively frequent. A surprising number of young women in their first confinements and older women with a number of children died from exhaustion, the fever, or other related causes.[68]

Gentlewomen such as Helen Macaulay and Mary Southby had other significant advantages. Helen Macaulay had full-time domestic staff and could, during her pregnancies, retreat from many of the day-to-day responsibilities of her household. After each birth, the family could afford to hire a full-time nurse to look after the newborn; another nursemaid cared for the other children. Mary Southby also had a maid. More important, she had the help of her sister-in-law and her mother-in-law who eagerly assumed most of the household duties before, during, and for some time after Mary's confinements. Thus, Helen Macaulay, Mary Southby, and other relatively affluent women or those with attending family had the opportunity to regain their health after each pregnancy. It appears that Helen Macaulay enjoyed the month of lying-in traditionally afforded confined women. Most women in Upper Canada were not so fortunate. Engaging a nurse or consulting a doctor was financially out of the question. And most women were obliged to continue their domestic or waged work throughout their pregnancies, and childbirth only interrupted their daily chores.

It is impossible to judge whether having servants to relieve them of their daily work or the attendance of a doctor made any real difference to the outcome of Helen Macaulay's or Mary Southby's confinements. What is clear is that in some households, especially relatively affluent ones, the rituals and circumstances of childbirth were beginning to change in the first half of the nineteenth century. Some women considered it both appropriate and necessary to consult a male doctor. Despite this, even wealthy women of the colonial upper class continued to rely primarily on the support of other women to see them through their ordeal.

Throughout that week in April 1840, the Macaulay household was "well filled." As John wrote to his mother, there were "four children, two nurses, two aunts, two Floras [the maids] besides the ordinary servants."[69] Though John assumed at least some of the responsibilities for nursing the triplets, he readily acknowledged that the assistance of Helen's sisters and friends was indispensable. "Poor Helen," he wrote after the death of the triplets, "had a very severe trial and I have had some new experiences of what life is ... I really do not know what I should have done during the illness of the infants if Ann [his sister-in-law] had not happily been here." While Helen recuperated,

Anne ran the household, oversaw the work of the servants, and nursed Helen and the children.[70]

During childbirth and perhaps for some time after, all colonial women relied heavily on the emotional and physical support they received from an often informal network of women that crossed class and ethnic lines. This community included family members, friends, neighbours, women who worked for wages, and women such as Helen Macaulay and Mary Southby who in turn helped their sisters and friends as part of their kinship with other women.[71] These female community networks were an essential part of all women's lives, and they continued to provide vital support to mothers as they coped with their domestic responsibilities and raised their children.

PREGNANCY AND CHILDBIRTH were essentially private affairs in Upper Canada (unless of course they occurred outside of marriage, in which case they were grounds for vehement public condemnation). How to raise the nation's children was always a public concern, however. Between 1800 and 1840, colonists went to considerable lengths in the press and from the pulpit to instruct mothers how best to carry out their onerous responsibilities.

In theory, the responsibility for rearing children and maintaining a well-ordered family rested with both parents. Given the innate differences between the sexes, however, it was asserted that the contributions made by a father and a mother to the enterprise differed significantly. Colonial fathers were the protectors, the providers, and the final authority within the family.[72] They were also expected to love their children, to take an interest in their activities, and to take pride "in their expanding virtues."[73] Moreover, it was believed that it was fathers who were best suited to assume "the office of a tutor" to their children.[74] Yet Upper Canadians accepted that a father was "less domestic" than a mother. "Worldly cares engross his mind; necessary cares engross his mind; necessary business calls him from home; and the kindnesses he bestows on his infant offspring are more indirect and therefore less obvious and impressive."[75] This was not to suggest that "the love of a father [was no less] deep and sincere" than that of a mother; it was, however, "more calculating and more fully directed in the great period and ends of life."[76]

Colonial leaders maintained that physically, emotionally, and morally, it was mothers who were best equipped to nurture and to train their children and who bore "the great[est] responsibility ... of forming their characters."[77] A mother, after all, was her children's "first friend." From infancy "she dispenses their food; dandles them in her arms, and assiduously guards their waking hours ... The name of a mother is our childhood's talisman, our refuge and our safeguard in all our misery."[78] A mother's love "transcend[ed] all other affections."[79] Even into adulthood, a mother was her children's "stay and solace when smitten by sudden calamity."[80]

Upper Canadians were quite clear on the attributes of a "good" mother. She was virtuous, discrete, pure, tender, and loving. When the need arose, she could also be strong, supportive, and untiring. A good mother, colonists believed, was "a fountain of life to her children."[81] An industrious mother was "sure to train up good children."[82] The mystique of motherhood was emphatic that "when so good and wise a being as a well-educated mother presides over the incipient stages of infant thought, the child is far on in the high road of knowledge and wisdom."[83] In fact, it was asserted that "a prudent and moral mother ... may, in a great degree, counteract in her family the unhappy consequences of her husband's intemperance or dissolute life." If a mother "walks in the path of virtue and religion, she is the safest support of a son." If, however, "she is unprincipled, the whole house is lost."[84] A brief article on "Female Responsibility" printed in 1834 stated emphatically, "Go visit the abodes of wretchedness and poverty! Go visit our gaols, our prisons, our alms-houses and without speaking hyperbolically, you can see these are the fruits of the negligence of mothers ... *Mothers*, upon you depend the future welfare of your children. You can see them the abject sons of poverty and shame or spring up like a well-watered plant, to warm your last days with *happiness, and peace.*"[85]

If they had time to consider the matter, most mothers in Upper Canada must have smiled ruefully or railed angrily at the press's depiction of the mystique of motherhood and its preoccupation with the virtues and responsibilities of a "good" mother. Certainly, the compelling image of a tranquil woman sitting in front of the hearth with a contented child at her breast and other smiling children grouped around hid the everyday reality of most women's lives. Raising children in Upper Canada was hard work. It required skill and energy and consumed an increasing proportion of women's time. As Mary O'Brien recorded in 1832, "the constant interruption of two babies" left her with "but little time" for anything else.[86] Frances Stewart ruefully commented in 1829, "I am in despair about being able to do anything but nurse or fuss a little over housekeeping." She explained that "even now I scribble with my little John sleeping on my arm, while the three elder ones are making all sorts of noises in the room."[87]

Initially, a new mother's time was taken up nursing and tending her newborn. In 1827, Frances Stewart remarked that her "little nursling Frank" needed to be watched constantly. She wrote home,

"All hours of the day and night I am engaged with him," to the detriment of her housework, her mending, and her older children.[88] Most women in Upper Canada appear to have nursed their own children for at least six months and in some cases as long as a year. The length of time that a child was at the breast depended on a number of factors. Many mothers used nursing as a way to try to delay a subsequent pregnancy.[89] For other women, their health, the demands made by other young children in the family, and the need to resume waged work forced them to wean the child early. Ann Macaulay's comment that her relative Jane was "behaving very badly in weaning her baby at six months" suggests that when there were no mitigating circumstances, six months was considered far too young to take a child off the breast.[90]

Mary O'Brien had little choice when she weaned her first born, Willie. "I have no trouble in deciding when to wean my present treasure," she wrote to her sister, "since the scanty supply of milk which I before had failed entirely."[91] Willie was about ten months old and Mary was soon to discover that she was pregnant for the second time. Mary had more trouble weaning her second child eighteen months later. "Weaning baby has led to two or three nights of broken sleep," she reported. The process was complicated and interrupted by an illness in the family.[92] But "baby being now ten months old & I am not over well, I believe I must seriously attempt to get another step in weaning her and in prosecution of this design, I have taken two walks today."[93]

If a mother did not have sufficient milk, was ill or, as often occurred, died during or after childbirth, a family was obliged to hire a wet nurse.[94] Anxious households, like the Macaulays in April 1840, relied on friends and neighbours to find "a good clean girl" who would live with the family as long as her services were required.[95] Others placed notices in local newspapers. "Wet nurse ... wanted immediately, a healthy young woman in the above capacity," a typical advertisement exclaimed.[96] It is likely that a number of families responded to advertisements of lactating women who "wanted a situation as a wet nurse" and promised "satisfactory testimonials as to character."[97]

A mother regained some freedom of movement after her child was off the breast (at least until the next child arrived) and many women looked forward to this. Frances Stewart predicted that once Frank was weaned, he would "be able to take care of himself." Certainly, she stated, he would require "less watching."[98] Toddlers still had to be fed, clothed, and carefully watched, however. Moreover, unavoidable accidents, injuries, and inevitable childhood diseases only added to a mother's work as well as increasing her anxiety for the life and health of her children.

The threats to a young child's life in early Upper Canada were many. Once the baby began to crawl and toddle, the mother or an older sister or brother had to be constantly vigilant to ensure a child's safety. Children had to be taught to avoid the open fireplace, the river, the well, or the medicine cabinet. Eli Playter recounted the incident of a young girl who tipped scalding water on herself and though she survived, was in constant pain and badly scarred.[99] Mary O'Brien recorded an incident of a child burned beyond recognition when left alone.[100] Curious children also got into medicines. In 1829, Mary O'Brien found her niece "eating some Pills." The family's considerable alarm was only assuaged when the child showed no ill effects after many hours.[101] Not all families were so fortunate. In 1823, Frances Stewart's youngest child, Bessy, ate some "raw Indian corn" and "was seized with dysentery." Frances frantically sought the assistance of a doctor for she was "quite ignorant of the treatment of this disease." Despite all her best efforts and the eventual ministrations of Dr H., Bessy died. As Frances Stewart recorded, "it was a bitter trial."[102]

Protecting children from accidents was possible, at least to some degree. Shielding them from disease was not. The hazards of Upper Canadian homes were overshadowed by the mother's knowledge that at least some of her children were likely to succumb to influenza, whooping cough, scarlet fever, measles, or after 1832, cholera. Thomas Radcliffe, an Irish immigrant, apologized to his father in December 1832 for taking so long to write. "But having heard of us all, from others of the family, you will make due allowances, and sympathize with us in the melancholy loss which has pleased God to afflict us. The despondency we suffer at having our dear little girl taken off in a few hours by the fatal pestilence and our anxiety for the safety of the other children caused our difficulties and privations to be doubly felt. We are now, thank God, in perfect health, our spirits beginning to revive."[103] Thomas Radcliffe was certainly not the only Upper Canadian parent to lose a child. It is estimated that on average, colonial families could expect that at least one of their children would die before they reached adolescence. As Mary O'Brien wrote, there were times when "the precariousness of [their] lives ... pressed painfully upon me as if it had occurred for the first time, altho' in fact it is never absent from my mind."[104]

Upper Canadian mothers dreaded the annual arrival of the fever or ague and the periodic appearance of measles, mumps, or other potentially fatal diseases. Households did what they could to avoid exposing themselves and their children to infection. In December 1831, for example, Edward O'Brien "horrified at the mortality amongst the children which [was] raging in York in the shape of Scarlet fever and measles," invited Mrs Herchmer, a family friend, and her children to come to the O'Briens to escape the epidemics.[105] Two months later, Mary left her new baby at home when she went visiting to avoid "infectious disorders." Many mothers had their children vaccinated.[106] Others such as the Macaulays took the children away from the city during times when "the fever" was present.[107] Yet no measures effectively stopped children from getting colds, influenza, or childhood diseases.

Nursing ill children appears to have been a constant occupation for mothers. Mary O'Brien's journal makes frequent references to tending a child who was teething, had a cold, or a more serious ailment. In November 1833, she recorded one day of "nursing, cooking, nursing again, sewing, nursing, eating, sewing, nursing, talking, nursing, singing."[108] Throughout late 1833 and well into 1834, Mary was also tending to her increasingly ill mother. In some cases, a child's illness was not particularly serious. There were many other occasions, however, when parents despaired of their child's recovery. In March 1834, Mary was "distressed about Willie," her eldest. "The impression that I shall live to miss him from my path is always present to me," she wrote. "Sometimes I can almost think of it with complacence, though my heart bleeds over it."[109]

Though often fearful of catching the complaint themselves, Upper Canadian mothers cared for the members of their families with whatever means and help was at hand. In many cases, all members of the family succumbed to a malaria-like fever and many diaries recorded its annual appearance. If the case was severe, the family might seek medical advice. More likely, however, and particularly in the backwoods, home-made remedies – perhaps ginger tea or the more powerful gum tea, pepper and whisky combinations – were taken.[110] In 1840 when her granddaughter Helen was ill with what seems to have been the flu and a bowel complaint, Ann Macaulay recommended "a little mutton broth every day." She also reminded her son that "a good nurse," meaning her daughter-in-law Helen, "was better than a doctor when one is recovering from an illness." And given the time of year, she concluded, sickness amongst children was only to be expected.[111]

As in the case of their confinement, colonial women relied on other women for advice and help when an illness was particularly severe or widespread. When the Johnson children and their mother came down with a severe bout of measles in the spring of 1832, for example, the captain called on a local woman and part-time midwife, Mrs

Elwes, to come and help nurse them. In addition, a neighbour, Mrs Wheeler, took James Johnson, the youngest son, home with her so that he might avoid the complaint; Mrs Wheeler then returned to help out, particularly after Mrs Elwes herself became ill. For the next three or four weeks, the house must have resembled a hospital, with the doctor coming and going, Mrs Elwes in residence and once she had recovered, helping to nurse the family, Mrs Johnson and some of the children convalescing, and others contracting the disease. It was not until mid-July that the captain was able to report, "Today I have much pleasure seeing Susan [his daughter] on her feet again and walking all over the house and into the orchard."[112] Ten days later, eleven-month-old James came home after being away for nine weeks. Neighbour Mrs Fairbourne stayed with the Johnsons for another week to ensure the family's full recovery.

The Johnsons' situation during the two months of illness was unusual only in that many of the women who joined the household for varying lengths of time to help with the nursing or keeping house were paid for their services. Most colonial families relied on the unpaid assistance of family members and neighbours.[113] Eli Playter's extended family was a case in point. In the pre-War-of-1812 period, the focus of the Playter family was the old homestead, just north of the town of York, where Eli's mother, father, brother George, and sister Mary lived. One brother John and his wife and children worked and resided on an adjacent farm. Another, James, and his family lived about half a day's ride north up Yonge Street. A sister with her husband had moved to the eastern section of the colony; and another brother lived near Philadelphia. Until his marriage, Eli resided for a time in York and part time with his parents. Once married, he and his wife purchased a farm about half a day's ride from his parents to the west. Eli's diary, spanning twenty years in Upper Canada, recounts the mundane daily events of meals and work in the fields, and those activities surrounding his various occupations, including being the clerk of York, a part-time farmer, and a maker of potash. The Playter diary also sketches the bare bones of an intensely close family that revolved around his father's home, but depended largely upon the efforts of his mother and unmarried sister Mary. During the numerous confinements of Eli's sisters or sisters-in-law, or when one of the children or grandchildren was ill, Mrs Playter was in attendance, often accompanied by Mary. When James Playter's house was destroyed by fire, his mother took in his wife and children. When John Playter was away, his mother ensured that her daughter-in-law was never completely alone with the children.[114]

For the Playter family, like the O'Briens, dependence on family was, in part, a matter of economics. Yet, even in those households such as the Johnsons and the Macaulays, which could afford to hire help, sisters, daughters, mothers, grandmothers, and women friends also rallied around to relieve mothers of the ongoing demands of nursing and child care. The role of wife/mother/nurse was not one which had to be or, indeed, could be performed alone. Neighbourhood and family networks were often an essential support to tired, worried, and overworked mothers. In the end, however, it was individual mothers who were considered the primary caregivers. In July 1840, little Helen Macaulay came down with a fever. The family had at least three live-in women servants, one of whom was a children's nurse. Despite this, Ann Macaulay advised her son that Helen should give her personal attention to her daughter's care. She should "see all the food [is] made under her own inspection and give *strict* order that nothing shall be given to the child but what she sees *herself*," Ann wrote. She also wanted John to remind Helen that the children "can be no better attended" than by their mother and "the only in short the real means of being well for a sick child" is her care.[115]

SHIELDING OR NURSING a child through the ravages of sometimes lethal childhood diseases was one of a mother's primary responsibilities. So too was providing children with that initial instruction and training necessary to ensure that they became upstanding, Christian, self-disciplined, and capable adults. "Bad morals are mostly formed in early age," Ann Macaulay wrote to her son John in 1839.[116] Like many Upper Canadian parents, she firmly believed that children needed both love and discipline.

In the first half of the nineteenth century, there was a growing acceptance among affluent Upper Canadians that childhood was a special time of life and that children required particular care and nurturing to ensure their happiness and success, both as individuals and as functioning members of society.[117] Publicly, at least, many colonists were somewhat ambivalent about how best to accomplish this. The debate revolved around whether children were "rational beings" or were ruled by their emotions and, therefore, always "desired supremacy."[118] At the beginning of the century, one commentator condemned "the modern whims about liberty and equality" in rearing the young and called for a clear recognition that children were dependent on their parents. Even the youngest child needed to be disciplined; her spirit had to be checked and, if need be, broken early. "The weakness of youth must be controlled by the hand of age and experience," it was noted. Believing that "parental tenderness is too oft to degenerate into parental weakness," the commentator advocated that parents be consistent in training their children and never use threats unless they were prepared to carry them out. The article sanctioned the use of corporal punishment; it was noted, however, that first "the reins of government should be always gently drawn."[119]

Most advice to Upper Canadian parents espoused rearing children by love, persuasion, and patience. "Use the rod sparingly," parents were told, and be judicious and reasonable in their expectations. "Arguments addressed to the heart" were more effective than "those addressed to the back." Moreover, parents must never punish in passion. Discipline was to be based on the child's fear and anxiety of giving the parents just cause for offence. To accomplish this, parents, and particularly mothers, were instructed to "begin early in your duties" and "to keep a steady hand with [your] children." Maintain "a mild but firm manner [when] issuing ... commands," it was suggested. And parents were reminded that "it is better and easier to command from their love and respect than fear."[120] In this way, the child's temper and waywardness would be subdued. "As the children grow up the discipline should gradually relax, till at length they are transformed into friends."[121]

Although advice on child-rearing was directed at both parents, in most colonial families, it was mothers who were primarily responsible for training their children and, when necessary, disciplining them. This is not to suggest that many fathers were not involved or were not interested in their children's development. Thomas Traill, John Macaulay, William Hutton, and many other fathers loved their children and were as much involved in their lives as circumstances and social practices allowed.[122] But fathers were frequently away from home, and many also spent much of their day working in the fields or in their shops. Though William Hutton of Belleville was delighted that his children were "entirely happy" in their new home, his work on the farm and in the classroom left him little time for his children. He barely found the opportunity to give them a few lessons.[123] In certain situations, when a mother was ill or absent, fathers were forced to be more directly involved in their children's lives. Yet, even then, men usually tried to find mother-substitutes to take on the day-to-day care of their children.

In 1836 and 1837, while Helen Macaulay made an extended visit to her mother in Scotland, Annie went to live with her grandmother in Kingston. As a member of the government, John apparently felt obliged to stay in York. He did keep in close touch with Annie's daily activities, however. "I shall expect a few lines from you each week" concerning Annie's activities and health, he wrote to his mother, in

December 1836.[124] Over the next few months, the correspondence between John and his mother was filled with accounts of Annie's life in Kingston and John's suggestions on how to care for his daughter. In February 1837, for example, having heard of a friend's child who had recently died of croup, John reminded his mother, who had already raised three sons, to "watch Annie closely, so that if attacked by the Croup it may be met as early as possible." A few days later, he sent his mother recipes for medicine to combat the disease.[125]

It was usually mothers who actually fed, clothed, and as time allowed, played with their children. In many households, it was also mothers who, when necessary, were expected to mete out the discipline. Some mothers found this latter responsibility difficult. When Willie was approaching three, Mary O'Brien recounted that she "had an unnatural struggle with my darling over a fit of childish obstinency." Mary obviously found the battle of wills trying. "I hope the good effects on him will last as long as the ill effects on me. I cannot get over it at all."[126] The Macaulay mothers, Ann in Kingston and Helen in York, confronted a similar dilemma.

Reports from family members in Kingston to Helen and John Macaulay throughout 1836 and 1837 indicate that young Annie was bright and inquisitive; at times, she was also a handful. In January 1837, Ann stated that her granddaughter, who was about four, was "getting a little self-willed." As yet, this was not a problem, for Annie was "so good natured that" her grandmother could "manage her very well." But Annie became more and more difficult. In February, she took off on her own to visit her uncle; she also refused to stay out of the cellar.[127] By May, Ann was reporting that "Annie is very well. I have some difficulty to manage her. She has grown so wild she watches the door being open when she is off in an instant but if she can get into the garden along side of Michael she is quite delighted and is as busy throwing sand." But, as Ann explained, "it takes more than one race around the garden before she is caught."[128] Ann did try to discipline her granddaughter. At times she stood her in a corner.[129] On other occasions Annie was scolded and sent to bed.

Annie's behaviour does not seem to have improved when she returned to her parents in York. John reported to his mother in November 1837, just after the family had moved into their new home, that Annie "is pretty wilful & fellish & I think her temper partakes of her mother's & Uncle William's. She will give us full employment in governing her for she is a restless little thing, with a quick active mind."[130] Helen, in an attempt to mend Annie's ways, tried reasoning and then scolding her daughter. Sometimes Annie was sent to bed early for misbehaving.[131] In February 1838, John reported that Helen had resorted to spanking her. "She was unruly this morning & Helen after trying all means of ruling her said 'Well Annie what must I do with you.' 'Hit me', she replied and she was whipped. The result was that she behaved remarkably well for the remainder of the day."[132] Corporal punishment was something that John and Helen used sparingly. There is no record that Annie's sister Helen was ever whipped. Yet, in the case of Annie, who continued periodically to be unmanageable, it was considered appropriate.[133]

Not all children in Upper Canada received the love, attention, and "considered discipline" that characterized the Macaulay, O'Brien, and Hutton homes. Although in most colonial households, children were a welcome addition to the family and a potentially valuable asset, the relentless demands of the land or the marketplace meant that many parents did not have the time, the energy, or the inclination to "nurture" or play with them. Indeed, having a number of young children under foot could be a distinct disadvantage. And "childhood" as a special time lasted only until a daughter or son was old or big enough to contribute in even a small way to maintaining the family. It is perhaps not surprising that in a number of households, the pressures of poverty, crowded living quarters, failed aspirations, personal disappointment in their new homes, and sheer frustration periodically erupted into violence against both children and women.

The official record of violence against children in Upper Canada is even slighter than that concerning battered wives. Some women, at least, had family to support them. Moreover, as adults, wives were valuable for their labour. Colonial children had no one other than their parents to assist them. The courts and society rarely challenged parents' authority to control members of their households, including their children. Fragmentary evidence nonetheless indicates that between 1790 and 1840, at least some children in Upper Canada were neglected, beaten, or otherwise abused by their parents. And it appears that mothers were as likely as fathers to be the offender. In 1830, for example, Elizabeth Burch was committed to jail for trying to kill her children while drunk.[134] A year later, Alexander Lemons was convicted of murdering his four-year-old step son.[135]

Most children in Upper Canada were not subject to such "discipline." Within the limits of their particular circumstances, the majority of parents probably did everything within their power to ensure that their children were healthy. They also tried to make sure that their offspring were capable of making their way in the world. And here, as in other aspects of child care, it was colonial mothers who assumed much of the responsibility for their children's basic education.

Middle- and upper-class parents such as Mary O'Brien and Helen Macaulay started lessons with their children early. In April 1835, Mary O'Brien noted that she had begun to teach Willie "to count his fingers."[136] He was about four. Annie Macaulay began to learn her letters at about the same age and at five her grandmother was trying to teach her "her book."[137]

The literacy rates in Upper Canada are still somewhat unclear. Teaching children to read and write certainly required that the mother herself could at least read and write, something many may have been able to do.[138] More significantly, teaching children required patience and time. As Frances Stewart discovered, though she tried "to attend to the education of my dear children ... it is tenfold labour" and "her obstacles are numerous."[139] Like many colonial mothers, Frances Stewart was already busy looking after a house full of children, nursing an infant, and trying to cope with the housework. Many mothers were also working with their husbands on the farm or in town and/or working outside the home to supplement the family income. Yet mothers did what they could. The children's classroom was often the family kitchen or porch; and the curriculum was a curious mixture of reading and copying from the Bible, counting household items, and learning to write one's name. Once children were old enough, lessons were often interrupted by a child's daily chores. At quite a young age, children began to help in the house. Boys then joined their fathers in the fields and girls stayed with their mothers in the home, looking after younger children, helping with the housework, and serving an informal apprenticeship with their mothers.[140]

This created a dilemma for a number of families, even ones of relative affluence. William Hutton wrote with pride to his mother that his eldest daughter Ann "is a remarkable fine girl with a very superior mind and understanding." She had little time or energy for her lessons, however. "I much regret that she is too often really fagged with nursing. We cannot afford to keep another servant, but she and her Mama have too much to do."[141] William and Fanny Hutton did try to ensure that their children had the opportunity to read and expand their knowledge, but the demands of the household too often intervened. In 1841, he reported that despite this, Ann had acquired sufficient knowledge to "teach the three little girls who are all quick and healthy in mind as well as in body."[142]

For Fanny Hutton, it was both gratifying and practically useful to have her daughters working by her side. Frances Stewart too found her eldest daughter of immeasurable help.[143] Daughters became surrogate or supplemental mothers. They helped care for younger children and did increasing proportions of the housework. Like Fanny Hutton, Frances Stewart recognized the cost, however. In April 1833, she wrote to a friend, "I find it impossible to attend to the improvement of the children with that quietness and regularity which alone can bring success." Her daughters were "amiable" and "very active and inclined to be useful and industrious as far as they are able." "This is all very pleasant," Frances continued, "but they are sadly deficient in general knowledge and education."[144] As Frances acknowledged, however, her daughters were acquiring skills that would be intensely useful after they married. Anna Jameson visited a family in Woodstock where her hostess had just given birth to her tenth or twelfth child (Anna was unsure). "Her eldest daughter," Jameson noted, "meantime, a fair and elegant girl, was acquiring at the age of fifteen, qualities and habits which might make ample amends for the possessing of mere accomplishments. She acted as a manager-in-chief and glided about in her household abdications with a serene and great grace that was quite charming."[145]

Fanny Hutton, Frances Stewart, and many colonial mothers had no choice but to cut short their children's education. Only the most affluent households could afford to let their daughters and sons pursue their studies beyond the age when they could be working beside their parents or working for wages in another household. Elite households had other concerns, however. Taking over the family business, receiving a government appointment, or entering one of the professions required more than an ability to read and write. And an upper-class wife had to be able to do more than look after children and run a house.

Many upper-class parents began to believe that home schooling did not provide all the education their children needed. Helen Macaulay and other prominent mothers often did not have the time, or the skills necessary, to prepare their children fully for the wider world. Some families hired nurses, governesses, and tutors to supplement a mother's teaching.[146] Others with the necessary financial means chose to send their children to school. Such measures did not mean, however, that mothers could abdicate their responsibility for overseeing their children's development.

At the beginning of the century, Ann Macaulay, now a widow, enrolled her two sons, John and William, in John Strachan's school in Cornwall. There, under the vigilant eye of the Anglican minister and his wife, "every care [was] taken of their learning and their morals."[147] Ann kept in regular correspondence with her sons and John Strachan concerning their health and their progress. When her son, John, moved to Montreal and entered an office with Mr McGill, she continued to provide encouragement and advice. "You are never a moment out of my thoughts," she informed him in January 1808, "and I am continually meditating on the happiness I shall enjoy if my boys continue to go on in improving themselves in learning and goodness."[148] "Youth," she advised him in a subsequent letter, "is too apt to forget the future in the present; youth is the season for study & observation, in order to lay the foundation for wisdom & knowledge and will certainly be the means of engaging in happy old age."[149] For Ann, such foundations could not be laid too early.

Given Ann's experience, it is not surprising that a generation later, she encouraged her son and daughter-in-law to send Annie to school. As she pointed out to John, only in school would Annie receive the discipline she was so sadly lacking. School would also introduce her to the benefits of formal education. Annie "is now near six years old and cannot read yet," her grandmother told John in 1840. Moreover, "she is compleatly spoilt child and all I have heard speak it so too, it is full time to commence a strict course and subdue her wilfulness or you will have a hard trial by and by I do not like to fret Helen in her weak state but I would have spoke my sentiments when I was up there."[150]

Ann was pleased when a few months later, John began "to think it necessary to send Annie to school." "I have been grieved to see her kept so long from it, the system of home teaching does not do where the mother has not time or ill health prevents from constant attention especially when there is but one child to attend to." As girls' schools in York were expensive,[151] John and Helen first decided to engage a part-time tutor for their daughter and have Annie take dancing lessons from a Mr Yeo. Her grandmother was only satisfied, however, when Annie was enrolled, full time, in Mrs Blake's school.[152]

Not all, or even most, Upper Canadian parents could afford to hire a tutor or to send their children to school. In the majority of colonial households, lack of means, distance from a school, and the need for a child's labour precluded formal education. Most children relied on their mothers for what education they received and in many households this included only the bare rudiments.

FOR MARY O'BRIEN, Fanny Hutton, and Ann and Helen Macaulay, being a wife and mother in early Upper Canada was apparently a satisfying experience. Marriage brought them companionship, personal security, and on the basis of their surviving correspondence, emotional fulfilment. Motherhood brought joy and a sense of achievement and pride in being able to cope with the seemingly endless responsibilities. But Mary O'Brien and other women in her situation knew all too well that the delights of family life were often fleeting. Marriage and motherhood could also be fearful, sometimes dangerous, undertakings. For a number of colonial women marriage was a prison that was at best difficult to leave. For all colonial women, motherhood evoked fear and sometimes resulted in tragedy. For all mothers, the joy in their children was always accompanied by trepidation and heartache.

The state of a woman's marriage and her experiences as a mother were directly related to the personalities in her household and her family's social and economic circumstances. They were also shaped by social attitudes, custom, and legal strictures. Women had little control over many of the external factors – the law, where her family lived, the occupation of her husband, or the onset of disease – that governed much of their lives. However, colonial women could and did assume some control over individual situations. When a marriage became intolerable, some women left. When accidents, illness, or other disasters struck a family, women turned to members of their families and to a community of women for advice and support. Individually and collectively, colonial wives and mothers coped; they usually had little choice.

Upper Canadian society defined women and judged their character by their relationships to their husbands and their children. Women, too, usually defined themselves within the context of their families. For the vast majority of women, marriage was the most important event in their lives. And its usual inevitable consequence, motherhood, governed their time, their energy, and their work for the rest of their lives.

This is not to suggest that women's work in Upper Canada was restricted to looking after their husbands and bearing and raising children. Colonial women also served as unpaid and paid domestic labourers, farm hands, and skilled domestic workers. Some ran businesses, either with their husbands and other members of their families, or independently. Others worked for wages as teachers, seamstresses, bakers, and builders. Inevitably, a woman's work as a wife and mother was directly influenced by the other work and responsibilities she was obliged to undertake. And her ability to keep her house clean, feed and clothe the family, and often work for wages outside the home inevitably had an effect on her experiences as a wife and mother.

PART TWO

"Woman is a Bit of a Slave in This Country": The Housewife and Her Help

Most women in Upper Canada lived and worked within a traditional family economy. Both in town and in the country, "family life was inseparably intertwined" with production and "the household was the centre around which resources, labour and consumption were balanced."[1] The unquestioned head of this economic/familial corporation was the husband/father who held the title of all tangible assets, including not only the land, the stock, the equipment, and the buildings on his farm or his shop and its contents, but also the fruits of the labour of all members of his family. No less essential working members of this basic social and economic family unit were, however, a man's wife, their children and, in many cases, other family and non-family members living in the household. Indeed, in most colonial homes, each able-bodied member of the household had to contribute energy and labour to ensure that the collective needs of the family were met.[2]

The importance of the family as an economic unit was not lost on early Upper Canadians. Most farms in the colony were small. Most shops and businesses in colonial towns provided only the barest means of support. Not only was this a pre-industrial economy, but most colonial families were, initially at least, obliged to be as independent and self-sufficient as possible. "The only salvation of a man here," Anna Jameson wrote in 1838, "is to have a wife and children."[3] Without a wife, a new settler had a difficult, if not impossible, task establishing himself in Upper Canada. A married couple without children were not by themselves capable of building and sustaining a

Illustration 4
Anne Langton, in later life
AO (S12753)

farm or a business. "Married persons were always more comfortable and succeed sooner in Canada than single men," traveller John Howison remarked in 1821. In fact, "a wife and family, so far from being a burden they are always proved sources of wealth. The wife of a new settler has many domestic duties to perform; and children if at all grown up, are useful in various ways."[4]

Even in relatively affluent rural households, like those of Anne Langton and Catharine Parr Traill, the work of women and children was important. As Catharine Parr Traill found, store-bought items were expensive and certain groceries and goods were frequently not available at all. Moreover, china and other fragile items often arrived broken in transit from store to farm, and although "you may send down a list of groceries to be forwarded when a team comes up," Catharine Parr Traill observed, often "our stores ... rice, sugar, currants, pepper and mustard [were] all jumbled into one mess ... You see, then [she wrote] that a settler in the bush requires to hold himself pretty independent, not only of the luxuries and delicacies of the table, but not infrequently of the very necessaries of life."[5] This was only possible when all members of the household shared in family production.

What actual work individual members of each household performed was determined primarily by their age and gender. Usually, men and boys worked in the fields or at their craft. Women worked in and around the home. In addition to the responsibilities of producing and caring for children, women's work in Upper Canada, like that in eighteenth-century New England, was usually "confined by space (a house and its surrounding yards), a set of tasks (cooking, washing, serving, milking, spinning, cleaning, gardening) and a limited area of authority (the internal economy of the family)."[6] It was, in fact, primarily the wife's responsibility to make sure that the basic needs of her family were met. For most women, this meant actually producing or procuring most of the food and clothing that the family needed to survive. For many women, it also meant helping their husbands and fathers in their shops or farms, assistance that was, in most instances, crucial for the operation's success. For all women, it also meant periodically "helping" a neighbour or friend with her work.

Few farms in Upper Canada were ever fully self-sufficient. Village households were rarely self-contained.[7] Even families with many children were usually obliged, at some time, to rely on neighbours, friends, and nonresident relations for help sustaining the family business. If possible, help was provided as part of that informal exchange of services that prevailed between family members, friends, and others in the immediate community. Farmers, small shopkeepers, mechanics, and artisans also sometimes hired a local man or woman, either part time or full time to fill an immediate need. And relatively affluent residents, such as the Langtons and the O'Briens, had full-time hired help, both for inside and outside work.

For thousands of less affluent settlers, working in the homes or businesses of their neighbours provided their only means of support or else an essential cash supplement to their families' incomes. Moreover, while male members of the household worked in the fields, at their craft, or as labourers and artisans in town, their wives, daughters, mothers, and sisters were often obliged or chose to take waged employment.[8] Some women pursued their own craft.[9] Others joined their husbands and fathers in their employers' fields, or depending on their age, their marital status, and the demands of their own households, took domestic employment working either part time or full time, as live-in help.

There is no question that in Upper Canada in the first half of the nineteenth century, "female labour" was often centred on production for the household.[10] To suggest, however, as Marjorie Cohen has done in her study of women's work in the Ontario dairy industry, that during the early period, the value of household work was that it freed "men to concentrate their energies on wage labour," and "to engage in production for exchange on the market"and the accumulation of capital is too simplistic.[11] Furthermore, to argue that the work of rural women was essentially "non-market-oriented" misrepresents relations and production within both rural and urban colonial households.[12] As Douglas McCalla has illustrated, agriculture in Upper Canada "was always a mixed farming system"[13] and "ordinary families" engaged in a variety of commercial activities to ensure the growth and viability of their farms. Certainly, while on most farms and in colonial towns, women's and men's work was different, it was always complementary. As Nancy Osterud stresses in her study of nineteenth-century farming in New York, most farm tasks were characterized by "mutuality and flexibility."[14] Women and men worked for a common goal and frequently made little distinction between production for the household and production for the market. At least until 1840, there was no sharp dichotomy between "reproductive" and "productive" labour and a wife's work was often related to the marketplace, either indirectly, as an unpaid domestic worker, or formally, as a waged employee.

We know a great deal about the lives and work of certain gentlewomen and farmer's wives such as Anne Langton and Mary O'Brien. The world and experiences of most other women remain largely a mystery, however. The vast majority of Upper Canadian women – those who lived all their lives in rude shanties or small two- or three-room log houses – left no record of their lives, had no land to sell, nor drew wills. We do know that, like their more affluent sisters, they too were wives, mothers, and daughters. They too looked after the family and tried to ensure that the household was fed and clothed. We also know that although unwilling to be considered servants, many of these women were willing to "help" their more affluent neighbours in exchange for a wage. It is in the brief, sporadic references in gentle mistresses' or masters' journals and pay ledgers, particularly those living in rural communities where "helping" prevailed,[15] that the lives and work of these shadowy, often illusive women come briefly into focus. For the lives of the mistress and her "help" intersected in that essentially women's world of the home, the kitchen, the garden, and the family. Gentle farming women's accounts of their own world also illuminate at least some of the world of their less affluent neighbours. They also provide a window through which to view colonial women's world of household work.

4 "Prime Minister of the House": Colonial Housekeepers

In July 1839, Anne Langton recorded that "we all joined in a little tirade against Canada this morning." Anne's mother's "ground of complaint" was "the slovenly nature of its inhabitants." "I grumbled a little," Anne continued, "at the necessity of storing all your summer provisions in the winter, and at the annoyance of unpacking and repacking barrels of pork, boiling brine etc, etc. Our caterer I find, instead of a box of candles, has brought us a cask of tallow, much to our disappointment, having already abundance of work on hand. I have sometimes thought, and I may as well say it, now that it is grumbling day – woman is a bit of a slave in this country."[1]

Anne Langton, like the majority of women in Upper Canada, lived on a farm. Though unmarried, she acted as primary housekeeper for her brother John for the first four or five years of her residence in the colony. Her collected journals and letters, spanning a period of almost ten years' residence at Sturgeon Lake, 1837–46, record the rhythms of a farm household, rhythms with which most women in Upper Canada between 1790 and 1840 would have been all too familiar. There were the daily tasks of baking, preparing meals, making beds, and generally keeping house, and the seasonal occupations of planting, tending, and harvesting the garden, pickling, preserving, and brining produce and meat, and the spring and fall cleaning. Anne Langton made candles and soap, and in her few spare moments, overhauled family members' wardrobes and made curtains, rugs, and furniture covers. Though unmarried, she also engaged in child care, periodically teaching the neighbours' children to read and write.

Most colonial women would probably have agreed with Anne that a woman in Upper Canada was "a little bit of a slave." Yet many might also have commented that Anne Langton's life was one of relative ease. Financially, the Langtons could afford to hire "help" for both outside and inside work (even though help was sometimes unavailable). Moreover, there was obviously sufficient income to purchase many goods such as candles, furniture, and food, which other households were forced to manufacture or grow themselves. Perhaps most important, Anne Langton had arrived in the backcountry accompanied by two other adult women, her mother and her aunt. From the outset, each of the three women assumed different responsibilities in the household; most wives were forced to cope with all the work on their own or with only periodic help from daughters, neighbours, and other relatives.[2]

Yet even the life of an affluent farm woman like Anne Langton was governed by constant physical toil.[3] As her journals and letters illustrate, even without the confusion of young children underfoot and with paid help in the house, Anne's days were fully occupied. Though usually unpaid and often unrecognized or explicitly acknowledged by their husbands, fathers, brothers, or society at large, the domestic work of colonial women was essential to the functioning and perpetuation of their households.

MANY COLONIAL WOMEN began their working lives in Upper Canada in a small shanty. Most early loyalists, later immigrants, and many young couples first lived in a one- or two-room house that might have had only "a piece of canvass" for a door "and a hole in the roof for a chimney." One resident wrote that "windows were unnecessary in such a dwelling, for such were the spaces between the logs that, when you were outside at night and the fire was bright, the shanty bore a striking similtude to a tin lantern."[4] Typically, an Upper Canadian shanty was ten by eight feet with ceilings six feet high.[5] As Catharine Parr Traill commented, "nothing can be more comfortless than some of these shanties, reeking with smoke and dirt, the common receptacle for children, pigs and fowl." But, as she continued, "I am happy to say all the shanties ... are not like this ... by far the large proportion were inhabited by tidy folks, and have one or even two small windows, had a log chimney regularly built up through the roof, and some were even roughly floored."[6]

As family fortunes improved, some families converted their shanty into a shed or gave it to the hired couple for their quarters and built themselves more substantial and relatively spacious quarters.[7] As

Illustration 5
Interior of John Langton's house c. 1838, pen and ink sketch by Anne Langton
AO (2401)

John Langton told his father, when discussing his plans to build a large house with eight rooms and a verandah, "the question" Upper Canadians first had to decide was whether to use "log, frame [or] stone." One traveller noted that many colonists preferred frame constructions. "When a man gets on a little in the world," Dr Dunlop observed, "he builds a frame house, weather-boarded outside, and lathed and plastered within."[8] John Langton chose to build his house of logs, even though this meant that the second storey could not be of full height. Stone he judged to be too expensive and frame houses were notoriously difficult to heat.[9]

Most residents were more restricted both in the choice of building materials and the size of their new home. The traditional log house, which for many farm and town women was their permanent home for a number of years, was really only "an elaboration of the shanty." It was about twenty by sixteen or eighteen feet and had two or three rooms, a rough-hewn lumber floor and perhaps one or two glazed windows.[10] Catharine Parr Traill's home had a kitchen, a pantry, a small sitting-room, and a bedchamber on the ground floor. "There is a good upper floor that will make good sleeping rooms," she reported to her family. She and her husband also planned to add "a handsome frame front ... which will give us another parlour, long hall and good spare bedroom."[11] Susanna Moodie's backwoods home, which had "a superior air of comfort to most dwellings of the same kind" was more spacious and had a "nice parlour, a kitchen and two small bedrooms, which were divided by plank partitions."[12]

To some degree the internal furnishing of Upper Canadian homes was determined by their size and structure. John Langton informed his mother shortly after he arrived in the colony that "chairs and tables are scarce articles" in the backwoods. "I may not have conveniences for writing a letter for a month to come."[13] For those first six weeks, he lived in a shanty and his bed consisted of two buffalo skins, "and empty barrels, chest, etc. served the purposes of chairs and tables." Initially, most residents had to make their own furniture. The bare necessities included a wooden table, chairs or benches, a shelf or two on the wall, "lock-up places," and beds (which were often shared).[14] Families who arrived with their household goods found settling in much easier. Catharine Parr Traill had a brass-railed sofa, Canadian painted chairs, a stained pine table, "green and white muslim curtains and a handsome Indian mat which covered the floor."[15] Anne Langton and her family brought all the furniture they needed from England – beds, chest of drawers, tables, chairs, curtains, and rugs. When Mary O'Brien moved to her new home shortly after her marriage, she proudly reported that her parlour had "two sides ... composed of whitewashed logs & the other two of planed planks." It was furnished with "two chairs, a sort of makeshift table, two guns, a whisky & a beer barrel, a box of nails & a few carpenter's tools, besides an ink bottle, a few books & a drawing of Edward's." Tongue-in-cheek, she concluded, "I am very smart and genteel."[16]

A settler's home was, in part, a reflection of the relative affluence of its residents. Its structure, size, and furnishings also determined the amount and the nature of the work done by its housekeeper. Cooking and working in a room dedicated as a kitchen was quite different than coping in a one- or two-room log house where the household table had to serve as a kitchen counter, a dining table, and a carpenter's workbench. Usually, the bigger the home and the more furnishings it had, the easier it was for the housekeeper to perform her duties. A large, well-appointed home, on the other hand, required more work in cleaning and keeping items in good repair than a shanty.[17] Yet even the most elaborate furnishings in the most affluent of Upper Canadian households could not keep residents warm throughout the Canadian winters.

Keeping homes warm was often a serious problem, particularly for those living in log or frame houses. Most Upper Canadians were forever having to re-chink or re-plaster walls which, as they settled and dried developed sometimes gaping holes that "let in daylight" and "quite too much of the winter blasts."[18] Shanties and small log cabins were heated by one open fireplace that vented either through a hole in the roof or through a wooden or clay chimney.[19] As financial circumstances and building materials allowed, the open fire was replaced by a partly enclosed and more efficient fireplace made of brick or stone. Wooden chimneys, which were very susceptible to catching fire, were rebuilt with brick or stone and equipped with a crossbar inserted above the roof line from which to suspend cooking pots and kettles. In the 1820s and 1830s, a number of households supplemented the heat and cooking surface provided by their fireplaces by installing a wood stove.[20] The Traill and Moodie homes each had only one stove which served both for cooking and heat. More affluent families such as the Langtons who lived in larger homes often had a Franklin in each room.[21] Yet, even with several stoves burning, families often woke to find frost accumulating on blankets and a pail of water in the kitchen frozen solid.

Cutting logs to lengths and splitting wood for the fire was usually considered men's work. Gathering the chips left over from clearing and bringing in wood was one of the many daily chores of housekeeping. In 1823, Frances Stewart described the ritual of building and maintaining the fire. First "a *back log* which is about a foot or eighteen inches in diameter" and about six or seven feet long was placed at the back of the fireplace by one of the men. "Then we [Frances and her children] need only add smaller sticks to keep up a good fire."[22] As Anne Langton commented fifteen years later, "firing is the most troublesome part of housekeeping in this country, the drying and cutting of the wood is endless. It is astonishing to see the piles that disappear in a day."[23]

In addition to providing heat, the central fireplace was often the residents' primary source of artificial light. Small shanties frequently had no windows at all. A log house might have one or two, which were shuttered throughout the winter and often at night. Work in Upper Canadian homes usually began before dawn and continued after dusk, however, and a fire alone did not provide housekeepers with enough light to perform most of their domestic chores. Most residents relied on candles for the light needed for sewing, reading, mending tools, and completing the work so necessary for the family's survival. Some colonists could afford to buy candles from the local village store or a travelling pedlar.[24] If the materials were available and time allowed, many women made their own. Few colonial journals and diaries made explicit references to candle making. It appears to have been one of those activities which many rural housekeepers did as a matter of course.[25]

Anne Langton made dipped candles, which she found was "a much more agreeable" process than making candles in molds. Anne's frequent journal entries on the subject indicate that she clearly took some pleasure in the process and was proud of the results, though she sometimes lamented her lack of skill in candle making. "I wish I could have an hours conversation with a tallow candler," she wrote to her brother in 1839. "Can you procure me some hints concerning the business, as to the temperature of the room, temperature of the tallow etc., what can prevent a drop from being thicker at the bottom than at the top? Also look at one properly made and tell me how near the wick reaches to the bottom of the candle."[26]

It is likely, however, that many women in Upper Canada had to battle constantly with poor lighting conditions. They also lived with drafts and cold that numbed the fingers, chilled the bones, and made cooking, cleaning, and sewing difficult at best. The problems of inadequate heat and light were only compounded by the actual structure and physical conditions of the workplace. Keeping a shanty with a dirt floor, open windows, and an open fireplace clean and neat was, to say the least, difficult. Women who lived in relatively spacious log or frame houses with plastered walls, glazed windows, and rugs on wooden floors did not confront the problem of dirt to the same degree; they also had a work place that was usually more adapted to performing various household tasks. Moreover, many such housekeepers possessed cooking pots, kitchenware, and other household equipment that was designed for particular tasks.

Even such women as Anne Langton still had to contend with the problems of providing adequate light and heat, however. And like less affluent women of rural and urban households, they were also responsible for feeding and clothing their families, work that was absolutely crucial to the household economy.

WHEN JOHN LANGTON arrived in Upper Canada in the early 1830s to homestead, he wrote to his father that "I mean to do all by contract, keeping no labour of my own til spring; the wife of one of the contractors or their men will be sufficient to cook and wash for me, and my own time will be fully taken up in superintending workmen, surveying the capability of the land."[27] Initially, John cooked for himself. As he described to his father in 1834, first wood had to be chopped,

Illustration 6
Cooking utensils in common use in Upper Canada c.1850
AO (ACC6326/s8486)

then "I began cooking, bringing in a pile of firewood" and within the hour a meal was ready. Baking, he wrote, "which is performed in a frying pan before the fire, requires constant attention, so I superintend that in the evening, having kneaded the dough during my cooking hour." John's enthusiasm for feeding himself quickly faded. In a later letter he reported that cooking and baking had become rather tedious and when his friend was not about, "I take no regular meals ... but I never have any cooking until after dark" (when work outside was impossible). "This task of baking, which I always disliked and which is a great interruption," he soon transferred to the wife of one of his labourers. And, he continued, "the other bore, the washing up ... I do all in a lump when I have used up my stack of plates, etc." Somewhat plaintively, he concluded, "in truth, I am almost tired of living alone."[28]

As John Langton had discovered, preparing meals was a never-ending task. Water had to be hauled at least once daily, wood had to be split or chips gathered, food had to be prepared, and the actual cooking process carefully supervised. Next to child care, preparing and cooking meals was one of the most important and time-consuming responsibilities of colonial wives. As soon as children were old enough or the family could afford to hire a girl or general servant, the housekeeper could assign someone to gather wood chips, tend the fire, or haul quantities of water.[29] But even with help, ensuring that meals were ready was, at best, difficult.

Most Upper Canadians, particularly in the pre-1812 period, had two substantial meals a day – breakfast sometime in mid-morning after a couple of hours' work had been completed, and dinner, which appears to have been served in the early- to mid-afternoon. Households also usually took a light supper or tea at the end of the day. The basic colonial diet consisted of bread, potatoes, and salt pork or beef. This varied considerably, however, depending on the particular circumstances and season of the year. In rural areas, hunting provided considerable meat for the larder; deer, bear, porcupine, ducks, geese, and various kinds of fish were also periodically available at the town market.[30] As land was cleared and as available cash allowed, colonists raised cattle, sheep, and pigs to provide meat and dairy products for the table, in addition to wool and hides for clothing. In addition, one of the first priorities of any new household, whether in town or country, was to establish a kitchen garden.

The division of labour in sustaining these activities was relatively well defined. Men hunted and ploughed the garden. Tending livestock was often shared by all family members. Though farmers and their children sometimes helped weed and harvest the garden, in even the most affluent of farm families it was the women who planted, tended, and harvested the garden. Women oversaw the poultry and worked the dairy. They also supervised or undertook themselves the butchering of meat and the preservation of meat, fruit, and vegetables. In town, if family income permitted, the mistress frequented the local market, and purchased supplies to supplement the family's provisions. And whether in town or in the country, women did the cooking.

Upper Canadian women baked bread, cooked meat and vegetables, and sometimes produced fancy sweets and desserts, either on an open fire, or increasingly on or in a wood-burning stove. Bread was baked in either a frying pan or in a closed kettle, buried in hot coals. Meat was roasted, boiled, or stewed.[31] The most common meal was a stew, cooked in an open pot over a fire. Only families with a variety of cooking pots that could be raised or lowered to adjust the heat could enjoy more than the basic one-pot meal. Only households with sufficient eating utensils and space could avoid having more than one sitting at each meal. When visitors arrived or workers were in residence, feeding them became particularly onerous. Mary O'Brien noted in December 1830, for example, that she had to make "three breakfasts and three tea parties" to feed their seasonal labourers as their tea kettle was scarcely big enough for the family.[32] When Anne Langton first arrived at her brother's, there was "no fire in the house" and feeding anywhere from six to ten residents was difficult, to say the least. "Every culinary operation, from baking bread to heating water, was performed on a dilapidated cooking stove, whilst eight or nine meals were regularly served each day."[33]

As Susanna Moodie, Fanny Hutton, and others found, baking bread, a staple of all Upper Canadian diets, required time, attention, and considerable skill. After having carefully combined the barm and salt in warm water and then mixing this with flour, Mrs Moodie ruefully wrote, "I did not understand the method of baking in these ovens." She continued, "it not only required experience to know when it [the dough] was a fit state for baking, but the oven should have been brought to a proper temperature to receive bread." (Moodie had also failed to let the dough rise a second time.) After putting it into a cold oven, she succeeded in burning the loaf entirely.[34] Anne Langton and Mary O'Brien were rather more skilled in the process. They were also aware, however, that even the most careful preparations, timing, and control of heat did not ensure success. As Anne Langton noted, "in case of failure, there is always a frying pan cake to resort to, namely, unfermented dough baked in one cake about half an inch thick."[35]

It is impossible to determine the amount of time women actually devoted to cooking. It appears that bread had to be baked at least every two days and in large households every day. Stewing and roasting required considerable lengths of time. And though food could be left to cook, it did have to be checked periodically to see that the pot had not tipped over or boiled dry.[36]

To make meals palatable and interesting required considerable thought. During those times when provisions were scarce – because of the season, the family's financial circumstances, or because they had been in the country only a short time – the wife's task was doubly hard. As Anne Langton wrote in her journal as late as April 1846, "this is the worst season of the year to provide" a good dinner. "At present provisions are at their lowest ebb. We are without fresh meat, the pork is done, for as we over-stocked ourselves last year, of course we rather under-stocked ourselves this year. We have no bacon, but what is two years old, and this year's hams are most indifferent, owing either to impure salt or impure molasses, or some other unknown cause ... Milk and butter will not be plentiful for a month to come, eggs are our chief luxury and with these we make as much variety as we can." As she observed, "the scarcity of the season is not regarded as much by anybody except the housekeeper, whose ingenuity is tasked to spread a decent table before the family."[37]

Such scarcity was particularly felt by townsfolk who could not maintain a garden or keep livestock and were restricted by their income and the season of the year as to what they could purchase at the local market. New settlers who had arrived too late to get in their garden, and households in which women and children were fully occupied with other domestic or waged work periodically went hungry. Even established farm households were often bereft of fresh meat and vegetables throughout the late winter and spring. Women just had to make do.

It was therefore one of the housekeeper's most important duties in summer and fall to ensure that the bounty of summer was available in the winter. In those households with pigs, sheep, and cattle, it was the wife's job, not only to cure the meat by salting or drying it for winter storage, but in many cases actually to slaughter and butcher the beasts. Anne Langton noted in October 1838 that she and her mother had killed and butchered a small porkling, "and we agreed, when on a small scale, it was more agreeable to operate ourselves than to stand by and give directions." The actual killing and cutting was only the beginning of the process. "When the butcher's part is over I know well from my own experience how much labour there is in turning head, heels, tallow, etc. to the best account."[38] Meat not only had to be cut and stored in brine, it also had to be examined periodically, tainted meat thrown out, and the remainder turned and put down again.[39] Some settlers chose to freeze their meat by packing it in snow.[40] Others smoked meat in their own or neighbours' smoke houses and made bacon, ham, and smoked beef.[41] But the most reliable means of preserving meat was to salt it.

Meat was not the only commodity that required special handling for storage. Produce from the garden also had to be put down for the winter. The largest part of most Upper Canadian gardens seems to have been devoted to growing potatoes, a staple of the Upper Canadian diet. Harvesting acres of potatoes was back-breaking work. The bushels of potatoes were sorted, packed in barrels, and then placed in a root cellar for use throughout the winter. Squash, pumpkins, carrots, onions, turnips, and yams might also be added to the winter supply. Throughout the summer and fall, children gathered fruits and berries from the surrounding woods. These and other vegetables had then to be processed for the winter. In early August 1839, Anne Langton recorded that "in the early part [of the week] we were preserving ourselves a good supply of raspberries. It is a fruit we have in plenty and much cheaper than in England. Pickling has also been the order of the day. We consume more in the way of ketchups, sauces, curry powder, etc. than we used to at home, on account of the many

Illustration 7
Boiling maple sap c. 1840, pen and ink from Ballingall Collection
Queen's University Archives

months we are without fresh meat."[42] Everything that could be was pickled or jammed or dried. Women spent days over hot stoves in August, September, and October hoping that the results of their efforts would last until the garden began to produce again the following summer.[43]

The autumn and early winter occupations of pickling and preserving fruits and vegetables and butchering and processing meat were bracketed in many farm households by the production of maple syrup in the spring. Though some families judged that tapping trees, collecting the sap, and then boiling the sap for long hours were not cost-efficient, many, like the Huttons of Belleville, produced sufficient sugar from the maple trees for a year's supply.[44] Catharine Parr Traill observed "where there is a large family of children and a convenient sugar bush on the lot, the making of sugar and molasses is decidedly a saving."[45] If the children were not old enough to do the job, the wife, with perhaps a little help from her husband, would collect the sap, tend the kettle over the open fires, and then finish the sugar indoors.[46] Although the running of the sap was a welcome first sign of spring, for many farm women it was also a harbinger of long and tedious hours over a sap kettle.

The daily and seasonal culinary duties of colonial wives were periodically increased when guests arrived, or when in rural areas a bee was organized for raising a barn, chopping trees, harvesting, or mucking out barns. Farm women would make preparations for days in advance for the men's arrival. Susanna Moodie remembered, "our men worked well until dinner time, when, after washing in the lake they all sat down to the rude board which I had prepared for them, loaded with the best fare that could be procured in the bush. Pea soup, legs of pork, venison, eel, and raspberry pie, garnished with plenty of potatoes and whisky to wash them down, besides a large iron kettle of tea."[47] The bee supper, so carefully prepared by the farm wife, was essential to labour relations in the Upper Canadian outback. Organizing and cooking such a multicourse meal on an open fire or cook-stove required skill and hard work. It was an integral part, however, of ensuring the development of the farm. It was also one of the central symbols of Upper Canadian women's role as housekeeper and undoubtedly the success of the dinner attested to her abilities.[48]

Women who lived in Upper Canada's towns and villages did not often have occasion to prepare for a bee. Like their rural sisters, however, many did cook for large households on a regular basis and could expect to receive a number of guests without notice. Most urban families also maintained gardens and kept a few chickens and perhaps a pig and/or a cow. Wives of artisans and labourers therefore shared with their rural sisters the responsibilities of producing, preserving, and, if space allowed, storing quantities of food to last the winter.[49] At the same time, village housekeepers were by necessity consumers. Increasingly, they were able or forced to rely on the proceeds of their family wage to buy butter, meat, flour, and other produce from the market or the general store. Therefore, where most of their rural cousins turned their skills to preserving goods, some urban women learned to bargain and barter. Both groups of women, however, had to turn the proceeds of their efforts into meals fit for the household.

THOUGH COOKING may have consumed the greatest percentage of time of any Upper Canadian housekeeper for at least part of the year, it was by no means her only task. Writing to her mother-in-law in 1837 to plead for a loan to tide the family over its hard times, Fanny Hutton explained how she intended to save money. In so doing, she provided a glimpse of her weekly routine. "I have come to the determination of doing without a servant for the fall and winter months ... I feel quite equal to do all the work except washing, with William's assistance evening and morning for lessons, churning, etc. I propose bringing in a woman one day in a fortnight to wash, and will do the ironing myself. The week free from washing, I shall be able to do a great deal of sewing. This can only be accomplished by early rising and employing every moment actively; but these things we have now got accustomed to, so that what three years ago would have appeared a monstrous impossibility, now appears light."[50]

Washing and ironing clothes and cleaning the house all required energy, strength, and skill. Travel accounts, diaries, and journals suggest that many Upper Canadian housewives were concerned to maintain a certain level of cleanliness and neatness.[51] British gentlewomen seemed to be particularly conscious of the need to preserve those domestic standards that they had been used to at home. After a day scrubbing her brother's house, Anne Langton emphatically commented, "I came back with a strengthened conviction of the importance of woman." And in a rather cryptic comment on the difference between men's and women's attitudes to housekeeping, she concluded, "[I was] congratulating myself, that though I might be an old maid, I never could be an old bachelor."[52]

In even the smallest Upper Canadian home, sweeping and scrubbing the table and kitchen area were daily tasks made all the more difficult by the constant movement of people into the home, dust and dirt leaking in through cracks in the wall, and sparks and soot from the open fireplace. Houses with dirt floors were almost impossible to keep clean. Open windows, doors and chimneys only compounded the problem.[53] Stone, brick, or frame houses may have been relatively easier "to keep;" their size and the often higher expectations of their residents meant that there was more work to be done, however.

Anne Langton and Mary O'Brien made frequent references to the daily and weekly tasks of sweeping, scrubbing, and washing. When time allowed, usually at least once and, in some cases, twice a year, women cleaned their houses thoroughly. Curtains, bedding, and rugs were taken down, washed, beaten, or aired, and replaced. Windows were washed; walls and floors were scrubbed and in some cases given a coat of whitewash or paint to help keep the dust down and the insects at bay.[54] On average, it seems to have taken Anne Langton two to three days to complete the spring or fall cleaning. Given the size of the Langton house, this must have meant long and hard work. And Anne could not possibly have completed it on her own. She always had at least one and often two women working with her. So, too, did Mary O'Brien. A number of households hired a woman by the day or the week to help them with a massive cleaning. Fanny Hutton, Frances Stewart, and many other women relied on their daughters for help. Some had to cope as best they could on their own. When this work was done, and "peace and quietness" was "at last restored and order also everywhere,"[55] Anne Langton and other Upper

Canadian housekeepers still had before them the more frequent demands of washing clothes.

Monday or Tuesday appears to have been the regular wash day in many Upper Canadian households. When her maid was away, Susanna Moodie discovered how difficult and often painful washing clothes could be. "After making a great preparation," which would have included heating the water, and mixing a lye-base soap into it, "I determined to try my unskilled hand upon the operation. The fact is, I knew nothing of the task I had imposed upon myself, and in a few minutes rubbed the skin off my wrists without getting the clothes clean."[56] Some colonial women hired the wives or daughters of their neighbours to help haul and heat the water and actually do most of the back-breaking work of washing, drying, and ironing clothes.[57] Most coped with the work on their own, however, or with the help of daughters, or their one "girl of all work."

Once clothes were washed and rinsed, they had to be hung out to dry. Gate posts, fences, and shrubs doubled as clotheslines, and women anxiously hoped that the weather would cooperate. Dried clothes then had to be ironed. Though the Langtons had a regular washerwoman, she apparently was not skilled with an iron. Anne did her own ironing, although, she commented, it was "an accomplishment I had not yet perfectly attained."[58] Heating the heavy irons to the correct temperature and managing them so that precious clothes were not scorched or burned beyond use was a skill that only came with considerable practice.

The basic tools of washing were hard work, water, and soap. Many Upper Canadian farm women took pride in their ability to make soap. William Hutton, who it should be remembered never actually made soap, rather glibly wrote, "home made soap costs nothing" but "the time and a little firewood." It was his wife Fanny who, using ashes from the annual burn and old bones and entrails from a recently slaughtered hog or sheep, regularly made the gallons of soft soap, suitable for everything "except for bedrooms."[59] A number of women colonists described to relatives and friends at home their efforts at making soap. Even those with the surplus cash to buy soap usually made their own.[60]

The care taken in washing clothes reflected in part the constant problem many Upper Canadians had acquiring new clothes. In the earliest days, loyalists and early American settlers carefully tanned the skins of local game and domestic animals to make trousers, shirts, and dresses, as well as shoes and boots for the family.[61] Some residents also bought imported flannel and broadcloth from a local merchant or relied on parcels from "home" for both cloth and new clothes.[62] But many of the earliest Upper Canadian settlers also "brought their spinning wheels and looms with them."[63] Though it was some time before the raw materials to work on the looms were available in the colony, by 1800, a number of farms had begun to raise sheep and cultivate flax.[64]

As in food preparation and cooking, it was the mistress of the house, often with the help of daughters and neighbours, who made cloth and fashioned it into clothes. Amelia Harris recalled that once the flax was sown, "the culture was given up to the women. They had to weed, pull and thrash out the seeds and then spread it out to rot When it was in a proper state for the Brake, it was handed over to the men who cracked and dressed it. It was again returned to the women who spun and wove it, making a strong linen for shirts, plaid for their own dresses."[65] Though Amelia Harris was perhaps exaggerating when she stated that "every thrifty farm house had a loom and both wife and daughters learned to weave," it is evident that certainly a number did. Neighbourhood women frequently gathered in each other's homes to spin and weave linen. The cloth was then fashioned into clothes for the family, and linen that the family could not use brought a good price on the market.[66]

Working the flax and making linen demanded skill and many hands. So too, did making woollen clothing. But if raw wool was available, either from the farmer's own flock or at the market,[67] a number of households found turning it into clothing a decided cost saving. Until the advent of carding machines at local mills, colonial women washed, teased, carded, and dyed the raw wool themselves. The work was labour-intensive and no housewife could hope to tackle the whole process on her own. Even after families could send their raw wool to the mill for primary processing, only a family with a number of daughters or other capable women in the household were able to spin and then weave or knit up enough wool to make it worthwhile.

In 1834, William Hutton commented to his mother that "I think there will be no harm whatever in our girls spinning wool bye and bye for two or three hours every day or knitting, for both of which they will be well rewarded by not being obliged to buy."[68] By early spring 1841, the family's large flock of sheep was providing meat, tallow for candles, but most importantly raw material for significant quantities of cloth. "We are all except Mama," William reported to his mother, "dressed in homespun." Fanny, he explained "is not yet reconciled to a dyed flannel gown and the supply sent from home at different times is not yet done." There was so much wool, in fact, that William Hutton had to hire a servant "to spin our wool in summer."[69]

The added expense was obviously worthwhile. Though home-made woollens did not usually bring in cash, they could be exchanged for other goods and services. In the fall of 1841, the Huttons' man "took his half year's wages in clothes, flannel etc. etc." A year later, William reported that "the cloth pays Tradesmen and Labourers and will possibly furnish us a carpet as the merchants will exchange excellent carpeting for home made cloth yard for yard."[70] For the majority of Upper Canadians who did not have the benefit of packages from "home" or the financial resources to buy their own cloth, facility with a spinning wheel, a loom, or knitting needles was important.[71]

In many families, it was not the making of clothes from new cloth that occupied so much of a woman's time and energy, but the repairing and re-working of old clothes. Frances Stewart frequently complained of "the everlasting, always increasing piles of needlework."[72] Anne Langton and her mother and aunt spent many of their "free" hours making and re-making dresses, corsets, and hats "to modern dimensions" in addition to manufacturing curtains and furniture covers.[73] Obviously at some distance from the nearest seamstress, the Langton women not only "got up" their own muslins (with arrowroot as a substitute for starch) but Anne also made "an attack upon [her] corsets ... and [I] feel a little appalled at the difficulties before me." Anne acknowledged that "I am no mantua-maker when out of the beaten track." Nonetheless she persisted.[74] Though not many women in Upper Canada would have had muslins "to be got up" or perhaps even corsets to worry about, all had to be capable with a needle and thread. Many a long winter's afternoon or evening were spent in front of the fire and by candlelight making or mending clothes. Only a very few colonial women could ever afford to have a seamstress come into their homes. One of the first skills mothers taught their daughters was plain sewing.[75]

Spinning flax and wool and making clothes, curtains and other household items seems to have been a seasonal occupation. "One ought to get all one's sewing done in winter," Anne Langton advised her family.[76] With a growing family, this was not always possible. Particularly on colonial farms, the inevitable piles of mending had to wait until inclement weather or dusk brought women indoors. For only the most affluent households could afford to hire workers full time to attend to the routine work outside the house. Colonial women and young children regularly assumed much of the work associated with actual food production. Thus, in addition to the daily work of cooking, cleaning, washing clothes, and child care, keeping house in Upper Canada, included "keeping" outdoors. In the spring, summer, and fall, mistresses were fully occupied.

AFTER THE MEN had ploughed the garden and perhaps helped to plant potatoes (and sometimes turnip), the women were left to get "the garden stuff in."[77] Carrots, tomatoes, melons, cucumbers, peas, beets, beans, and turnip were sown and carefully tended.[78] When ripe, vegetables and wild fruit were harvested and put down. Rural families often planted orchards and berry bushes from stock that was bought at the local store, sent from overseas by family, or donated by neighbours. While gardens were an important source of food for the table, they were also a place of relaxation and enjoyment for many women, particularly when there were flowers and ornamental bushes to tend.[79] Keeping a garden was hard work, however, and it also took considerable time away from other duties. Many housekeepers found that their indoor responsibilities and especially the demands of a young and growing family left little time to work outside, regardless of how much they might wish to do so.

In 1837, Mary O'Brien lamented that for a number of years, she had not managed to put in a garden at all. "The first year, I went so far as to sow a few seeds but by the time the weeds grew I was too ill at ease [as a result of her first pregnancy] to pull them & so my plants were choked; the second my baby was too young and delicate to be exposed to the damp earth; the third I had no garden to make & the fourth, fifth & sixth I have been far too much occupied to admit of me doing anything except at very long intervals & rare occasions."[80] It is not surprising that, particularly in the first few years of settlement, many gardens included only those items that required little tending.[81] It was only when the family had increased and the number of hands available to weed and harvest had grown that gardens could be enlarged and diversified. A number of women then found that they had more fruits and vegetables to be preserved than the household could consume or needed. In such instances, they were able to turn their labour into cash by selling excess produce to neighbours or by bartering it at the nearest market.

The seasonal work required in a garden was only one aspect of keeping food on the family table. Many Upper Canadian households kept poultry and it was usually the wife's or daughter's responsibility to feed the flock, find, collect, and wash the eggs and, as required, kill and prepare a chicken or goose for dinner. If carefully housed and tended, chickens, ducks, and geese provided not only fresh meat and eggs for the table but sometimes a supplementary income.[82] Fanny Hutton reported to her mother-in-law in 1837, "our poultry yard is also increasing. We have now twelve young chicks, four goslings, and upwards of forty chickens. Our hens have given a good supply of eggs for the family and some to spare, for which we got 7s8d per dozen. We shall also be able to spare some poultry to supply little necessaries for the children and myself; our wants are not many. Geese are very profitable. I hope next year to rear a great many."[83]

Of equal and perhaps greater importance to the family table as well as to the pocket book was the dairy. One of the first investments many Upper Canadians made was to buy a cow in calf. This assured the family of milk, butter, and other dairy products and once a small herd was established, fresh meat for the pantry.[84] Managing the dairy was one of the many duties of the farm wife. It was often women who fed the beasts and oversaw calving and weaning. A wife also often had to retrieve a wandering cow before she could be milked. Many newly arrived immigrants from Great Britain were never comfortable in the dairy. Susanna Moodie's first experience as a "pupil of cows" convinced her that though she could, after considerable trial and error, milk a cow if she had to, she preferred that someone else do it.[85] Most women did not have this option.

Milking was only the first step in the process. The milk then had to be separated. Some was kept for the family table; the slops were fed to the pigs; and the cream had to be churned into butter or processed into cheese, both monotonous and time-consuming exercises. In most households, dairy equipment was primitive. Women worked "under difficult conditions," in the kitchen-parlour or on the porch.[86] Inevitably, they were interrupted frequently by their children or by the ongoing demands of other housekeeping chores. As Marjorie Cohen has ably illustrated, dairying was not in itself a commercial enterprise in Upper Canada. Many households were fortunate if they had sufficient milk and butter for their own daily needs. There were, however, a number of colonial women including Fanny Hutton and Mrs Playter who periodically made enough butter to sell to neighbours or at the local market.[87]

For women in Upper Canada, housekeeping was clearly not restricted to the physical confines of the home. Most women could not avoid yard work and a woman's skill and patience in the dairy, the garden, the hen house, or the piggery were a substantial benefit to her family. As Catharine Parr Traill commented in the mid 1830s, "here it is considered by no means derogatory to the wife of an officer or gentlemen to assist in the work of the house or to perform its entire duties, if occasion required; to understand the mystery of soap, candle and sugar making; to make bread, butter and cheese or even to milk her own cows, to knit and spin and prepare wool for the loom."[88] Indeed, "the occasion" *always* required that Upper Canadian women work in the garden and in the yard as well as in their home. Without their efforts, no farm or town family could hope to attain a basic level of subsistence and limited self-sufficiency. While farmers and their sons cleared the land, ploughed, planted, and harvested, and village artisans, shopkeepers, and workers sold their skills and labour, it was left to their wives, with the help of their daughters and perhaps a hired woman, to ensure that the family was fed and clothed.

Colonial wives took their work outside the home seriously. In 1833, Mary O'Brien had a litany of "housekeeping woes." "The cattle cannot be found, the girl is not to be had, the butter is all disposed of at the store, the large peas in the garden are forgotten, the hen which is just going to sit had been driven off her nest & the eggs destroyed & worst of all our house calf on whose interest his mother and we depended alone for milk has run off and cannot be traced."[89] And as "the occasion required," Mary O'Brien and other women also stepped outside of their traditional roles – as wives, housekeepers, and providers of food and clothing – to work for and beside their husbands, fathers, and brothers in the fields or, as shall be discussed later, in village shops at what was usually considered men's work.

EVEN THE MOST gentle farming wife sometimes found herself helping to make hay or planting and harvesting. Particularly in the first few years of settlement when children were small or where households lacked cash or goods to hire labourers, it is probable that most women regularly worked in the fields, in addition to keeping house. In 1835, when their children were small, William Hutton reported to his mother that "labour is enormously expensive and children's work must be done by men. We finished last week putting down two acres of Indian corn ... Fanny and I put a good deal of it down ourselves."[90] Two years later, he wrote, "I am daily surprised how Fanny stands the constant hard work she goes through both inside and out. She spread and filled manure in the cart; cut very nearly the whole seventy bushels of seed potatoes; laid them nearly all ... She is up between five and six and with all her unparalleled exertions she is quite strong." Not only did she work in the fields, Fanny also apparently took full responsibility for calving and lambing.[91] This was, of course, in addition to looking after six children and maintaining the house and garden.

Initially, Fanny Hutton may have found it very difficult to even think of taking on such work. Certainly other gentlewomen settlers found it hard to accept. "I had a hard struggle with my pride," Susanna Moodie wrote "before I would consent to render the least assistance on the farm; but reflection convinced me that I was wrong." In 1835, after three years of struggling, the Moodies' money was exhausted and "it was not only my duty to obey that call, but to exert myself to the utmost to assist my husband and help to maintain my family."[92] Susanna and her maid dug and hoed potatoes and during harvest carried sheaves of wheat by hand.[93] In hindsight, she concluded that "manual toil, however distasteful to those unaccustomed to it, was not after all such a dreadful hardship ... If we occasionally suffered severe pain, we as often experienced a great pleasure and I have contemplated a well-hoed ridge of potatoes on that bush farm with as much delight as in years long past I had experienced in examining fine paintings in some well-appointed drawing room."[94]

It is somewhat ironic that Susanna Moodie and probably other British immigrants considered field work "manual toil" and yet, by implication, would not have described their work as mothers, housekeepers, and gardeners in this way. But to Moodie, the necessity of working in the fields and engaging in "manual toil" symbolized a fall in class and standing that was shameful. It went against all her experience and her expectations of the proper conduct of a gentlewoman, expectations, it must be remembered, that were being reinforced in the colonial press.[95] Not all women shared Susanna Moodie's dilemma. Mary O'Brien, Mrs Playter and her daughters-in-law, and numerous other wives and daughters willingly helped gather hay, tend the livestock, and pick rocks. Indeed, Mary O'Brien bemoaned the need to cope with "domestic arrangements"and frequently mentioned her preference for working outside.[96]

Mary O'Brien's and other women's willingness and ability to work with their husbands often made the difference between the success or failure of the family business. As will be discussed later, wives and daughters in town regularly assisted their husbands and fathers in their shops; some took part-time waged employment to supplement the family coffers. The same was true of farm wives. Moreover, it was not unusual for a wife to act as a surrogate husband and to assume full responsibility for the family business while her mate was away. As Marjorie Cohen and other historians have noted, men in Upper Canada often had to leave their farms for varying lengths of time to work for wages, to fulfil military responsibilities, or to go to market or the mill.[97] On colonial farms, however, livestock still had to be tended and field work done. It was up to the farm wife, with or without the help of her children, to manage as best she could.

Shortly after her marriage, Mary O'Brien began overseeing the farm work while Edward was away for extended periods of time superintending the opening of a new settlement. Her journal makes frequent and matter-of-fact notations of her "various jobs in charge" – including managing a number of male workers.[98] Initially, she was conscious that the workmen resented taking instructions from the mistress of the house. They "look rather disposed to laugh at my interference, so I took care to look as undismayed as possible," she wrote in July 1831. Mary was "impressed with the disadvantages under which I must manage the farm." But she was determined "to establish [her] character of being a good managing body."[99] By the end of the summer of 1831, Mary appears to have successfully established her authority and gained the respect of the workers.

While acting as a surrogate husband, Mary O'Brien still had to cope with her own work. In an entry in her journal, Mary recorded a typical day while Edward was away. "I was up as soon as the day dawned to give Connally [the hired man] a message." The first thing she noticed was that it was raining, "so I dispatch another to fetch home a stray pig & go into the barn to see if Hunt is going on right with his job." She then went to the dairy "to skim & arrange milk – all this time the baby is in bed awake playing." Her mother and niece were also in bed, though Mary's maid, Flora, "is cleaning the house & getting breakfast for both parties." As the baby was getting restless, Mary dressed him, and took him with her to the barn to check on Hunt again. Then "we have prayers & go to breakfast whilst Flora is gone to milk."

After breakfast, Mary sent the man who had come back without the pig off to try again. Before dinner, the early afternoon meal, Mary made three more trips to the barn to supervise Hunt and the two thrashers who had arrived. She also helped "Flora to strain the cream into the churn," gave her niece Mary a lesson, looked again at the thrashers and checked on her favourite sow and her new litter. After dinner, she churned butter which would "not *come*," gave Mary a lesson in geography, made tea, sewed "a little," helped Flora with her evening chores and went to bed.[100] It should be noted that Mary's infant son accompanied her in all her activities.

Mary O'Brien was not the only farmer's wife who periodically found herself acting as farmer as well as wife and mother. During the War of 1812 and the Rebellions of 1837–8, women were regularly left to look after the family and maintain the farm or family business as best they could while their husbands served with the local militia.[101] Men were also often away working in the bush, on the roads or canals, or on someone else's farm. Particularly for new settlers living on land that was only partly cleared and with few financial resources, off-farm income was essential for the family's survival. In their husbands' absence, women automatically turned their attention to work that was not "naturally" women's work. Though some such as Susanna Moodie found such circumstances difficult to accept, many others like Mary O'Brien took on these added responsibilities without complaint.

IT IS NOT SURPRISING that for many women, being a farmer's or artisan's wife exacted a heavy physical and emotional toll. "The labour involved in feeding, clothing and caring for large families" or households was considerable.[102] After only six years in the colony, William Hutton reported that Fanny "is indefatigable, but looks many, many years older than she ought to look at her time of life."[103] Anne Langton mused in 1838 that "I have caught myself wishing an old long-forgotten wish that I had been born of the rougher sex. Women are very dependent here, and give a great deal of trouble; we feel our weakness more than anything else."[104] It took more than physical endurance to be a settler's wife. Housekeeping, in the broadest sense, also required considerable skill. Many women in Upper Canada, like those American settlers moving from one frontier to another, learned their work at their mothers' knee. Others, however, acquired the skills necessary to sustain the family only after painstaking trial and error. Indeed, for some British women who came to the colony in the post-1815 years, even the most basic skills of housekeeping remained a bewildering mystery.

The work nonetheless had to be done. It did not have to be, nor indeed could be, accomplished by one woman on her own, however. Clearly, Mary O'Brien would not have been able to manage her own work and oversee that of her husband's without help. Indeed, even when her husband was home and particularly when her children were young, many found it next to impossible to fully complete the most basic daily chores. As William Hutton remarked in 1842, "What a difference it makes when the farmer's own family can do *all!!!*"[105]

Fanny Hutton depended on the efforts of her daughters to help cook, clean, make clothes, and look after the younger children. Anne Langton relied extensively on the help of her mother and aunt to run her brother's household. But, even with adult women or older daughters in residence to help them with housekeeping, Anne Langton and Fanny Hutton and all other farm wives had little time to relax and to rest. And many discovered that even a large family could not cope with all the work.

In emergencies, Upper Canadian women turned to friends and extended family to help them meet the needs of their households. Within the informal community of working women, help now was exchanged for help in the future. But in many households, the demands of young and large families, absent husbands, and large homes often required a somewhat more formal and extended arrangement. Then, colonial housewives looked for a "help" to join their household – a local girl or a widowed woman who became part of the family, and in exchange for her board and a small wage joined the woman of the house in her work.

5 "The Ordinary Sort of Canadian Servant": Helping and the Neighbour's Girl

In January 1831, Flora, a young woman from the Isle of Mull presented herself at Mary O'Brien's door looking for work.[1] After consulting with Wilson, the hired man, as to Flora's reputation, Mary decided to take her on. Though Flora spoke "imperfect English," having only heard "the language for the first time in the vessel which brought her to Upper Canada," she seemed, Mary wrote, to be energetic and eager to work and "there was a chance of her being more efficient than the child" Mary already had.[2] After some rather protracted negotiations, which included agreeing to hire Flora's brother "to take care of her during my absence," Flora arrived to take up her duties.[3] Flora worked for and with Mary O'Brien for the next eighteen months, and during that time, she became a trusted and treasured member of the O'Brien household.

Flora was a "help." She was hired by the O'Briens to assist with the domestic work. And it is clear from Mary's diary that Flora, like many of the other women who helped in Upper Canada, was essential to the functioning of her employer's household. Generally, the help (or the maid or girl as she was referred to in some country diaries) assisted her mistress with cooking , cleaning, child care, and any other duties that farm women were obliged to undertake. Mothers especially needed help when their children were small or when some other short-term circumstance overwhelmed the woman of the house.[4] Reading the diaries, letters, and journals of Anne Langton, Mary O'Brien, John Thompson, Hamnett Pinhey, and other employers leaves one with the impression that farm households in particular were often desperate to find a girl. But they were also resigned to the fact that acquiring the services of a really "good" girl or woman was next to impossible. Mary O'Brien appears to have been very fortunate when she accepted Flora's offer.

It is often difficult to discern the exact identity of these women who "helped" for wages. We know little, for example, of Flora's background and nothing of her life after she left the O'Briens. What we do know of her suggests that she was reasonably representative of many women who sought waged work in Upper Canada. She was young, probably under twenty-one; she was also single, a recent immigrant, and her family lived in the immediate vicinity of the O'Briens.

Young single girls in Upper Canada frequently worked for a neighbour's family when their labour was not required at home. As traveller Basil Hall observed in the late 1820s, "all those members of each family who can be spared from field work, go off to neighbouring towns, villages, or even the better class of farm houses, and engage themselves as servants. Most of the young women are thus employed at first, and frequently also the boys."[5] For some young women, this was a way to earn a little cash before they married. More often, their meagre wages were necessary to help sustain their families.

Helps in Upper Canada were not always young and single, however. There were a number of older and widowed women who helped in exchange for a home and some limited security. The wives and daughters of newly arrived settlers, small farmers, rural artisans, and landless labourers also helped a neighbour or their husband's employer on a part-time basis. The wages they received for domestic or farm work were small, particularly when compared to those earned by men. The extra cash was nonetheless always a welcome addition to the family coffers. In some circumstances, it enabled families to purchase what would otherwise be luxury items. In still others, their wages meant the difference between feeding and clothing their children or going hungry.

Regardless of their financial circumstances, the vast majority of women who helped for wages in Upper Canada consciously maintained a certain degree of personal independence and self-worth. Women who worked as helps refused to consider themselves servants. And very few "hired girls" expected that any domestic employment would be permanent or long term. Both in town and in the country, helps were aware that prospective employers needed their assistance. Finding work was not in itself particularly difficult, although finding a good situation with a congenial family was sometimes more problematic. Thus if and when a woman became dissatisfied with her situation, she did not hesitate to leave because she was fairly confident that she would be able to find another position when she wanted to re-enter the workforce. Moreover, domestic helps always expected to work with, as well as for, their employers. Flora's work was intended to supplement, not to replace, that of Mary O'Brien. And Flora and other girls made sure that their employers realized the distinction.

WOMEN LIVING in rural Upper Canada where the practice of helping was most prevalent were surprisingly restricted in what type of waged work they could get.[6] The frontier conditions of the colony did permit a few exceptional women to cross into what was unquestionably "men's" work. Mary O'Brien reported hearing of a pair of women loggers.[7] But unlike the custom in rural Great Britain in the eighteenth and early nineteenth centuries, relatively few colonial women were employed as general farm hands.[8] Skilled dairy maids did appear to have been in some demand in Upper Canada in the first half of the nineteenth century.[9] Contemporary diaries and account books indicate that women sometimes found work haying, digging potatoes, shearing sheep, or helping plant and harvest.[10] Yet when Mary O'Brien hired "a great tall black girl" to take up potatoes in 1832, she commented not on her colour but on her gender. "It is the first time we have ever had female Canadians as farm servants, though in my farming days I got some day's work at odd times from some English girls who were living on the farm, but this rather as a freak than anything else."[11]

Some colonists attributed the absence of women farm labourers to the fact that women chose not to accept such work. Writing two years after her arrival to Upper Canada, Mary O'Brien observed that "amongst the varieties and unsettled habits of this new land, the employment of the women are remarkable. Some confine themselves entirely to household employments, including however spinning & weaving & are almost too inactive beyond that route to walk." These, she observed, "were chiefly the Yankee settlers or generally those residing in the most settled parts." There were others, however, "the uncorrupted Dutch or rather German tribes" and the Scots living "more generally in the remoter situations" who considered "not only gardening ... exclusively their [women's] province, but shearing & in harvesting, sugar-making and as I have just heard [in] logging, the most laborious of all employments, they take their share with men."[12] Surviving diaries and government reports suggest that although rural women frequently worked without pay with their fathers, husbands, and brothers, farmers were reluctant to *hire* women field workers individually.[13] Only when male workers were in relatively short supply or a woman was in some way already attached to the household, as perhaps the wife of a hired man, did farmers turn to women as waged labourers. Rural women were more likely to find waged work home making; and women domestic workers were in considerable demand.

It seems to have been the custom, especially in rural Upper Canada, for a prospective employer to initiate the work relationship. Some newly arrived immigrants did state in their notices in local newspapers their willingness to work "in the country."[14] And it was certainly not unknown for women such as Flora to apply personally to be a help. But Flora was one of the few girls Mary O'Brien hired between 1828 and 1840 who actually came to her door soliciting work. "Girl hunting" was a constant occupation of many rural Upper Canadians. All that most available girls had to do was wait for an offer.

"One of the troubles of the backwoods," Anne Langton observed in 1833 was "so much expense and lost time in hunting for a servant."[15] Mistresses and masters would travel for miles and often spend days looking for someone to help them at home.[16] In May 1828 after a day of looking, Mary O'Brien was somewhat disconcerted to discover "that the girls have just gone back into the woods."[17] Two years later, she was vexed that after making an arrangement with a local girl, the maid's father refused to let her go because her labour was more useful at home.[18] A few rural employers tried to entice girls from the nearest village to come to the country by placing advertisements in local newspapers.[19] Some even went to the village to make a personal appeal. But as Anne Langton reported in 1842, "servants are very scarce just now," and "none of the Peterboro servants will come so far back, so that beyond what the neighbouring townships offer there is small chance."[20] Three years earlier after looking unsuccessfully for a woman to work as a cook, Anne Langton had turned to her young maid, Kitty, to help her in her search. And though she realized that relying on Kitty's recommendation was rather unusual, she knew that it would save her brother invaluable time in not having to continue their search.[21] Mary O'Brien often asked friends and family if they knew of a girl willing to work for her. In one instance, she even engaged a young woman she encountered by chance on the street.[22]

In some cases, rural mistresses resorted to hiring young boys or men to serve as "maids." In the late 1830s, the Langtons, for example, kept both a boy and a girl servant. Though the boy was hired specifically to cut wood and look after the pigs and the poultry, he also assumed duties in the kitchen when the maid was away.[23] In 1829 Mary Gapper's soon-to-be husband, Edward O'Brien, kept only a man for household chores.[24] A year later, Mary reported that an Irishman was one of the best kitchen maids she had ever had. And soon after her marriage, Mary hired a Yorkshire lad to act as her kitchen maid.[25] Not surprisingly, hiring a man to do women's work was highly unusual.[26] Rural gentlefolk preferred to engage women for indoor work. And given the problems of travel in the back country and the particular demands of rural households, most wives also tried to find someone from their own neighbourhood.

Amelia Ryerse Harris remembered that in the early years, "the native American would not and will not ... go out to service." She noted, however, that "almost any of the neighbour daughters would be glad to go as helps, doing the same work only eating at the Table with their mistress."[27] The Ryerses first hired Barbara Troyer, the daughter of their neighbour. They subsequently employed the daughter of a local labourer, Polly Spragge, who Amelia remembered as a "merry, laughing, who cares sort of a Girl."[28] Over the next few years, Mrs Ryerse had a succession of "helps," all local girls, who ate at the family table and according to Amelia, subsequently became "the wives of Squires, Captains, Majors, Colonels in the Militia and are owners of large properties; and they and their descendants drive in their own carriages."[29]

Amelia Harris's implication that girls who "helped" were usually of the same class as their employers may have reflected the situation at the turn of the century. Certainly, a generation later this was less likely to have been the case. In 1830, Mary O'Brien recounted the instance of the Southbys' hesitancy in taking "one of the young Seagers." "The difficulty," she noted "rested on employing as a hired servant a person who they could not receive in their family but as an equal." Mary O'Brien found nothing wrong with this and, indeed, "the thing appeared to me very feasible."[30] The fact, however, that the decision required "private consultation" among the family before the boy was employed indicates that the Southbys were uncomfortable with the proposition. Upper Canadian diaries and letters suggest that rural hired help were usually the sons and daughters of local labourers, artisans and smaller, less prosperous neighbouring farmers. These households could not usually afford to hire help themselves and, in fact, often depended on the wages of their children to supplement the family income.[31]

For farm wives, hiring a local girl to help had a number of immediate advantages. As a farmer's daughter or sister, a neighbourhood girl was already familiar with the work of a farm household. Working in someone else's home was very similar to working for and with her own family. Though usually not "trained" as a servant, a girl would have received informal instruction in housekeeping from her mother. Moreover, a girl recruited from the community was less likely to be overwhelmed by backwoods conditions. With her family close at hand, there was less chance that she would become lonely and want to leave her employer. As Mary O'Brien commented after she had hired a young child as a maid in 1830, "as her mother lives near, I can send [the little girl] home when I go out."[32] Perhaps most important, however, a local girl was not a stranger to her new mistress. Within the closely-knit rural communities of Upper Canada, a farmer's wife invariably knew something of the prospective girl's situation and her family's reputation. She also knew or could find out from the neighbours if the girl was likely to be "a steady & well recommended person."[33]

A help's personal reputation was important to a prospective employer. In January 1829, Betsy Garland, a young girl recommended by the Reverend John Strachan, arrived at Mary Gapper's door looking for a position or at least help in finding one. Clearly, Betsy was not from the area. Much more troubling, however, was the fact that Betsy "had lost her character" and was accompanied by a young child. Moved by both Betsy's "misfortune" and Strachan's evident concern, Mary attempted to help Betsy find a "respectable service."[34]

At the first farmhouse the two approached, the young mistress considered Betsy "too bad for her purpose." Over the next few days, other households echoed this judgment.[35] For Betsy, the situation must have been devastating. Unlike many other girls in her situation, she was obviously alone in the world with the exception of the child who accompanied her. And given that both Strachan and, as a result, Mary Gapper knew her circumstances, she could not attempt to pass herself off as a recent widow. Mary Gapper did not record whether or not Betsy managed to find a place.

Even women who were widows or who were accepted as such but were accompanied by very young children often had considerable difficulty securing employment. In 1830, Mary Southby refused to take on a widow with a child, as she did not "approve."[36] Five years later, Mary O'Brien was not pleased that her new help had arrived with a five-month-old child. Mary had been led to believe that the youngster was fifteen months old and she feared that the woman's attention and time would necessarily be distracted from her work.[37] Single or unattached women rarely had such problems. They frequently did have difficulty finding situations that paid well, however.

In 1841, Anne Langton considered that "on the whole" servants were not badly paid in Upper Canada, "but" she acknowledged, "there is no scale of remuneration according to merit." Pay was determined loosely by age. "You give a girl less than a woman," Anne re-

Illustration 8
Sketch of Peterborough from White's Tavern ("an unlikely source of 'help'"), pen and
ink by Anne Langton
AO (s13285)

ported, "but when they consider themselves women they must have
four dollars a month." It is clear that this basic scale was implicitly accepted throughout the Langtons' neighbourhood. As Anne noted,
"more than this you could not give them without exciting the wrath
of all the housekeepers in the neighbourhood for raising wages."[38]

Indeed, it appears that this rate of pay was standard throughout
the colony. Between 1815 and 1840, a full-time female help received
between three and four dollars a month plus her room and board. If a
girl was very young, her wage was correspondingly less. An older,
experienced woman might be paid slightly more.[39] Many farm families such as the Huttons paid their help in a combination of produce
and cash.[40] Others like the Pinheys of March Township allowed the
help to buy items from the local pedlar or the village shop and put it
on their account.[41]

It is not clear why wages for female helps did not change or actually may have decreased over time. The wages for men who worked
on the farm increased over the period. And there does appear to have
been a continuing demand for domestic help. Marjorie Cohen at-

tributes the fact that women's wages remained static in part to "the lack of alternative income sources for women" who lived in rural communities and this undoubtedly influenced the situation.[42] But her explanation that "women's labour remained [largely] out of the market place" and that farm families were therefore reluctant to spend money "increasing the productivity of female labour" misrepresents the role and the work of helps and the nature of work relations on colonial farms. It is more likely that the reluctance of at least some rural women to move far from home to earn cash compromised their ability to negotiate a higher wage. Moreover, the very nature of "helping," which presumed a level of equality between employer and employee, may have precluded some girls and their families from demanding more than the market would bear. For as shall be discussed, unlike men who worked for wages in the fields, domestic helps usually considered themselves part of the family. Moreover, for a girl without skills who intended to work for only a limited period of time, her wage was only part of her remuneration. She also received training and, for some at least, a greater measure of independence than if she was living at home.

The apparent inability of a girl or her family to negotiate individual wages was offset to some degree by the influence the family maintained over the actual conditions of work. Before hiring a young girl, the mistress always had to discuss the matter with her parents, both to obtain their permission and to negotiate basic terms of employment.[43] Moreover, the proximity of an employee's family also encouraged the farm wife to treat her help fairly.[44] A farm wife was well aware that if her girl became disgruntled or upset by her work or her employer's treatment, she could and would leave to go home. This could sour relations within a small community and might jeopardize a mistress's ability to gain help from other families.

There were disadvantages for a young girl in helping a neighbour. Young daughters often had no choice but to accept work on their parents' insistence. Moreover, a girl was not legally entitled to retain her meagre wages. They were owed to her father or mother who could and often did collect them.[45] Despite the relatively low rate of pay and the fact that helps were not always able to keep what they had earned, hired girls nonetheless resisted the trappings of servitude that were beginning to be evident in some urban homes. Even as the economic and social gap between the farm wife and her help widened, helps maintained and exercised a sense of personal independence, both in assumptions about their work and how they carried it out.

Mary Gapper reported to her family shortly after she arrived in the colony that her sister-in-law Mary Southby had "a man who lives in the house and two females who choose to be called girls as a more dignified appellation than servant." From the vantage point of her British experience, Mary considered that these girls were "unworthy of the title servant." Among other things, one of them refused "to wear a cap or keep her hair neat." The girls were also far too casual about their work and in their relations with the family for Mary's liking. Nonetheless, Mary reported that one of these independent girls "has been with them since Christmas & is very good as times go."[46] In fact, Mary implied, her sister-in-law was fortunate to have them. Farmer's wives knew that although they might control salaries, they could not often control a girl's attitude. They were dependent on the willingness of such women to come into their homes and provide the assistance that in many cases was essential for the family's well-being.[47]

WHEN A GIRL arrived to take up her position, she immediately became an integral member of her employer's household, sharing both "the conditions of the family" and the work of the farm wife.[48] Even when there was "no actual kinship tie between a woman and her 'hired girl'," in many households, "the relationship between them was, in part, modelled on kin relations."[49] Not surprisingly, the duties of the "help" varied from one household to another, depending on the season of the year, the number of children in the family, and the household's economic and social circumstances. In most cases a help's days, like those of her mistress, were long and her work onerous. But as Faye Dudden argues, it must be remembered that "'helps' denoted less an occupation than an activity."[50]

A typical workday probably began before dawn and ended only after dark. The girl was usually expected to be up before the rest of the household to get the fires burning and make early morning tea or coffee. Then the day's real work would commence. In 1835, Mary O'Brien described to her family in Great Britain "a regular detail of my daily proceedings." At that time, the O'Briens had a young girl who had been taken on partly in exchange for her education. "We breakfast [at] six before which I expect my little lassie [the help] to dust & arrange the parlour whilst I am helping the children to dress, skimming the milk & looking at the cows and poultry which now in the hatching season requires a more experienced hand than Willie's [her son] to adjust all their affairs." After breakfast Mary O'Brien "arranged my household affairs" which included giving orders to the help. While Mary gave Willie his lessons, the girl, Helen, "furbished their apartments." Throughout the rest of the day the young girl helped with ironing, making meals, and the general cleaning.[51] Periodically, Helen, together with her sisters (who came to the O'Briens to help by the day) had their lessons, which sometimes continued into the evenings.

As with any member of a rural household, the work expected of the help depended to a large degree upon her age and her particular skills and ability. Young girls, like young daughters or sisters, could mind the children, help prepare meals, and see that dinner did not prematurely end up in the fire. They also helped with cleaning the house and washing clothes. Very young "damsels," as Mary O'Brien often referred to them, had, of course, to be supervised and often taught how to do many tasks. When Kitty came to the Langtons in November 1838, she was a "strong and stout" fourteen-year-old, who, Anne believed, was "very capable of *being made* a good servant."[52] Five months later, Anne was pleased with Kitty's work. "I do not think many girls of fourteen would have done as well for us this winter as [Kitty] has done," she wrote in her diary. But, Anne continued, "Not that her capabilities are anything very great except in the cleaning way, and she is a capital scrubber, and so stout and strong that one did not feel that a little hard-working occasionally would do her any harm, as one would have done with most girls."[53]

The girl hired by Anne on Kitty's recommendation in the spring of 1839, ostensibly to take over the kitchen, was "by no means promising," however. According to Anne, "she is too young in the first place, only seventeen," and did not have the experience necessary for the work. But, as Anne lamented, "a person of steady years is difficult to obtain, and one with any but the commonest sort of knowledge is quite out of the question."[54] Moreover, Anne concluded some time later, because girls did not stay long in one place, "they are too uncertain to be worth teaching, at least it seems quite customary to leave them untaught." As a result, she was "inclined to make the best of them, and expect nothing more."[55]

An industrious and skilled girl such as Mary O'Brien's Flora was a real help to her mistress. Within a week of her arrival in February 1831, Flora had settled into a routine. She helped cook and Mary recorded "is so active that I am not only obliged to resign to her all my accustomed share of the household duties but to teach her to read lest she should suffer from *ennui*."[56] As Mary entered the last trimester of her first pregnancy, Flora assumed more and more of the household management. After the birth of Mary's second child, Flora not only helped look after the children, but as Mary explained to her family, did not give her "room to spend time in householdry if I wished it."[57]

Flora and Mary obviously worked well together.[58] When Flora went away periodically to visit her family, Mary either tried to manage on her own or hired the wife of a neighbour to replace her temporarily. Neither arrangement was satisfactory. Over Christmas 1831, for example, Mary stated emphatically, "I wish I had Flora back, the outrageous piece of mortality I have to supply her is a tissue of blunders."[59] When Flora left the O'Briens for good in September 1832, three weeks after Mary's latest confinement, Mary complained that even with the help of a second young girl, Amelia, she was swamped with work.[60]

Flora appears to have been able to turn her hand to anything. Many girls were not so versatile. Mistresses did try to capitalize, however, on whatever skills their helps possessed. As already mentioned, Anne Langton's Kitty was a "capital scrubber." One of the girls who replaced Flora in 1832 was apparently capable with a needle, and Mary willingly relinquished her work basket.[61] If a girl showed facility with livestock, she might become the dairy maid, responsible for tending the cattle, milking, and making butter.[62] Sometimes a girl was hired to perform a specific task. Anne Langton considered herself fortunate in 1837 to have Mary who was responsible for cooking and baking.[63] In August 1831, Mary O'Brien hired a second girl (in addition to Flora) primarily to cook and wash.[64] Her sister-in-law, Mary Southby, had a "cook" as well as a general maid. Yet in most colonial households, the help's work was undifferentiated. Most performed a wide variety of tasks. Even Anne Langton's Mary, for example, frequently turned her hand to general cleaning and sewing. Mary O'Brien's cook helped in the dairy.

Inevitably, the rhythms and demands of various seasons and changing circumstances in the household had an impact on the work of a general help. Though a woman might be hired primarily for indoor work, when the situation demanded, she joined the rest of the household in the garden or in the fields. In 1837, old Jennie, Susanna Moodie's maid who had come to Upper Canada with the family, worked for a number of days with her master and mistress making hay.[65] Flora regularly tended Mary O'Brien's garden.[66] A new girl hired by the O'Briens in February 1834 helped with reaping.[67] Jane Jordan who worked for Mrs Thompson of Lake Simcoe in 1833 as a general maid helped dig potatoes in the fall.[68]

Women who contracted to work as helps on Upper Canadian farms were important working members of the household. Like their mistress, they were homemakers, who could, and were expected to, turn their attention to any and all tasks normally undertaken by the farm wife. As directed by their mistress, they washed clothes, cleaned the house, looked after the children, made preserves, and helped put down meat.

Even the most enterprising girl was never expected to tackle all the work on her own. In response to a comment made by her sister Lucy, Mary O'Brien rather indignantly informed her that having a good servant like Flora did not preclude Mary from working in her own dairy. She explained that this summer, 1831, there were three to six men to provide with board and lodgings "besides our own parlour party." Further, "Having no cook, my lassie has to bake almost every day besides which she washes for us all so that I now find myself frequently obliged to take some share of the household employments," including the dairy.[69] Two years later, with five or six men, in addition to her family, living in their home, Mary O'Brien, in an interesting reversal of roles, "helped" the cook. "We have to bake an oven full of bread every other day, then there are puddings to be made for supper to save the pork barrel &c &c. so the cook can not get on without help which all goes out of my work basket."[70]

Even in those rural households that could afford to engage more than one servant, the girls assumed that the mistress would do her share. Anne Langton recorded in 1840 "we ladies are as busy as the servants rubbing furniture, etc ... You lose no respect in such exertions." Comparing the attitude to such activities in both Britain and to that in Upper Canada, Anne continued, "here one of our domestics would be surprised and perhaps think herself a little ill-used if, in any extra bustle we should be sitting in our drawing room. They are apt to think it quite right that we should be taking our due share and are certainly our 'helps' ... I cannot perceive that anything like disrespect is engendered by the relative position of mistress and maid."[71] When in March 1835 Mary O'Brien was able to keep three full-time helps, "a boy & girl assistant in the parlour" and a "pretty little Scotch girl" of about seventeen, she still had her own work to perform. Three servants "give me pretty full employment as superintendent," she wrote, "but [will] I hope relieve me from the greater part of my household labours." Moreover, Mary continued to be primary care-giver for her children. She also tended a large garden and in April, she started a school for neighbourhood children.[72]

By 1834, after having spent many of her early years in the colony without any help, Frances Stewart managed to acquire two "comfortable servants." The eldest girl, Frances wrote to a friend, "does the milking, baking, cooking, washing and cleaning in all parts of the house adjacent to her belongings in the kitchen ... Occasionally, in her spare hours ... [she also] attends to spinning wool." The youngest help, "a tiny little girl of sixteen, takes care of the other rooms, lays the table, cleans knives and candlesticks, washes cups and saucers, irons all the clothes and nurses Charlie [the youngest child] if she is at a loss for employment ... This "does not often happen," Frances ruefully acknowledged.[73] Yet, even with two girls in the house, Frances, who was again pregnant, was not idle. She and her eldest daughters, Anna and Ellen, looked after the younger children, made cloth, sewed, mended clothes, and generally supervised the household.

Unfortunately, Frances Stewart soon discovered that she could not escape the dilemma that periodically confronted all rural employers. Within a few months of her letter, Frances had to report that the two girls had left, and she now had "a little girl of fifteen" to cook, bake, and do "the rough work of the house." Though a woman came in to wash every fortnight, Frances and her daughters now did the ironing and the rest of the housework.[74]

Although Frances Stewart may have found the situation frustrating, to the little fifteen-year-old girl it probably did not seem particularly unusual; nor would it have changed her expectations of her work. Although both women and men accepted board and wages for their work, domestic, parlour, and often farm labourers shared the conditions of the family and "address[ed] their masters with a tone of perfect equality."[75] Indeed, as Nancy Osterud concludes in her study of farm women in nineteenth-century New York, being a hired girl "did not in itself, create social distance." Certainly, Osterud notes, the relationship between employer and employee was hierarchical. But, she continued, "questions of authority were handled as much in generational as contractual terms."[76] In many rural homes, the help ate at the family table and relaxed with the family at the end of the day.[77] If the girl fell ill, she was nursed by her mistress. In her turn, the girl expected to take on extra work if another member of the household became ill. At the end of June 1831, for example, Flora was forced to her bed and Mary noted that, as a result, her day was taken up with nursing Flora and doing the work of two.[78]

In many rural households, "the conditions of helping ... made service less obnoxious" than being a "servant" in an urban household. The informality of the relationship was reinforced by the expectations both the girl and her mistress had of the relationship. A "help" did not require special living quarters or a uniform. Moreover, a girl's "provisions did not require much cash outlay for farm families who produced many of their own goods."[79] In short, the farm mistress assumed that the help would share the living conditions of the family. For her part, a girl expected to receive room and board and a small wage in return for her work. She also expected to be treated, if not as one of the family, at least as a member of a neighbour's family.

In many instances, a close personal relationship developed between the mistress and her help. Mary O'Brien and Flora were more than co-workers. They were also bound together by affection and mutual respect.

DESPITE SUCH informality between employer and help, the difference in status or authority between them was never completely erased. The girl was, after all, an employee. She had little choice in her activities and was subject to the disciplines and rhythms of another's household. And despite the relative informality of the arrangement, many farmer's wives seemed to have little real confidence in their helps' abilities, intelligence, or diligence.

Shortly after arriving in the colony, Mary Gapper assumed responsibility for superintending the Southby household. Her sister-in-law, Mary, was in the middle of her second and very difficult pregnancy. A record of one of Mary Gapper's "typical" days noted that she was up shortly after six and immediately went "into the dairy to see the milk etc. put right." Then, while dressing her niece, she walked "once or twice into the kitchen to see that the servants do not forget to put on the tea kettle." Once breakfast was over, Mary took "all convenient opportunity to look into the kitchen to see that the cook is doing the right thing at the right time." Her journal continued, "before 9 1/2, I take my bible again but about that time go regularly the rounds of kitchen, cellar & dairy, with the cook, examining into such minutiae as would never enter into the head of a person who had to conduct servants instead of girls – order dinner or so much of it as I think she can remember at once telling, directing what is to be done first, what next & so on for that & laying out the day's work altogether." Mary's account of the rest of that August day in 1829 included frequent references to having to oversee, interrupt, and correct the help. Even in the evening "after tea," she continued to visit the kitchen periodically "to see that my orders have been obeyed."[80]

It must be remembered that in 1829, Mary Gapper was still very much an English gentlewoman. She expected her sister-in-law's domestic staff to be like servants at home, where the maid would have worn a cap and the cook would have been a trained and experienced professional. Like many gentlewomen who lived in the Upper Canadian back country, Mary was initially frustrated by the attitudes and seeming ineptitude of many of the girls who worked for her sister-in-law.[81] She was never reconciled to the "American" practice of sharing a table with her help.[82] And like William and Fanny Hutton, she expected women to "know their place."[83] However, by the time she had married Edward O'Brien and had set up housekeeping on her own, her expectations of the help had begun to change. But Mary, like Anne Langton and many other farm wives, continued to believe that the girl usually needed constant supervision and direction. In 1839 Anne Langton complained that her new girl was "not promising" and both her helps had "to be perpetually reminded." In what was perhaps a typical attitude of colonial mistresses, she concluded, "the more we do it the more they depend on us, and the less we trust them, so that, like the vibrations of a pendulum, the thing is kept up ad infinitum. Such as ours, I suppose, is the ordinary sort of Canadian servant."[84]

Many women who "helped" their mistresses must have found such attitudes galling, particularly if they believed that they knew more about keeping a colonial household than did their mistresses. In 1829, the Southbys' Fanny, the old dairy girl, was "in a state of insurrection," and Mary reported "[she] very logically maintaining that having been thirty summers in the practice of making sour butter, she must know how to make sweet butter better than her young mistress who has never made any."[85] Susanna Moodie's maid must have laughed quietly to herself when her mistress had difficulties with the washing or making bread. And Mary Southby's girl also probably watched with carefully concealed glee as Mary Gapper, the woman who presumed to tell her what to do, had herself to learn how to cook on an open fire, churn butter, and milk.

The nature of the rural domestic workplace and the differing expectations of the mistress and the help tended to complicate the situation. Colonial farm houses were small and cramped. For the most part, the girl worked within sight or hearing of her mistress. Like all other members of the household, she had little real personal privacy or "free" time. Though working as a help was usually task- rather than time-oriented,[86] in most farmhouses there was almost always too much work to be done to allow much opportunity to relax. A number of girls may have managed to order their work so that they had an evening and perhaps part of a day free. Time off for a half or full day appears to have been granted by many mistresses only irregularly, however.

Many girls did attempt to assert some control over their working lives. Anne Langton commented in 1838 that "women are very independent here and give a good deal of trouble."[87] Many girls tried to set their own terms of work. Helps often avoided tasks they did not like or worked at their own pace. In 1829, for example, Mary Gapper reported that one of the Southby maids "had got into the habit of neglecting to milk the cows." She had also convinced her companion, the nursery girl, "to lie on this subject."[88] When her antics were dis-

Illustration 9
"Blythe Farm," John Langton's farm, sketch by Anne Langton
AO (s13285)

covered, the dairy maid was firmly scolded for her laziness and neglect; ironically, she also found herself under a greater degree of
supervision than before. Despite this, the girl's behaviour continued.
A few months after the first incident, Mary discovered that when the
dairy maid was "observed in her work, [she] got three or four more
quarts each time than when left on her own."[89]

Given the living conditions in rural Upper Canada and the attitudes of many wife-employers, it is not surprising that colonial
households were periodically racked with tension and acrimony.
When Kitty first came to the Langton household in January 1839, the
older couple already in service clearly resented her presence. In less
than two months Anne reported that "the crisis came and the old
people left." Anne Langton recognized that the couple's determination to leave the Langtons was only in part a result of their unhappiness with Kitty. "The old woman was evidently tired of service,"
Anne noted "and is now rejoicing in the tranquillity of her own
shanty."[90] Yet Anne realized that relations among the help were frequently strained. Personalities often clashed. A girl might feel that
she was doing more work than her companion; helps sometimes became apprehensive about their place in the household when a new

girl arrived. Some months after Kitty was first hired, Anne expressed concern that Kitty, now the "senior help," might be unwilling to accept any other girl in the kitchen.[91]

All rural mistresses sometimes had to cope with parlour squabbles. In the fall of 1830, Mary O'Brien was "a little bothered by a gentle dissatisfaction between the married pair in the kitchen." As she explained to her family in Britain, "according to custom, to make peace with each other they made war upon me." Mary was very cross when the two threatened to leave and the husband also refused to attend family prayers. The couple left, unceremoniously, two days later.[92] Mary immediately engaged an "old Irish woman" to replace them. It was clear from the outset that this new arrangement had its own difficulties. Not only was the Irish woman reluctant to perform various duties in the manner that Mary O'Brien considered appropriate, but she openly questioned Mary's instructions. Her mistress, pregnant for the first time, put up with such behaviour, obviously aware that if she protested too much, the woman would leave.[93] For a month, the two women managed, quite often amicably, to work together. Their mutual forbearance did not resolve the situation, however. After only three months with the O'Briens (Mary had hoped she would stay for at least nine), the Irish woman left, though not before she informed her mistress of her general unhappiness with the O'Brien household.[94] There is no question that the old Irish woman's abrupt departure was in part a result of her differences with her mistress. Mary believed, however, that it was also prompted by loneliness for her brother and her dissatisfaction "with the attentions of her fellow servant."[95]

With Flora's arrival in February 1831, the situation in the O'Brien household eased for a time. Then, in July 1831, Mary recorded that "I have been congratulating myself on the good behaviour of my household but today a flame broke out, it seems that it has been long smothered, my family is all in discord & I can neither understand or appease the discord – I fear it must end in our losing one or two valuable servants."[96]

Tensions within colonial households were sometimes relieved momentarily, at least, when the girl was given or took a few days off. All mistresses appear to have recognized that a help's family responsibilities superseded her duties to her employer. Maids received or took leave to care for sick parents or to attend a family wedding.[97] In August 1831, Flora received word that her brother was ill and as Mary recorded, "I could not but send her off to see him."[98]

Whether the employer and employee formally agreed on holidays or regular time off is unclear. In 1838, Anne Langton noted that the previous winter, "we spared our only woman twice, once for a week and again for a fortnight."[99] In many households, including the O'Briens', the help were away on some Sundays, for part of a day each month and usually for high holidays such as Christmas.[100] And some diaries and account books record that the help received time off as demanded and was convenient for the household. At the same time, it is clear that mistresses could do little to stop a girl from taking a holiday, even if it was not convenient. Moreover, some girls obviously left their work without first asking for leave. Farm diaries frequently recorded "the girl absent," or "the servant girl missing."[101] Maids also often exercised considerable independence when it came to returning to their employment. In September 1834, for example, although Mary O'Brien had expected her maid, Mary, to return that evening, she stayed with some "new come friends" instead.[102] In April 1839, Anne Langton awaited the arrival of Kitty "who will be back again in a few days, I fancy."[103] Though many mistresses and masters usually deducted pay for their girl's absence, there appears to have been little they could do to prevent her from going or ensuring her speedy return.

The girl's ability to take time off as required or desired undoubtedly helped to relieve some of the tediousness of her working situation. So too did the knowledge that she did not intend or have to work for the same employer for an extended period of time. Girls who expected to be married before they were twenty or twenty-one also expected to have had a number of situations before that important event.[104] As Anne Langton noted somewhat ruefully, "Girls never expect to remain long in service and seldom do so long enough to gain much experience."[105] In October 1838, Anne Langton's "housemaid" informed the family that she was leaving. Apparently, Anne recorded, "she never intended to remain more than three months" and she "never stays from home in the winter." This, Anne concluded, "I suppose is one of the troubles of the backwoods."[106] It is not surprising, therefore, that if a girl considered that the conditions of work were not acceptable or she could not get along with another member of the household, she did not hesitate to leave. In May 1829, Mary Southby's cook left the day after she had been severely scolded by her mistress.[107] Sometimes, a girl left without warning or notice; a few were willing, in the short term at least, to forgo their wages.[108]

It was not always the help who chose to terminate the relationship. Although colonial women were willing to put up with a great deal to try to keep their help, there were occasions when a girl's behaviour was considered so outrageous that she was discharged for being "unfit" or "unsuitable."[109] When John Thompson's maid was discovered "beneath the kitchen floor ... drunk," she was sent away, and "of course & I did not pay her."[110] More serious was the predicament that George Leith's maid Mary found herself in March 1838. When Mrs Leith discovered that Mary was pregnant, she and her lover Donaldson were summarily dismissed.[111] Whether John Thompson's anonymous maid or Mary (or Donaldson) subsequently had any difficulty in securing work is unknown. Certainly they would not have received any references from their employers. However, given the informality of rural Upper Canadian hiring practices and the apparently high demand for full-time, live-in help, it is likely that neither woman would have been short of work, if she wanted it.

Surviving diaries and letters suggest that households rarely fired their help. A help's apparent incompetence or inability to do the work were not usually considered sufficient grounds for dismissal. In August 1839, Anne Langton stated emphatically that "the new girl [Bridget] will not do" for "I never had, I think, one so thoroughly useless. She is inconceivable and indescribable." Anne did not dismiss her, however. At least they had a girl, and as she explained, "we continue ... to like her and therefore must consider ourselves comparatively well off."[112] Anne noted that many of their neighbours were without help altogether. Bridget stayed with the Langtons until March 1840. When she finally left of her own accord, Anne recorded that though "her deficiencies were many," she had remained with them an unusually long time, nine or ten months, "something longer than any other we have had." Moreover, she did have "some good points for which I regret her."[113]

This is perhaps the essence of the relationship between a girl and her employer. In rural Upper Canada, the girl was more than hired help. She was also the daughter, sister, or wife of a neighbour and, although her pay was meagre, her treatment "reflected her status as a member of another family." It also reflected the fact that she and her employer shared much of the housework as well as whatever leisure time they could steal from the day's activities. In Upper Canada, as was the case in the United States about the same time, "helping was, if not an ideal relationship, not an arena of great conflict." For those young women willing to work as domestic helps, their "recruitment was optional" and it was accepted that their "treatment ought not to be demeaning." Certainly, "help were more likely to be treated with personal consideration than domestics would be later."[114]

For many young unmarried girls, joining a neighbour's household and performing work that would otherwise have been the responsibility of an older daughter or sister was a natural part of adolescence.

Helping was not restricted, however, to young, unmarried women, nor was it always a full-time, live-in arrangement. In Upper Canada during the first half of the nineteenth century, many older women also took on domestic paid employment on a part-time or temporary basis. Obliging a neighbour while remaining at home permitted especially married women to provide a welcome and often necessary supplement to their own families' incomes.

WIVES AND DAUGHTERS of labourers, small farmers, and squatters could apparently find as much part-time work as they wanted or could cope with. The annual or biannual house cleaning required many hands and strong backs.[115] So too did the weekly or bi-weekly clothes washing.[116] Women also found temporary work during the busy times of a particular season or during a neighbour's crisis, such as her confinement or an illness in the family. Women contracted their services by the day, the week, or longer, or for a specific task. Often part-time helps returned to their own home each night. On occasion they boarded temporarily with their employers. Although they worked to supplement their family's income, it was also clear to their employers that they were helping out as a favour to a neighbour.

In 1838, Mrs Daniels, one of Anne Langton's neighbours, was prevailed upon to "oblige" the Langton household and provide assistance "for a grand day of scrubbing." "She promises to come," Anne commented, "though she seems a little overwhelmed with business herself as they had killed an ox a day or two before and she had had to assist her husband in flaying, cutting up etc; and when the butcher's part is over, I know well from my own experience how much labour there is in turning head, heels, tallow, etc all to the best account."[117] When Bridget, the girl who would "not do" but stayed for ten months, left in March 1840 with only a day's notice, neighbour and "friend in need Mary Scarry" arrived "to see us over our party tonight." Anne also relied on the part-time help of Sally Jordan, one of her neighbour's daughters, until "we get a servant" to replace Bridget.[118] Sally Jordan had worked for the Langtons part time since January 1839 and she continued to oblige the Langtons, probably on a daily basis, throughout 1840. When Sally married in September of that year, Anne acknowledged that, although delighted at Sally's happiness, "we shall miss her very much. There is no other person near us who can come and lend us a helping hand on every occasion so I cannot but lament the circumstances on our own account."[119] Anne need not have worried. Sally Jordan, now Mrs Woods, continued to be the Langtons' "help in need" for some months after her wedding.[120]

Sally Jordan's and Mary Scarry's willingness to help Anne was probably a result of that sense of community that prevailed among rural women. There is no question, however, that Sally Jordan and Mrs Daniels also expected to be paid for their work. So too did those women who regularly found part-time employment in Captain William Johnson's household in Georgina.

Between 1830 and 1840, the Johnsons appear to have kept at least one girl full time to do the washing, cope with the dairy, and generally help out.[121] Yet, from time to time, Mrs Johnson also required additional help, and there were a number of women in the area who were more than willing to oblige. Mrs Elwes attended Mrs Johnson during at least two confinements, in 1832 and 1835. In both instances she stayed for a number of weeks to ensure that mother and child were fully recovered. In 1832, she also served as a nurse-housekeeper for six weeks, and in 1839, she came to the Johnsons to "wash and scrub."[122] Between July 1835 and August 1841, a Mrs Climkskill periodically sewed and cleaned for the Johnsons. During that same period, when the children were small and Mrs Johnson was particularly busy, Mrs Nugent, Mrs Bramble, and Mrs Griffin and her son were hired for varying lengths of time to do the laundry, scrub floors, make candles, and clean the house.[123]

The Johnson and Langton households were not unusual. Mary O'Brien frequently called on the wives of Edward's labourers or her neighbours to help her in the house, or to relieve her "from some of my usual associations."[124] Mrs Thompson, also of the Simcoe region, relied on the help of a neighbour, Mrs Broomsmead, during her confinement in 1835. Mrs Broomsmead stayed for at least three weeks and acted as surrogate housekeeper while Mrs Thompson recovered.[125] During her next pregnancy two years later, Mrs Thompson was attended by another neighbour, Mrs Fraser.[126]

Part-time helps were not restricted to domestic work. When time and the season pressed, wives and daughters of labourers or neighbours worked at "getting up potatoes," clearing brush or gathering the hay and the harvest for some of their neighbours.[127] Mrs Broomsmead piled brush and worked in the Thompson barn in September 1835. She also helped clean wheat and dig the potatoes.[128] A Mrs Holland and her husband John worked together bringing in George Leith's wheat in August 1836. Though John Holland was discharged for insolence at the end of that month, Mrs Holland continued to "help" the Leiths, killing and butchering hogs. Following this, she appears to have lived with the family as a general servant.[129]

Mrs Holland was relatively fortunate. It seems that the Leiths had engaged her independently of her husband and she received a separate wage. A number of women in Upper Canada did not. Many farmers tried to hire married men as outdoor labourers on the understanding that their wives would help the farmer's wife with the housework, and as required, would work beside her husband in the fields. Certainly, if a man understood farming or "taking care of stock" and his wife was willing "to manage a small dairy and to do housework," they could readily find employment in rural Upper Canada.[130] Married couples frequently worked for a year or two on someone else's farm so that they could accumulate the capital necessary to purchase or to lease land. It appears that the Broomsmeads, who worked for the Thompsons in 1835 may have been engaged as a couple after Mrs Thompson's confinement; Mrs Broomsmead may have earned no extra wages for work in the house or in the fields.[131] In July 1830, shortly after her marriage, Mary O'Brien engaged a woman and her husband to come for a year for one hundred and fifty dollars. "At the end of which," she wrote, "they proposed going to the land for which he has been working for the past year."[132]

Such arrangements worked well for both the employer and the employees. For slightly more than the wages of a single man, Edward O'Brien and other masters gained the services of two adults – one to work in the fields and the other to work indoors.[133] In return, the couple received a wage and sometimes housing separate from that of the family. The O'Briens' couple actually lived with them for a couple of months before moving into their own shanty.[134] In most cases, the husband was contracted as the full-time worker. His wife and perhaps his children worked according to the dictates of the season and the farm household.

Whether a married woman did or did not receive a wage for part-time domestic work does not appear to have influenced how she was regarded by the farm household. Certainly, she did not consider herself, nor was she considered by her employer as a servant or merely a "girl." Those who periodically cleaned, nursed, or worked in the fields were usually afforded the dignity that came with their status as married women. In diaries and letters, mistresses almost always referred to them formally by their married names. Moreover, those neighbourhood women who were engaged individually to perform specific household tasks received a wage commensurate with their age, their skills, and the length of their contract. A woman who contracted to clean for a week could receive as much as two dollars and her board, twice the rate of a live-in girl. Women hired especially to sew, or to act as a nurse, or midwife received even higher wages. Even those doing heavy or what was considered unskilled domestic work such as washing or cleaning were paid better than a girl.

Many women who worked by the day also had the advantage of living in their own homes or shanties. They were not subject to constant supervision and they retained a crucial element of privacy. In short, they were mistresses of their own households in addition to being one of the help in someone else's home. And though they always had to juggle their own domestic work with their waged work, these women did maintain a degree of independence and respect not available to live-in help.

"ALTHOUGH MONEY changed hands, helping was not primarily a market transaction" in either Upper Canada of the United States.[135] It was a personal arrangement between neighbours and sometimes friends. It was also a transaction whose terms and parameters were fundamentally shaped by the life cycle of both parties. Wives, mothers, and housekeepers needed help. If possible, they turned to female family members for assistance. When daughters were too young or sisters and mothers not available, women were obliged to turn instead to neighbouring women for either paid or unpaid help. For their part, girls considered joining some local household when their labour was not needed at home. Wives worked for wages as the financial needs of their families demanded and the domestic work of their own households permitted. Yet, whether mistress or maid, the farmer's wife and the girl were both working women. They shared a workplace and they shared the work. They also shared a personal relationship that was an integral part of the network of community support that was so important in the life of rural women.[136]

This is not to say that there were not often sharp social and economic differences between the mistress and the girl. Though farm wives needed the help, women who sought domestic employment needed the wages they received.[137] Some also needed a home. Young girls who worked in neighbours' households did so to relieve their parents and particularly their fathers of the cost of their upkeep. But though there was considerable opportunity to "help" on either a part- or a full-time basis, such women's wages remained low and their ability to move out of domestic work limited.

"Helping" for wages in Upper Canada was an arrangement that appears to have been relatively restricted in time and place. Although the wives of artisans, mechanics, and shopkeepers who lived in Upper Canadian towns and villages must also have relied on the daughters and wives of neighbours to help perform their domestic work, "helping" as such appears to have been largely a rural practice. And with the arrival of growing numbers of gentle and relatively affluent farming families after 1820, there were indications that some households, at least, were trying to inject a greater degree of formality in the relationship of the mistress and her girl. At the same time, a growing number of urban households also began to want women "servants" rather than "helps" to work in their homes.

"The transition from help to domestic was neither rapid nor complete" in Upper Canada between 1790 and 1840.[138] Throughout the period, however, elite households had always sought women who were willing to be "servants" to do their domestic work. Like middle- and upper-class families in Great Britain and the United States, prominent colonial women wanted their domestics to work for them, not with them. In part, having servants was a sign of a family's affluence. But the lifestyle enjoyed, and endured, by elite families also required that affluent women have a staff to relieve them of at least some of their domestic responsibilities. Not surprisingly, living and working in an elite Upper Canadian household was quite different than living and working on the farm.

PART THREE

"A Sense of Decorum" and "Service": The World of the Colonial "Aristocracy"

Elizabeth Russell, the half-sister of Peter Russell, one of the executive councillors of the new colony of Upper Canada, wrote to her lifelong friend in England in 1793 that she was most uncomfortable in her new Niagara home. It only had two rooms in which she, her brother, and their servants had to "sleep and do everything else." Moreover, they, like their friends the Simcoes, were "exposed to continual interruptions by people coming in on either Business or as visitors."[1] She further explained, "we are in a continual dirt and litter notwithstanding. We have plenty of morning and tea visitors who often puts me to the blush to be caught in such disable but there is no help for it and they are kind enough to make allowances."[2] By the end of that first year, some of Elizabeth's concerns were resolved when she and Peter moved into a "very comfortable" and expensive new home in Niagara. "[We also have] a nice little farm about us," she wrote to Lizzy Kiernan, "[and are thus able to] eat our own Mutton, and Pork and poultry."[3] In 1797, the Russells moved for the last time. In York, the colonial capital, Elizabeth presided over a "good House ... in a most charming situation in the front of the town."[4] They also owned a farm a few miles away.

Forty years later, in October 1837, Helen Macaulay and her family moved into a large, newly renovated house in York. Almost immediately, Helen assumed her place as the wife of the surveyor general of Upper Canada. York, and indeed all of Upper Canada, had changed considerably in the years between Elizabeth Russell's arrival and that of Helen Macaulay. The colony had almost quadrupled in size; York, the capital, had been transformed from a struggling village to a busy government and commercial town. In 1793 Elizabeth Russell had been one of the few women of some means; in 1837, Helen Macaulay entered a society that was firmly established and socially intricate.

Elizabeth Russell and Helen Macaulay never met, and in many ways their lives in Upper Canada took quite divergent paths. Despite the differences in their marital status and their time of residence in the colony, they nevertheless shared similar experiences. Because they were attached to men of relative affluence and considerable political influence, both women belonged to the select and closed world of the Upper Canadian elite. Whether living in a two-room log house or a large, lavish home, they and others like them were women of the town, and women of the "big" houses. Their lives were defined to a large degree by their class and the work of their husbands or brothers. Thus, in addition to being housekeepers, and in Helen's case, a wife and mother, these two women were also managers of increasingly complex households, hostesses for their husband or brother, and public representatives of their class.

To outsiders, women of the colonial upper class were easily identified by their homes, their servants, their dress, and their often exaggerated sense of decorum. To most Upper Canadians, women such as Elizabeth Russell and Helen Macaulay seemed to pursue a life of leisure and, at times, frivolity amidst the constant toil of the Upper Canadian frontier.[5] Elite women in Upper Canada were not part of a pre-industrial family economy. They did not actually produce the goods needed to sustain their families. Instead, like their middle-class sisters in Great Britain and the United States,[6] they depended on their husbands' earned income to purchase the goods and services that their families required. Certainly, neither Elizabeth Russell nor Helen Macaulay regularly had to scrub, cook, or tend livestock. Neither woman ever worked for wages. Rather they engaged in rounds of visiting, drinking tea with friends, and entertaining business and personal associates. They went to balls, the theatre, and formal dinners dressed in feathers and evening gowns. Publicly, their lives resembled that of "the angel in the house" – women who were preoccupied with their appearance and protocol, and who actually lived those ideals of domesticity so assiduously promoted from colonial pulpits and in local newspapers.

From within the walls of the big house, however, such women knew that there was considerable work involved in being a member of the colonial upper class. A mistress of a big house was also usually a wife and mother. The merchant's household had to be fed; the lieutenant-governor's home had to be kept clean; and the bishop's children had

Illustration 10
"Russell Abbey," home of Elizabeth and Peter Russell, from engraving by Henry
Scadding, in *Toronto of Old* (Toronto, 1878)
J. Ross Robertson Collection, MTL (T11480)

to be cared for. While managing these tasks, elite women also had numerous public responsibilities that resulted from their husbands' professions and their families' place in the social order. They were obliged to entertain formally and to attend numerous public functions. They had to understand and conform to rigid social rituals and protocols. They were also expected to assume personal, religious, and class-based responsibilities to help those less fortunate than themselves.

The public demands of society and the influence of class and status on women's lives were most apparent in York, the colonial capital. Here senior government officers and their households inhabited a social and political world that self-consciously copied that of London and other large British cities. Being attached to what some considered the Upper Canadian "aristocracy" demanded a level of decorum and an outward display of status far beyond that necessary in any of the regional centres of the colony. Nevertheless, the difference between "society" in York and that in Kingston and Niagara was one of degree, not of kind. Ann Macaulay and Harriet Cartwright of Kingston were, within their own community, members of the elite. They too established and oversaw the working of various philanthropic and religious organizations. They too had to abide by a rigid set of social conventions that confirmed the community's hierarchical structure and symbolically illustrated the relative ranking of its members.

Elite women would not have considered their lives carefree and frivolous. Performing their many public responsibilities required skill, considerable effort, and often endless patience. It also required sufficient income to dress well, to entertain, and to maintain a household that was a suitable reflection of their husbands' rank. Even within the apparent privacy of their homes, upper-class matrons such as Elizabeth Russell or Helen Macaulay could not escape from their public duties. In the colony's early years, their homes frequently served as government offices or as venues in which to entertain personal and official visitors.[7] Moreover, they were well aware that a successful wife, housekeeper, and hostess materially aided her husband in the furtherance of his career. Her inability or unwillingness to fulfil these duties could well bring disaster, not only to herself, but to the entire family.

Elite women could not cope with all their work alone. Not only were they dependent on their husbands for the family income as well as for their social status, they were also obliged to rely on other women to do much of the physical work of the household. Having "servants" was a symbol of a family's affluence.[8] Domestic workers were also essential for any upper-class household in Upper Canada to function properly. While Helen Macaulay and Anne Powell entertained, their servants cooked, cleaned, and looked after the children. In addition to being a supportive wife and caring mother, Helen Macaulay was therefore by necessity also an employer, a household manager, and a supervisor. She had to find and hire a staff, determine what domestic work needed to be done, and then ensure that it was performed to her satisfaction. There is no question that having servants alleviated the mistress of some of the drudgery of household work, but having servants also presented its own series of problems and responsibilities.

Women who worked for wages in Upper Canadian elite households could not help but be aware of their mistresses' dependence. They were also increasingly conscious of the wide social and economic gulf that existed between themselves and their employers. Unlike women who "helped" in rural colonial communities, an urban maid was usually not the daughter of a neighbour or the wife of a local labourer. More often, servants who worked in town were the daughters, wives, or sisters of members of the "labouring" classes, the "poor," or recently arrived immigrants. They were part of a pool of women wage-earners who were clearly dependent on their income "for the necessities of life."[9] Moreover, being a member of an urban parlour staff was very different from working as a help on the farm or in a small-town household. Such a maid's relationship to her elite mistress was formal, as befitted that between an employee and her employer. Her work was intended to replace, not to supplement that of the female head of the household.

Most servants must have resented this arm's-length relationship with their employers. Working as a maid, cook, or housekeeper in someone else's home was also not a particularly lucrative or appealing prospect. The days were long and the work was physically demanding. As employers in the big houses constantly rediscovered, women who went "into service" in the first half of the nineteenth century tried, sometimes quite successfully, to assert their independence and exercise their very limited power. Mistresses' diaries and letters indicate that a servant in the big house, like helps who worked on the farm, often tried to take advantage of her mistress's vulnerability to establish her own conditions and pace of work. Servants often resisted instructions and demanded more pay. Advertisements in newspapers and mistresses' constant references to "the servant problem" also suggest that there was abundant opportunity for domestic employment. Thus, if a maid or cook was unhappy with her work or her employer, she could take the ultimate action and leave her situation, relatively confident that she would find other work.

The women who lived and worked in the big houses came from two distinct economic classes. They worked, however, within the common constraints imposed upon those of their gender. Both mistress and maid were performing women's work, and did so within the socially acceptable workplace of home and hearth. They were, moreover, working at a common enterprise – to ensure that the needs of the upper-class household were met, either within the privacy of the home or publicly, in society. What made elite households different from less affluent homes in Upper Canada was the manner in which women's work was carried out and who actually did it.

6 "No End to the Wants": Living and Working in the "Big" House

On moving into her new home in York at the end of October 1837, Helen Macaulay was immediately saddled with a host of new duties. As the wife of one of the colony's most influential citizens, Helen was expected to take an active part in York society. Within days of her arrival, she was already receiving guests and making calls; within weeks, she was fully involved in a host of social activities. But Helen was also a mother; and one of her first responsibilities on coming to York was to make a home for her family and to ensure that the ongoing needs of her husband and children were met.

For Helen Macaulay, setting up housekeeping was in many ways less onerous than for most women in Upper Canada. She was taking up residence in a large home that had been specially built and equipped to meet her family's needs. She had the financial resources necessary to buy furniture, kitchen equipment, and other household items that many families had to do without. She could also afford to hire women and men to help her settle into her new home and to do most of the housework. But like other affluent women in Upper Canada, she was also aware that her situation had some decided disadvantages.

No elite woman in Upper Canada could manage her work as a wife and mother and take her place in society without domestic workers "to underwrite these ... activities."[1] Thus, employers such as Helen Macaulay had first to find, then train, and constantly supervise an increasingly differentiated and specialized domestic workforce. While the women who actually performed most of the work willingly took their wages and many were grateful to have a home, most were not working in the big house by choice; few servants found much satisfaction in their jobs.

Although they had the power to hire and fire members of their domestic staffs, Helen Macaulay and other upper-class household managers in Upper Canada frequently found themselves at the mercy of their servants. Unlike their sisters who "helped" on a farm or in a small urban household, women who worked in affluent colonial homes often had little real sense of belonging to the community or to their employers' households. And although the elite mistress and her maids formed one economic and working unit, they did not share the work itself or the family table. They did, however, share their place of work. The "big" house was not just a symbol of its owner's affluence and influence on colonial society, although this was important.[2] It was also a residence for both the upper-class family and their servants. The big house was, moreover, an increasingly demanding and complex business.[3]

IN THE EARLY YEARS of settlement, members of the colonial elite had to manage without proper housing. Elizabeth Simcoe spent much of her time in Upper Canada living in tents. Hannah Jarvis and her husband William, the registrar of Upper Canada, first lived in a three-room log house.[4] As Elizabeth Russell and Hannah Jarvis discovered, it was impossible to fulfil important social obligations when living in a two- or three-room log house. There was no one room in which to dress properly or which could be dedicated to receiving visitors or conducting business; the kitchen was not large enough or adequately equipped to prepare meals for guests. Moreover, as Elizabeth Russell reported, in her first home, she had "nowhere to put a female servant, except she was to sleep with the male servant – who are at some distance from the house."[5] Elite households needed "superior accommodation."[6]

As soon as circumstances allowed, prominent Upper Canadians built and moved into homes that were more in keeping with their station, and perhaps more important, far more suited to the work of their residents. The two-storey stone houses of Robert Hamilton of Queenston and Richard Cartwright of Kingston each had a dining room, a drawing room, and a kitchen on the first floor, and bedrooms upstairs. When former Attorney General William Firth put his York house up for auction in 1811, it was described as having "eleven commodious, large and lofty Rooms on one Floor, and two Chambers, and ample space for four others on one pair of stairs, fit for the reception of a large Family." This "Mansion" also had "two Barns, Stabling,

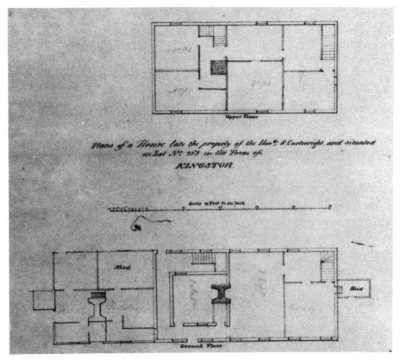

Illustration 11
Plans of house belonging to Richard Cartwright by M. Dixon, 1815
National Map Collection, NA (C51519)

Coach House, and extensive Outhouses, together with a small Cottage, and four Acres of Land."[7]

A typical "big" house had room for servants, as well as enough space for a growing family. It also had larger "public" rooms – a parlour, a drawing room, and a dining room – that were appropriately furnished, in which to receive visitors and to conduct business. Yet the larger the house, the more expensive it was to build or rent, and to keep up. A big house had to have more lavish decorations and furniture than would be found in most homes in the colony. It required more help to maintain, both inside and out. And residents of "the big house" were still subject to the same problems, though on a larger scale, that all Upper Canadians faced – heating, cleaning, and lighting.[8]

The choice of which house was suitable for the family and whether to build, buy, or rent rested with the head of the household.[9] Moreover, it was men such as Peter Russell and John Macaulay who made many of the crucial decisions about necessary renovations. Wives and sisters undoubtedly had their say in the matter, but the basis of the decision seemed to rest on cost and the male head's perception of the needs and status of his household.

After his marriage in 1833 and his subsequent appointment as legislative councillor, John Macaulay, who maintained his home in Kingston, considered establishing a permanent residence in York. Initially he and his wife Helen intended to buy a house.[10] The decision was postponed, however, until after Helen returned from an extended visit to see her mother in Scotland. In the interim, John decided to keep the Kingston house and to live in rooms while in the capital. It was not until after John accepted an appointment as surveyor general in 1837 that the family moved to York.

John Macaulay had been conscious for some time that living in York would be an expensive proposition. Indeed, this was one of the factors he had taken into account when deciding whether he would accept the new government appointment or return permanently to Kingston. Living in York would provide John with far greater opportunity to influence colonial affairs.[11] However, a salary of "six [hundred] at Kingston will go farther than £800 here," he wrote to his mother early in 1837. He judged that even with careful managing, "I shall not find it easy to save anything out of my salary if I remain here."[12]

It has been estimated that in the early years, building a "modest" house in York cost at least £1000.[13] Elizabeth Russell had reported to her friend that as early as 1795, her brother had "expended a large sum of money in procuring himself comfort and conveniences."[14] And William Dummer Powell, a justice of the Provincial Court, commented in 1806, that "even with a bare salary of £750 per ann," it was only by "steady dunning" that he was able to maintain a satisfactory situation.[15] When his salary increased in 1817 to £2500, the family continued to live up to their income, for as Anne wrote to her brother, "Mr Powell's station obliges him to see all strangers who come to the place," and the family home had to be enlarged.[16]

It was not surprising that in the late 1830s, John Macaulay decided to rent a home "for some years to come," believing that this would be considerably cheaper than having to borrow money to buy a lot and build.[17] In January 1837, while his wife was staying with Ann Macaulay in Kingston, John leased and began to renovate the Denison house, a two-storey, wooden home with extensive gardens. Even before the alterations were complete, John, believing that with a rent of £80 a year, the house was going to be too expensive to keep up, began to look for another house.[18] In August 1837, he rented the Powell establishment, another two-storey house, that, he reported to his mother, had the same number of spare bedrooms as the first house; its dining room, kitchen, and drawing room were, if anything, however, "better," and the pantry was "more convenient." The Powell house also had a "small kitchen garden & neat grass plot," and, John assured his wife, "I think we shall be far more snug in it than in the other extensive and aristocratic premises."[19] Moreover, at a rent of £75 a year, he believed that the Powell house was a good bargain, particularly as he anticipated saving "£15 a year in fuel alone compared with Mr Denison's house."[20]

Throughout September and October of 1837, John supervised the renovations that he considered necessary. The house was enlarged by adding an outer kitchen, a new servants' bedroom, and a small utility room for storage and cleaning boots.[21] John also had some minor alterations made to the central portion of the house. He faithfully reported the progress of the renovations to his wife, consulting Helen about the colour of paint and wallpaper for the downstairs rooms, and about curtains and carpets.[22] Helen was also involved in decisions about furnishing the new house. To help defray some of the costs, John borrowed furniture from his mother. The couple ordered new carpeting, curtains, and stoves from New York, Rochester, and Buffalo and dining-room furniture was made to their particular specifications.[23] The house was finally ready for Helen and the children to take up residence at the end of October 1837.

The family's arrival from Kingston marked the end of John's active responsibility in finding a home for his family. He did continue to pay the bills. A week after the family moved in, he noted that he still had to make some "large dispersements to be comfortable." Indeed, he lamented to his mother in November that "there seems to be no end to the wants."[24] John did not have to actually "make a home" for the family, however. It was up to Helen to cope with the day-to-day confusion of moving and the problems that inevitably came with the continuing renovations.[25] And it was up to Helen, with a two-year-old at her side, to finish the decorating, hire most of the staff, and establish and maintain the daily household routines.

ONE OF HELEN'S first responsibilities was to engage domestic staff. While renovations were going on in the house in 1837, John Macaulay had hired a "butler and groom." One of these men, John reported to Helen, was to be "the man of all work ... who will keep the grounds in order & hoe the potatoes, etc." The other was engaged as a butler who would "assist us in the pantry."[26] John had refused to hire indoor female staff, however. When individual women had presented themselves looking for employment, John told them to come back when his wife was there.[27]

The number of domestics any Upper Canadian elite household "needed" depended on the size of the home and the family and the master's social and political status. All affluent homes had a cook, at least one other woman to help with the housework and perhaps to serve as a maid, and if there were young children in the house, a nursemaid or governess.[28] If possible, the family also hired a manservant to act as butler, and if they could afford it, a second man to look after the garden and other outside work. As finances allowed and their households' political-social commitments increased, affluent women supplemented their parlour staff with additional full-time workers, if available, or daily or weekly part-time help.[29] A year after her husband was appointed chief justice, Anne Powell had two menservants and two maids in addition to her "little girl."[30] At the time of her confinement in 1840, Helen Macaulay had a cook and at least two housemaids, a nurse-governess for the children, and at least one manservant who worked in the garden and probably acted as the butler. At about the same time, Helen's mother-in-law in Kingston kept two maids and a full-time gardener.

Identifying their household staffing needs did not necessarily mean that elite women could find women and men to fill them, however. Like their less affluent sisters, women of the big houses had a constant problem getting and keeping good help. "The worst inconvenience in this country," Elizabeth Simcoe complained in 1793, "is the want of servants which are not to be got."[31] Her sentiments were echoed by many others throughout the first half of the nineteenth century. The "servant problem" was particularly acute in the early years of colonial settlement. Before the War of 1812, Upper Canadian towns were small; most residents and new arrivals were settled on the land; and the vast majority of Upper Canadians were preoccupied with the problems of settlement. Though women were willing to help a neighbour, most were not willing to go "into service." Some prominent families brought a maid or two with them when they came to the colony. Elizabeth Russell, for example, arrived in Niagara in 1793 with her brother and a young companion, Mary Fleming. During her first year in the colony, she also had a cook and one other servant.[32] As Elizabeth explained to her friend Lizzie Kiernan in 1793, she still did not have a proper maidservant, however, and was her own "Chamber Maid, Housekeeper, etc. and [I] am grown quite an expert mantua-maker."[33] When the Russells moved to their new home in Niagara, Elizabeth still had to do much of her own housework. She also acted "the part of the Dairy Maid," and probably helped to plant and to harvest the garden and to prepare and process meat and vegetables for the table and storage.[34]

For the first few years of colonial settlement, the servant problem was partly resolved by the availability of slave labour. Elizabeth Russell's first cook was black and after they moved to York, the Russells maintained a slave family who worked both in their town house and on their farm.[35] In 1793, however, the Simcoe administration abolished slavery. Though families who already had slaves did not lose their property, no new slaves could be introduced into the colony. Elite mistresses, including Hannah Jarvis, were dismayed by Simcoe's "piece of Chicanery."[36] For though many colonists complained that slaves were idle and prone to running away, they at least did not have to be paid or have the legal right to abandon their households. Some households tried to replace slave labour with indentured servants.[37] Most of the time, however, affluent colonial families were forced to find "free" workers for domestic work. In 1793, Hannah Jarvis was so desperate that she pleaded with her father, who was living in the United States, to let "*Caesar & Family come to us.*"[38] Though Hannah recognized that Caesar and his family, who were slaves, would be free as soon as they crossed the border, the servant situation was so bad in Niagara that she was willing to pay them wages.

As the colony developed, the number of women willing and able to go into service gradually increased. Especially after 1815, tens of thousands of immigrants began to arrive in colonial centres looking for work and many of them, together with a growing number of native-born Upper Canadians, sought positions in urban households.[39] But colonial mistresses continued to complain that "the want of good servants" remained a "serious evil." Anna Jameson ruefully commented in 1837, "I could amuse you with an account of the petty miseries we have been enduring from this cause, the strange characters who come to offer themselves, and the wages required."[40] For it was not enough to find women willing to work. Helen Macaulay and her friends wanted domestic workers who were clean, presentable, physically able to perform their work, and had previous experience. Colonial mistresses were also concerned about a servant's character. Often, in fact, personal characteristics and willingness to work were of greater importance than skill or training.

Ann Macaulay advised her son to look for good "honest" servants when he was setting up his house in Toronto in 1837.[41] A good servant was one who exhibited "honesty, industry and *sobriety.*"[42] When praising her manservant in 1839, Ann did not commend him for his ability as a gardener. Rather she commented to her son, "he suits me he is slow but steady and honest and as Mr Marks says, has come from good stock."[43] If a mistress was willing to expend the time and energy, a good, honest, willing girl or woman could, after all, be trained to become a good servant. After one of their lengthy periods without a cook, John Macaulay reported to his mother that "Helen, has, I think at last found a girl ... She promises to become a very passable cook."[44] This promise depended on Helen's ability to train the girl.[45]

The question of character was important enough to some colonial mistresses that they were willing to do without a servant rather than engage someone who did not satisfy them. In 1811, Anne Powell complained that "I am experiencing the agreeable of Housekeeping without a Woman Servant & no chance of finding out that will suit me."[46] As a result, Anne and her daughters had to do some of the daily housework. In 1838, Helen Macaulay reported to her mother-in-law that one of her servants had left. Though "we have not got a person in his place, I shall not take one that is not likely to suit, but do without until a good one offers."[47]

This policy had its limits, however. Affluent households could not function without some domestic workers. In certain circumstances, the question of a woman's character had to be weighed against her skills, experience, and the family's needs. John Macaulay was pleased to report to his wife in September of 1837 that Elizabeth Haye, who had applied for the job of cook, had two years experience with Colonel Foster and had presented him with an excellent character reference. Catharine Purcell, who was applying for the same position, had experience with the Drapers and though she would not do washing, John commented that "I like her appearance."[48] Which woman Helen finally chose to hire is unknown. However, she did not always have the luxury of having a choice of women who had both skills and a good character.

Finding a servant could be a time-consuming and frustrating undertaking. In addition to interviewing women who came to their doors, elite women often relied on family and friends to find a suitable domestic. Ann Macaulay searched fruitlessly for a replacement for Mary, the maid who had been dismissed in disgrace in the late summer of 1838, then turned to her sons for help.[49] In 1839, Helen Macaulay tentatively appealed to her mother-in-law to give up her own personal maid, Flora. "If you would like to part with Flora I think I would like to get her ... she is so well principled." Helen, in her third pregnancy, explained rather plaintively that she desperately needed another experienced servant. Helen assured her mother-in-law that "I have no wish to get her without you would rather give than keep her." Ann must, nonetheless, have been rather startled.[50] Flora did not go to Toronto and Helen was forced to look elsewhere.

Some society matrons were not adverse to using outright subterfuge to entice a good servant away from a neighbour with promises of higher wages and better working conditions. In 1839, John Macaulay reported that their cook Eliza had been "spirited away" by Mrs Strachan. "Cooks have been very scarce" in Toronto, he continued, and "there are families here who do not stick at trifles & go behind their neighbours in wages in order to get their choice. How we shall get on without Eliza I don't know. It would perhaps have been a real saving to have allowed her £6 a year additional."[51]

The problem that elite households confronted in finding suitable domestic staff was compounded in the 1820s and 1830s, because of the growing number of urban households looking for women to work in their homes. The wives of most "respectable" middle-income families – artisans, small shopkeepers, and mechanics – were undoubtedly looking for a "help." Like their rural counterparts, small urban households probably tried to find a neighbour's daughter to meet their domestic needs. Such arrangements did not satisfy the requirements of upper-class households or perhaps even those middling families who aspired to upward mobility. They needed, or at least wanted, women who were willing to define themselves as servants.[52] Such women were increasingly difficult to find, however. As colonial towns increased in size and the social and economic distance between various classes grew, hopeful employers had less and less regular contact with "the labouring classes." In the 1820s and 1830s, the marketplace was also becoming more complex and formal. A growing number of Upper Canadian urban households were forced to turn to the press or to employment agencies to help them find suitable domestic workers.

In the mid-1820s, W. Meckham of York established the first "intelligence office for servants" in Upper Canada.[53] By 1830, there were rudimentary employment agencies in all major colonial centres.[54] Editors of local newspapers, emigrant societies, and land agents encouraged prospective employers and women and men looking for work to register at their agency. For a fee they would arrange a suitable match or permit employers to view their list of hopeful workers.[55] Unfortunately, no records of these agencies have survived. The hundreds of notices for "situation wanted" or "help wanted" that appeared in local newspapers do, however, provide a general profile of what types of domestic employees Upper Canadians were looking for, and what types of work women and girls were willing to undertake.

Most domestic employers sought young girls who were willing to become general servants or maids of all work.[56] A typical notice read, "Wanted: an active, clean woman as a maid of all work in a family of moderate size." The successful applicant had to be honest and "a good getter-upper of linen and kind to children."[57] A notice usually concluded that liberal wages would be offered to a woman of good character.[58] Though experience was obviously an asset and in some cases English or Scottish girls were expressly canvassed, neither qualification was absolutely necessary.[59]

Most help-wanted notices were placed anonymously and interested applicants were instructed to reply to the newspaper, to an accommodation address, or to the agency. The tenor of these advertisements suggests, however, that many of prospective employers were small urban families who required or could only afford one servant. The same may well have been the case for those ads looking for a "steady" (often middle-aged) woman to act as a housekeeper for a "genteel family" or to "take charge of a small family" including cooking and looking after the dairy.[60] Some households may well have needed a substitute wife-mother, due to the illness or death of the natural mother.[61] Advertisements from prospective employers who were hoping to hire a couple, the wife to cook or be a housekeeper and her husband to serve as coachman or gardener suggest a somewhat larger and more affluent household.[62]

There is no concrete evidence that elite women such as Helen Macaulay resorted to newspapers or employment agencies to find suitable servants. However, notices in local newspapers do suggest that at least some advertisements were placed by relatively wealthy families. Advertisements calling for women with specialized skills – experienced cooks, for example – indicate employer households that had a number of servants. Only affluent households could have afforded to hire a dedicated nursemaid or a governess.[63]

Prominent women, like other urban mistresses, may also have responded to the growing number of notices placed by women who were looking for work. In the 1820s and 1830s, there were many young women seeking a situation as "a cook or House Maid," or who indicated their willingness to serve as "a general indoor servant."[64] Others clearly wanted a more elevated position as a lady's maid, a children's maid, or a general nurse.[65]

Notices in local newspapers indicate that women looking for work in domestic service were of all ages and marital status and, by their own admission, possessed varying degrees of skills. But as was the case in rural communities, domestic service in Upper Canada was really a "life-cycle occupation."[66] Most notices were placed by young, apparently unmarried girls, many of whom were looking for their first position. After 1815, an increasing number of notices were from women who had "recently arrived" from the old country and were willing to do any work in or with "respectable families."[67]

There were, however, also older women who were looking for work – as cooks, cook-housekeepers, or governesses.[68] These women obviously did not consider themselves common servants, and were clearly hoping to gain a situation where their skills would be appreciated or their age and experience recognized. A large proportion of these notices were from widowed women or "ladies" who had fallen on hard times. Their notices implied that although they were obliged to work, their age, in some cases their education, and their claim to being gentlewomen fitted them for domestic positions of responsibility.[69] At the same time, it is evident that many of these women were desperate for employment that would provide them with some personal security and a home. Indeed, many were explicit that "the permanency of the situation [was] more an object than the emolument of it."[70]

In 1832, Mrs Lyons, a widow "without any encumbrance" was one of a number of women who wanted "a situation to superintend the management of a small family or assist in Needlework or make herself generally useful."[71] In York in 1834, a widow who was "capable of acting as a Housekeeper, or to take charge of a nursery," was most direct in her objectives. "Has no objection to Town or Country," the notice stated, and "a respectable and permanent situation being the principle object of the Advertiser, emolument not so much consideration."[72]

There was a somewhat smaller group of women who wanted specialized domestic work as governesses. For the most part, these women do not seem to have been just "ladies in distress." Although they were young and usually single, almost all of them claimed to be skilled and/or experienced teachers and were looking for positions and salaries commensurate with their qualifications.[73] In 1838, "a Lady from England" wanted a position as a "DAILY or RESIDENT GOVERNESS." Her advertisement stated that she was "experienced in the education of children" and was competent "to instruct in English, in all its branches, MUSIC, SINGING, FRENCH, DRAWING & NEEDLEWORK, etc." The notice concluded, "Salary not so much an object as a comfortable home."[74] Women who sought work as governesses were apparently well-educated and competent to teach both "the ordinary branches of education" (reading, writing, grammar, geography, arithmetic, etc.) and the "accomplishments."[75] Some explicitly stated their ability to teach English "in all its branches," arithmetic, history, and geography. A few hopeful governesses stressed that they were able to teach a combination of singing, music, drawing, and plain and fancy needlework. Some advertised their ability to teach French.[76] A number of these women obviously hoped that working as a governess would only be temporary; what many really wanted was a position teaching in a ladies' academy or to save enough money to begin their own school.

Whether any of the women looking for work actually found positions is unknown. It is evident, however, that after 1820, job opportunities for domestic workers were increasing, as was the pool of women willing to accept such work. Advertisements in local newspapers suggest that in the 1820s and 1830s, women had no trouble finding domestic work in Upper Canada. The number of notices from hopeful employers looking for domestic staff was far greater than those placed by women who were seeking a situation. However, this does not necessarily provide an accurate reflection of the relative state of supply and demand, since it is likely that many women seeking work did not place notices in local newspapers. Some women undoubtedly relied on their reputations as good workers to obtain a situation. Others may have been unable to afford the cost of advertising and may have responded directly to notices from families wanting help. They may also have applied personally at a mistress's home, or relied on contacts made at the local market or on the street.[77]

Although we cannot determine with any degree of certainty what proportion of prospective employers and employees actually relied on advertisements in local newspapers or on the services provided by local intelligence agencies to fulfil their household needs, it is apparent that the manner of recruiting household staff was beginning to change after 1820. Urban mistresses never record actually going out "girl hunting." Many probably relied on women coming to their doors looking for work; others may have hired women they met at the market or on the street. But the opportunities for such contact were diminishing, particularly for upper-class mistresses. Increasingly, the mistress and her maid came from increasingly divergent social and economic worlds.[78] Women willing to consider themselves servants were part of a pool of "foreign" labourers. In most cases, they were not previously known to their employers and often had no permanent connection to the community.[79] The only way for such women to find work and for affluent mistresses to find servants was through increasingly formal and impersonal agencies.[80]

The result was that both employees and employers lost a crucial element of control in defining their needs and choosing with whom they would work. Once staff were engaged, the relationship between the mistress and her maids was often quite formal, as befitted an employer and her workers. As Davidoff and Hall have concluded in their study of middle-class life in Great Britain, middle-class women were forced on a daily basis to cope with "the contradiction of operating across class lines in a family setting."[81] Inevitably, the sense of personal and mutual responsibility that existed between a farm woman and her help was lost in many urban households, particularly in those of the upper class. In addition, both the nature of the housework and the persons who actually performed it were quite different in urban households than they were in most rural ones.

FROM THE VERY beginning of settlement, elite women were expected to run their households and meet the needs of their families in a manner that ignored the physical conditions of frontier settlement or the difficulty of getting servants. Their social status and the political prominence of their families dictated that they themselves had "higher," more important, tasks to perform than struggling with the actual housework, although they were expected to make a home and meet the physical needs of their families. They were also expected, as shall be discussed later, to assume an array of social, religious, and philanthropic responsibilities outside their homes. Elite women's relative wealth afforded them the opportunity to hire homemakers; their rank, their public responsibilities, and the prescriptive dictates of domesticity presumed that they would be household managers – supervisors of a number of domestic workers. Helen Macaulay's work was not actually to cook, clean, or look after the children. She was to order her domestic world and ensure that her staff did the work, carefully and efficiently. As Anne Macaulay of Picton cryptically commented, "there is no manager like the mistress of the house."[82] But as her sister-in-law and other elite women in Upper Canada knew all too well, being a mistress of a large house was no easy matter.

Affluent women did receive some advice in local newspapers and increasingly from "household guides" published in Great Britain and the United States on how to manage their home.[83] A short excerpt from *The English Housekeeper*, reprinted in one York newspaper, told colonial mistresses that "Servants, like children and indeed like all dependents may be made good or bad; you may, by your management, cause them to be nearly what you please."[84] Wives were reminded that servants were from the lower social and economic orders. Not only would they have different and usually somewhat lower moral standards than their employers, but servants were almost always lazy, vexatious, and dishonest.[85] To forestall maids' apparently inherent "temptations to be dishonest," the mistress was

Illustration 12
"Elmsley Villa," a big house in York c.1840
J. Ross Robertson Collection, MTL (T 11395)

advised to "lockup" drawers and cupboards.[86] Elite women were also to expect that their servants would try to take advantage of them. Mistresses were therefore counselled to insist on and maintain the highest standards of work and behaviour from their staff from the beginning. They should establish strict daily routines and clearly delineate the responsibilities of each servant.[87] In short, servants in a "big" house were first and foremost employees. Though they resided in the same house as their employers, servants and their mistresses lived very different lives and their work was usually quite separate. From the time they first took up their positions, maids and cooks were left in little doubt about this.

The homes of prominent Upper Canadians provided for quarters for the domestic staff that were separate from those of the family.[88] Although their rooms were usually cramped and situated at the back of the house or in the garret, mistresses were careful to provide the staff with at least the basic necessities. In 1837, Ann Macaulay sent her son John "a bedstead & clean bed tick (he will need straw) blankets & pillow, two pillow cases & counterpane" for his new manservant's room.[89] When a second man was hired, John requested more bedding. "My intention is to give them good straw mattresses with a little wool outside & I only want additional sheets etc if you have any of ours yet in hand ie Blankets, sheets, pillow cases & for a change."[90]

Not only did the family and the staff live apart, they also ate at separate tables and may have had separate diets. For the Russells, the Macaulays, and the Powells, it would have been unthinkable to have servants join them for meals. As Faye Dudden has noted, "the dinner table was the one chance the family had to be together in privacy."[91] At other times, when guests were present, the dining room was where the public world of society and politics intersected with the private world of the family. In neither instance was it appropriate for servants to sit down with their "betters."

The growing sense of distance between the elite mistress and her domestic employees was further accentuated by a servant's dress. In 1830, Mary O'Brien told of calling at a "very handsome house" just outside York. She was met at the door by "a not very smart maid servant." Mary noted that "this ... was perhaps [an] accident, as I believe the establishment of the house includes men in livery."[92] Throughout the first half of the nineteenth century, it is likely that only a few affluent households required their staff to be in livery. A servant's appearance was important, nevertheless. Servants were a visible symbol of the relative affluence and importance of the family for whom they worked. A servant's appearance also made a statement about her mistress's ability as a household manager. When mistresses paid and received formal calls during the endless social routines of York or Kingston, it was the maid who first opened the door to receive visitors. It was the maid and perhaps the butler who formally served family and guests often elaborately prepared meals. Maids, butlers, and other servants obviously had to be neat and clean. Female servants also undoubtedly wore aprons and some may even have had caps as badges of their work and status.[93] A well-turned-out servant was clearly an asset to an Upper Canadian household.

Where a servant slept and ate, and what she wore were important symbols of her status in a colonial home. They were also indications of her relationship to her mistress and the work she was expected to perform. Elite urban mistresses hired women to work for them, not with them. The mistress established the household routines and assigned work; it was the servants who actually carried it out. Only in emergencies would an elite wife do her own cleaning or cooking.[94]

The workday of a domestic servant, even within a relatively large staff, was long and onerous. In 1840, the Macaulays' housemaid Sarah, worked from morning until 9 PM each night.[95] The cook and the children's nurse, Elinore, undoubtedly kept similar hours. The cook (whom Helen never named), Sarah, and Elinore appear to have had relatively well-defined responsibilities. The cook prepared meals, kept the kitchen clean, and may have been responsible for the marketing. Sarah was the general housemaid and probably helped serve meals. Elinore's primary responsibility was looking after Annie and little Helen; she also helped with dusting and, in her free time, other cleaning.[96]

The work required in keeping an affluent Upper Canadian home was, in part, determined by some colonists' rising expectations of orderliness and cleanliness. A good household manager was always prepared to receive guests. Maintaining a mistress's reputation and meeting the new standards of housekeeping was accomplished, however, "at the expense of the domestic labour."[97] Though Helen Macaulay's cook would have had the most up-to-date equipment, including a new cook stove, she was also expected to produce intricate and varied multi-course meals for an indeterminate number of guests; though Sarah had help from Elinore and perhaps another woman part time, to clean and dust, the Macaulays had a large and elaborate home. Keeping heavy curtains, carpets, and furniture clean was burdensome, never-ending work.

In addition to doing the housework, Sarah, Elinore, and the cook were expected to function "in specific ways to secure and protect their employer's status." It was Sarah who answered the door and on Helen's instructions either admitted visitors or took their cards. It was the cook who was always prepared to feed extra guests at dinner or who could produce tea and confectionaries for visiting ladies. Servants were "buffers, transmitters and facilitators" of their elite employers' social status. They gave their mistresses a crucial element of control over their social lives and enabled them to participate fully in society. The servants, however, remained "non-participants in the proceedings";[98] they were anonymous, impersonal household fixtures – efficient, characterless, and often faceless.

An upper-class mistress was well aware that having a good servant was a very real asset to her household. In 1818, after years of making do with too few or indifferent servants, Anne Powell was pleased that at last, "we are as well prepared as we can be." She reported that she now had "two good female Servants besides a little English girl who has been with me more than a year, and makes a good housemaid; we have two men Servants who both attend table."[99] Given the considerable time and effort required to find and train good servants, a number of colonial mistresses went to some trouble to keep them. It is unknown what provisions were negotiated between maids and mistresses with respect to holidays. As resident servants, maids were probably expected to be on duty most, if not all, waking hours. Days off may have been sporadic and certainly in some households, payment of wages was irregular.[100] When a good servant became restless or unhappy, her mistress often, however, made special arrangements to entice her to stay.[101] She might offer her a higher wage or time off. When Sarah complained to Helen Macaulay in 1840 that her days were too long and there was too much to do, Helen began to look for additional help.[102] Helen Macaulay and other mistresses also took a personal interest in the welfare of their servants. Sometimes a mistress helped to nurse a maid who was ill, or made sure that they received proper medical attention.

Soon after she arrived in the colony, Elizabeth Russell became increasingly concerned about the health and habits of her young servant/companion, Mary Fleming. For two years, Elizabeth tried to break Mary of her "nasty night habits," wetting the bed, "of which [she] was not at all ashamed or concerned about." Elizabeth was much more concerned, however, when Mary contracted consumption in 1795. Elizabeth provided Mary with the best medical help available and took her to the country for a change of air. In the end, nothing Elizabeth did brought Mary back to health. Elizabeth was devastated when Mary died. "I have lost a pleasing companion," she wrote to Lizzy Kiernan.[103]

In 1841, Helen Macaulay was faced with a similar, but apparently not so serious, dilemma. The family was planning to travel to Sarasoga Springs, and Elinore, the family nursemaid, appeared to be too ill to go. "I don't know what to do," Helen wrote to John in June of 1841. "Were she able to do her duty for us at the Springs, the benefit to her health no doubt would be great." Helen continued, "She is a good girl and I do not like casting her off when she is poorly but doing her upmost to do her duty."[104] Elinore, whom John Macaulay had described as "a very decent girl," had been with the family since they had come to York in 1837. Over the years, she had become a coveted member of the household. "She is a most respectable young woman & complete trust woman being very good tempered, good judgement and most worthy of the charge of the children," Helen commented to her mother-in-law.[105] In the end, Elinore did go to the Springs with the family and moved with them to Kingston later that fall.[106]

For Helen Macaulay and other elite mistresses, the benefits of a good servant did not offset the frustration and at times serious distress that a bad servant could evoke. A maid's or cook's deficiencies could not only make life very uncomfortable for residents of the big house but they also impinged on her mistress's ability to entertain or perform her other public duties. Hannah Jarvis, for example, complained to her father in 1793 that "we cannot get a Woman who can cook a Joint of Meat unless I am at her Heels – at the Price of Seven

Eight & Nine Dollars per Month." At that time, Hannah also had "a Scotch girl, from the Highlands – sulky, faulty ill-Tempered Creature, – she had nearly killed the other girl the other Day – Struck her with the Tongs and beat her intolerably – and had not Mr Jarvis happened to pass the window, at that moment, in all probability would have laid up if not murdered her."[107]

Elizabeth Russell found herself in an even more precarious position in 1806. She related in her diary that her brother Peter entertained rarely, despite his position near the top of Upper Canada's social circle. "His constant application to Business and having such bad servants is greatly the cause," she noted. Peggy and John Beecher, her couple, were "customarily very dirty, idle and insolent." In addition, the young maid, Milly, "exactly copies their manner." Elizabeth's frustration with her servants was compounded by her brother's attitude to the problem. "Peter talked of letting his servants go on as they please without saying very much to them but now and then gets out of patience with them & lets them go on again."[108] Peter's vacillation and "indifference about conditions" clearly only exacerbated the situation.

Upper Canadian mistresses were all too aware of the difficulties involved in replacing any servant, however. Many women were willing to put up with a great deal from members of their staff. In addition to finding her servants dirty and "insolent," Elizabeth Russell complained that they didn't perform their work and "were much addicted to pilfering and lying."[109] Yet it was only when the Russells' servants (some of whom, at least, were slaves) became overtly abusive and physically threatening that Peter finally took action. In January 1806, their man, Jupiter, was jailed for threatening the Russells' farm tenant, the Denisons.[110] At the end of the month, Elizabeth recorded, "Jupiter was released from prison today and contrary to orders, was brought into the house, but was sent off home with Pompodore who was very drunk today and impertinent with Peter who was very angry at Jupiter being brought into the house. He behaved so ill when he was here that I am determined that he shall not come at all to the house which Peter is good enough to comply with. He is a thief and everything that is bad and since he has been in jail he is over-run with lice." Her diary entry concluded, "he is to be sold."[111] Ironically, two months later Elizabeth Russell was again complaining of drunken servants.[112]

The willingness to overlook or tolerate the actions of a bad servant did have its limits. Immoral behaviour among servants could not be condoned. Both Anne Powell and Ann Macaulay dismissed their maids after they had given birth to children out of wedlock. It should be noted that Ann Macaulay also dismissed the father of the child.

Helen and John Macaulay had other problems with their servants. While Helen was confined in the spring of 1840 after the birth of the triplets, her sister-in-law, Anne, reported to the family in Kingston that she could not leave Helen "to the mercy of the servants."[113] With Helen prostrate and in bed after a lengthy and difficult delivery, three desperately ill newborns requiring full-time nursing, and John frantic with worry, "Helen's cook & a stout woman Rose I think, as two regular thieves ... took advantage of their mistress's illness to purloin all they could while they had not even the grace to cook John a good dinner."[114] The two servant women were subsequently discharged; sister-in-law Anne and Helen's sister temporarily filled the breach.

Helen, or given the circumstances, perhaps John, managed to replace the two thieving servants within a couple of weeks; the new cook and housemaid both required training, however.[115] Moreover, the cook was discharged only three days after she was hired. Helen, by then beginning to resume her household duties, engaged "an elderly Black woman named Victoria, as Cook." Victoria, John reported to his mother, had experience "and is perfect in all culinary accomplishments." He had to admit, however, that "she has defects, of course in her character against which we have to guard, such as an occasional dispute with another servant, but she is represented as being honest and sober to as great degree as her class of person can reasonably be expected to be. We have had to sustain a good deal of waste since Helen became unable to superintend, owing to the want of a trusty 'queen of the Kitchen.' If therefore this woman answers our purpose we shall have more than one solid reason in joining in the cry of 'Long Live Victoria.'"[116]

The hiring of Victoria in the spring of 1840 apparently solved the Macaulays' cook problem until the family moved to Kingston eighteen months later. John's reservations about Victoria seem to have been well-founded, however. John reported to his mother in February 1841 that the black cook was "honest but in other respects is indifferent enough, being old & slow & not particularly clean. In fact, we never had a set of servants so inferior as our present – but we have not seen company & the uncertainty about our movements have rendered us by no means anxious to improve their qualities."[117] John Macaulay's reluctance to "improve the quality" of his staff was not unique. Mistresses' diaries and letters suggest that only in the most unusual or dire circumstances was a servant let go.[118]

What to employers was a servant problem was to many domestic waged workers a problem with the mistress. In reply to a scathing indictment of the "serving classes" made in the *Kingston Gazette* in 1812, "Servitia" noted that "persons that are under the hard necessity of working for their daily bread in the houses of people no better than themselves are subjected to contumelies, and insults enough without being exposed in printed papers." Servitia continued, "it is very easy for poor servants to retort [to the earlier charges] with interest, they have only to give the history of a few of their employers to turn the laugh completely in their favour." Servitia then described a former mistress who had been a camp follower, and though able to buy herself fine dresses, had distrusted and been niggardly with her staff. Her next employer had been a lady of education who had considered herself better than her neighbours, in addition to her servants. Her last position had been with a merchant and his wife who continually fought among themselves and their children, while presenting a public face as devoted lovers.[119]

As Servitia concluded, putting up with mistresses who were ill-tempered and inconsiderate only made the servants' work much harder and more disagreeable. Maids or cooks resented taking instructions from a mistress who they believed was "no better than themselves" or did not know how particular tasks should best be performed.[120] Helen Macaulay's Sarah, her cook, and other servants in elite homes must also have "often resented their use in status competition" so endemic to York society.[121] Moreover, they were undoubtedly frustrated that the presence of guests meant more work with no extra pay and often no acknowledgment of their performance. Aware of their employers' latent distrust and perhaps even more of the wide economic gulf that separated them from their employers, it is not surprising that servants attempted to take whatever advantage they could of their situation. As in the country, servants in town avoided certain tasks and "stole" time for themselves. Many also undoubtedly tried to work at their own pace. Indeed, diaries and letters of exasperated elite women suggest that domestic workers resisted the social implications of being "in service."

Given the mistress's dependence on her servants and the difficulty of finding good ones, a servant in an elite household did have some real bargaining power.[122] The Macaulays' maid Sarah could not have been the only maid in Upper Canada to complain to her mistress.[123] Some servants also refused to do certain kinds of work. They sometimes ignored instructions and when the domestic situation became too difficult or onerous, servants could and did leave.[124] Upper Canadian households were resigned to having servant girls leave to marry. And even when she left with the well wishes of her mistress, as John Macaulay wrote to his mother, "It is unfortunate ... for I find that it is not very easy to pick up another girl."[125] Maids frequently left without any explanation and at sometimes very inopportune times for their mistresses. Elizabeth Russell complained in 1807 of an "ungrateful" mulatto "wench," hired by her friend and tenant Mrs Denison, who had "forsaken her & gone to the Governors" just after Mrs Denison had given birth.[126]

Particularly in the 1820s and 1830s, skilled female domestic workers were in great demand, and many took advantage of this. Even those who had no family or friends in the area to offer them a home for the short term were confident of their ability to find other employment. John Macaulay did not seem particularly surprised when he reported to his mother in his first letter from their new home in the fall of 1837 that "we have got a good House maid & a passable plain cook – our first hired Cook came on Friday morning & left at night without saying a word, not a pleasant way of opening House. We were not aware of it until we were moving in on Saturday. Fortunately we had another string to our bow."[127]

Mistresses clearly resented what they considered a servant's lack of loyalty. There was often little they could do to forestall the problem, however. Like rural helps, most women who became resident servants, either in the big house or in smaller urban households, did not expect to remain with their employer for ever.[128] Some married women often became domestic workers only until their families had saved sufficient funds to set up their own business or could buy land.[129] Others moved in and out of the labour force and often worked part time, as their own family situation demanded. Even formal contracts did not always solve the problem. Slaves and indentured or contract servants frequently "ran away," much to their owners' disgust.[130]

As was the case in the back country, paid domestic service was a highly mobile occupation. It was rarely as binding an arrangement as employers would have liked. Yet many mistresses also resisted committing themselves fully. Servants in Upper Canada were usually hired for an unspecified time. Wages were paid by the week, the month, or even the year, and both parties could and did terminate the relationship without notice or cause. Nonetheless, in the majority of cases, it seems to have been the servant who chose to terminate the relationship rather than the employer.

It is not surprising, therefore, that diaries and letters frequently revealed friction between the Upper Canadian elite mistress and her servants. The potential for conflict between the two was high. The parties entered into the relationship with distinct and often conflicting expectations. Elite mistresses naturally wanted women workers who were skilled, industrious, and compliant. In return for what they considered "liberal" wages, employers expected hard work and loyalty. Domestic servants wanted waged employment and respect for their work. Many needed a home. Their loyalty to their work or their employer was secondary to their own needs.[131] Many never intended to remain in service for any length of time. Moreover, it was clear that despite the inherent inequality of the situation, the mistress did not completely control the relationship. Given the number of households that required or desired domestic workers, servants had considerable latitude in choosing their employment and establishing at least some of the conditions of work. In 1840, the Macaulays were particularly conscious of their vulnerability. As William Macaulay commented, "John ... I can see has very heavy expenses of living there [in York] & must look sharp as his family increase." Servants could relieve a mistress of much of her housework, but, William continued, in a rare flash of insight, "It is bad though to have too many servants." John and Helen had become "a slave to their own domestics & no slavery is worse – or more costly ... Is not that a fine chapter in economy from the Prince of Economists,' " William wryly concluded.[132]

As a minister in the village of Picton, living in a small household with no children, William Macaulay believed he was unlikely to be subjected to such indignity. Yet his wife's correspondence indicates that they too had their domestic problems. For though they lived in a small community and had fewer formal social responsibilities, Anne and William did need assistance in the house. It appears, however, that Anne's girl was more often a "help" than a servant. In the late 1830s, Anne obviously worked with Jane Armstrong, who had been hired to wash, make soap, and scrub the floors.[133] In York, Helen depended on her servants, and did not work "with" them. They worked for her.

THE NEW PATTERNS of domestic service were most apparent in Upper Canada's elite households. Only the most affluent women could afford to keep more than one or two servants, and indeed, only the wealthiest and most prominent households needed to do so.[134] As women such as Ann and Helen Macaulay and Anne Powell became increasingly involved in social, philanthropic, and public affairs, they became more and more dependent on other women to do what had traditionally been their work. Ironically, as elite women embraced the dictates of domesticity inherent in the cult of true womanhood, they were forced to rely on other women to maintain this. This is not to say that elite women lived a carefree life of leisure. Managing the homes of Upper Canada's most prominent residents was a full-time occupation. This work was made all the more difficult because the women who were engaged to carry out the actual work in the house did not nor could not share the same values, aspirations, or beliefs as their employers.

Colonial women servants were increasingly drawn from the lower ranks of the economic and social order. They could not aspire to the life of the "angel" in the house. Their financial situation and often their own cultural baggage precluded this. But they could not escape being influenced by the presumptions inherent in the new social ideology. Being a wife and mother was an honoured vocation. But a woman who was obliged to accept a wage for this work and answer to the title of servant had little social or economic status. It is not surprising that domestic wage-earners were often reluctant employees. Although they needed their meagre wages, they not unnaturally often resented the attitudes and expectations of their employers. Many asserted their independence in whatever way they could. As Helen Macaulay prepared to enter the world of York society, she must at times have wondered if the power of the purse made any real difference.

Yet, in the end, power did rest primarily with the employer. This was not only evident in relations within elite households. It was also becoming increasingly apparent as Helen Macaulay, Anna Jameson, Anne Powell, and their friends and associates moved and worked outside their homes, in the public world of Upper Canadian "society."

7 "Social Obligations" and "Angelic Ministrations": Society Matrons and Crusading Ladies

After seven years of separation, Anna Jameson joined her husband, Robert, the attorney general of Upper Canada, in York in December 1836. Anna moved into the couple's temporary home and immediately began to assume the duties incumbent on the wife of a leading colonial official. She entertained the "first" families of York; she attended the official opening of the House of Assembly and, suitably attired, she received and made calls on the wives and daughters of the members of the Upper Canadian elite. By February 1837, Anna Jameson rather scathingly concluded, "There is no *society* in Toronto ... 'But,' you will say, 'what could be expected in a remote town, which forty years before was uninhabited swamp and twenty years ago only began to exist?'" Anna Jameson had not really known what to expect when she came to the colony. "But I will tell you what I did *not* expect," she wrote. "I did not expect to find here in this new capital of a new country, with the boundless forest within half a mile of us on almost every side – concentrated as it were the worst evils of our old and most artificial social system at home, with none of its *agremens* and none of its advantages."[1] Anna Jameson considered that York was "like a fourth or fifth provincial town with the pretensions of a Capital city. We have here a petty colonial oligarchy, a self-constituted aristocracy, based upon nothing real, nor even upon anything imaginary; and we have all the mutual jealousy and fear, and petty gossip, and mutual meddling and mean rivalship which are common in a small society of which the members are well known to each other."[2]

Illustration 13
Portrait of Anna Jameson
J. Ross Robertson Collection, MTL (T15767)

Given her views on the matter, it is rather ironic that Anna Jameson had come to the colony, not to effect a reconciliation with her husband, but to provide him with "the appearance of normalcy" which the small self-conscious society demanded of its leading members.[3] During her nine-month sojourn in Upper Canada, Anna acted as her husband's housekeeper and hostess. She coped with moving his household into a new house, hiring indoor staff, and generally ensuring that his domestic requirements were met. She also assumed, outwardly at least, the many public responsibilities of a conventional wife of a senior member of the colonial elite.[4] It was obviously very important for Robert Jameson, who in February 1837 was promoted to the position of vice-chancellor of Upper Canada, to have his wife running his home and standing publicly by his side. Not only was Anna's work necessary for his physical comfort, but she also provided her husband with a crucial element of social respectability. By attending balls, affairs of state, and private parties, Anna was representing his interests in York society and was a visible symbol of his political rank and social status.

The wives of other affluent Upper Canadians would have recognised and respected Anna Jameson's efforts on behalf of her husband. Helen Macaulay, Anne Powell, and Elizabeth Russell also had special duties that resulted from their husbands' work and their families' rank in the social hierarchy. They too had to take an active part in the often closed world of "high" colonial society. Of equal, and for some of greater importance, was their work assisting those less fortunate than themselves. In the 1820s and 1830s, members of the Upper Canadian upper class became increasingly involved in efforts to reform colonial society, morally, religiously, and socially. Initially, as was befitting members of their sex, women such as Anne Powell and her daughters worked in the shadow of their husbands and fathers. By the mid-1820s, however, as prominent women devoted an increasing proportion of their time, energy, and organizational skills to the reforming crusade, they also began to assume public leadership roles independent of their husbands.

Not surprisingly, elite women found it increasingly difficult to balance their domestic responsibilities with their growing public work on behalf of family, class, and God. Some, like Harriet Dobbs Cartwright of Kingston, tried to concentrate their efforts on philanthropic and religious endeavours. Avoiding the elaborate rituals of society altogether was not possible, however. Regardless of personal preference, Harriet Cartwright and other upper-class women, including Anna Jameson, who only expected to be in the colony for a short time, knew that they could seriously harm their husbands' political standing and influence if they did not conform to community dictates and take their rightful place in Upper Canada's "artificial social system."

THE FOUNDATION of the Upper Canadian elite's intricate and rigidly structured social world was initially laid down by Elizabeth Simcoe and her husband, Lieutenant-Governor John Graves Simcoe.[5] Though living in tents or in log cabins, the colonial "aristocracy" of the late eighteenth century attended formal balls, received visitors and personal guests and maintained social conventions reminiscent of large European centres. Within the artificial environment of the Upper Canadian upper class, calling, attending state functions, entertaining the "right" people, and knowing how to address associates and subordinates were essential duties of any responsible wife. First calls, for example, were to be made by the relatively social inferior household on one that was socially superior. At state occasions, rank was reflected in the placement of guests and the order of who began the dancing or initiated conversation. Failure to accept one's rank was considered outrageous and led to public snubs. It could result in the complete ostracism of the offending party. Elite women had to be aware of the protocol and of the changing of rank. They also had to "keep up their end" by their dress, their conduct, and their ability and willingness to entertain.[6]

A newly married woman, a recently arrived wife, or a visitor to an elite household was introduced to Upper Canadian society by the formal visit. Within a week of her arrival to York in December 1836, Anna Jameson reported that "All the official gentlemen have called, and all the ladies have properly and politely left their cards." The ceremonial calls, which in some cases meant no more than leaving a card at the door, had all to be returned promptly. Anna Jameson found the rituals of arrival a nuisance. She recalled that "in a sleigh, well capped in furs and buffalo robe, I set out duly to return these visits. I learned something of the geography of the town," she admitted but learned "nothing of the people. Those whom I did see looked somewhat formal and alarmed, but they may be excellent people for all that."[7] The obligations could not, however, be avoided. When Julia Lambert arrived in 1828 to visit her sister, the wife of a legislative councillor, she reported that "most of the ladies of the place called" and she also called on the lieutenant-governor's wife, Lady Maitland.[8] Five years later, when Harriet Dobbs Cartwright arrived at her sister-in-law's home in Kingston shortly after her marriage to Robert, a Church of England clergyman, she ceremoniously offered "cake and wine to those who made their calls" even before moving into her own house.[9]

The question of who called first was very important to the best families of Upper Canada. As wife of the attorney general, Anna Jameson had few social superiors. Though she undoubtedly called first on Lady Bond Head, the wife of the lieutenant-governor,[10] the wives of other members of the government made first calls on Mrs Jameson. In some cases, however, the question of precedent was unclear. Katherine McKenna relates that in 1827, Lady Mary Willis, wife of the new associate justice of Upper Canada, assumed for some time that she was superior in rank to Mrs Maitland, the wife of the lieutenant-governor.[11] It was only after some careful manoeuvring by a third party that the situation was resolved and Mrs Willis made the first call. A similar situation seems to have emerged a decade later. John Macaulay reported to his wife that it had been decided that members of the Executive Council were to take social precedence over all other members of the government. The result was, he noted, "that some have taken umbrage."[12] Part of the problem was that Lady Bond Head, wife of the new lieutenant-governor, had not yet arrived in the colony to take over "as Head of our female Society."[13] It was anticipated that when she took up residence, she would "make some changes in the ceremonies."[14]

Once first calls were made, the new arrivals had to return the courtesy. John and Helen Macaulay were fortunate that, despite the time of year, they had good weather while returning their calls in November 1837.[15] Even in good weather, however, returning calls could be tiresome and time-consuming. During her first visit to York in the summer of 1833, Harriet Dobbs Cartwright stayed at Archdeacon Strachan's, and in the absence of Mrs Strachan, was de facto mistress. "It would have saved much trouble" if the Archdeacon's and Robert's friends "had been a few days in discovering our arrival, and a few more days longer in calling in on us ... As it was ... half our time was occupied in paying and receiving visits, which generally speaking [is] a very profitless occupation." Harriet conceded that there might be some benefit to the protocol. "I do not say that [it] is always or necessarily" a waste of time, she wrote, "but few people possess either the ability or inclination of turning conversation to good account and redeeming the time devoted to the intercourse of society and interchanges of civility, perhaps still fewer make the endeavour."[16] Profitless or not, the proprieties had to be maintained.

Not all formal visits were attended with such impatience. When Elizabeth Russell visited Mrs Gore, the wife of the new lieutenant-governor in 1808, she was charmed by her reception and pleased with a gift of feathers.[17] Ten years later, Anne Powell was delighted to find Mrs Sarah Maitland "a most unaffected woman."[18] She was subsequently flattered to become part of the inner social circle of the Maitlands. To Anne Powell and many other elite women of Upper Canada, the conventions of formal calling were extremely important.[19] Formal calling was an elite woman's first introduction into her new society. It established her place in the social order and set the parameters of her public life, which would prevail as long as her husband maintained his position or the family remained in the community. Thus, for those who expected that Upper Canada would be their permanent home, setting the protocol and proprieties at the beginning was essential. Many upper-class women undoubtedly enjoyed the status that such rituals illustrated to society at large. For some, the formalities of calling also confirmed their sense of whom they were, personally as well as publicly. Although it is clear that a number of prominent women did not take such protocol seriously, some women jealously guarded the rules of society and enforced them zealously.

Once precedence was established and initial visits made and returned, the wives of the elite settled into their work of entertaining, attending public functions, and doing good works. John and Helen Macaulay seem to have been relatively unusual in their lack of social activity. In part, this may have been a result of Helen's pregnancies and frequent bouts of ill health. Helen Macaulay also travelled a good deal, visiting her sister in Niagara and her mother-in-law in Kingston; she also made two extended trips home to Scotland. Society wives were undoubtedly excused from much of the formal socializing during their pregnancies and when their children were ill. At other times, however, women were expected to take part both in large "state" functions and in smaller, more "private," though no less ritualized occasions.[20]

Even in its earliest years, official Upper Canadian society prided itself on its public functions. As early as 1793, Mrs Simcoe reported that every fortnight men in formal suits and women with "a great display of gauze, feathers & velvet" danced, sat down to a supper and danced again.[21] For one of the first balls, the Simcoes added to their own establishment by building a room "60' long, for the eighteen couples to dance." In addition to subscription balls, the lieutenant-governor and his wife annually hosted a levee or ball in honour of the king or queen's birthday. A touring American, General Lincoln, attended the first celebration of the king's birthday in Upper Canada in June 1793. "General Simcoe," he wrote, "is exceedingly attentive to these public assemblies, and makes it his duty to reconcile the inhabitants, who have tasted the pleasures of society, to their present situation, in an infant province." The general noted that the lieutenant-governor "intends next winter to have concerts and assemblies very frequently."[22]

Subsequent lieutenant-governors and other high-ranking colonial officials continued to host such celebrations and entertainment. These events provided affluent women and men of the community with an opportunity to dress in their best and to partake of an evening's entertainment with their associates. It was also an opportunity for women whose lives were often busy coping with children, servants, and household affairs to meet and share their problems, concerns, and delights. Such functions were also very important public affairs, however. Invitations to these events were coveted by many colonial families; attendance was a visible symbol of one's acceptance into society.

Writing to her brother in 1806, Anne Powell remarked that "the follies of *little* York will if we meet serve to you who know us, for an hour's ridicule." She continued, "Rank will be settled [at the president's hall tomorrow] ... I fear some who claim precedent, will find themselves of less importance than they expect, – for me I am fortunately out of the scrape, – I shall get my Rubber, & whether I eat my supper at the upper or lower end of the table, is a matter of the most perfect indifference, perhaps my Neighbours will feel more interest, as wherever I am she is below me."[23]

The "neighbours" Anne Powell was referring to were Justice and Mrs Thorpe – a couple who had recently arrived from Britain. And Anne Powell's cryptic, yet pointed, criticism of "the follies of York" was the result of ongoing tension that had divided York society for more than a year. When the Thorpes had first arrived in the summer of 1805, Anne Powell had been insulted when Mrs Thorpe had refused to call on her. She also resented the Thorpes for their social informality and political pretensions. Believing that the justice and his wife had offended against community protocol, Anne Powell refused to accept any social invitations from them. The next year was a difficult period for Anne. For although they appeared to snub the Powells, the Thorpes consciously courted other members of York society and Anne and her family felt increasingly isolated.[24] Anne's problem was only resolved when the couple left the colony altogether after the justice had slipped from public favour in 1807.[25]

The tension between the Thorpes and the Powells was but a minor social skirmish when compared to the scandal that revolved around the wife of the clerk of the Executive Council, Mrs Small. The Small affair had begun in 1799 when John White, then the attorney general, had been outraged by the conduct of Mrs Small to his wife at a ball. White, unable to gain any satisfaction from the Smalls, whom he considered social inferiors, set out to destroy Mrs Small's reputation. Rumours flew around York that Mrs Small had had numerous sexual liaisons. Mr Small was understandably upset; he challenged White to a duel and killed him. Though Small was subsequently acquitted of murder, his appearance in court made what had been whispered rumours public knowledge.

From that time on, "Mrs Small and her husband lived in a kind of social twilight."[26] And when the new lieutenant-governor, Francis

Gore, attempted in 1806 to bring the couple back into York society, Anne Powell resisted vehemently. As Katherine McKenna has so ably recounted, Anne engaged in guerrilla-like warfare with Lieutenant-Governor Gore over the "Small affair." Anne was determined to uphold her rank and maintain social and moral propriety. Despite personal invitations from the lieutenant-governor, she refused to attend social functions when the Smalls were present. Although Anne Powell won the battle in the end,[27] it was not without some cost to herself and her husband's career. McKenna notes "that the Lieutenant-Governor assumed that Anne was at the head of a conspiracy to thwart his effort of restoring social harmony. This in turn affected William's relationship with Gore."[28] For the next eighteen months William Dummer Powell was out of favour with the lieutenant-governor. It was not until Anne's assessment of Justice Thorpe was vindicated that the lieutenant-governor conceded that she might also have been right in the Small affair.

Not all formal occasions were so fraught with potential pitfalls and tension. In 1838, Anna Jameson "received about thirty gentlemen" on New Year's Day, who in keeping with the "custom" had come to offer congratulations of the New Year. "To gentlemen luckily for me the obligation is confined," she commented rather cryptically. She had never met most of her guests and many were never introduced. "Some of them, on being ushered into the room, bowed, sat down, and after the lapse of two minutes, rose and bowed themselves out of the room again without uttering a syllable; all were too much in a hurry and apparently far too cold to converse." Anna found herself "almost giddy" at these "strange faces" who "appeared and disappeared in succession so rapidly." By the end of the day she was exhausted.[29]

Women in other parts of the colony were also expected to host New Year's levees. In Kingston, Harriet Dobbs Cartwright reported to her two sisters that "this is the second day of the observance of Canadian fashion of paying and receiving New Year's visits." Harriet hoped to finish the letter she was writing to her sister between "exits and entrance of visitors ... although yesterday Mary [her sister-in-law] and I were sitting in state, receiving our gentlemen visitors of whom we had upward of fifty between twelve and five o'clock." As Harriet explained, "all the ladies are expected to remain at home, and sit in state for two or three days with cakes and wines and whatever other good things they please, to present to their Cavaliers Servants ... yesterday we had several whom I had never seen before and probably will not again til some similar occasion."[30]

The practice of the at-home was not reserved for New Year's. In 1833, John Macaulay received a card from Mrs Colborne (wife of the lieutenant-governor) stating she was "at home." He was obviously obliged to attend. "I found all the world assembled & the rooms filled with near three hundred, perhaps 250+ people of whom more than one half were perfect strangers to me & even to many of the people of York."[31] John Macaulay and other gentlemen had only to attend such functions. Mrs Colborne, Anna Jameson, and Harriet Cartwright had to prepare for them. They then had to be on their best behaviour, greeting guests, and ensuring that refreshments were ready and available.

Preparations for a ball, a levee, or a formal at-home could be onerous. When Sheriff Jarvis had a ball in February 1839, it drew "an immense crowd" and went off, according to one guest, "remarkably well."[32] Anne Macaulay attended a party at Mrs Sherwood's that same season. In her letter to her mother-in-law, Anne reported that "Mrs Sherwood was a very good hostess." There was a large crowd of people at the event. "A receiving room had been established and there were two dancing rooms, a card room and a supper room." Clearly, Anne concluded, "a great deal of trouble" had gone into preparing for the event.[33]

Probably only those few "aristocratic" women whose husbands were most prominent in colonial affairs were obliged to host such grand and large functions. All upper-class women, however, had to give and attend formal dinner parties. As wife of the chief justice, Anne Powell "expected to give large dinner parties two times a week for members of the legislature."[34] In 1827, John Strachan hosted a "Dinner" for "22 persons consisting of Fish, soup, venison, Turkey, 3 entire courses, served on a complete service of china, side dishes, silver, champagne, claret & cider."[35] John Macaulay reported that he and Helen had been two of twenty at the lieutenant-governor's for dinner in November 1837.[36] At the beginning of 1840, he told his mother that "here the GG dined with Hagerman on Monday; on Tuesday there was a musical entertainment at Lady Arthur's. On Wednesday evening the GG had a ladies party. This evening Colonel Foster has a large evening party to which we were invited but have not gone."[37]

For each of these events, considerable time and energy were required to prepare. Food had to be purchased and cooked; wine and other beverages made ready; musicians had to be hired; the house had to be thoroughly cleaned and then had to be arranged to accommodate often large number of guests. Even for those who did not themselves host such events, the continual round of entertainment must have been exhausting. It was also expensive. John Macaulay noted in 1840 that being at least five months pregnant, "Helen cannot

at present think of every amusement, but must take care of herself."
John explained to his mother that he and Helen had given up serious
entertaining anyway. This was not because of Helen's condition, but
rather "my salary will not admit of it & I shall not run into the follies
of some of my neighbours." Within the previous three weeks, the
Macaulays had given at least two formal dinner parties.[38]

The Macaulays could not avoid some of the more informal entertaining that resulted from John's work. Before the War of 1812, the
mistress of an elite household always had to be prepared to receive
her husband's business associates. Elizabeth Simcoe recorded in her
diary the arrival of seemingly endless numbers of guests – the wives
of officers and members of the government, foreign dignitaries, European travellers, and political and military associates of her husband.
Elizabeth Russell also commented on the frequency of visitors.[39]
Once the Russells had moved to York, it was not usual for Elizabeth
to receive guests before breakfast, and frequently the cook would be
informed only moments before the household sat down that there
were extra numbers for dinner.

In the 1820s and 1830s, when John Macaulay and other government officials began to conduct most of their business from offices in
the legislative buildings, elite homes did begin to resemble that private domestic domain so indicative of middle-class society in Great
Britain and the United States.[40] Lack of formal occasions or invitations to dinner parties did not preclude prominent Upper Canadians
from receiving business associates into their homes at all times of the
day, however. The mistress of the house always had to be prepared
to present a public face to the world, regardless of any domestic
crisis.

The need to complete public duties within what was ostensibly a
private domain was not restricted to the elite. All women in Upper
Canada, regardless of class, found themselves in a similar situation.
What was unusual, however, was that for women of the Upper Canadian elite, the ability to make the private home publicly acceptable reflected very much on their husbands' careers. Moreover, it was
important to have at least the appearance of a leisured life, while still
managing a large household and coping with a growing family. This
was never easy to do. It required skill, considerable flexibility, and often much hard work to be a successful upper-class wife.

FOR ELIZABETH RUSSELL, Helen Macaulay, Anne Powell, and other
elite women in Upper Canada, their big houses, fine clothes and involvement in a whirl of social activities was only part, and often a
small part, of their lives. There were also obligations to family and

friends. And as women of wealth and prominence, many also felt obliged to assume, personally and collectively, a responsibility to help the poor, the destitute, and the abandoned.

In September 1832, the *Brockville Gazette* published a brief report of the work of "a number of young ladies" in Trenton, New Jersey who were ministering to "afflicted strangers" who had been stricken with cholera. The editor of the *Gazette* commented "this is only one act in a long, long catalogue of angelic ministrations, for which we are indebted to women – What would our wretched career of existence be without their smiles and the moderating influence of their gentle councils?" Without the society of women, "men are mere brutes," he stated emphatically. Indeed, the world would be a much cruder and ruder place without women's work and their ministrations.[41]

Ann Macaulay, Mary O'Brien, and their friends and associates must have been gratified by such tributes. But they knew that the work of the young ladies of Trenton was little different than what was already happening in Upper Canada. While charity might begin at home, women who presided over the big house had always assumed that it should not end there. Since the formation of the colony, many affluent families had financially supported their churches and assisted distressed individuals in their communities. When the occasion had required, wealthy women and men had also donated funds and their time to special philanthropic causes.[42] During the War of 1812, for example, elite women had, among other things, actively supported the Loyal and Patriotic Society of Upper Canada which had been formed to help supply the military hospital in York.[43] Anne Powell had also provided food for the wounded, and as she told her husband in 1813, "the Females here are all employed making Barrack Sheets."[44]

Between 1815 and 1840, however, it had become increasingly evident that private charity was not enough. In addition to the devastation that war had brought to some parts of the colony, a postwar depression and the influx of British immigrants had stretched private resources to their limit. Moreover, while the rapid growth of the colony had brought prosperity to some residents, an increasing number of Upper Canadians were destitute.

"The poor and the infirm demand our particular attention," Joseph Scott, a surgeon in Kingston, reminded inhabitants in 1818. "We are duty bound," he continued, "to inform their minds; to repress their vices; to assist their labours; to invigorate their activity; and to improve their comforts. These are the noblest offices of enlightened minds; offices which are the very essence of virtue and patriotism; offices which will obtain the favour of the Eternal Being, who is the

Great Father of us all."[45] Following the example of others in the Anglo-American world, Upper Canadians of all classes joined the crusade for social reform.[46] Prominent men and women began to establish Bible and missionary societies to combat the apparent religious and moral dissipation that prevailed in the colony. They also formed benevolent and aid organizations to help the "deserving" poor.

For Anne Powell and other elite women and men, their God required them, as Christians, to help those less fortunate than themselves.[47] Their affluence obligated them both to be charitable and to try to bring others to the realization of society's needs. Their attachment to gentlemen of colonial influence undoubtedly heightened their understanding that, in order to protect their families and their status in the society, colonial society had to be reformed and stabilized.

Initially, as befitted persons of their sex, prominent women who joined the reform crusade worked silently and in the shadows of their husbands and fathers.[48] Yet the same ideology that promoted "separate spheres" and the presumption of women's inherent weakness also asserted that women were morally superior to men. It was assumed that women had a duty to safeguard and promote social morality; one of the best ways to do this was to consider the community as one large family. The growing acceptance of the cult of true womanhood encouraged elite women into social activism[49] and it sanctioned the formation of independent female philanthropic organizations and activities. In addition to supporting more traditional colonial benevolent organizations, upper-class women began to identify and to addresses particular areas of social need that were of special concern and interest to them. And in doing this, they were joined by, or found themselves in the company of women from other ranks of society who too had a vision of a new world.[50]

One of the traditional roles of a good wife in Upper Canada was to be a Christian neighbour. Colonial women had long been active members of their churches. And since the settlement of the colony, many women had promoted, both in their homes and at church, the importance of the scriptures and an acceptance of God's divine purpose.[51] In 1817, an anonymous contributor to the *Kingston Gazette* suggested that such private efforts were not enough. "The present age so fertile for charity [has] produced wonders in the modern world. Bible Societies, Missionary Societies & Tract Societies have been formed in almost all principal parts of Christendom." Many believed that it was now up to Upper Canadians to come together and exert "their influence" in this international crusade "to cleanse the moral darkness from the minds of benighted men."[52]

On 3 December 1816, "the principal Gentlemen and Inhabitants of the Town of York" drew up a constitution for a society whose purpose was to "distribute Bibles and Common Prayer Books throughout the Province."[53] Auxiliary societies were soon established in Kingston and Niagara and other communities throughout the colony.[54] The need for such organizations was all too apparent to their founding members. Immediately after the War of 1812, Upper Canadians had only a few "Christian Protestant Clergy" and "in many places, the great ignorance of the people and their total disregard of all religious observances [was] rapidly increasing."[55] As Archdeacon Strachan noted in his address at the first meeting in York, "To increase the Ministry of the Word requires time and is not immediately in our power; the dissemination of the Scriptures is within the compass of our exertions and will be productive of the greatest advantages."[56] The constitution of the Upper Canada Bible and Common Prayer Book Society invited all Upper Canadians, regardless of religious denomination, "religious tenets, opinions or modes of worship" to join the cause.[57]

The Bible and Common Prayer Book Society of Upper Canada and various missionary societies that were formed somewhat later in the decade were a conscious attempt by members of the Upper Canadian elite to defend their own view of the world and to promote certain social and religious values. The moving force of association, its officers, and those individuals who were responsible for collecting donations and distributing tracts were some of the colony's most influential male residents. But as the first subscription list for the York branch of the Upper Canada Bible Society illustrates, prominent women publicly joined their husbands in support of the cause.[58] Though restricted by reason of their sex from actually leading the crusade for reform, Mrs Gore, wife of the lieutenant-governor, Mrs Powell, wife of the chief justice, and her two daughters Elizabeth and Mary, Mrs McGill, Mrs Strachan, wife of the rector of York, Mrs Bolton, wife of the attorney general, Mrs Jarvis, wife of the secretary of Upper Canada, Miss Cruickshank, Mrs Allan, and Mrs Sturmont all gave their time, their energy, and when possible, direct financial contributions to promoting the cause of Christianity and the work of God.

For the next twenty years, many upper-class women attended annual meetings of the Bible Society and Missionary Societies and collected contributions for the cause. For some including Anne Powell, her daughters and granddaughters, their support of this work undoubtedly rested on personal conviction. Mrs Gore's public support of the York Bible Society signalled to her associate sisters that open support of such organizations was also socially imperative.[59] When

Mrs Sarah Maitland, wife of the lieutenant-governor, arrived in the colony in 1818 and began actively to promote the "advancement of true religion,"[60] the wives and daughters of government officials, principal merchants, and colonial professionals were left in no doubt that they too were expected to become involved.

Yet the need to be seen at the annual meeting of the Bible and Common Prayer Book Society and to have one's name recorded as a principle contributor was, for many prominent women, of secondary importance. Such an interpretation fails to acknowledge the time and energy that women of all classes devoted to religious endeavours. An evangelical revival in Britain and the United States highlighted to many men and women such as Mary O'Brien and Harriet Dobbs Cartwright the need to bring God into the daily lives of their neighbours. A growing number of elite women were thus determined to take a more active part in the evangelical crusade. Of particular concern to many was the lack of religious instruction available to colonial children.

Sunday schools were first established in the colony shortly after the War of 1812.[61] At that time, it seemed clear to many that there was a "need to instruct children, to live counting the dignity of human beings, respect and revere God and worship, to be obedient to parents, to respect superiors, and in short [to] instill into their minds the principles of piety and virtue."[62] Sunday schools, it was believed, would provide "a few hours of instruction in the Bible" to children of the poor who had no other means of education, or of learning piety or "the glad tidings of Salvation."[63] By the mid-1820's, hundreds of children were attending Sunday schools established by the Methodists, the Presbyterians, the Anglicans, and various interdenominational groups throughout the colony.[64] By the early 1830s, Sunday schools had developed into formal educational institutions. Local Bible and Sunday school societies donated Bibles and other suitable books; some teachers and local ministers established libraries for use by area children.[65] Increasingly, lessons, which went on from two to four hours each Sunday, included instruction in reading and writing.[66] Girls and boys were taught separately and classes were organized by age and ability.

Although for the most part Sunday school associations were organized and run by men, many Upper Canadian women served as teachers and donated money and books. Mrs Maitland's public support for Sunday school associations in the colonial capital between 1818 and 1828 undoubtedly encouraged other elite women to become involved.[67] Anne Powell, her daughter Eliza, and her niece Mary regularly taught at the local Sunday school.[68] So too did Harriet Cartwright of Kingston and Mary O'Brien of the Simcoe region. The O'Brien journal records that Mary regularly "went to school" throughout 1829 and 1830. The children, she wrote, were "of all sorts of persuasions of religion"; most of them were "very ignorant" and "unaccustomed to think on the subjects which we propose to them." To help keep the children's interest, Mary O'Brien led the children in the singing of psalms.[69] She and other Sunday school teachers also awarded prizes of a New Testament to pupils who learned the greatest number of verses, or showed the most improvement.[70]

It appears that most women who taught in local Sunday schools were single or older widowed women.[71] Once married and with children, many women did not have time for such work. Certainly Mary O'Brien stopped teaching Sunday school once she began to have a family of her own. For unmarried women such as Eliza Powell, the single daughter of Anne, teaching Sunday school was "a fitting occupation," however.[72] As the single daughter of one of Upper Canada's wealthiest and most prominent families, Eliza was quite restricted in her personal and social life. Without the "benefit of a husband," not only did her class and the dictates of domesticity preclude her from working for wages but it also restricted her and others of her status from many social activities. Throughout her life, Eliza, like Mary Gapper before she married, provided considerable support to her mother and married sisters. She often served as resident nurse/companion when her sisters were confined or found themselves in the midst of a domestic crisis. And Eliza was also her mother's constant companion and helpmate. But she, like other women in her situation, also looked for other avenues through which to gain personal fulfilment. Working in the Sunday school movement and in other religious and philanthropic endeavours provided such an outlet.[73]

Colonial women's involvement in Upper Canadian Sunday schools was accompanied by their growing assertiveness in other aspects of evangelical reform. An article in the *Kingston Gazette* in March 1817 reported the creation of the Clinton Female Missionary Society of New York. The editor of the *Gazette* encouraged "the fair daughters of Upper Canada" to "go ye and do likewise."[74] Initially, colonial missionary societies were organized by men.[75] Women regularly donated money in their own names, however, and also collected money on behalf of particular projects.[76] Upper-class women also took in donations of clothes and made socks and mittens for distribution to needy individuals.

In 1830, Lady Colborne, wife of the lieutenant-governor, became a principal contributor to the York Female Missionary Society and three years later, the patroness and largest contributor of the York Ladies' Bible Society.[77] The list of subscribers and committee members for both organizations included the wives and daughters of the first citizens of York.[78] In late 1823 or early 1824, women in Kingston formed the Kingston Dorcas Society, a Christian women's organization. The purpose of the society included encouraging attendance at Sunday schools and promoting the welfare of needy children in the area. In addition to making and distributing clothing, the accounts presented in 1825 showed payments made to cover the cost of wet nurses for motherless children.[79] In its first public report, the Kingston Dorcas Society was careful to point out that there had been no partiality in determining which children received support; fully one-half of the recipients were Roman Catholic. The only condition of charity was that the children had to attend one of the Sunday schools in the area. In reply to criticism in 1829 that this latter stipulation was unjust, the directress of the society stated emphatically that it was not wrong to reward children for attending school. Moreover, "the clothes offered by our Society are offered not merely as a reward ... but also as a means by which attendance of many destitute children would be impossible."[80]

Dorcas Societies appeared in other parts of the colony over the next fifteen years. In 1829, "the Indian females at the Credit Mission" formed a Dorcas Society to make goods for sale and to teach sewing to Indian women. The proceeds from this work were then used "to promote the cause of missions among tribes more remote."[81] As the Reverend Egerton Ryerson observed in his address to the John Street Church Dorcas Society in New York, by 1830 Christian women in all parts of the colony were combining good works and veneration of God in the noble crusade to help other women and children.[82]

Methodist women were especially active in mission work and the scope of the evangelical women's groups was very broad. As the members of the Cramahe Female Missionary Society declared at their fifth annual meeting in 1831, "our field is the world – our object is the Glory of God in the salvation of sinners – our motive is Christian love."[83] Methodist women of all classes made significant donations to the Canada Conference Missionary Society, which supported various Indian missions throughout the colony. By the mid-1830s, many of these societies were openly acknowledging women's contributions and, in some instances, appointing them official collectors, members of local committees, or managers. But clearly women were not satisfied working only at the behest of their husbands and fathers. By the mid-1820s, evangelical women, like their affluent sisters, were establishing separate ladies' auxiliaries of various Bible and missionary so-

cieties. By 1830, they were forming their own independent organizations.[84]

Upper Canadian women could not escape the disability of their
sex, however. Though women held executive positions in exclusively
female missionary and Bible societies, their annual meetings were
usually chaired by the husbands of office-holders or by local preachers.[85] A number of women may also have considered that, given their
God-given lot in life, this was only fitting. Certainly, it did not seem to
discourage women from expanding their Christian work.

For many women in Upper Canada, their support of Bible, missionary, and tract societies and their work as members of the Dorcas
Society and other Christian organizations was an extension of their
personal commitment to God. For elite women, including Sarah Maitland and Anne Powell, it was also a responsibility which came with
their class. The state of Upper Canadians' souls was not the only concern that captured the attention of the colony's leaders, however. A
growing number of Upper Canadian women, together with their husbands and fathers, were becoming increasingly conscious of the social
and economic ills that existed in their communities. As the aim and
work of various Dorcas Societies illustrates, for many women there
was little distinction between the need to convert the irreligious and
the need to feed and clothe the destitute. Being a good Christian
meant doing good works and providing tangible material aid to those
who could best use it.

IN NOVEMBER 1817, an anonymous Kingstonian observed in a letter
to the *Kingston Gazette* that though Bible, missionary and tract societies were successfully addressing "the moral state of man" and the
needs of his soul, there was also a necessity to give "a helping hand
towards the relief of the body." He went on to explain "if reports are
to be credited, numbers of our fellow men lately arrived in these
Provinces are now literally starving, through want of food and shelter." Many new arrivals, he continued, having lost their possessions
in transit or having come to the colony "fully expecting to obtain
maintenance for themselves and their families" were reduced to beg-
ging for bread "for their perishing families." Others were quietly
starving to death. It was time, he wrote, for "the rich and the noble"
who had given "mighty sums towards the support and spread of the
Gospel" to turn their attention to the needs of the poor and the destitute. "Every man" must give "according to his ability" to rescue
"men, women and children, from going down into an untimely
grave." He concluded, "Reader, imagine thyself in the situation of
some of those objects of charity, who have come into a far country, ex-

pecting to find employment – but who are now without money, without shelter, without Food, without Friends – and thy soul will at once be stirred within thee to give them a helping hand."[86]

In 1817, Upper Canada was in the middle of an economic depression that would persist until the early 1820s. At the same time, thousands of immigrants were arriving annually, seeking land, employment, and improved opportunities for themselves and their children. While colonial leaders welcomed the arrival of new settlers, beggars were beginning to appear on the streets and at the doors of the big houses; crime was escalating, and the promise of peace and prosperity, so painfully won in 1815, seemed threatened. The plight of the poor was heart-rending to many women and men. Colonial leaders also began to fear that if nothing was done to alleviate the problem, the rising discontent would erupt into violence.[87]

The residents of Kingston and York had already begun to take action when the anonymous Kingstonian made his heartfelt plea. In October 1817, the members of the York elite under the patronage of the lieutenant-governor had formed the "Society of Friends to Strangers in Distress."[88] At the beginning of December, prominent Kingstonians had organized the Kingston Compassionate Society.[89] For at least the next decade, members of the Society of Friends, the Kingston Compassionate Society, and other emigrant aid organisations established throughout the colony raised and distributed funds, food, and clothing to the needy. In an attempt "to prevent pauperism" and "to promote industry, economy and sobriety among the lower orders," officers, appointed managers, and visitors also undertook "to assist" bewildered and needy immigrants "to procure employment."[90]

Upper Canadians were initially optimistic that their efforts on behalf of destitute immigrants would alleviate the situation quickly. However, in 1820, although the directors of the Kingston Compassionate Society applauded local residents "on the great benefit and utility of your charitable institutions," the annual report also stated emphatically that the society was seriously short of funds and the relief it had been able to provide was "imperfect."[91] There were still fathers with hearts "broken" and "agonized by the surrounding cries of the famished children." "Upwards of fifty sick persons" had been restored to health, but in the past year, the report stated, "agues and dysenteries and fevers" continued to disable victims and claim lives. The Society of Friends of Strangers in Distress in York was having similar problems. In December 1820, the treasurer reported that he had had to beg for old clothes to cover children's nakedness.[92]

Leading Upper Canadians redoubled their efforts. In 1826, "the respectable gentlemen of York" under the patronage of Lieutenant-

Governor Maitland, formed a "Society for Promoting Education and Industry in Canada."[93] Following the lead of the parent organization in London, the mandate of the York group was to "supply needy objects" in the vicinity. Surplus funds were to be sent to the parent society in Montreal. Two years later, in recognition that it was not just immigrants who needed help, the Strangers' Friend Society of York was reorganized into the Society for the Relief of the Sick and Destitute. At its initial meeting, with its new patron, Lieutenant-Governor Colborne in attendance, the membership considered establishing a soup kitchen in the old jail. The editor of the *Colonial Advocate* rather sarcastically reported that "after a parley of two hours, the good sense of the meeting" rejected the proposition, for it was argued, "such a standing rendezvous for indiscriminate pauperism" would not obtain the support of local citizens. [94] After further consideration, a soup kitchen was opened and, despite periodic protest that it encouraged riots and raised the price of goods in the market,[95] for the next ten years, the society provided hot meals to paupers, the indigent, and the dispossessed.

The Kingston Compassionate Society, the Society of Friends in York, and other aid organizations were established and run by local magistrates, government officials, and various prominent men. It was, after all, their responsibility to ensure public safety and security. But from the beginning, colonial leaders were actively and ably supported by their wives and daughters.

A number of prominent women made a point of donating funds to various societies in their own name. They also gathered food and clothing to help "to relieve the distresses of destitute emigrants and others" in their region.[96] In delicate situations, some women were called on actually to distribute the assistance required. In December 1817, for example, Eliza Powell "served as an intermediary" between the managers of the Society of Friends and a young Mrs Irvine who "had just delivered of twins."[97] A year later Eliza's mother, Anne, was "particularly kind to two Scottish families who had fallen on hard times." At the request of the society, she "judiciously expended" a small amount of money for their benefit and continued to oversee their welfare on the society's behalf.[98] In 1828, at the same time that Lieutenant-Governor Maitland helped to start the Society for Promoting Education and Industry in Canada, Lady Maitland and other prominent women organized a separate ladies' society. All "the Ladies of the Members of His Majesty's Executive and Legislative Councils, and the Lady of the Speaker of the House" were deemed "honourary members." In addition to supplying "needy objects," the York Ladies' Society also proposed to open "A Depository of Clothing and Manufactured Articles" which could either be sold to raise money or distributed to the poor.[99]

In the 1820s, prominent women in Upper Canada also began to expand their philanthropic efforts into areas that were of particular concern to them, as wives and mothers. In 1820, Lady Maitland led women residents of York in the formation of the "Society for the Relief of Women during their Confinement." Society matrons solicited funds, clothing, and food from the community for distribution to needy mothers and their newborns. The organization also ensured that the destitute women in their care had the services of a "midwife and physician, if needed."[100] The first annual report of the society, published in November 1821, noted that the actual distribution of aid was carried out by members who had been appointed governesses and visitors. It was women such as Eliza Powell who gave out "comfortable clothing" and "the best nourishment" to destitute women during their confinements. Certain members of the society were also charged with the responsibility of visiting these women frequently "during their illness to see that every thing was as comfortable as the situation of the patients would allow."[101] Prominent women in York were also concerned about the plight of local widows and orphans. Although the Society for the Relief of the Orphans, Widows and Fatherless caused by the Cholera of 1832 was initiated by Archdeacon John Strachan, Anne Powell, Mrs Boulton, and the wives of other affluent citizens gave liberally to the cause.[102] It is likely that in addition to donating money, food, and clothing,[103] many of these women were also directly involved in distributing aid.

While the women of York were occupied with helping destitute mothers, in the fall of 1820, Ann Macaulay, her sister-in-law Anne Kirby, and a number of their friends established the Kingston Benevolent Society.[104] Patterned, it would appear, on a similar organization that had been established a year earlier in Montreal, "the Ladies of Kingston, deeply impressed with the destitute situation of the sick poor and being solicitous to mitigate their suffering ... formed a society for relieving them as far as in their power." Ann Macaulay and Anne Kirby invited local residents to donate money and other goods that would be distributed to the "sick poor" by two lady managers, who would be appointed weekly. The Benevolent Society intended to maintain "a store of clothing and other necessaries."[105] To meet the growing demand for medical services for destitute residents in the area, the society also proposed to open, manage, and supply a local hospital.

Throughout the 1820s, the Female Benevolent Society held its meetings at Mrs Kirby's home. From here, the society's officers and managers organized the distribution of provisions and medicine to needy families and, with the support of local doctors, ran the only charity hospital in the region. The society's limited funds meant that the hospital was closed during the summer and early fall. When, however, the "autumnal fevers and inclement weather" recurred each November,[106] dozens of indigent women, men, and children were admitted to hospital, and were fed, treated by doctors, and nursed by local ladies. In 1825, the managers, who at that time included Ann Macaulay, were, because of financial constraints, obliged to curtail their activities. It was announced that the society would "in future give assistance only to as many sick as can be accommodated in the Hospital."[107] Home visits and the wide distribution of medicines would stop. The Female Benevolent Society ceased to function altogether ten years later when the hospital was destroyed by fire. Its effectiveness had been diminishing for some time, however, because the officers of the society had had increasing problems raising sufficient money and by the mid-1830s, many of the organization's founding members were women who were now well into their sixties and were understandably becoming tired. The society was revived four years later, however, by the efforts of Harriet Dobbs Cartwright and a younger generation of Kingston's prominent women.

As Katherine McKenna has chronicled, Harriet Dobbs Cartwright was firmly committed to both evangelical and philanthropic work. Like a number of other elite women in Upper Canada who shared her firm religious convictions, she considered that helping the less fortunate was not just a social responsibility that emanated from her class and relative wealth; it was also a vital part of her duty to God.[108] Under Harriet's leadership, the work of the Female Benevolent society was significantly expanded. In addition to "working to reestablish the hospital," the women of Kingston began to visit the poor to assess their needs before distributing financial aid or provisions. The society also began a regular program "of distributing raw material to the poor" so that they could make "useful" goods for sale.[109]

Harriet's work with the Female Benevolent Society was only one of a number of philanthropic organizations that she supported. Though a mother of four and wife to a prominent clergyman, Harriet also found time to supervise both a Sunday and a day school, host weekly sewing parties in her home, and hold singing meetings every other week. As wife of one of Kingston's leading citizens and a member of one of its most prominent families, Harriet could not avoid taking part in at least some of the social events of Kingston society. Whenever possible, however, "she sought to minimize her social obligations."[110] She also relied heavily on her sister-in-law Mary (whom Harriet referred

Illustration 14
View of Kingston from her home, by Harriett Dobbs Cartwright
NA (C2753)

to as "Robert's first wife"[111]) to manage her home. This allowed her to
concentrate her energy and time on meeting the needs of her family
and helping others, both materially and spiritually.

Harriet may have devoted somewhat more time than some other
upper-class women to charitable and religious work. Certainly, as an
evangelical Anglican and the wife of a prominent Kingston clergyman, she felt compelled to witness her faith by supporting her husband in his work and spreading the blessings of God. She was not
alone, however. Many of Upper Canada's most prominent women
found the time and the energy to go to countless numbers of meetings, and to canvass their husbands, their friends, and even strangers
for donations to various charities. Some shared Harriet's religious fer-
vour. Others appear to have been fulfilling what were really class and
social responsibilities. Regardless of motivation, however, one of the
most important contributions that elite women made to benevolent
reform in Upper Canada was raising funds.

In 1830, a brief notice in local York newspapers stated that "The
SALE of LADIES WORK FOR THE BENEFIT of the POOR will take place
at the Court House on Thurs, the 13th of May." What came to be
known as Lady Colborne's Bazaar opened a new era in fund raising
in Upper Canada. In the spring of 1830, women from all parts of the

region were encouraged to donate goods for sale, the proceeds from which would be donated to the poor. The organizers of the bazaar also intended to charge admission to the event.[112] The response from middle- and upper-class women was significant. A subsequent report of the 1830 bazaar noted that "the collection of elegant fancy articles furnished by the benevolent ladies of York and its vicinity was large and arranged with much taste."[113] Mary O'Brien and her sister-in-law and neighbours sewed clothes and sent down parcels from Lake Simcoe for the sale. It is likely that Anne Powell and her daughters and granddaughters also donated fancy goods, jewellery, and needlework. Part of the event's success, which raised £209.14,[114] was the influence of Lady Colborne's "very pleasing and interesting manners." Her sponsorship of the bazaar clearly indicated to women in the York region that this was an important social as well as charity event. Her actual presence at the sale, and her ability to promote "the good feelings of the company"[115] undoubtedly prompted those who attended to spend their money liberally.

Lady Colborne's Bazaar became an annual event and affluent women used their prominence and their organizational skills to good effect. Sometimes, two bazaars were held in a year and after each one, organizers were able to report that a substantial amount of money had been raised.[116] The proceeds from the bazaars were at first channelled to the York Lying-in Society. After 1838, the funds were donated to the local House of Industry, which had been established in 1838 under the auspices of the Committee for the Relief of the Poor and Destitute.[117]

Ladies' bazaars were not restricted to York.[118] In the 1820s and 1830s, prominent women throughout the colony used their rank and their substantial organizational skills to convince colonists to support other charity events. Leading Upper Canadians organized and supported benefit concerts and certain theatrical performances.[119] Prominent women and men also continued to lend their names, their money, and their managerial skills to the by now well-established benevolent societies.

Between 1815 and 1840, women in Upper Canada and especially prominent women were increasingly active in trying to better the lot of Upper Canadians who were in desperate need. These women were encouraged and supported in their work by their churches, their class obligations, and their personal convictions. Many upper-class women believed that they had little choice but to become involved. Personal faith, a sense of duty to womanhood, to families, and to class – all of these factors motivated individual women. For as the colony developed and many residents prospered, the incidence of poverty, destitution, and unemployment among immigrants and the lower ranks of society seemed only to increase. Reports from the Female Benevolent Society, the Committee for the Relief of the Poor and the Destitute, and other organizations indicated that more and more families depended on charity to survive. Women and men of the Upper Canadian elite were compelled to respond to such distress. For women such as Lady Colborne, Anne Powell, and Harriet Cartwright, neither their conscience nor their public duty would allow them to do anything less.

BECAUSE WOMEN of privilege were attached to men of property and standing, they enjoyed significant advantages over the vast majority of women in the colony. Not only did they live in a large house but they had considerable disposable income. Moreover, in very real terms, the mistresses of the big houses had more power than most in the colony. They hired and fired employees; they helped dictate social customs and behaviourial norms; and through their husbands, they had some influence on colonial affairs.

Wealth and privilege brought social and religious responsibilities, however. Anne Powell's and Harriet Cartwright's apparent freedom from the drudgery of housework was offset by their duty to uphold and to support the public position of their husbands and families. They also had an obligation to ensure that less fortunate members of their communities were looked after. It is likely that, because of their wealth and influence, elite women exhibited a growing sense of paternalism to the "lower orders." Certainly, Anne Powell, Ann Macaulay, Harriet Dobbs Cartwright and many other prominent wives and mothers believed that they knew best who deserved aid and what recipients needed. Benevolent and religious organizations did create a community of women in Upper Canada; it was a community however, whose membership was self-selective. It was also a community that, by its very formation, accentuated differences between the various social and economic classes.[120]

Yet elite women were also well aware that they could not perform their efforts to reform and do other work in "society" without help. Though at times seemingly isolated from the rest of colonial society by the walls of their spacious homes, wives, mothers, and daughters of influential Upper Canadians were dependent both on their husbands' salaries and the work of their maids, their cooks, their nurses, and their governesses. The elite household was another community of women, one that encompassed women of varying classes, though class differences were never really negated. It was a community, moreover, which regularly reached beyond the walls of the big houses. It touched and was influenced both by the poor and the destitute, and by the work and lives of women who worked for wages in the public world of commerce. School teachers, innkeepers, and "she merchants" made up their own, at times distinct, community of working women. And although this world appeared to challenge the beliefs and prescriptive social norms of many upper-class women, it was one that was both dependent on and catered to the needs and aspirations of elite and lower-class households.

PART IV

Beyond the Bounds of Domesticity: Surrogate Husbands and Independent Business Women

By 1833, the capital of Upper Canada had become a bustling market town. Although many of York's approximately 9,000 residents continued to depend directly on the government for their livelihood, a growing proportion of the local population relied on the retail, manufacturing, or service trades to earn a living. William Ware, for example, sold spirits, wines, and groceries; William Cormack and Co. was a wholesale and dry goods firm. When Anna Jameson arrived in York in 1836, she could purchase supplies at Donald Ross's retail shop on King St. If she did not want to go to the Market House for fresh produce, she could go to Holmes and Co., which was located on Yonge St. The 1833 *York Directory* included twenty-two such retail and wholesale businesses in the community; it also listed dozens of small specialty shops, numerous inns, taverns, hotels, and many small manufacturing establishments.[1]

Almost hidden among the growing number of retail outlets were Mrs Owen's boarding-house, Mrs Bell's candle and soap factory, and the York Hotel, owned and operated by Mrs Jane Jordan.[2] Though many women were probably aware that Mrs Claris' millinery and dressmaking shop had a new supply of the "latest fashions" in August 1833,[3] probably only a few frequented Mrs Shaw's millinery business, which she ran out of her home. Despite the diminutive size of their businesses, these, and many other women were a vital part of the local economy. Like many of their male neighbours, they provided goods and services that residents of this government town needed.

Illustration 15
The market in York, 1831, by Stanley Francis Turner
MTL (T31828)

The eclectic commercial scene that was characteristic of York in the 1830s was also apparent in other colonial towns and villages. Small communities such as Cobourg, Picton, and Peterborough supported a butcher, a baker, and a candlestick maker, as well as a number of general stores. An increasing number of towns and villages, including, of course, Kingston and Niagara, also had at least one millinery and mantuamaking shop and a school for young ladies. And it was not unusual for one of the local boarding-houses, inns, and hotels to be owned by a woman.

In the pre-industrial economy of Upper Canada, women were frequently involved in the marketplace. Although women were "by definition basically domestic,"[4] this did not preclude them from assuming economic as well as familial responsibilities. Many colonial wives were, by necessity, actively involved in the economic affairs of their husbands.[5] Just as Mary O'Brien, Fanny Hutton, Susanna Moodie, and other farm wives helped their husbands plant and harvest, urban women too assisted their husbands in their shops and at their crafts. As was the custom in Europe in the eighteenth century, some artisans' wives "prepared or finished material on which [their] husbands worked."[6] Others cooked and served guests of family inns. When their husbands were ill or away, wives became their "representatives" and even their "surrogates." As Laurel Ulrich has noted, "female responsibility ... was ... very broad ... the role of housewife and the role of deputy husband were two sides of the same coin."[7]

For many women, working beside and with their husbands, fathers, or brothers was not always enough to sustain the family, however. Particularly in Upper Canada's towns and villages, families were units of consumption as well as of production and the family economy was a wage economy.[8] Households depended increasingly on cash to buy goods and services that they did not or could not produce themselves. Women together with the children were often obliged to find waged work to supplement the family income.

In the premodern world, "any task was suitable" for a woman "as long as it furthered the good of the family" and if she was married, it "was accepted by her husband."[9] A woman's opportunity to earn a wage in Upper Canada was determined by a number of factors, including her age, her marital status, her skills, and her available capital. Women were also restricted in their choice of work by where they lived. (Only in urban areas was there sufficient custom actually to set up a dress shop or open a girls' school.) Wage-earning women were also influenced by colonial assumptions about what type of work was appropriate for persons of their sex. Women were not admitted to most crafts. Married women could not own property; legally, they could not hire employees.

As in rural areas, "domestic service was probably the most common waged employment" open to women living in town.[10] To meet the vagaries of seasonal unemployment or those fluctuations in market demand that inevitably affected the income of the family business, married women often sewed, took in washing, became a char, took in a few lodgers, or marketed other "homemaking" skills on a part-time basis.[11] Usually considered unskilled labourers, such women received minuscule wages for their work and coped with often appalling working conditions. Yet a wife's ability to earn even a little money was indispensable to ensuring an adequate family wage.[12]

Though domestic service was the most prevalent type of women's waged work, it was by no means the only one. Many widows who were left "solely responsible for maintaining the family" tried to continue with the family business. With the help of their children, they managed family farms, village stores, or their late husbands' craft shops. In some and perhaps most instances, the death of a husband meant "the destruction of the family economy," however. A number of widows were forced into service; others opened their homes to boarders. After 1820, a growing number of widowed women entered, or often re-entered, one of the "female trades."[13]

Particularly in the second generation of colonial development, a number of women – widowed, single, and married – opened schools for girls, dress-shops, and millinery and mantuamaking establishments. Some of these women were recent immigrants who had come to Upper Canada to take advantage of expanding business opportunities and perhaps to escape some of the social and economic strictures that were emerging at home.[14] They were well aware that the chatelaine of the big house needed appropriate clothing, and that Upper Canadian mothers wanted proper schooling for their daughters. Either alone or with female relatives or colleagues, such women opened businesses that consciously catered to these demands.

Nevertheless, relatively few women had the financial resources, skills, and personal confidence necessary to embark on what was inevitably a risky enterprise.[15] The majority of Upper Canadian women were not independent merchants, shopkeepers, or craftswomen who sold their skills in the open marketplace; they were wives and mothers whose primary responsibility remained "the well being of ... husband and children."[16] Even so, many urban labouring-class women took part in "the common commerce of life" at some time in their lives.[17]

Evidence of women's varied market activities is, for the most part, available only indirectly. Most women who were homemakers for hire, assistants in their husbands' businesses, or small independent tradeswomen were part of the "hidden economy" of Upper Canada.[18] They relied on their local reputation or on contacts made on the street or at the market to gain work. Many of them were undoubtedly part of an informal economy of barter and exchange. However, a growing number of women did sometimes place notices in local newspapers advertising their business. It is these notices, together with brief references in gentlewomen's diaries and aside comments printed in local newspapers that allow us to begin to piece together the world of wage-earning women in Upper Canada's towns and villages.

8 "Requesting Their Patronage": Milliners, Mantuamakers and Wage-earning Women in Upper Canada

A small notice appeared in May 1808 in the *Upper Canada Gazette*, calling for the creditors and debtors of the late Paul Marion, baker and innkeeper, to present their claims. Jane Marion, widow and sole executor of her husband's estate, returned "her sincere thanks to the public for past favours" and announced that she intended to carry on the family "baking business and keeping a house of entertainment." She requested the good people of York to continue their patronage.[1]

Jane's decision to try to carry on the family business after her husband's death was not particularly unusual. Jane, after all, had undoubtedly been actively involved in the business for some time. While Paul was alive, Jane would have worked as hostess and cook at the inn. In addition to managing her household and caring for their children, she had probably also helped with the baking, coped with customers, and sometimes done the accounts. And when Paul was ill, it was probably Jane who had stood "in his place" and managed the business.[2]

It is likely that most of the time, Jane's effort in support of her husband and family had gone largely unnoticed. As Paul's wife, she would never have received remuneration for her work. She also had had no claim to ownership in the business, other than her one-third dower right. Jane had nonetheless made a significant contribution to the viability of the family enterprise. While working as Paul's assistant, she must also have gained valuable experience running the business, knowledge that she now intended to put to good use as an independent proprietor.

Whether Widow Marion was successful in her endeavour is unknown. In 1808, York was still only a tiny village and the demand for
her services may have been, at best, unreliable. More important, depending on the size of her family and the ages of her children, Jane
may not have had the time or the energy necessary to devote to the
business. Jane Marion probably had little choice but to try, however.
For, throughout the first generation of Upper Canadian development,
the options open to women in Jane Marion's position (apart, of
course, from remarriage) were quite limited. If, on the other hand,
Jane had been widowed twenty years later, she would have had a far
greater range of commercial opportunities.

Depending on their family's economic position and their individual skills, between 1820 and 1840, widowed, single, and even married
women were increasingly involved in the colonial marketplace. Certainly, most women who were engaged in public commerce continued to do so as their husbands' assistants and any proceeds or
financial benefits of their efforts were directed to helping sustain the
family. But there were a number of women who ran local inns, taverns, and hotels apparently on their own. Others opened provision
and grocery shops; many women took in boarders. And as the colony's population grew, a growing number of women with recognized
skills opened millinery,[3] mantuamaking and hat shops. For at least
some women proprietors, their involvement in commerce provided
them with personal independence and the possibility of earning a living. A few women actually became prosperous.

THROUGHOUT THE FIRST half of the nineteenth century, it was taken
for granted in Upper Canada that wives would work in family businesses. A proprietor and his customers expected that women would
help serve customers, perhaps maintain the accounts, and at times
supervise workers. A reference to the "female staff" of a local prison
that appeared in the *Hallowell Free Press* in 1832 would have passed
without comment, for the "staff" were undoubtedly the wives and
daughters of prison guards.[4] Most Upper Canadian proprietors could
not have succeeded without the active assistance of their wives. This
was clearly evident in Upper Canada's burgeoning hospitality industry, which, between 1790 and 1840 was dominated by small, family-
owned, and family-operated enterprises.

The most basic form of accommodation available in Upper Canada
was the family boarding-house. There was always a demand for
lodging,[5] and taking in boarders was a convenient and "natural" way
for colonial families to supplement their income. Without any significant capital expense, a family could expand its household as their fi-

nancial needs required. In most circumstances, living arrangements were informal. The newly arrived immigrant looking for work or a single artisan or labourer unable to afford his or her own home became a member of the household. She or he joined the family for meals and perhaps shared a room with a daughter or son. Having extra adults in residence undoubtedly strained the physical limits of the home. It also meant that the family's privacy was compromised. However, adding one or two adults to the family brought in scarce and often much needed hard currency.

Most boarding-houses in Upper Canada were limited domestic businesses that did not advertise publicly, no doubt because placing a notice in a local newspaper was relatively expensive. Moreover, as late as 1840, Upper Canadian towns and villages were still small enough that proprietors had only to make it known that they had space for a lodger and their local reputation or the demand for accommodation was sufficient to gain custom. It would have been "common" knowledge, for example, that Mrs Parsons, whose house was mentioned in the report of the fire in Kingston in 1833, or Mrs Oliver, whose tenant Dr Turner of York advertised in the local paper, took in boarders.[6] It is therefore interesting that in the 1820s and 1830s, a few Upper Canadian households nonetheless chose to advertise their boarding facilities formally.[7]

In 1833, for example, "a respectable private English family" in York offered "Board and Lodging for Gentlemen."[8] Another "small respectable family" was willing to board two or three "ladies" in "one of the best and most agreeable situated Houses in Town."[9] Five years later, "A LADY and GENTLEMAN without family" tried to take advantage of their proximity to the new boys' school in York, Upper Canada College. They offered to take "two or three Boys as Boarders" and assured parents that their children "would find this a comfortable home for them."[10] Two years later, this anonymous couple was looking for "two or three Gentlemen as Boarders." Failing this "they would be glad to receive the same number of Boys who are attending College to whose comfort every attention would be given."[11]

A number of advertisements were placed by women, at least some of whom were widows. Mrs Fitzgibbons of Niagara, for example, offered in 1829 "convenient lodging in a refined part of town" for gentlemen of "refined habits."[12] Mrs Handy of Toronto was willing in 1834 to "give good accommodation to 6 Genteel Boarders" for a period "up to the 1st of May 1835."[13] Mrs Fitzgibbons, Mrs Handy, and a few other women were emphatic that they were looking for clients who were "genteel" and of "retired habits."[14] For presumably gentle or at least respectable women, opening their homes to boarders was a socially acceptable way to earn a living.[15] It enabled them to remain in their homes and use their "innate" womanly talents to gain a small income.

The boarding-houses advertised in local newspapers were probably not representative of most of these businesses. By stating their preferences so specifically, such households were obviously trying to exercise some control over whom they would accept into their homes. They were also trying, to some degree, to formalize the enterprise. The tenor and specificity of the notices also suggest that not only was the accommodation being offered superior to the norm, but the proprietors considered themselves a better class than most boarding-house keepers. Indeed, one is left with the impression that although they were willing and perhaps eager to accept payment from clients, if no suitable person came forward, such households could afford not to take in any lodgers. There seems little question, however, that like labouring families and widowed women who eked out a living by taking in lodgers, these families were in business.[16] Not only were they consciously trying to cater to the demands of the local marketplace, but they too wanted and probably needed, the extra income.[17] Most often, the extra income came at the expense of the boarding-house keeper's wife. The same was true in those households which offered accomodation on a short-term, rather more formal basis.

In the earliest years of settlement, everyone's home "served as an inn."[18] And for the next fifty years, European travellers frequently reported that most taverns and inns in Upper Canada were "a burlesque upon what they profess to be."[19] John Howison complained as late as 1821 that not only was the accommodation inferior, but "a tolerable meal can scarcely be procured at any one of them."[20] As the number of Upper Canadians and tourists looking for temporary accommodation increased, local regulations were instituted that made it necessary for taverns to be licensed to sell alcoholic beverages. Tavern-owners and innkeepers were also expected to provide "wholesome provisions and Drink" as well as "clean beds for their guests."[21]

After the War of 1812, travellers did begin to report an increase in the number of "tolerable accommodations" run by "good families" who provided, in even the barest of abodes, "a delectable repast."[22] In some of Upper Canada's larger communities, proprietors began building taverns, inns, and hotels that were specially designed to accommodate guests. In 1821, John Howison toured a hotel near Cornwall that had a large upper room fifty feet long. "The apartment was a ball room," he was informed, "and as it occupied the whole upper floor, [the hotel keeper] had made his bedchamber in his house." Howison concluded that "to have a ball room ... seems to be the height of every publican's ambition in Upper Canada," to the point that "convenience, comfort and symmetry" were sacrificed.[23] In small inns and taverns, however, travellers and patrons continued to report having to share the family table. In many cases they also had to sleep on the floor or share a bed.[24]

Keeping even a small colonial inn required considerable work, most of which seems to have fallen on the proprietor's wife. As traveller Isaac Weld commented in 1797, "the wife is generally the active person in managing the tavern, and the husband attends to his farm or has some other independent occupation."[25] The innkeeper's wife, perhaps with the help of her daughters or a maid-servant, cooked and waited on an indeterminate number of guests. It was the wife who was responsible for keeping the premises clean, washing the bedding, and attending to the daily chores of the household. As hostess, it was the wife who usually greeted visitors and clients on their arrival and had to cope with customer complaints. And travellers did not hesitate to complain about the quality of service they received.

John Howison recounted that "it is immaterial what meal the traveller calls for, as the same articles will be set before him morning, noon and night." In some places, a customer was "not even provided with bread." As to service, Howison continued, "none of the minor public houses are provided with servants to attend travellers who put up at them and therefore, when the landlord is absent or in an *independent* humour, one is obliged to unsaddle, feed and take charge of his own horse ... for the women disdain to do anything of this kind."[26] However, most innkeepers' wives would have had little time to pass "pleasantries" with the guests or the energy to take on extra work. It was difficult enough to meet the demands of their own families, to serve meals and drink to customers, and maintain the standard of domestic order needed to receive guests. Mrs Davis, who in the late 1820s ran the Amherst Hotel in Cobourg while her husband, a tailor, worked in his own shop, would have been hard-pressed to find time to stable a customer's horse.[27]

Not all innkeepers' wives were so directly occupied with domestic work. The wife of the owner of Walker's Hotel in Kingston, the Mansion House in York, Howard's Hotel in Niagara, or any other large urban establishment was probably more a hostess and manager than a domestic worker. Certainly in the 1820s and 1830s, a number of inns and hotels in Upper Canada hired cooks, kitchen maids, general servants and washerwomen to perform much of the menial work.[28] This was also true of some of Upper Canada's most prestigious boarding-houses, which in the 1830s, rivalled large hotels in size and in the type of accommodation they provided.

In 1833, Mr and Mrs Morgan opened a "FAMILY BOARDING-HOUSE" at No. 96 Bishop's Building, Newgate St., York, in the "immediate vicinity of the Government House, Public Offices and Upper Canada College."[29] That same year, Mr and Mrs Grieg purchased "Richmond House" and patrons were offered "refined" surroundings and almost palatial accommodation. Individuals could rent a private room; families could obtain separate quarters which included their own sitting room.[30]

The establishments maintained by the Morgans and the Griegs and Mr and Mrs Baynon who ran a similar boarding-house in Kingston in the 1830s[31] were clearly specialized businesses that were trying to cater to the needs of the best families in the colony. In 1836, John Macaulay may well have boarded at one of the York houses while his wife Helen was overseas. He and his family stayed briefly in a local hotel before moving into their new home in November 1837. Such establishments offered their tenants all the amenities of home, including their personal privacy. Certainly, the Griegs only accepted clients who could produce suitable references. Moreover, guests were required to pay for accommodation in advance, by the week, the month, or the year.[32]

The fact that advertisements clearly stated that the businesses were owned and run by both the husband and his wife suggests that Mrs Morgan, Mrs Grieg and Mrs Baynon were recognized as making important contributions to the enterprises. In addition to ensuring that their guests were content, these wives would have been responsible, at least partly, for hiring domestic staff and overseeing their work. It must also be remembered, that such boarding-houses, like most inns and taverns in the colony, were family businesses.[33] The essential work performed by keepers' wives was obviously supplemented by the efforts of their husbands, who not only owned the businesses, but probably coped with the accounts and looked after the upkeep of the premises. Children too would have helped as they were able, since the viability of such businesses depended up on the combined efforts of all members of the family.

Thus, when one of the couple became ill to the point of being incapacitated or died, the surviving spouse was often hard pressed to continue the business alone. It was not unusual for a widowed proprietor, whether a husband or a wife, to remarry quickly in order to secure assistance in the family business. Some proprietors hired waged workers to perform some of the work, while widowed women often appear to have relied on their children or other family members for assistance.

Laurel Ulrich has observed that "few women" in premodern America "were prepared either by education or by experience to become 'independent women of affairs'."[34] It is clear that in Upper Canada a number of widowed and single women did try, however, and given their central role in maintaining inns, taverns, and boarding-houses, this is not surprising. For some women, the hospitality industry in Upper Canada offered a limited degree of financial security. A few widows even became prosperous. For many, perhaps most, however, running an inn or boarding-house was a difficult and risky business and provided only a precarious existence.[35]

IN 1828, Mrs Scantlebury informed residents of Kingston that despite her husband's death, she would continue to run the Commercial Hotel.[36] Four years later, Mrs Elizabeth Bell informed York patrons that she intended to carry on the business of her late husband and "keep the Inn … open … as usual."[37] Within a few months of their husbands' deaths, however, the two hotels had been sold.[38] We can only speculate as to the reason for this. Both the Half Moon Inn and the Commercial Hotel appear to have been extensive operations, offering accommodation, "the best provisions … the best of Liquors, Wine and Beer" and full stabling for horses.[39] Both Mrs Bell and Mrs Scantlebury must also have been familiar with the business that they took on. They probably had at least some helpers to assist them with the work. But one wonders if their previous responsibilities as innkeepers' wives had included such tasks as ordering supplies, bargaining with customers, and coping with legal affairs. As Mrs Post of Pickering explicitly pointed out when she gave up her tavern in 1832, the hotel business usually required the active participation of both a wife and her husband. When Mrs Post's son also died, she was "under the necessity of discontinuing her tavern."[40]

Such disappointments did not seem to deter other women from continuing or entering into the hospitality industry. Although she had lost the income from her husband's tailoring business, Mrs Davis of Cobourg was determined in 1831 "to carry on the tavern as usual."[41] Sarah Moore of Kingston, Elizabeth Reid of the Gore District, and Jane Marion of York also announced their intention of carrying on as usual.[42] They were joined by an indeterminate number of women, mostly widows, it seems, who started a new hotel or inn.[43]

The number of women who owned and operated boarding-houses, taverns, inns, or hotels in Upper Canada in their own right is difficult to discern. Women proprietors were undoubtedly outnumbered by men.[44] Though a few women advertised their establishments in the local newspapers, most did not.[45] Neither, it should be noted, did male proprietors. Like boarding-house keepers, most women inn-keepers did not find it necessary to advertise. For many, the location of their inn and their reputation assured them of custom. Unlike operating a boarding-house, however, running an inn or tavern thrust women proprietors into the "public" world. Upper Canadian inns and taverns were usually local landmarks, community centres, and public meeting places, and women keepers of such establishments were therefore at the centre of much of the day-to-day activity in their communities. Many innkeepers allowed and appear to have encouraged their patrons to run businesses from their rooms or from the inn's public areas.[46] In addition, colonial inns often housed local courts, salesrooms, and theatres. Mrs Petrie's inn in Barriefield, for example, was the site of the special session of the Township of Pittsburgh in 1831.[47] Public auctions to sell Crown land were held at the Widow Pierce's Inn in Maria in 1833, and at Mrs Hill's tavern in Richmond in 1835.[48] Mrs Roger's hotel in Niagara frequently hosted auctions and meetings of the local gentry.[49] These women proprietors were women of affairs. Even had they wished it, it would have been next to impossible for them to retreat into the limited privacy that boarding-house keepers enjoyed.

It is unclear whether most widows who owned inns, taverns, or hotels in Upper Canada managed to succeed in the business. There were certainly a few women who managed to sustain their enterprises for a number of years. Mrs Patrick's inn in Kingston, for example, was viable throughout the late teens and well into the 1820s and was highly recommended to travellers.[50] One of the most successful hotel-keepers in the colonial capital in the postwar years was the widow Jane Jordan.

Jane Jordan's career as a hotel-keeper began with the death of her husband. In 1821, within a month of being widowed, Mrs Jordan repaired and enlarged the family hotel.[51] The York Hotel, which was sometimes referred to as Mrs Jordan's Hotel, subsequently became a local landmark and for the next nine years it was a regular place of business for travelling salespeople.[52] Jane Jordan sold the hotel to John Martin in July 1829.[53] A year later, however, she published the following notice in the Colonial Advocate: "To TRAVELLERS and others – The subscriber respectfully begs leave to inform her numerous friends and the public in general that she has again opened a TAVERN in that old established house owned, formally occupied by herself and known by the name YORK HOTEL where she is constantly supplied with Liquors, Wines etc of the first quality. Gentlemen from the country will find it to their advantage to put up at this hotel, the

Illustration 16
York Hotel, 1804, later known as Jane Jordan's Hotel, from lithograph by
Stanley Francis Turner
MTL (T11034)

charges being moderate and the accommodation not excelled in York.
Being in a retired part of the Town, it is admirably suited to those resident gentlemen, who would prefer a House of Entertainment, secure
from the noise and bustle usually attendant on the more frequented
part of the city."[54] For the next ten years, Mrs Jordan took in boarders
and provided meals and entertainment to travellers and residents of
York. Then in April 1840, she offered to let her "LARGE, SPACIOUS
and COMMODIOUS HOUSE" and apparently retired.[55]

There may have been a few other women who managed not only to
sustain themselves economically by running an inn or hotel but who
were able to gain some degree of financial security.[56] The relatively
rapid growth of the colony in the postwar years and the increased
commercial activity, especially in such centres as York, Kingston, and
Niagara, provided new opportunities for both families and widowed
women to earn their living catering to the needs of travellers. The

thousands of immigrants who joined labourers, students, and business people in colonial towns all had to be housed and fed. At the most basic level, all that was required of women willing to engage in housekeeping for hire was to provide an extra bed and meals. Those with capital could aspire to much grander establishments.

For most widowed women, it may have been difficult to grasp these new economic opportunities.[57] "Deprived of a husband's assistance," a number of women were forced to abandon the family inn or hotel. Many discovered that remarriage was "the happiest solution to the threat of insecurity." Others tried to find "new kinds of work."[58] Advertisements in local newspapers and brief references in news stories do indicate that women in Upper Canada did engage in a wide variety of business activities, however. Some were farmers. Mrs Field of Niagara ran a candle and soap factory in the 1820s.[59] Nancy Robert ran a brick factory in Hallowell.[60] In 1831, Mrs MacPhail of York announced "to her friends and the public that having employed a competent person she would carry on the business of her late husband, *Bookbinding*."[61] There were a number of women who ran small shops or dry goods stores or combined their provision shops with a boarding-house.[62] Jane McLeod of Kingston may well have had to compete with Mrs Tolkien, whose "DRY GOODS SHOP" was damaged by fire in 1833, or with Mary Ann Reid, a forty-year-old spinster shopkeeper.[63] In the mid-1820s, Mary Miller ran a general store in Niagara. This may have been the same Mary Miller who, in a notice looking for her parents in 1833, called herself a druggist.[64]

It is likely that the majority of these women proprietors were widows.[65] Many may have been trying to maintain the family business until their sons were old enough to take over. In 1833, Mary Barker and David Stevenson ran an advertisement in the *Hallowell Free Press* for their dry goods store. A new notice a month later announced that David Barker, probably Mary's son, would continue the business on his own.[66] But in a few instances, it is clear that a woman owned and operated the business in her own right. Although Rafaela Gabiott was obviously not a skilled chairmaker, in 1835 she nonetheless purchased "the Chair Factory and Paint Shop of Patrick Stedman" in Niagara and "employed Mr Joseph [Pencott] to superintend the business."[67]

There is no question, however, that in Upper Canada in the first half of the nineteenth century, male innkeepers, shopkeepers, and proprietors far outnumbered those who were female. The one enterprise that a growing number of women could and did engage in with some expectation of success was catering to the fashion needs of other women. As the colony matured, working for wages as a dressmaker, milliner, or mantuamaker offered at least some skilled women the opportunity for personal satisfaction and a potentially lucrative career.

REGARDLESS OF CLASS or location, all women in Upper Canada were expected to be able to sew. Needlework was one of the domestic arts that was both a symbol of true womanhood and an absolutely essential skill for all wives and mothers. Sewing was one of the first things a mother taught her daughter. For some women in Upper Canada, making and repairing clothes or doing fancy needlework was also more than a domestic occupation; it was a marketable asset. For example, the Huttons of Belleville sewed and knitted in exchange for goods and services, and they were not alone. Between 1790 and 1840, married, single, and widowed women frequently supplemented their families' incomes or earned their living making and mending clothes for clients, neighbours, and friends.[68]

Advertisements in local newspapers suggest that in the first twenty years of colonial development, the work available to seamstresses was relatively limited. Although a few women found work sewing, most Upper Canadians could not afford to have their clothes made. And those upper-class women who did need to dress well often had clothes sent from Montreal or New York. The first specialized "mantuamaking business in all its branches" in Upper Canada was opened in York in 1808 by Maria de Dieman.[69] Although Frances Murray opened a second millinery and mantuamaking shop in the capital two years later, it was not until after the War of 1812 that the demand for ladies' clothes had grown sufficiently to support a local fashion industry, and dressmaking and millinery came to be "recognized and respectable crafts."[70]

Between 1817 and 1840, millinery, mantuamaking, dress, and hat shops were opened in most towns and villages throughout the colony. Until about 1820, milliners were, not surprisingly, located in Upper Canada's principal commercial centres. After 1817, the ladies of Kingston could buy their clothes from Mrs Lambie's, who sold imported goods from Mr Barnett's store, at Miss Read's who had brought in "the most fashionable spring articles" from Montreal, or at Miss Barker's, who opened a Millinery Store with the "latest summer and fall fashions" in 1818.[71] If Kingston women wanted clothes made-to-measure, and a more personal touch, they could attend on Mrs Kurtshalts, who also sold cloth and other millinery goods.[72] In Niagara, women could shop at Mrs Ritter and Miss Culver's who, in 1818, had ready-made "ladies Caps, Bonnets, etc" for sale and offered to make ladies' gowns "after the most approved fashions."[73] Two years later, Mrs Ferguson opened a millinery business in the community and promised her clients that "every pain will be taken to procure the latest fashions from New York and Montreal."[74] By 1820, Mrs Frances Murray of York was having to compete with Miss Page, who "had on hand an assortment of Hats & Dressed Caps & Ostrich Feathers" and with E. Turquand and M. Carey, who offered millinery, fancy dresses and corset making.[75]

The growth of an indigenous fashion industry in Upper Canada was initially supported by the periodic appearance of a number of itinerant businesswomen from the lower province. In December 1816, a Miss Lewis arrived in Kingston from Montreal with "a large and fashionable assortment of clothes" which she displayed and sold from the upper part of Mr Macdonald's house. Two months later, she was in Fort George, having "come up with the first sleighing" with "a large and fashionable assortment of Merino Cloth, Plessies, Dresses."[76] Miss Lewis may have visited the colony annually. It was not until 1826, however, that she again advertised that she was at "the House of Mr Thom's Wells" in York, with a wide assortment of "fashionable Millinery, Dresses, Pelisses" for sale.[77] A year earlier, Mrs Metzner had joined the ranks of itinerant businesswomen. In a notice in the Kingston *Upper Canada Herald* in June 1825, Mrs Metzner announced that she intended to arrive in the community on the fifteenth or sixteenth of that month with "an extensive and elegant assortment of Millinery and Fancy Goods." Three weeks later, she was in York.[78] Mrs Metzner visited York again in January and later in August 1828. On both occasions, she stayed and sold her goods from Mr Well's cabinet shop.[79]

Mrs Metzner and Miss Lewis obviously found that for a time, at least, business in the upper province warranted their attention. But as more and more milliners and dressmakers located permanently in the colony, the trade of the travelling saleswomen correspondingly diminished. For though they did not have the capital or overhead costs of those who maintained permanent shops, these rather high-class peddlers could not offer the variety of clothes, the specialized services, and the personal attention that women consumers could obtain from local milliners. Itinerant saleswomen could also probably not match Kingston, Niagara, or York prices. After 1830, only a few travelling saleswomen made brief appearances in Kingston.[80]

By then, the colonial fashion industry had become highly competitive. York, Kingston, and Niagara each had a number of specialty shops that sold ladies' hats, dresses, and millinery goods. Most small towns and villages had at least one ladies' clothes shop and a number of women who encouraged customers to come to their homes for fittings and with mending.[81] As more and more skilled craftswomen opened small businesses, the colonial clothing industry also became increasingly specialized.

In the 1820s and 1830s, most women merchants advertised themselves as milliners and dressmakers, or mantuamakers.[82] This meant that they made and sold women's clothing; some probably also sold fabric, thread, and other dressmaking supplies. As the market expanded, a growing number of milliners also stocked and sold ready-made ladies' clothing. Miss Cochrane of York, for example, not only promised "strict attention to Fashion and Taste" but noted that she was "regularly supplied with the NEWEST FASHIONS."[83] As competition increased, a few imported dresses from Montreal and New York. Others, like Mrs Claris also of York, claimed that they were in regular contact with fashion developments in London, Paris, New York, Montreal, or Quebec.[84] Proprietors also used other means to distinguish themselves from their competitors. In addition to having an assortment of millinery goods in stock, Mrs Phillips of Kingston offered in 1834, for example, to make clothes to measure and to embroider children's dresses.[85] To encourage potential customers, a few general milliners sold lace or fans; Mrs Fern of Kingston carried ladies' and children's boots, in addition to her regular supply of ready-made dresses.[86] There were also a few milliners and dressmakers who kept ladies' hats and bonnets in stock or who offered to make them for their clients.[87]

Making, cleaning, or supplying hats, bonnets, and caps was usually a distinct craft, however; and this was reflected in the growing number of shops that sold exclusively hats that were opened in Upper Canada after 1820.[88] Like many general milliners, bonnetmakers were quite competitive. Mrs Connell, for example, sold or cleaned "Fur, Tippets and Boas."[89] In addition to having in stock "Ladies Hats and Bonnets of all Kinds," in 1827 Miss Shelton informed the residents of Ancaster that she expected to receive "a General Assortment of Laces, Veils, Combs, Reticules fans and Bonnets" from Montreal and Rochester. Moreover, for those not wanting to buy a new hat, Miss Shelton offered to turn, whiten and press hats and bonnets as required.[90] In the 1830s, ladies in York could buy hats at Mrs Davidson's.

A small but highly specialized segment of the colonial clothing trade made or supplied stays. It is likely that a number of the larger millinery and dressmaking shops in Upper Canada sold women's foundation garments. Only two proprietors, Mrs Cooper of Cobourg and E. Turquand specifically advertised that they had them in stock or could make them.[91] In 1831, however, Miss Jane McBradney opened a business exclusively for making stays-to-measure for women in

"Brockville and the vicinity."[92] Seven years later, Mrs Steed of York announced that she was "prepared to serve [the ladies] with English, French and Habit Stays, and sitting up stays on the shortest notice."[93]

The growing diversity in the fashion industry of Upper Canada was, in part, a result of the economic development of the colony. It was also a reflection of the increasing consumer demand by colonial women for the latest fashions. Although a number of elite women continued to take periodic trips to Montreal, Quebec, and New York to visit friends and to shop, they undoubtedly also began to patronize local businesses. This was not only more convenient, but by 1840, it is likely that the quality of merchandise was relatively high and the selection improving. Yet, it was not just the most prominent women in Kingston, Niagara and York who needed or wanted to dress well. The number of specialty clothing shops in Upper Canada suggests that the wives of small businessmen, local artisans, shopkeepers, and even farmers could both afford and preferred to have at least some of their clothes made for them.

THE WOMEN who provided such goods and services were a diverse lot. Being a skilled dressmaker, mantuamaker or hatmaker was a respected and accepted way for any woman to earn some cash. For women with skills, some capital, and the personal confidence to enter the public marketplace, owning and operating a women's specialty shop could be a lucrative and satisfying career. Dressmaking was also a craft that a woman could continue to pursue after she married, working either part or full time as the demands of child care and her other domestic responsibilities allowed. Many seamstresses in Upper Canada worked from their homes; others shared premises with their husbands. And there were a few married milliners who opened businesses quite independently of their husbands.[94] This was obviously often more convenient for many women than working as an assistant in their husbands' shops. For many families, it was probably also more lucrative and a better use of a woman's training and skills.

While her husband built cabinets in his shop, Mrs Fox of Brockville began to sew "at her home" in 1830.[95] Four years later, Mrs Watson of York advertised herself as a dressmaker; her husband was a local stone mason.[96] Mrs Caffry, of Brockville made and sold inexpensive silk, straw, and leghorn bonnets while her husband painted signs.[97] Mrs Willard was a Belleville milliner; her husband was a watchmaker.[98] Quite frequently, the wife and husband's waged work was complementary. Though Mrs Fowler, a milliner and dressmaker in Kingston in 1831, had her own shop, she probably relied on her husband's contacts as a cloth merchant to obtain supplies and customers.[99]

Often the couple's crafts were directly related and wife and husband shared work space. Mrs Isaac Robinson of York made hats and bonnets from her husband's tailoring shop.[100] Mrs Parsons made and sold dresses from her husband's tailoring shop in the capital.[101] In such instances, the husband and wife may well have helped each other in their respective work.[102] Mrs and Mr Robinson probably also shared client families. While Mrs Robinson took orders from colonial women for new bonnets, her tailor husband could be making jackets and trousers for the "gentlemen." Sharing workspace and working in related crafts in no way implied that a wife's business was necessarily less important or remunerative than her husband's work. Mrs Robinson's business survived for at least five years; by 1840, she had sufficient capital or credit to begin to import "a large assortment of straw and tuscan bonnets of the latest fashions."[103] Mrs Morse, a dressmaker in Brockville who shared a shop with her tailor husband, had enough business in May 1833, to need "a hand" so that she would "be able to give general satisfaction to all those who will favour her with their custom."[104]

For a few married women, their work was in fact a career. Mrs Robinson and Mrs Morse may well have had hired help to do their domestic work so they could devote more time to their businesses. Some milliners and dressmakers maintained their own shops;[105] they must often have had to pass on at least some of their housekeeping duties to other women. When Mrs Claris opened her millinery shop in York in 1832, she probably had someone doing her housework.

Like many other milliners, Mrs Claris began her dressmaking career working out of her home. At the end of 1832 she had sufficient capital and credit and a large enough clientele to open her own shop. Her notice to the "good Ladies" of York stated that she intended to keep "an elegant and fashionable MILLINERY, CLOAKS etc," in stock. She was also looking for a knowledgeable young woman to be her assistant and to be trained in the business.[106] A year later, Mrs Claris moved to new premises, apparently as a result of "the desire of most of the Ladies of York." At that time, she announced that she had on hand a new supply of fancy goods and had engaged two milliners from London and an embroiderer from Paris, who were expected to arrive before the autumn.[107]

By the end of that year, however, Mrs Claris' business had collapsed, as had her husband's wholesale and retail establishment, "London House."[108] In December 1833, John Claris and his associate, John Moule, announced the dissolution of their partnership.[109] A notice that appeared a month later indicated that Mrs Claris had died and that John Claris and John Moule had been forced to declare bankruptcy. In the ensuing legal proceedings, Mrs Claris' assets, her shop, and all its stock, together with that of her husband's former business were auctioned off to pay creditors.[110]

Whether Mrs Claris' death precipitated the end of her own business as well as the financial ruin of her husband is unknown. Mrs Claris and/or her husband and his partner had obviously overextended themselves financially. Yet it seems that for the last year of her life, Mrs Claris may have headed a flourishing and perhaps expanding business. Her repeated calls for apprentices and the hiring of professional, skilled assistants suggest that she had quite a large and probably well-heeled clientele.[111] Her shop must have been large enough to provide workspace for the staff, to house her stock, and to serve clients. Although in law, the assets and liabilities of the millinery shop belonged to her husband, the residents of York must have thought of the establishment as Mrs Claris' millinery and dressmaking business.

Mrs Claris was not the only married woman to establish what was, for all intents and purposes, a business independent of her husband. But she-merchants in Upper Canada did work under definite legal restrictions. Unless Mrs and Mr Claris had worked out a marital property agreement, Mrs Claris' shop, its contents, and its profits all belonged to John. The same was true for Mrs Robinson; in the 1833 *York Directory,* her bonnet business is not even acknowledged. The business registry listed J. Robinson (Mrs Robinson's husband) as "tailor & Straw-hat-manufacturer."[112] Usually only single and widowed "women of affairs" could and did have legal title to their own enterprise.

In the 1820s and 1830s, a growing number of independent milliners and dressmakers established careers and, in some cases, lucrative businesses catering to the demands of middle- and upper-class women. Some of these women appear to have been young, single girls who considered sewing a more attractive way to earn a living than going into domestic service. More and more of these women were skilled and mature craftspeople, however, who came to the colony, in part at least, in order to pursue a career.

IN 1828, Mrs Jones and Miss Rose Anne Osbourne arrived in Upper Canada from Quebec for the express purpose of establishing a "Millinery, Bonnet and Dressmaking" shop in York.[113] They brought with them their skills, their experience, and it appears, sufficient funds to buy or rent premises, purchase supplies, and generally establish the business. Over the next ten years, at least six other milliners or bonnetmakers relocated from Montreal or Quebec to various centres in

Upper Canada, including the Misses McCord and Miss Stillman. During the same period, over a dozen women who were "recently arrived from the old country" set up dressmaking and bonnetmaking businesses in the colony.[114]

Many of these women, such as staymaker Jane McBradney, had "served a regular apprenticeship" in their craft or had received some training in their business. Some, like Jane Arnold of Brockville, were "experienced" seamstresses and may have owned or worked in a shop before they emigrated.[115] Although a few women arrived in the colony with sufficient capital to open shops and cover their initial expenses, most began their careers in Upper Canada working from their homes or a room in a boarding-house.[116] Yet even working from one's home required some capital. Supplies had to be purchased and advertisements paid for. Married women who were able to share their husbands' shops and could perhaps rely on their husbands' wages had a significant advantage over those who had to work alone. Miss Wilson of Kingston and others were obliged to work at home for some time before they had saved enough money to open a shop.

Some women attempted to resolve this financial problem by combining their resources. A mother and daughters or two sisters frequently opened a shop together and shared expenses and labour. In 1826, for example, the Misses S. and R. Parsons "commenced the millinery business in Niagara," providing the newest fashions and repairing leghorns and bonnets. The Misses S. and J. Ross and the Misses M. and P. Warren each established a business in Brockville.[117] It was also not unusual for two apparently unrelated women to form a partnership. In March 1825, Mary L. Stroughton and Phoebe A. Dayton opened a millinery and manutamaking shop in Kingston at "the old stand of Miss Dayton's."[118] Partnerships involving family members appear to have survived for some time (perhaps until one of the two was married). Some of the non-familial associations were more difficult to maintain. The Stroughton-Dayton partnership only survived two weeks after which Miss Dayton resumed business on her own.[119] In 1834, the partnership of Mrs Laing and Miss Langley in York was abruptly terminated with Miss Langley's death at the age of eighteen, only a few months after the two first joined forces.[120]

Whether many businesses suffered the fate of the Stroughton-Dayton partnership is unknown. Indeed, it is impossible to determine what percentage of all millinery businesses were financially viable. The appearance or disappearance of advertisements in local newspapers is not a reliable guide. As was the case with innkeepers and hotel-owners, milliners, dressmakers, and others involved in the fashion industry did not always or perhaps even usually depend on public notices in local newspapers to solicit business. Most plain seam-stresses probably never advertised. Even well-placed and prosperous business women placed notices in local papers only when they wished to inform residents that their business was starting up, had received new supplies, had moved, one of the parties had left, or the shop was forced to close. As late as 1840, Upper Canadian towns and villages were relatively small, and news and information was transmitted as much by face-to-face communications as by the printed press. Women shopkeepers and craftspeople depended on their reputation and the satisfaction of their clients to gain and keep customers. Advertising was expensive, and for many it was probably not cost-effective.[121]

It is known that some businesses did fail, for one reason or another. One rather curious situation was that of the Stonehouses, who arrived in York from Kingston at the beginning of August in 1833 with an assortment of goods from London and Paris for sale. In the same notice, Miss Stonehouse offered to give lessons "to a limited number of young ladies in the elegant art of Oriental Tinting." A week later, the two women called for several apprentices. In mid-September, however, Mrs and Miss Stonehouse announced that they were "dispensing with their present stock" for they intended to close the business the first week of October.[122] The Stonehouses may have been the equivalent of itinerant peddlers. They may also have discovered that they could not compete with the many milliners and dressmakers already in the colony.

One of the ways to gauge the size and relative success of a millinery or dressmaking shop is by the number of apprentices or trained assistants it had on staff. Up until the 1830s, no dressmaker or mantuamaker publicly called for skilled or experienced assistants. Some owners may have employed and trained a general servant to help them, but the market for skilled wage work in the trade was very small. It was not until well into the 1830s that a few larger establishments such as those of Mrs Steward or Mrs Claris began to hire expert needlewomen or "sewing" girls.[123] In 1836, Robert Wightman, the only man who "crossed" into this female trade and ran a "Straw Bonnet Manufactury and General Drapery" business was looking for two or three "superior straw bonnet makers."[124] Most proprietresses could not afford such assistance, however. Those who needed help usually took on inexperienced but "respectable" girls as apprentices.

Although Frances Murray took on at least one apprentice in 1811,[125] it was not until the early 1830s that there was a regular demand for millinery apprentices. Most milliners, like Mrs Cochrane of St Catharines, wanted only one or two girls who would help in their shops as part of their apprenticeship.[126] When Miss Conrey and Miss

Donlevy opened their business in York in 1832, they wanted two apprentices, "to whom they would give liberal encouragement." A few proprietors were looking for a number of girls. In January 1833, for example, Mrs Claris advertised for five or six "respectable girls" and that spring she hoped to hire ten "indoor apprentices." In 1838, one business took on the appearance of a minifactory. S. Mayhew, who ran a "Millinery and Dress Establishment, Baby Lines Manufactury and Toy Warehouse," wanted twelve apprentices "immediately." A year later, she and probably her husband were once again interviewing girls for apprenticeships.[127]

In the 1830s, working in a dress, millinery or hat shop was one of the few skilled occupations open to Upper Canadian women. And there were a number of girls who were willing and able either to work as assistants in a shop or to serve what could be a lengthy apprenticeship. In 1831, the *Colonial Advocate* printed a notice from a "young woman" who wanted "A SITUATION ... as Assistant to the Millinery and Dress making."[128] Five years later, "a Respectable English female aged 21" stated she wanted work "in some Commercial Establishment where she could be actively employed." The girl noted that she had "a thorough knowledge of the Millinery Business and had served in a retail fancy goods store."[129]

It is clear that by the 1830s, Upper Canadians were supporting a mature and, for some at least, prosperous fashion industry. The women who owned and operated the growing number of millinery and manutuamaking shops, hat and bonnet businesses, and dressmaking establishments in the colony were "women of affairs." For those single and widowed women with skills, capital, or credit, meeting the fashion needs of colonial women offered them a career, and if they were fortunate, financial security.

ONLY A MINORITY of women in Upper Canada managed to become she-merchants of some means. The careers and successes enjoyed by Jane Jordan or Frances Murray were not shared, or perhaps even desired, by most women in the colony. The vast majority of women who worked in inns, taverns, or boarding-houses, or sewed for wages in Upper Canada did so as part of a family strategy of survival. These women were first and foremost wives; they worked for and with their husbands, or if they engaged in a female trade, they did so with his consent and "had the support of a familial environment."[130] In many instances, women's work in the marketplace was also "informal" and "personal." Business transactions were between friends. Goods and services rather than cash changed hands and women worked from within a domestic base.

But for at least some women, opening or running an inn or hotel or establishing a dress, hat, or millinery shop provided a viable alternative to marriage or remarriage. This was especially true for women who had a recognized expertise that could be converted into cash.[131] Many women, including those girls who served apprenticeships may, in the end, have chosen to marry and leave the business. Given her financial circumstances, it is likely that Jane Jordan could have remarried if she so chose. She and a number of other hotel-keepers, milliners, and skilled craftswomen appear to have preferred their independence. They may well have gained considerable personal satisfaction from working in the public marketplace.

At least a few of these career women were stretching the limits of domesticity, particularly as prescribed by the emerging cult of true womanhood. In the end, however, women hotel-keepers and milliners were merely exchanging what were considered traditional female skills for an income. And it is clear that a growing number of women in Upper Canada required their services. In fact, such women proprietors were, to some degree, working within what might be described as a women's economic world. They were working with women to meet the needs of other women. It would be going too far to conclude, however, that Upper Canadian merchants were part of a "women's culture" that was closed or isolated from the rest of the marketplace. Although they too had to cope with families, household chores, and children underfoot, it is unlikely that either the seamstress or the widow-innkeeper ever forgot the economic and social chasm that separated her from her upper-class clients.

Managing a hotel or running a dress shop were not the only acceptable options open to women who needed or wanted to work for wages in Upper Canada. Women were also able to sell their mothering skills on the open market. And as the colony matured, a growing number of women with education and expertise in a classroom found that teaching the colony's daughters was another way both to support themselves and to retain their independence and respectability.

9 Ladies' Academies and "Seminaries of Respectability": Training "Good" Women of Upper Canada

Wanted – Housekeeper and Governess

A respectable, well educated female (if from England or a member of the Episcopal Church, it would be preferred, though these are not indispensable) from 30 to 45 years of age, to take the charge of a small family, where two servants are kept & to superintend the education, when at home, of a young lady, 12 years of age, who goes to school in the city; & a little girl of about four years of age, of whom she will be expected to take the exclusive management. It will be preferred that she be competent to teach music.

A suitable person desiring such a position will find a comfortable home & will receive a liberal salary.

Apply either personally to or by letter (post paid) to the care of the editor of the Courier.[1]

The plight of George Gurnett, the editor of the *Courier*, seems clear. There was no adult female to run his home and to superintend the care and education of his children.

For a mature woman, looking perhaps desperately for employment and a home, such an advertisement offered a possible solution to her dilemma. So too might have the simple notice, "Wanted – A Governess to superintend the education of 3 children," that appeared in the Toronto *Patriot* in September 1833; or the advertisement a year later offering employment to someone "competent to TAKE CHARGE OF and INSTRUCT SIX or SEVEN YOUNG CHILDREN," and able to teach "Reading Writing, Grammar, Geography, Arithmetic, etc." and preferably "acquainted with Music."[2]

In Upper Canada in the first half of the nineteenth century, caring for and instructing the children of others was an acceptable and respectable way for a woman to earn her living.[3] Almost all Upper Canadian women had assumed the responsibilities of governess, nurse, or teacher, at some time in their lives. Exchanging those skills considered inherent in persons of their sex for a home and/or a wage was but a natural extension of this traditional and highly respected aspect of women's work.

The editor of the *Courier* probably had little trouble finding a suitable candidate for his position. Notices in local newspapers suggest that between 1790 and 1840, there were many women in Upper Canada who were willing and apparently able to undertake such work. Advertisements in those same newspapers indicate that, particularly after 1815, "respectable" and "educated" ladies also looked for other ways to take advantage of Upper Canadians' growing desire to educate their daughters formally. Instead of going into "service," a number of married, single, and widowed women opened day and boarding schools for young girls. Others established seminaries of respectability that tried to cater to the requirements of the best families in the colony. For many of these women, teaching for pay or establishing a small school was a convenient and often temporary measure, intended only to supplement their families' incomes. Other schoolmistresses obviously considered teaching a long-term career. For a few, owning and operating their own school promised the possibility of independence, financial security and personal fulfilment.

This is not to suggest that between 1800 and 1840 most women who taught in Upper Canada would have considered themselves pofessional teachers. As Alison Prentice notes, during this period "domestic or private teachers ... predominated in most parts of Canada."[4] In most colonial homes, mothers continued to fill the role of teachers. In affluent or motherless homes, governesses or nursemaids oversaw the children's education. The majority of women who were paid to take children into their homes for schooling had no particular expertise and their "schools" were quite informal. Many schoolmistresses in Upper Canada probably intended to teach only until they married, remarried, or their financial circumstances improved sufficiently to permit them to leave the labour market. There seems little question, however, that for women who considered teaching a career, Upper Canada was increasingly attractive.

In the first four decades of the nineteenth century, Upper Canada supported a wide variety of schools, particularly for girls. The women who owned or taught in these schools came from diverse backgrounds and had at times sharply differing expectations of their

Illustration 17
Downtown York c. 1824
MTL (10426)

work. In the end, however, Upper Canadian women who taught for wages were performing work that both they and other members of colonial society considered appropriate for persons of their sex. And in so doing, these working women were helping to promote, through the curriculum they offered at their schools, the precepts of "good" womanhood that leading Upper Canadians considered so important.

UPPER CANADIANS had been concerned about the education of their children since the loyalists had first arrived in the colony. Within a generation of settlement, residents had established common and district schools in the most populated parts of the colony. In smaller and newly opened-up areas, parents raised subscriptions and built one-room school houses. Between 1790 and 1840, the local school was an important symbol of a community's progress.[5] But even as late as 1840, many Upper Canadian children still did not receive any kind of formal education. Moreover, as has been discussed, although many parents considered that education was important, few mothers or fathers had the time or the energy to pass on much more than the basics of reading and writing to their children. It was therefore with some relief that a number of Upper Canadian families accepted the help offered by those neighbours such as Anne Langton and Mary O'Brien who were willing to transform their kitchens and parlours into classrooms.

In January 1839, Anne Langton recorded, "I had Menzie's two little girls for a lesson today. I have lately begun to teach them a little." Anne's "school" convened "for about an hour three times a week."

Her first pupils were "two very pretty little girls about five and seven." Anne reported that "as yet we are not all perfect in our letters and I sometimes feel that, unaccustomed as I am to teaching, I shall not accomplish much in my short school." Anne believed that her school had one "good effect," however. It encouraged the children's parents to give them "a little more teaching at home."[6]

Anne continued to teach between two and ten young neighbourhood girls and boys their ABCs until a "real" school was opened in the Sturgeon Lake area in 1841.[7] Interestingly enough, she noted that though many of the children did not know how to read or write, even the youngest girls had already been introduced to some of the basic skills of housekeeping.[8] Anne characterized her methods as "humdrum, old fashioned." As the number of her "scholars" increased, she wondered whether the children were getting any real benefit from their lessons. At least, she concluded, "they are put into the way of learning and rendered capable of improving themselves."[9]

Mary O'Brien started her "school" in 1836, when it was arranged that four of her new neighbour's children would "give us work for teaching." Within a week of the girls' arrival, Mary had begun "to form more regular habits of school."[10] Maintaining regular hours for lessons was next to impossible, however. As in the Langton home, Mary's school was conducted in her kitchen, the parlour, or on the verandah. Lessons were often interrupted by the demands of younger children and periodic domestic crises. The birth of her fourth child at the end of 1836 seems to have cut short Mary's career as a schoolmistress. She then only had enough time to give lessons to her own children.[11]

Neither Anne Langton nor Mary O'Brien would have considered themselves teachers, in the formal sense of the word. And, although Mary received some remuneration for her work, neither she nor Anne kept a "school" to earn money. Both women were, however, following a pattern that had been long established in Upper Canada, Great Britain, and the United States. Educating children was primarily women's work. Taking in neighbourhood children for lessons was but an extension of the traditional responsibilities of motherhood and was an integral part of that exchange of services and community assistance on which so many colonial women relied.

Both Anne and Mary recognised that their efforts to educate neighbourhood children were only temporary measures. The relatively rapid growth of local schools in Upper Canada between 1790 and 1840 was a reflection of colonists' determination to ensure that the general population was both literate and educated. By 1820, many in the colony considered that it was no longer "enough that the children of the settlers know how to read and cast accounts." John Strachan, chairman of the General Board of Education for Upper Canada, asserted in 1829 that all children "ought likewise to enjoy the pleasure as well as the advantages of intellectual employment."[12] In addition to training sons and daughters "for their own professions," Strachan and other colonial leaders encouraged parents and teachers to expose their children to "good authors," to encourage them to "converse and write in good style," and teach them, among other things, geography, history, natural science, and geology.[13]

Strachan took it for granted, however, that boys and girls required different kinds of education. A boy, after all, had to be able to support himself and cope with the wider world of the market. Depending on his family's class and the occupation of his father, a boy either had to be taught a trade or craft, or he had to pursue "higher" education that would fit him for business or one of the professions. Girls obviously required different skills.

All Upper Canadians accepted that girls, like boys, had to be able to read and write. To enable them to become supportive wives and attentive mothers, daughters also had to be well grounded in the "domestic arts."[14] But, as with a boy, it was recognized that what was considered an appropriate education for a girl depended to some degree on her family's status in society. Many believed that the daughters of labourers and artisans should receive some training in one of the "female" trades. Young ladies of the middle and upper classes, on the other hand, had to be able to converse well, act as a hostess for their husband, and generally be capable of taking their rightful place in "society." They also had to be capable of reflecting and promoting virtue and morality to members of their families and to the community at large. "Girls ... require much more care and attention in bringing up than parents generally suppose," articles in local newspapers frequently asserted.[15] Certainly, a young lady did not become a "good" woman without some training. Mothers, who bore the primary responsibility for ensuring that their daughters were adequately prepared for adulthood, were reminded that "the education of your daughters is of the first importance," for the "very character of the country was at stake."[16]

Such assertions immediately raised the question of how this was to be accomplished. Should girls be educated formally? Indeed, could girls be educated at all? Women, after all, were different from men. They were timid, feeble, and, some suggested, "their minds are not so strong and they are less capable of reasoning."[17] A number of Upper Canadians argued vehemently that a girl's biology made her incapable of "higher" learning. There were others, however, who emphatically defended a woman's intellectual capabilities.

"It has never been proved to me that women are in any respect inferior to men," an anonymous Acetum explained to the residents of Kingston in 1812, "except in a few particulars connected with their Physical texture." Certainly, he continued, these physical differences did have "a peculiar influence on their nerves," making them "more liable to irritation."[18] It did not impair a woman's ability to reason, however. "You are not henceforth to consider us all frivolous creatures, incapable of serious reflection," one young woman vehemently asserted. Replying to charges that women were intellectually as well as physically weak, she stated, "Believe me, Sir, the natural ability of the sexes are equal." Apparent differences were the result of "their different education." It was the specific "purposes for which [men and women] are destined in life which accounted sufficiently for these distinctions."[19]

Between 1790 and 1840, a growing number of Upper Canadians, especially those in the upper and middle ranks of society, began to accept that not only were women capable of "higher education" but that the training that they could receive at home was no longer sufficient to prepare them for the responsibilities of adulthood. Ann Macaulay believed passionately that her granddaughter should go to school; so too did Anne Powell, who had herself gone to Mrs Palmer's boarding school in Norwich in the late eighteenth century. It is therefore not surprising that Anne Powell sent her granddaughter Mary to a local school in York in 1811 over the objections of her husband. After the War of 1812, Mary attended a girls' school in Litchfield, Connecticut. Anne Powell's purpose was clear. Her granddaughters needed to receive training suitable to their station. They also had to acquire some practical skills so that in the event of "a future emergency" they would be able to "obtain a respectable support."[20]

"Nothing short of the refinement of education can give dignity and elevation to the female character," one article on women's education, printed in 1828, began. "Nothing can so well qualify them for participating to advantage in all pleasures desirable for mutual intercourse with the polished circles of life."[21] Increasingly, parents were told that "a woman's senses are generally as quick as ours, their reason is as quick as nervous and their judgement as secure and solid." A brief article on "Female Education" published before the turn of the century considered that barring women from "the privilege of ingenious education" was an inhuman tyranny.[22] It also hampered women from fulfilling their God-given responsibilities in life. "Men of sense," it was asserted, "naturally seek companions possessing corresponding qualifications."[23] Moreover, "by concentrating the power of their minds" through education, "the cares and anxieties evident in [the] connubial state are consequently diminished and the union is attended with all those happy results which characterize it above all others as the most felicitous."[24]

It is obvious, however, that as late as 1840, not all Upper Canadians were convinced of the efficacy of educating women. Proponents of formal education for women went to considerable lengths to reassure men that they would not "lose [their] empire" over women whose "natural abilities" had been improved. In fact, a man's position as head of the household and master of the family was even more secure. "Where there is most learning, sense and knowledge, there is observed to be the greatest modesty and rectitude of manners," it was contended.[25] Far from being a threat to family order, an educated woman was an asset to a discerning man, to his home, and to the future of their community. "She whose mind has been expanded and feeling so elevated," an address by a teacher to her pupils printed in the *Farmers' Journal* in 1829 stated, "will have neatness, economy and regularity in all her domestic avocations; she will never debase herself by associating with the vulgar and the mean; she will cheerfully discern that her dwelling is the centre of her companion's happiness."[26] In short, a well-educated girl made the best wife and mother; she was, indeed, far more valuable to her husband than a wealthy or beautiful spouse.[27]

By the 1830s, more and more Upper Canadians had become convinced that it was necessary to educate the colony's future wives and mothers formally. Only if a girl was educated in the finer arts of womanhood as well as in the basic skills of housekeeping could she properly assume her role as a good woman, secure in her special domestic role. Elite families had been sending their daughters to school for some time. After 1820, members of the middling ranks of colonial society began to believe that their daughters' attendance at a ladies' academy was both a sign of their growing affluence and a means of promoting their children's social mobility.

Upper Canadians continued to accept, however, that girls needed different skills than boys. The curriculum of the new girls' schools or ladies' academies was expected to be "useful." For example, in order to be a suitable companion to her future husband, a woman had to have a good general knowledge of the world. Thus, instead of training in the classics, girls needed to be exposed to modern languages, geography, history, and biology, subjects that, as Marjorie Theobald has noted, formed the basis of a modern liberal education at a later date.[28] In addition, it was presumed that upper- and middle-class girls should receive some instruction in those social skills – the "accomplishments" – that were necessary for everyday life. These included vocal and instrumental music, dancing, painting, and fancy needlework.

The opportunities available to women to earn their living as teachers in Upper Canada were directly influenced by the evolving expectations that middle- and upper-class families had for their daughters' education.[29] Such opportunities were also dictated by the changing economic and social circumstances of the colony. During the first generation of settlement, Upper Canada was too small to support many schools, especially schools for girls. After 1815, however, as the population grew, as towns and villages developed, and as disposable income increased, more and more women turned to teaching to help support their families and themselves.

IN 1827, Mrs Margaret Powell, widow of Major Powell, announced to the residents of York that she was opening a school for children three to ten years old.[30] Eight years later, Mrs Campbell, "the Widow of a Clergyman ... of Belleville" notified local residents that she was willing to take six young ladies "into her house ... to educate with her own children."[31] Mrs Powell and Mrs Campbell were apparently "gentlewomen" of reduced means. Although neither woman claimed to have any formal experience in a classroom, to resolve their financial difficulties, each had turned to what was considered in Upper Canada a "natural" way for a woman to earn her living – teaching neighbourhood children.[32]

Mrs Powell and Mrs Campbell were not the only women who pursued this course. Between 1790 and 1840, dozens of widowed and married women opened their homes to young children, and in exchange for a small fee, provided students with the care and instruction that any mother could provide. Classes were informal and the curriculum was limited to the rudiments of literacy.[33] It is likely that attendance was erratic and the teachers' income meagre.

It is difficult to estimate how many of these small "dame" schools existed in the colony.[34] Most widow- or wife-proprietors did not advertise their establishments. Like those "schools" run by Mary O'Brien and Anne Langton, students, who usually included both boys and girls, were drawn from the immediate neighbourhood. Any woman with a room large enough to accommodate a number of students could open a school. She needed no particular expertise, other than her sex, a good reputation, and the confidence to begin. For widowed and married women in the colony, opening such a business was a relatively convenient way to supplement their families' incomes. And it is likely that these "schoolmistresses" moved into and out of the classroom as the needs of the household economy dictated and their domestic responsibilities allowed.

Women who did appear to have some education and more confidence in their own abilities aspired to somewhat greater things. Particularly after 1815, a growing number of both women and men tried to tap into what appears to have been a more lucrative and undoubtedly more "respectable" market – teaching young girls how to be ladies.[35]

One of the first private-venture schools offering a curriculum specially tailored for girls was opened in Niagara in February 1802 by Mr and Mrs Tyler. The school, which was situated "in a healthy and agreeable location," took both boys and girls over the age of four for either regular day or night school classes. The Tylers also intended to take a few boarders into their home. "Nothing will be neglected," the notice assured prospective clients, "for the health, instruction, religion and good morals" of the pupils.[36]

The notice for the Tylers' school provides some insight into early Upper Canadians' expectations of their daughters' education and the women who taught them. A girl's training had to be useful. In addition to a basic curriculum that included "reading, writing and arithmetic," the Tylers proposed to provide "the young ladies" with instruction "in all that is necessary for persons of their sex, to appear decently and be useful in the world, in all that concerns housekeeping, either for those who wish to live in town or country." No one presumed that Mrs Tyler had any special qualification to teach. In fact, her notice ended with the announcement that "having been bred in the line of *mantua makers*," she also sought work as a seamstress and offered "to execute her work in the neatest manner, to the satisfaction of those who may honour her with their custom."[37]

It is not known if the Tylers managed to attract students and make a go of their new business. Like most women in Upper Canada, Mrs Tyler's waged work was probably undertaken as one of her wifely duties. The family needed to be supported and Mrs and Mr Tyler obviously hoped that the combined income from sewing and teaching would be sufficient. What is interesting is that this couple were offering services that at the time appear to have had only limited appeal. There were few colonial families in 1802 who could afford formal training for their daughters, or for that matter, to have their clothes made to measure. It was not until after the War of 1812 that the demand for special education for girls really blossomed. Then, the number and variety of girls' schools quickly grew.

For a married couple with their own home, establishing a school in Upper Canada was a respectable way to earn a living and one that may well have been more appealing than opening a boarding-house. For Mr and Mrs Pringle and Mr and Mrs Woolf, who opened boarding schools for young ladies in Kingston between 1814 and 1817, and for Mr and Mrs Roberts, who had established a similar business in Niagara before 1820, their choice of business is understandable.[38] Like the Maitlands, who opened a girls' school in York in the 1830s, the Roberts, the Pringles, and the Woolfs were teaching couples – both husband and wife claimed to have "had long experience in the instruction of youth."[39] In these family-run girls' schools, it would have been Mrs Pringle or Mrs Roberts who, like Mrs Tyler a generation earlier, taught the "ornamental" and womanly arts; they probably also shared the teaching of some of the academic subjects with their husbands.[40] But as such wife-teachers undoubtedly knew only too well, running a school meant more than just working in a classroom.

All schools in Upper Canada needed the services of a working wife in order to succeed. Inevitably, it was the wife-teachers and wives of schoolmasters who were responsible for all household affairs. When the Rev. M. Marcus opened a district school for boys in Picton in 1833, for example, he observed that it was Mrs Marcus who would superintend all "the domestic arrangements," including ensuring "regularity and discipline," and providing students with "the care and comfort of a private family."[41] Those wives who did teach also had to ensure that their houses were clean, meals were cooked, and other daily chores were done.[42] The mistress of the business undoubtedly also acted as a mother-substitute for her charges. Moreover she provided a vital element of respectability for the establishment. No conscientious parent would enrol either her daughters or her sons in a school that did not have an obviously respectable mother-figure. It must have been difficult at times for many teaching wives to find the patience and energy to prepare lessons. Mrs Roberts, Mrs Pringle, and Mrs Woolf at least had the full-time support of their husbands; most women who taught in Upper Canada did not.

Advertisements in local newspapers indicate that many girls' schools were run by women who were sole proprietors.[43] A number of married or single women took a few students into their homes to supplement the income earned by their husbands or fathers. For example, in 1830 Mrs Sturdy opened a school in Port Hope, while her husband, a weaver, worked in his shop.[44] In 1833, Mrs Denham ran a "Ladies Seminary" in York; her husband, Christopher Richard Denham, worked from the same premises as a brass-founder and smith.[45] In 1832, Mrs Montjoy and her daughter opened a small day school in Hallowell. While Mr Montjoy made and repaired clocks and watches, his wife and daughter taught a maximum of fifteen young ladies geography, history, French, and drawing – a relatively standard curriculum for a girls' school.[46] What may initially have been a way to bring in a little extra money seems to have become the sole means of support for Mrs Montjoy and her daughters two years later. "A Card" to the public of York (where the family had obviously moved) announced Mr Montjoy's death in 1834. After expressing her "heartfelt gratitude" to those kind friends who had supported her and her family through "their last afflicting trial," Mrs Montjoy asked the inhabitants of York to continue their patronage of her school. To supplement their income further, Mrs Montjoy and her daughter announced that they would now take in a few boarders.[47]

Mrs Montjoy was, of course, not the only woman who turned to teaching to support herself. Widows often took in a few boarding students to help make ends meet. Nor was she the only schoolmistress who turned to members of her family – or joined with associates in similar circumstances to share teaching, costs, and the many other responsibilities involved in running a school.[48] The majority of women who ran schools together were, like the Montjoys, members of the same family – either mother-daughter or sister-sister combinations. Such cooperation did not guarantee the success of the business however.

In March 1833, a Mrs Taylor offered to give private lessons in music and French to local Peterborough girls. At the same time, she and her daughter started a school for girls. Their joint venture was very short-lived, however. Eighteen months after opening her school, Mrs Taylor was forced to announce that she was discontinuing it "in consequence of Miss Taylor's departure." Thereafter she would continue to teach only music privately.[49] The Scotts of Sandwich seem to have been no more successful. Mrs Horton Scott and her daughters started a "Young Ladies Institute" in 1834, offering girls "a finished education." Though Mrs Scott employed "the most approved teachers" and offered a wide variety of subjects, within three months they were forced to lower their fees "on the advice of friends." And there is no mention of the school in the local press after 1835.[50]

Some of the women who headed these households were, like skilled mantuamakers and milliners, recent arrivals to the colony. Mrs Weatherstone and her sister "just in from England" ran a school for girls in Kingston for at least two years in the mid-1830s. Mrs Marshall and her sister, Mrs Davidson of Scotland, now of Belleville, offered to take in a few young ladies and teach them "the useful and ornamental branches of education."[51] A most successful pair was Mrs and Miss Street, who, within months of arriving from England rented

Ontario House in Niagara Falls for the express purpose of starting a school. By the end of July 1833, their school was called the Ancaster Boarding School for Young Ladies and within a year they had the patronage of both Lady Colborne, the lieutenant-governor's wife, and of the lord bishop of Quebec.[52]

Such ambition and success seem to have been unusual. Most schoolmistresses in Upper Canada did not profess to have any previous experience in the classroom or any particular skills, other than those that any gentlewoman would possess. They taught because they needed the income. Undoubtedly many would have been relieved if their financial situation had improved sufficiently to allow them to close the doors of their schools. For the majority, however, this was unlikely. Most schoolmistresses had to struggle just to keep their school going.

Between 1815 and 1840, women who aspired to owning a girls' school in Upper Canada were entering an increasingly competitive market. Even those who had the relative security of their husbands' incomes or the active assistance of a partner still had to convince colonial parents to patronize their school. It is not surprising that proprietors of ladies' academies and seminaries often went out of their way to point out those features of their schools that made them worthy of patronage.[53] And in so doing, these women revealed a little more about who they were and the nature of their work in Upper Canada.

SOME TEACHERS obviously believed that their schools' location was a valuable asset. Mrs Newall announced to the residents in the eastern portion of the province in 1820 that her new location in Brockville, did "in respect to health, possess superior advantages." She explained that, compared with her old location in Cornwall (and by implication, the location of other local seminaries), the school now had "the benefit of pure and uncontaminated air, which gives to the necessary exercise an innocent recreation of the students during the intervals of the day."[54] The Streets of Niagara Falls emphasized their proximity to two churches (a "Scottish" church and Church of England) and the availability of "excellent medical advice."[55] Such factors may have been important to some parents. It is likely, however, that most families were far more concerned about the schoolmistress's reputation and the curriculum she could offer their daughters.

Almost all notices of hopeful schoolmistresses made specific references as to their personal character and respectability. Although women who took students into their homes for pay were obviously not of the upper ranks of society, most professed to be "respectable" ladies sharing the beliefs and attitudes of the best families in the col-

ony. Being able to state that one had the public patronage and support of prominent residents in the community or the colony was one
concrete way that schoolmistresses could illustrate such stature.[56] In
keeping with the sensibilities of the time, almost all proprietors of
girls' schools also assured parents that close attention, or as Mrs Black
of St Catharines noted, "strict regard," would be paid to the "Moral
and Religious instruction" of those students entrusted to their care.[57]
Moreover, classes in the Bible, daily prayers, and regular attendance
at a local church were standard fare at many girls' schools.

So too were classes in reading, writing, and needlework. In even
the smallest and most informal girls' school, such as Almira Ewing's
day school, which opened in York in 1816, teachers also provided lessons in arithmetic and fancy needlework.[58] Increasingly, however,
Upper Canadian parents wanted more for their daughters, and many
mistresses of girls' schools responded by offering a broad array of
"the ornamental branches of Female education."[59] In 1831, for example, Mrs Upton of Brockville announced that although she would
only take one or two boarding pupils and a few day students, she
would personally teach her young charges English, arithmetic, German, history, geography, and plain and fancy needlework. Only a few
months later, Miss Farrand, also of Brockville and probably a compet-
itor of Mrs Upton, offered her daily scholars lessons in English, grammar, geography, composition, rhetoric, geometry, and algebra. Music
and drawing were available for an extra fee.[60]

Such relatively extensive curricula did not mean, however, that
Mrs Upton's and Miss Farrand's schools were formal educational institutions. Like many others in the colony, their schools were probably only one step removed from traditional dame schools. Most
proprietors of girls' schools in Upper Canada worked in their homes.
The classroom was their parlour, or any other room large enough to
accommodate the group. Lessons were informal, and in the end, the
curriculum was restricted by the mistress's ability and her facilities.
Very few schools had any "specialized" equipment. Texts for reading,
for example, were either provided by the students or were part of the
teacher's private library.[61] Lessons in history were probably taken
from local newspapers. Only a limited number of the larger schools
advertised that they used globes or maps in the teaching of geography.

Some of these schoolmistresses did attempt to emulate the structure and formality indicative of a "real" school. For example, Miss
Farrand of Brockville did demand the "punctual attendance of each
scholar ... during the hours of Instruction and no allowance [will be
made] ... for occasional absences."[62] She and a number of other

teachers also divided their students into primary, junior, and senior "departments."[63] Lessons were scheduled and taught by age and academic ability, with more advanced students helping the juniors.

Many Upper Canadians probably considered that elaborate equipment and formal classroom schedules were unnecessary. What their daughters needed was the company of their social peers or "betters," lessons in basic literacy, training in the "useful accomplishments," and a secure domestic environment. This last requirement all proprietors were able to provide.

Most ladies' academies were boarding schools. Because they were also located in the teacher's home, by necessity they were small. Having even a few students must have strained the physical limits of any household, however, and they must also have taxed the resources and the energy of the most devoted teacher. Girls who attended a colonial boarding school usually had to provide their own beds and linen; in some cases, they brought their own cutlery.[64] In addition to conducting "lessons," a schoolmistress also had to plan and cook meals, regularly clean her home/business, and generally make sure that all her domestic chores were complete. It is likely that in most schools, students were almost considered members of the extended family. And like all daughters, they were probably expected to assume some of the domestic responsibilities. Only those schools run by a husband-and-wife team, such as the Pringles or the Maitlands or by teachers whose mothers or sisters acted as housekeepers could avoid having either student or paid help.[65]

Some proprietresses such as Mrs Marshall and her sister, Miss Davidson of Belleville tried to make a virtue of a necessity. They claimed that they were limiting the number of students to six or eight so that the instruction could be almost individual.[66] Other schoolmistresses tried to impress parents with the homelike atmosphere of their school. "In point of domestic comfort," Mrs Fraser of Newmarket observed, "the young ladies placed under her care enjoy all the privileges of home."[67] This may well have meant that students received instruction in the basic accomplishments and were required, or had the opportunity, to "practise" their homemaking skills.

To avoid at least some of the domestic problems associated with taking in boarders, a few women in Upper Canada opened schools exclusively for day pupils. This created other difficulties, however. Day students' attendance was often erratic and the schoolmistress's income therefore fluctuated accordingly. To attempt to gain some security and predictability in the numbers of pupils, some mistresses found they had to offer to board one or two pupils in their own homes; others made arrangements to have students board with neighbouring families.[68] Even well-established boarding schools that accepted a few day pupils to try to increase revenues found that student attendance was a problem.[69]

Some women with specific and recognizable skills in one of the accomplishments tried to avoid the problems of running a "regular" school altogether by tutoring girls on a part-time basis. However, there were surprisingly few women who taught for pay part time. Most private tutors or proprietors of "specialty schools" in Upper Canada were men. Only men, for example, offered tutoring in the classics and penmanship. Male tutors also predominated in teaching dancing and French.[70] Madam Harris, who owned a dancing school in York in the late 1820s, was apparently the only woman in her field. Although she offered lessons to both young ladies and gentlemen, classes were segregated and students came together only once a week for a carefully supervised practice.[71] In even the most basic of the "accomplishments" – teaching instrumental and vocal music and drawing – the number of women offering private lessons was fewer than men.[72] While it appears that middle-class women in Upper Canada, like their sisters in Australia, were expected to acquire the ability to dance, sing, or play the piano, it was not socially acceptable for them to display their talent publicly, or to offer to sell these skills too openly.[73]

The relative dearth of women advertising to teach just one or more of the "accomplishments" may, in part at least, have been because most women who had to teach did not have the financial flexibility to work only part time. Moreover, there may have been only a few who had any real expertise in their subject. A greater impediment may have been that it was apparently unacceptable for women tutors to have both boys and girls as students. Such was not the case for men. Social mores dictated and middle- and upper-class parents determined that wage-earning female teachers were suited, by reason of their sex and their ability, to instruct only young children and adolescent girls.[74] Notices from women teachers always made it clear that they did not teach "older" boys. Moreover, it was assumed that any self-respecting middle-class or aspiring-to middle-class schoolmistress both preferred and ought to earn her living within the confines of her own home.

Thus, those relatively few women who were able to trade their skills in one of the accomplishments for a part-time income were clearly fortunate. Most women who wished to or had to earn their living by teaching colonial girls were obliged to sacrifice their privacy and open their homes to students on a full-time basis. They relied on their respectability and their personal reputation to attract students.

Success must have been precarious. Most schoolmistresses probably had little business experience and families could never depend on the income from their schools alone. Many probably did not try to. But even when a school succeeded, teacher-proprietors still had numerous other domestic responsibilities that competed for their time and energy. It is likely that most women taught for wages in Upper Canada because they had to, not because they wanted to.

Some schoolmistresses in Upper Canada clearly did aspire to greater things, however. Between 1820 and 1840, a growing number of ladies' academies and seminaries offered both a rigorous academic curriculum and a full range of the "accomplishments." In the "best" schools in York, for example, girls took classes in English language and literature, arithmetic, composition, music, geography, history, one of the sciences and, of course, needlework. Then, depending on the size and clientele of the school, girls also had lessons in two or three of the "accomplishments," including dancing, embroidery, drawing, and painting (of various kinds), instrumental and vocal music, French, Italian, German, and sometimes Latin. Instruction in many of the ornamental arts was provided for an extra fee and taught either privately or in small groups, by the proprietor or an assistant engaged specially for that purpose.

Sustaining such a curriculum obviously required that a schoolmistress have considerable talent and wide-ranging skills, or that she have assistants trained in each subject. Certainly few, if any such mistresses were "poor ladies" reduced to teaching, or young women with little experience. After 1820, a growing number of the single and widowed women who opened girls' schools in Upper Canada were career teachers and they offered colonial parents the services of a "professional."[75] Despite specialized training or experience in the classroom, there was no guarantee that these schoolmistresses would succeed. Their "qualifications" probably did give them a significant advantage over their less well-prepared competitors.

IN NOVEMBER 1824, a "Lady having lately arrived from England" proposed to establish "a Seminary of respectability" in Kingston, Upper Canada. In notices widely distributed throughout the colony, she solicited "the patronage of those Ladies who [felt] disposed to place their Daughters where the most useful & polite Branches of Education are taught." "Having been accustomed to the best established methods of Tuition [she trusted that] an assiduous and unremitting attention to her Pupils and their Interests [would] ensure her success."[76]

When Mrs Twigg solicited the ladies of Kingston for her new "School for Young Ladies" a year later, she carefully outlined the merits of her new establishment. "For many years" she wrote, she had "conducted a Boarding and Day School in the North of Ireland." She had resigned from "a large School in that Country" after she had been "induced" to emigrate to Upper Canada to open a school there. Mrs Twigg trusted that her "long experience and the credentials which she has brought with her" would induce parents to place their daughters into her care.[77]

Between 1820 and 1840, an increasing number of women came to Upper Canada, either alone or with their husbands, mothers or sisters to try to take advantage of the growing demand for specialized education for colonial girls. Many of these women, such as Mrs Hamilton of Toronto, Mrs Bickerton of Picton, Mrs Weatherstone of Kingston, and Mrs Crookshank offered testimonials of their previous experience teaching; others provided prospective clients with evidence of their professional training or explained to Upper Canadians their "philosophy of education."[78]

Mrs Grattan of York, for example, stated that she had "completed her studies under the guidance of the most eminent masters."[79] In 1829, Mrs Breackenridge and her new associate, Mrs Fenwick, an English lady of "considerable experience," explained that in their school, they intended to proceed on the assumption that "the great object of an instructor is to inspire a taste for knowledge, and to cultivate the power of acquiring it."[80] In 1834, Mrs Nash, a "late Teacher of the Central School in London," planned to initiate Doctor Bell's System in her new school. In particular, she informed residents, "we might produce many testimonials from some of the most eminent men of science in Europe and America, to prove the superiority of this system to the 'old way' ... That instruction which is brought to bear upon the mind, is superior to that by which the memory only is called into action; or that it is better to store the mind with absolute definite ideas, than to burthen the memory with unintelligible words."[81]

An increasing number of such teachers in Upper Canada would have considered themselves professional women. As Marjorie Theobald's work on lady teachers in Australia illustrates, these schoolmistresses were seeking a viable and respectable means of earning their living and establishing new careers. For some, the move to Upper Canada promised financial security; a few gained prosperity.[82]

One of the oldest and most successful girls' schools in Upper Canada was begun in September 1817 by Mrs Goodman. With twenty years' experience teaching in England and Montreal, Mrs Goodman chose to settle in York apparently because of its lack of schools for girls. Initially, her boarding and day school was small and its curriculum limited to reading, writing, and grammar, with lessons in music, dancing, and fancy needlework. Mrs Goodman probably taught most classes herself, though a master was engaged part time to give lessons in dancing.[83] Mrs Goodman retired in the spring of 1822. Her school continued, however, under the direction of Mrs Cockburn, a doctor's widow from Quebec City.[84]

Over the next eighteen years, Mrs Cockburn's Boarding School developed into one of the premier girls' schools in the province.[85] By 1835, the school had forty pupils, most of them from the best families of York. At that time, Mrs Cockburn employed four teacher-assistants – three women and one man – and the school curriculum included both the "useful" arts and the standard accomplishments. Girls at Mrs Cockburn's could also take lessons in painting on velvet and flower and card work. At a public examination that year, attended by the Archdeacon of Toronto among others, the young ladies were questioned for four hours on a wide variety of subjects, "reading, English grammar, composition, geography, civil history, arithmetic, etc." and "the principles of the Catechism." The result, an admiring commentator noted, "was highly pleasing and satisfactory." The girls displayed an "accurate knowledge of their subject," and modesty and diligence.[86] A year later, Mrs Cockburn increased her establishment. She hired additional assistants and expanded the boarding facilities.[87] The seminary continued to prosper until well into the 1840s.

The Goodman-Cockburn Boarding School was not the only academy of such calibre in Upper Canada. In September 1826, the Misses Purcell and Rose announced the re-opening of their girls' boarding school in the capital.[88] Under the patronage of the lieutenant-governor's wife, Lady Sarah Maitland, the York Boarding School offered twelve boarding students French, drawing, and dancing (taught by a master) in addition to the standard curriculum. New mistresses and masters were hired over the next five years,[89] and though the school remained relatively small, its curriculum expanded. In 1830, one of Miss Purcell's assistants, a Miss Beynon, left the school to strike out on her own.[90] Both the Purcell-Rose school and the Beynon school continued to be viable for at least the next three years. And when one of the last announcements for the Purcell and Rose school appeared in the local press in September 1833, a separate announcement from Miss Beynon stated that she had "removed to a handsome new house" in a "fine, wholesome, airy situation" that was "well adapted for boarders."[91]

As the capital and, by the mid-1830s, the largest community in Upper Canada, York offered considerable scope for lady teachers. In addition to the Cockburn Seminary and the boarding schools of the

Misses Purcell and Rose and Miss Beynon, there were a few other establishments of note. The Misses McCord opened a girls' boarding and day school in 1831. Conscious that competition in the capital was brisk, they carefully distinguished their establishment from others. "The system of teaching which they propose to follow will be found different from the plan generally pursued, but as it is one which is now adopted in the most respectable seminaries in Great Britain and Ireland, and one by which they have always taught, they ... feel confident that on trial it will be approved here."[92] And approved it seems to have been. For at least the next ten years, the Misses McCord "trained the minds [of young women] by intellectual exercises, and making all the exercises of the school subservient to religion."[93] Another school which enjoyed similar success was that of the Misses Winn, "an English family of respectability and strictly moral principles," who arrived in York in 1834 and taught young ladies well into the 1840s.[94]

York was not the only community that supported more than one ladies' academy. Miss Leah operated a seminary for young ladies in Kingston from 1831 to at least 1840 under the patronage of the "Archdeacon Stewart," while her brother (or father) was master of a commercial school in Cramahe.[95] The Niagara Seminary, owned and operated by Mrs Breackenridge and Mrs Fenwick started in 1829 under the patronage of "the principle families of Niagara." With the help of "suitable assistants," the two women instructed students in the standard curriculum of the time and held annual public examinations throughout the 1830s.[96] By mid-decade, the Niagara Seminary was competing with a Miss Butler, who, with an assistant, offered, "instruction in the various branches of a polite education." When Miss Butler was forced to retire due to illness in 1835, Miss Christle, a former assistant, and her partner, Miss Chettle, took over.[97]

In the postwar years, single and married women also opened girls' schools in smaller colonial towns and villages including Peterborough, Newmarket, Brockville, St Catharines, and Cobourg. The growing demand for "superior" education for women also encouraged a few teachers to move from one community to another, either to gain a better location for their school, or to take advantage of new opportunities for employment. A case in point was that of Miss Radcliffe.

In 1823, a brief account in the *Niagara Gleaner* described an evening "of the finest treats ... The young ladies under the tuition of Mrs and Miss Radcliffe exhibited specimens of their industry and improvement, to an assemblage of nearly all the finest families of the Town."[98] The next month, it was announced that Mrs and Miss Radcliffe's school would re-open. Nothing more was heard of the Radcliffe school or its proprietresses until 1829, when a notice in the *Brockville Gazette* noted that a Miss Radcliffe was now directing the Brockville Seminary.[99] In the intervening years, the Niagara school had apparently closed (perhaps Mrs Radcliffe had died, as there was no subsequent mention of her) and at least one of her daughters had found her way to Kingston to teach at the high school for ladies. Then either she or her sister moved to Brockville. The Miss Radcliffe in Brockville was accompanied by her brother, or father, who was teaching at the boys' high school. The editor of the *Brockville Gazette* was clearly pleased with the community's acquisition. "We beg to congratulate the gentry of this place" on the new seminary, he wrote, and particularly as Miss Radcliffe possessed "great abilities and accomplishment."[100] Two years later one of the Miss Radcliffes re-surfaced in Cobourg, where she had "undertaken a share in the direction of the Cobourg Ladies Academy."[101]

Such women were part of a growing number who owned girls' schools or ladies' academies or who were employed in them. They taught for a living and, given the durability of their schools, they were able and expected to continue to teach throughout much of their lives. Their success was the result of a number of factors. They must have had some ability to teach, and perhaps considerable knowledge of their subjects. They also had gained a reputation, both in their local communities and, in some cases, throughout the colony, as women of integrity, respectability, and ability. Mothers of the middling and upper ranks of colonial society could quite safely entrust their daughters to their care and instruction.

These teacher-proprietresses must also have possessed some considerable skill in administration and management. Like any other successful business person, they had to hire and fire employees, keep accurate accounts, establish and maintain certain routines and work schedules, and generally invest their time, energy, and financial assets wisely. Not all lady teachers were so capable. It is estimated that most girls' schools in Upper Canada did not survive for more than two years.[102] For even if some women had training and experience in the classroom, not many had the economic resources to sustain their enterprise.

Upper Canada did provide considerable opportunity to a number of young, educated, and often single women who wished to teach, however. Many such women found positions as a resident governess with a good family. Others found waged work as assistant teachers or after 1830, as a preceptress or teacher in one of the new coeducational academies. Some of these women managed to accumulate enough capital to open a school of their own.

IN APRIL 1829, four trustees of a privately endowed organization announced to the public their intention of opening a new Elementary and Classical School – Grantham Academy in St Catharines. The substantial two-storey building for the "Academick Institute" was almost complete and the trustees were now calling for applications from qualified gentlemen ("graduates of some college or university") to take over the teaching. It was also announced that the trustees required the services of "a competent female teacher" with "respectable references or recommendations" to assist him.[103] Four months later it was announced that Mr William Lewis had been appointed principal and that a Miss Cornelia Converse would supervise the ladies' department. School would begin on the second Monday in September 1829.[104]

For the next four years, notices regularly appeared in local newspapers advertising the curriculum and various rates of tuition for pupils enrolled in either the male or female departments. Miss Converse taught at Grantham Academy for a year; then, without explanation, she was replaced by a Miss Anderson.[105] Miss Converse returned, however, in the fall of 1831, only to lose her position two and a half years later when the school failed.[106]

Both Miss Converse and Miss Anderson were part of that new group of single working women, the professional teacher. In addition to overseeing the female department and teaching plain and fancy needlework, both Miss Converse and Miss Anderson appear to have taught some of the basic subjects – spelling, reading, writing, arithmetic, grammar, geography, and mapping – though the young ladies were taught some of the "branches" of their education by masters.[107] The curricula changed as the teachers changed, however. In the fall of 1831, Miss Converse was acclaimed for her ability "in the higher and more useful branches of female literature."[108] While she was in residence, students could take classes in chemistry and geology, and probably history and natural philosophy. Miss Anderson's abilities were more "traditional." Considered "a young lady of ability and experience," during her tenure at the school she oversaw "the different branches which are usually taught in Female Institutions" and gave instruction in "Musick, Drawing and Ornamental Needlework."[109]

Grantham Academy was the first of a number of coeducational, private venture day and boarding schools established in the colony in the 1830s. A professional woman teacher might also find employment in the Commercial and Classical Academy founded in 1833 in York, the Bay Street Academy, a day school begun by Mr Boyd, or "the Toronto Academy," established in 1837 by Mr Scanlon.[110] All these schools maintained a separate "Ladies Department," supervised by "a Governess" or, as in the case of the Toronto Academy, the founder's wife, Mrs Scanlon. Potential patrons were assured that the women teachers in these schools were "of unquestionable ability and respectability" and their daughters would be taught needlework and other appropriate subjects.[111]

Women willing to move out of the York area could also apply to Upper Canada Academy, a coeducational boarding school in Cobourg. Sponsored and financially underwritten by donations from the Methodist Church, Upper Canada Academy opened its doors to boarders in 1833. The school was officially non-denominational; it did dedicate itself, however, to promoting "the health, morals, comfort and instruction of the children committed to its care," under a "parental government." To ensure that the students were truly regarded as "members of the same family," a Methodist preacher and his wife catered to their daily comforts. Masters and mistresses, whose duties were apparently restricted to teaching, superintended the students' education.[112]

The founders of Upper Canada Academy fully accepted the belief that girls needed special and separate education; and from the beginning, "young ladies from the country" were afforded "Genteel accommodation."[113] "Parts of the building and premises [were] assigned exclusively to the young ladies";[114] parents were also assured that the girls took their lessons in a "separate and spacious apartment." "The course of instruction prescribed for young ladies" enrolled at the academy was, a notice explained in 1840, "as complete in all the solid and ornamental branches of female education as any in America."[115] In 1832, parents were informed that "the young ladies were constantly under the supervision of the Preceptress" and a considerable part of their evening was spent "in the presence of an efficient monitress ... preparing their lessons for the following day."[116]

Being a teacher in a relatively large school in Upper Canada was considerably different than owning and operating a seminary. Miss Anderson, Miss Converse, and others in their position received a specific wage for their work, remuneration which was negotiated and did not depend on their ability to attract students or manage a business. In return for their pay, teaching assistants had to maintain the highest levels of respectability. They were also expected to have ability and in some cases experience in the classroom teaching the ornamental accomplishments and certain academic subjects, probably English, writing, and composition.[117] Unlike teacher-proprietors, such assistants had almost no independence or authority. Despite their expertise and experience, it was clear that from the outset, they were subject to the dictates of the board of trustees and the supervision of the principal of the school, who apparently visited "the Female Department ... daily."[118] Moreover, when students were put through their annual examinations,[119] the performance of Miss Anderson and Miss Converse was also being assessed by the trustees and parents. Their private lives too would have been scrutinized carefully. Only women of proven and clearly evident decorum and ability could be entrusted with the care of patrons' daughters.

Many of the single women who taught at one of the new coeducational schools or at one of the larger ladies' academies undoubtedly expected to marry and leave the paid work force. Others, such as Miss Barnes, who taught at Upper Canada Academy in 1840 and 1841, had ambitions to open their own school and gain greater freedom of action.[120]

THE GROWING number of lady teachers in Upper Canada, whether they were employed as assistants or owned their own schools, had a significant impact on the development of women's education in Upper Canada. Their presence also reflected the increasing demand of colonial parents that their daughters be "properly" educated. Yet even in the 1820s, there continued to be some debate on what "properly" actually meant. The editor of the *Farmers' Journal* commented in 1827 that the "*fashion* of educating young girls ... has often been a subject of consideration with us." There were, he judged, a number of "good or excellent schools" in the colony. But, he was distressed that many girls, even some of those in school, were still not able to read, write, or do their numbers adequately. The problem, asserted the editor, was that parents were encouraging their daughters to devote their time to "dancing, musick, embroidery, drawing, etc." He recommended that girls remain in school until they were at least seventeen or eighteen. More important, he advised parents that they ensure that their daughters receive a "useful" education. A girl needed, he believed, "the cultivation of mind to render her a pleasing companion to the husband of her future choice, and a knowledge of a housewife's duties, to make his home agreeable, or of the first moment ... With such a course, we will see not only more intelligence but also more happiness in society."[121]

Many colonial parents probably agreed with these sentiments. But Mrs Tyler and her husband, whose school appeared to have met such criteria, would have been hard-pressed to compete in the academic world of the post-War-of-1812 period. Indeed, to many colonial parents in the 1830s, the Tylers' 1802 school would have seemed hopelessly old-fashioned. They wanted their daughters to be able to dance, draw, sing, and do fancy needlework as well as have some grounding in English, history, literature, and mathematics. Mastery of the fine arts was, after all, a visible symbol of belonging to the upper ranks of society. In Upper Canada, as in Great Britain and the United States, the accomplishments were emerging as "the dominant mode of education for middle-class girls."[122] And it was in the new ladies' academies and the prestigious girls' schools that their daughters could receive the training necessary for persons of their sex and station in life.

It is somewhat ironic that the emergence of the cult of domesticity, which placed such a high premium on women being restricted to the private sphere and thus fulfilling "natural" roles as teachers of their children, relied increasingly on wage-earning women to transmit these values and skills. Certainly many women, including the children's nurse and the governess, actually inhabited the private world of the home and they participated only marginally in the public workplace. The same might be said of most women who opened schools in Upper Canada. Many wife-teachers were merely opening up their domestic private world to include their neighbours' children. Moreover, many women teachers undoubtedly expected to teach only until their financial circumstances improved. Young women teachers probably married and left the job market. Widowed women and their friends and daughters too may have hoped to remarry, or to realize their husbands' assets and thus regain the privacy of their homes and the rhythms of apparent leisure.

Yet after 1820, an increasing number of very capable and skilled women hoped to establish a career in teaching. For them, teaching was more than a short-term solution to their financial problems. Owning and operating a girls' school offered the possibility of financial independence and personal satisfaction. Although they were relying on skills considered inherent in their sex and their private-venture schools followed a "domestic pattern," schoolmistress-proprietors were a vital part of the public world of commerce. In their academies, lady proprietors subscribed to and actively promoted the skills and attitudes of true womanhood. Most were, after all, products of these new social values; they not only accepted the dictates of domesticity but jealously guarded their status as gentlewomen. Nonetheless, these women were implicitly challenging the accepted rubric about a woman's relationship to paid labour. Though supporting and in some cases embracing the "dictates of domesticity," they also seemed unwilling to give up that personal independence that came with working for wages.

10 Epilogue

Given the small size of York in the late 1830s, it would not be surprising if hotelkeeper Jane Jordan, staymaker Jane McBradney, schoolmistress Mrs Cockburn, and society matron Helen Macaulay had at least a nodding acquaintance. Certainly, Helen Macaulay must have known of Mrs Cockburn's school; she or her husband John may have attended a social event at Mrs Jordan's hotel; and Helen, Jane Jordan, and Mrs Cockburn may well have been clients of Miss McBradney. But even if these women were complete strangers to each other, they lived in a society that encouraged them to seek, or at least to recognize, a common cause. Indeed, as women, they belonged to a clearly identifiable community in Upper Canada whose membership was determined by gender and by the work its members performed.

This is not to suggest that women in Upper Canada viewed themselves, or should be viewed, as one homogeneous group. Between 1790 and 1840, colonial women, like men, came from diverse ethnic, linguistic, social, and economic backgrounds.[1] Differing personal beliefs and expectations sometimes brought women into pointed conflict with each other. And there is no question that women's experiences in the colony varied, at times quite sharply. Despite such differences, no women in Upper Canada would, or indeed, could have denied their membership in the community of colonial women. Because of their sex, they all shared certain fundamental experiences.

Women in Upper Canada could never really escape the fact that, legally and politically, they were subordinate to men. Regardless of their class or social stature, they could not vote; married women

Illustration 18
Portrait of Mary Boyles Powell, granddaughter of Anne Powell
"In Good Faith" by Julia Jarvis
MTL (BR9292)

could not own or control property. At the more immediate and personal level, all women were subject daily to the authority of their fathers, husbands, and in some cases brothers and sons. While the power of the patriarchy was muted for many women, few ever avoided being confronted by their political and personal subordination at some time in their lives.

The bonds forged among colonial women by this basic reality were strengthened by their common experiences as wives and mothers. Whether living in a big house or eking out an existence in a small shanty, almost all women shared the delights and trials of marriage and the physical and emotional demands of motherhood. They also shared similar domestic responsibilities ensuring that members of their families were fed, clothed, and their welfare generally assured.

The physical and emotional focus of this community of women was the family home. At its working centre was a woman fulfilling her role as wife and mother. But this did not mean that single and widowed women, such as Ann Macaulay of Kingston and Eliza Powell of York, or labouring women – Helen Macaulay's maid Sarah and Mary O'Brien's "girl" Flora, for example – or women merchant-proprietors such as Jane Jordan and Miss Steward were excluded from the community. Even in the earliest years of Upper Canadian settlement, colonial homes were never isolated, closed units. Women rarely worked alone. Households frequently included members of the extended family and unrelated individuals of diverse social and economic classes. Colonial women depended on female relatives, friends, neighbours, and in many cases, employees for emotional, physical, intellectual, and economic support. They often worked together as wives, mothers, and housekeepers. The framework of this women's community, which rested on past experience coping with similar situations, was reinforced within colonial homes. And the ongoing and at times intensely personal relationships that developed among working women reinforced the bonds of the greater women's community.

For although centred in individual homes, the bonds forged by domestic work linked all colonial women. Flora, Sarah, and other helps and servants were not only integral members of their employers' households but they also had homes of their own. Business women such as Jane Jordan and Mrs Cockburn earned their wages by performing tasks that were considered primarily "women's" work and most often, did so within a domestic environment. Even female shopkeepers and teachers usually (though not always) worked with other women to meet the needs of female clients. The lives and work of all women intersected at many points in time and in many ways. It should not be surprising that the emotional, physical and economic bonds that linked all colonial women together were strong and enduring.

At first glance, it would appear that what Nancy Cott has termed the "bonds of womanhood" were reinforced in Upper Canada between 1790 and 1840 by the promulgation of the new social rhetoric of domesticity.[2] For many colonial leaders, the cult of true womanhood clearly established what an ideal woman in the colony was supposed to be and do and also identified her proper place in the social and economic order. She was to be submissive, amiable, and virtuous; she was to celebrate her subordination to men, and find fulfilment and happiness in the private world of her home.

Between 1790 and 1840, the rhetoric of true womanhood was still largely a *prescription* of desired behaviour, however. It certainly did not reflect the reality of most colonial women's lives. Given the economic realities of Upper Canada, few women could retreat into the private and leisured world of the home and the hearth. Most women worked beside their husbands in the fields or with them in their shops. Frequently, married and widowed women went "out to work" for wages or started their own business to ensure their families' economic viability. Single girls left home to go to school, to help a neighbour, or to work in a shop or in an affluent home. And although the vast majority of women in Upper Canada did marry, some did not, preferring to pursue a career and maintain their independence.

Yet colonial women could not entirely escape the prescriptions of the cult of true womanhood. The growing acceptance that women and men did, or at least should, inhabit a separate sphere, and that good women were always "virtuous wives" and "caring mothers" restricted some of women's actions. It also raised personal and social expectations that in many cases neither women nor men could meet. Some British gentlewomen immigrants, for example, had great difficulty accepting that social graces and "knowing one's place" had no place in the Upper Canadian backwoods. The rhetoric of the "well-regulated family" notwithstanding, many marriages in Upper Canada were unhappy; some were obviously dysfunctional.

When women attempted to cope with their personal situation by refusing or failing to abide by the new social rules, they were condemned for their actions. For example, women who chose not to marry at all, or who left what were often abusive relationships were considered "unwomanly." Those who produced children out of wedlock were "unnatural." Ironically, such a standard of behaviour was enforced by women as well as men. Elite women such as Helen Macaulay and Anne Powell not only seemed to embrace the cult of true womanhood in their daily lives, but increasingly accepted it as the basis of social respectability and economic success. Thus, while the image of the "angel in the house" seemed to bind women in Upper Canada within an all-embracing social definition of whom they were or should be, it actually divided women by accentuating those social, economic, and personal differences that already existed.

It could be argued that indirectly the cult of true womanhood did help to provide the basis for a new sense of community among colonial women. After 1815, the need to convert the heathen, nurse the sick, and save destitute mothers and children prompted some women in the colony to formalize what had previously been loose networks of community support. The assumption that women were morally superior to men and had a responsibility to promote social order encouraged upper- and middle-class women to extend their work within the "private" sphere to include those in the larger community. By 1818, these women were actively supporting a growing number of religious and aid organizations. By 1820, they had begun to act independently of their husbands and fathers and to establish separate ladies' auxiliaries and benevolent aid societies. For the next twenty years, women in Upper Canada raised money, gathered clothing, taught Sunday school, visited the poor, and generally used their considerable organizing and "innate" nurturing skills to help those less fortunate than themselves.

For the most part, this work was led and carried out by relatively affluent women, including Macaulays, the Powells, and the wives and daughters of Upper Canada's middle and upper classes. Some of the projects that these women undertook did attempt to address issues that concerned "ordinary" colonial women. Women's organizations were established to help destitute widows and orphans, and to target the problems that excessive use of alcohol had on women's lives. In fact, the one social reform movement that perhaps most clearly illustrated women's growing sense of common cause and their determination to take collective action was the temperance crusade.

Intemperance began to be seen as the great social evil in Upper Canada in the late 1820s. It destroyed the health, the happiness, and the morals of all who came in contact with it, particularly, some suggested, of innocent women and children. Intemperance caused a man to "neglect his business ... His property is wasted, his parents have broken hearts, his wife is pale and emaciated, his children ragged and squalid, and ignorant."[3] Though it was acknowledged that sometimes women drank to excess,[4] drunkenness was believed to be most prevalent among men. Women were primarily its victims. A drunkard "is useless, worst than useless; he is a pest to all around him," an address in the *Farmers' Journal* emphatically judged in 1830.[5] A man under the influence of intoxicating spirits "has lost all shame ... he staggers through the mud, through the filth to his hut; he meets a weeping wife and starving children; he abuses them, he tumbles into his straw, and he rolls and foams like a mad brute, til he is able to go again."[6] One anonymous Upper Canadian noted that "the misery entailed upon family and society at large by this pernicious custom exceeds all the calamities inflicted by war, pestilence and famine."[7]

Following the example of American neighbours and British associates, Upper Canadians began a concerted campaign against the demon rum. Initially temperance societies, which began to appear in various colonial centres in 1830, were established and run by men. From the beginning, however, women were urged "to undertake to be the formers as well as the polishers of mankind" and use all their powers to discourage their husbands, brothers, fathers, and sons from heading down the evil path. One of many articles in local newspapers asserted that "the influence of the female sex, in favour of the temperance cause, has had a high salutary effect upon all classes and community, and especially upon those who are the hope of future generations, children and youth, and that should the influence ... be ... universally exerted in favour of this cause, they would do much to perfect and perpetuate the moral renovation of all human family."[8]

Colonial women joined community temperance organizations in increasing numbers between 1830 and 1840.[9] They also began to form temperance committees and societies of their own. Unlike other benevolent and religious organizations, ladies' temperance organizations do not seem to have been dominated by elite women. Although Mary O'Brien and her sister-in-law Mary Southby were active members of societies in the Simcoe region, Harriet Dobbs Cartwright, one of Kingston's leading social activists, was not. Harriet did not believe in prohibition. She did, however, campaign to diminish the number of licenses for taverns and close down the many shops that sold spirits without a license.[10] For the most part, it was women and men of the middling ranks of colonial society who led and mounted temperance campaigns. Methodist, Baptist, and Anglican women encouraged their friends and neighbours to become involved and in the end helped to make temperance a special women's crusade.[11]

The emergence of hundreds of temperance societies throughout Upper Canada in the 1830s was one indication of the growing maturity of the colony. It was also evidence of colonial women's increasing social activism and their ability to use the dictates of domesticity to further various social causes that were of particular interest to persons of their sex. The rise of reform crusades also provided many women in Upper Canada with a formal sense of community, one that made them conscious of their shared status and work in society.

Ironically, however, women's growing involvement in the crusade to reform both individuals and society as a whole also accentuated the impact that class had on all colonists' lives. The very existence of aid and religious societies illustrated that some Upper Canadians had the financial means and presumed they had the moral and social responsibility to help "them" – members of the "lower" classes – who individually or collectively were economically or morally wanting.

Moreover, with perhaps the exception of the temperance movement, the actual organization and control of various benevolent groups reflected the social divisions in the colony. Ladies Maitland and Colborne and other elite women who headed women's aid organizations assumed that they had the right and the responsibility to define social ills. They also presumed to determine which causes most needed to be addressed and how best to do this. And women such as Anne Powell and Harriet Cartwright assumed that they had a duty to enter the homes of aid supplicants and to decide, not only *if* they were deserving of aid, but also *what* aid these families needed.

Women in Upper Canada did belong to a distinct female community and to some degree they did share a common culture that was based on their sex, their gender (as defined by individual men and the state), and similar experiences. But their class, their economic and their social position, the location of their homes, and their time of arrival in the colony also all had a very real impact on their lives and their work. And as women themselves were aware, such factors often divided or at least distinguished one group of women from another.

It was obvious to Mary O'Brien that the nature of her life and work on the farm was quite different from that of Helen Macaulay in town. Women who worked for wages also knew that their experience differed from that of women who worked without receiving a wage. And although almost all women in Upper Canada performed some kind of "domestic" work, there were significant variations in exactly what they did, how they did it, and how they felt about it. For example, it made a difference if a woman was an employee or an employer, or if she worked in a town or the country. Being an "independent" woman of affairs might provide some personal freedom; it did not guarantee a woman economic security or social respectability.

The impact that social and economic factors had on a woman's life was perhaps most evident to neighbours and employees of women such as the Macaulays and Powells. Their attachment to men of property and standing not only provided them with a life of apparent leisure, but it gave them real power over their domestic workers and over the lives of many in their communities, including many men. But even artisan, farming, and labouring families recognized fine social and economic differences between themselves and others in their communities and this had a direct impact on their wives' and daughters' lives and work.

The effect that time of settlement had on a colonial woman's life was somewhat less pronounced. The story of women's work in Upper Canada between 1790 and 1840 tends to be a story of continuity, in which age, marital status, and familial economic situation had most significance. The experience of becoming and being a mother in 1790 was, for example, not much different from bearing and looking after children in 1840. Although Frances Stewart arrived in the colony thirty years after Margaret Ryerse, both women's lives were governed by the repeated cycles of pregnancy, childbirth, and lactation. The sense of continuity and commonality of women's work over the first fifty years of colonial development was also the direct result of the nature of the colonial economy. Between 1790 and 1840, Upper Canada was a pre-industrial society. As Catharine Parr Traill discovered when she arrived in Douro in 1832, being a farmer's or artisan's wife was little different in the 1830s than it had been for Margaret Ryerse in the 1790s. Although they arrived in the colony some thirty years apart, Anne Powell and Helen Macaulay found that the duties and responsibilities they were expected to perform as wives of influential men were much the same.

Certainly the time of settlement did have some influence on how women carried out their work. The tools they acquired to help them in their work, the physical condition of their workplaces, and in some instances what work was expected of them did change over the period. In the 1830s, Helen Macaulay had the advantage of living in a big house in a relatively sophisticated urban community. Forty years earlier, Elizabeth Simcoe had had to make do with a tent in the backwoods. While Margaret Ryerse and her family initially coped without the benefit of roads, close neighbours, or even a village nearby, Mary O'Brien visited York regularly and almost always had help in the house. Time of settlement also made a significant difference in the lives of skilled and wage-earning women in the colony. In 1800, it was next to impossible for a woman to establish herself in a business or to find skilled work. By 1820, women had increasing opportunities to earn their living teaching, making clothes, or running a hotel.

None of these women lived in any golden age, however. And the story of women's lives and work in Upper Canada is not one of progress. It is one of gradual change – change that made some aspects of women's lives "easier" and others "more difficult." One might judge that Helen Macaulay had greater freedom of action than most of her contemporaries because of her wealth. She benefited from having the most up-to-date equipment in her house and servants to do her housework. In one sense her life was easier than Anne Powell's had been a generation earlier. Yet Helen Macaulay was under greater social and personal constraints than were prominent women who lived in Upper Canada before 1815. And though she and others of her class had far greater access to goods and services than did their mothers and their neighbours, they were also expected to be more involved in the lives of their families, more active in society, and more responsive to the needs of the community at large.

The changing nature of women's work in Upper Canada and its increasing variety and complexity over two generations of development is a reflection of the changes that were happening in Upper Canada was a whole. Over the next two generations, the pace of change would greatly accelerate; and many women would find themselves under even greater social and personal constraints. By the turn of the century, it would seem to some that women's work had been completely transformed. And yet in 1900, most women were still wives and mothers. Women continued to work in certain areas and fields that were deemed appropriate for individuals of their gender. And some women were still resisting such strictures.

It must be remembered, however, women's work in Upper Canada must be regarded within the context of its own times in order to be fully appreciated. Class, location, and time of settlement must all be considered in conjunction with evolving social attitudes and changing relations between the sexes. In 1840 as in 1790, women's work and the economic, social, and personal roles that they assumed were multifaceted. Women could be and were, all at once, mothers, daughters, sisters, wives, Christians, neighbours, housekeepers, and, as the situation demanded, shopkeepers, farmers, teachers, or society matrons.

Appendices

Patterns of Women's Part-time Employment, 1832–40

"Help"	Household of Captain William Johnson			
	Arrived	Left	Paid	Comments
Mrs Elwes:	17 May 32	14 June 32	–*	ill, 22 June 32
	15 June 32	17 June 32	$1.00	–
	–	14 July 32	$5.00	period of wife's confinement
Mrs Wheeler:	21 May 32	25 May 32	$1.00	–
Mrs Fairbourne:	21 May 32	25 May 32	–	–
	22 July 32	28 July 32	$2.50	for unkeep of James Johnson
Mrs Climskill:	–	7 March 33	yes	for washing
	25 July 35	5 August 35	–	–
	–	6 March 36	yes	3s.2d
	31 May 37	16 July 37	no	–
	–	2 Feb. 39	yes	for 14 days work
	22 April 39	28 April 39	yes	for 5 1/2 days
	–	8 August 40	–	owed 5s.
	8 Sept. 40	19 Sept. 40	yes	to sew
	2 March 41	28 March 41	$4.00	with Elizabeth Morton
	17 August 41	–	–	to sew

Patterns of Women's Part-time Employment, 1832–40 (Continued)

| "Help" | Household of Captain William Johnson | | | |
	Arrived	Left	Paid	Comments
Mrs Nugent:	22 May 37	several weeks at a time	–	–
	2 Oct. 37	30 Oct. 37	–	owed $5.00
	23 Nov. 37	28 Nov. 37	–	–
	10 May 38	13 May 38	–	with "Hogan's girl" who stayed for an extra week
	–	9 June 38	–	3 1/2 days
	–	23 June 38	–	3 1/2 days
	–	15 July 38	–	4 days
	15 Oct. 38	–	–	–
	4 Dec. 38	–	–	–
	21 Jan. 39	30 Jan. 39	–	9 days
	8 April 39	15 April 39	–	–
	5 May 39	–	–	–
	–	23 June 39	–	11 days
	26 Nov. 39	–	–	–
	27 Nov. 39	–	–	washing and rendering tallow
	–	29 Nov. 39	–	3 days
	13 Jan. 40	20 Jan. 40	–	–
Mrs Bramble:	23 Dec. 1838	–	–	to wash and clean
	29 Nov. 37	1 Dec. 37	–	–
	4 Dec. 37	17 Dec. 37	–	to wash
	18 Dec. 37	24 Dec. 37	–	–
	16 Sept. 38	–	–	–
Mrs Griffin and son:	3 Nov. 40	7 Nov. 40	yes	she for 5 days son for 3 days
Miss Smith:				sewer
	2 Nov. 40	10 Nov. 40	5s.	–
	28 Nov. 40	29 Dec. 40	–	–

Source: Information, including dates, payments, and comments are taken from Dairies of Captain William Johnson, Archives of Ontario, MS18.

* Signifies no reference in the Diaries.

APPENDIX TWO

Women in the Needle Trades in York, Upper Canada

Milliners, Mantuamakers	Date of Notice	Marital Status	Additional If Available
Maria De Dieman	1808	–	–
Francis Murray	1810–15	–	–
Miss Page	1817	single	–
E. Turquand/Carey	1820	–	B. Turquand clerk, 1833 Directory
Mrs Smith	1830	–	–
Misses Rubergall*	1830	single	–
Mrs Sewers*	1830	–	–
Mrs Claris*	1832	married	separate business
E. Butler	1833	–	a John Butler, saddler, 1833 Directory
Mrs/Miss Stonehouse*	1833	widow/single	–
Mrs Armstrong**	1833	married	shared premises with husband
Mrs Phipps**	1833/1837	married	shared premises with Thomas, grocer
Mrs Thatcher**	1833	–	–
Jane Wilkinson**	1833	married	shared premises with John, plasterer
Miss Lane	1834	single	–
Mrs Conrey*/ Miss Donlevy	1834	married/ single	–
Mrs Cochrane	1834	–	–
Mrs Steward	1834	–	had expert help
Miss Hall*	1836/1837	single	–
Mrs Price	1837	–	–
M. McCord	1838	–	sister/mother of teacher?
Miss Cochrane	1840	single	–

Women in the Needle Trades in York, Upper Canada (Continued)

Bonnetmakers	Date of Notice	Marital Status	Additional If Available
Mrs Jones/Miss Rose	1828	–	arrived from Quebec
Anne Osbourne		single	–
Mrs Carpenter	1830	–	–
Mrs Coleman/ Miss Boucher	1831	–	William Coleman, boot- and shoemaker, 1833 Anne Boucher had children's school, 1833 *Directory*
Miss Parsons	1833	single	perhaps daughter of Timothy Parsons, straw bonnetmaker and draper, 1833 *Directory*
Mrs Parsons	1833	married	–
Margaret Elliott**	1833	–	–
Mary Horlden*	1833	–	–
Ann Mitchelson**	1833	–	–
T. Nagle**	1833	–	–
Mrs Davidson	1833	–	–
Mrs Stockdale**	1833	married	shared premises with William, carpenter
Mrs Dickson	1834	–	–
Mrs Laing/ Miss Langley	1834	married	husband, drawing instructor; father, shoemaker, 1833 *Directory*
Mrs Robinson	1835	married	husband, tailor, straw bonnetmaker, 1833 *Directory*
	1837*	married	business listed separately
Miss Rankin/ Miss Chestnut	1836	single	John Rankin labourer, 1833 *Directory*
Mrs Scott*	1836	married	–
Miss Madden	1837	single	–
Mrs Connell*	1837	widow	–
Mrs Miller	1838	–	–
Mrs Porter/	1839	married	–
Miss King	–	single	–
Mrs George & Co.	1840	–	–

Women in the Needle Trades in York, Upper Canada (Continued)

Staymakers, Seamstresses	Date of Notice	Marital Status	Additional If Available
A. Adams*	1833	–	–
Mrs Short*	1833	–	–
Mrs Steed*	1838	married	shared with husband, boot- and shoemaker
Miss Stillman	1837	single	–
Mary Ann Hardy**	1833	–	–
Misses Hill**	1833/1837	single	lived with Samuel, carpenter
Mary Hord**	1833	–	–
Mary Lyness**	1833	–	lived with Kennedy Lyness, lathmaker
Rebecca Shattock**	1833	–	–
Mrs Watson	1834	married	husband, stonemason
Mrs Shaw	1834	married	husband, watchmaker
S. Mayhew*	1838	married	husband, drygoods merchant

Source: Lists compiled from advertisements in local newspapers, and businesses registered in the 1833 and 1837 York Directories.

* listed in 1833 or 1837 York Directory, in addition to a local newspaper.

** reference found only in either the 1833 or 1837 Directory.

Notes

PREFACE

1 *United Empire Loyalist*, 15 December 1827, taken from the *Gore Gazette*.
2 Mary Consitt, *Weekly Register*, 17 June 1824.
3 *Upper Canada Gazette*, 25 November 1819 (Mrs McGill's first name was never given).
4 On the death of Mrs Maria Buell, *St Catharines Journal*, 15 October 1835.
5 See *Brockville Gazette*, 23 October 1829, on the death of Mrs Rachel Wiltse, "relick" of Col Benom Wiltse.
6 This begins with Craig's seminal history of the colony, *Upper Canada*, and is evident in many subsequent scholarly works, including my own *The Lion, The Eagle and Upper Canada*.
7 This is not to suggest that historians are not now recognizing and considering the lives of the "little" people, both women and men, of Upper Canada. Much of this has appeared in selected articles in *Ontario History*, *Labour/le Travail* and *Social History/Sociale histoire* and in volumes of collected works, including Johnson and Wilson, eds., *Historical Essays on Upper Canada*. But we historians still tend to "read" our history backward. We often take not only the questions but also the concerns and the understandings of the twentieth century and apply them, sometimes indiscriminately, to the early nineteenth century. A case in point is the renewed interest in the rebellions of 1837 and the rise of responsible government in the colony. As Alan Greer commented in "1837–38: Rebellion Reconsidered" (Calgary: CHA Annual Meeting, 1994), 4, too often, we assume that "history [has] a discernable direction and flow." Things happened be-

cause they *had* to happen; the future developments make this self-evident. As Greer points out, 9, what many recent accounts and examinations of the rebellions lack "is an appreciation of context." I would argue that the same is true of our understanding of other events and circumstances in the colonial period. Our preoccupation with "the real history of the nation," that of the periods following 1841, 1867, or 1900, has frequently led us either to ignore or distort the colonial past.

8 See discussion in Kerber, "Separate Spheres, Female Worlds and Woman's Place," for an assessment of what our use of the "cult of true womanhood" has done to the writing of women's history, particularly in the United States.

It must be noted that although very little has been done in colonial women's history, the discipline generally has matured immensely in the last ten or fifteen years. In addition to a number of general histories, including Prentice, Bourne, Brandt, et al., *Canadian Women*, and volumes of collected articles, such as Strong-Boag and Fellman, eds., *Rethinking Canada*, Trofimenkoff and Prentice, eds., *The Neglected Majority*, and Light and Prentice, eds., *Pioneer and Gentlewomen of British North America*, there has been a plethora of detailed studies of Canadian women in the late nineteenth and twentieth centuries. See Gail Cuthbert Brandt, "Postmodern Patchwork: Some Recent Trends in the Writing of Women's History in Canada," *Canadian Historical Review*, 72 (4, 1991), 441–70.

9 See for example the work of Scott, *Making the Invisible Woman Visible*.

10 For a discussion of the challenges that this poses, see Pierson, "Experience, Difference and Dominance and Voice."

11 See for example Fowler, *The Embroidered Tent*, which is a collected biography of five prominent women, Elizabeth Simcoe, Catharine Parr Traill, Susanna Moodie, Anna Jameson, and Lady Dufferin; Fryer, *Elizabeth Postuma Simcoe*; McKenna, *A Life of Propriety*; Innis, ed., *The Clear Spirit*; Morris, *Gentle Pioneers*; Needler, *Otonabee Pioneers*; Thomas, *Love and Work Enough*.

12 A notable exception to this is the work of McKenna, *A Life of Propriety*, whose consideration of Anne Powell does consider fully all aspects of her long and often difficult life. For further discussion of the importance of women's biographies, see McKenna, "The Union Between Faith and Good Works"; Prentice, "Writing Women into History: The History of Women's Work in Canada," *Atlantis*, 3 Pt 2 (Spring 1978).

13 I use the term "apparent" advisedly. When I started this project, I too accepted that sources were limited. However, over the past five or six years, I have discovered that though it is often difficult to piece information together, there is much more available than one might suppose. In addition to the traditional manuscript sources that do include a wealth of information by reportage and in the many account books, newspapers are also invaluable – both for the rhetoric that they included and for the information

that can be garnered in advertisements, court reports, and references to women in other stories. In addition, for the post-1815 period, police, surrogate, and probate court records include a wealth of information.

14 John, ed, "Introduction," *Unequal Opportunities*, 3.

15 Tilly and Scott, *Women, Work, and Family*; Ryan, *Cradle of the Middle Class* and other works cited throughout this volume. For an exceptional study of the relationship of women, work, and family in Canada in the latter half of the nineteenth century, see Bradbury, *Working Families*. Marjorie Cohen, in *Women's Work, Markets, and Economic Development*, does begin to address the problem posed by dividing work into "productive" and "reproductive" and she notes that women's work in the colonial period "sustained the family in the basic consumption needs"(8). Her discussion of the early period is limited, however, and then includes only an examination of women's "productive" labour. This is also true of the Canadian Women's Educational Press publication, *Women at Work: Ontario, 1850–1930* (1974). As the title suggests, the focus is clearly on the latter half of the nineteenth century. In the one article that even mentions women's work in Upper Canada, Leo Johnson, "The Political Economy of Ontario Women in the Nineteenth Century," 13–32, only eight pages are dedicated to the subject.

16 Even here, eulogies can be a valuable source. See for example those printed in the local Methodist newspaper, the *Christian Guardian*, which often graphically described not only a woman's deathbed experience, but also her earlier conversion.

CHAPTER ONE

1 Mary Quayle Innis, *Mrs Simcoe's Diary* (Toronto: University of Toronto Press 1965), 15 March 1792, 54–5. Unless noted, all subsequent references to Elizabeth Simcoe's diary and her correspondence are taken from Innis. J. Ross Robertson, ed., *The Diary of Mrs John Graves Simcoe* (Toronto: Ontario Publishing 1934) is not as complete and does not include a number of her letters.

2 Ibid., Letter to Mrs Hunt, 26 April 1792, 58.

3 Innis, *Mrs Simcoe's Diary*, 86. Our knowledge of the numbers of residents in the colony in the prewar period is still incomplete. It appears that there were between 5,000–6,000 loyalists whose numbers had increased to about 14,000 by 1792: McCalla, *Planting the Province*, 249. At the invitation of Lieutenant-Governor Simcoe, the number of settlers rapidly increased. Michael Smith, *A Geographical View of the Province of Upper Canada* (Philadelphia, 1810) estimated 75,000 residents at the outbreak of the war. McCalla states that there were approximately 60,000 residents of European ancestry in 1811. See also Craig, *Upper Canada*, 51.

4 Innis, *Mrs Simcoe's Diary*, 27 June 1793, 96. The italics are mine.

5 Fowler in *The Embroidered Tent*, 17–47, explores the "awakening" of Elizabeth Simcoe as a result of her contact with the wilderness. Fryer has recently published a full-length biography, *Elizabeth Postuma Simcoe*.
Though Fryer does not place Elizabeth sufficiently into her time and
place, this biography does chronicle much of her daily life, including her
lengthy stay in the colony.

6 "Documents Relating to Catharine White," in J. J. Talman, ed., *Loyalist
Narratives from Upper Canada* (Toronto: Champlain Society 1946),
351–60, 354. Potter-MacKinnon, in *While the Women Only Wept*, 133–4, considers the case of some loyalist women from the time of the outbreak of
the American Revolution to their arrival in Upper Canada. She notes that
for most women "the decision to go was clearly not [theirs] to make."

7 La Rochefoucauld Liancourt, *Travels in Canada, 1795*, ed. Alexander Fraser.
Thirteenth Report of the Bureau of Archives for the Province of Ontario
(Toronto: A.T. Wilgress 1917), 28.

8 "Historical Memorandum by Mrs Amelia Harris," in *Loyalist Narratives*,
109–48, 110. It should be noted that the Ryerses were relatively fortunate.
Margaret Ryerse did not experience life in the Quebec refugees camps,
though she undoubtedly experienced the dislocation and disorientation
of being attached to an active loyalist during the revolution. See Potter-
MacKinnon, *While the Women Only Wept*.

9 "Mrs Amelia Harris," 110.

10 Ibid., 113, 114. In most instances, I have not corrected the spelling or punc-
tuation of the early nineteenth-century accounts. Where corrections have
been made, in exceptional cases, this is noted.

11 Russell, "Wage Labour Rates in Upper Canada," 61–80, 62. McCalla estimates in *Planting the Province*, 249, that the population in 1842 was 487,000.

12 "Mrs Amelia Harris," 145.

13 George Heriot, *Travels Through the Canadas* (1807) (Reprint, Edmonton: M.
Hurtig Ltd. 1969), 138–9. For a graphic illustration of the growth in popu-
lation and changing settlement patterns in the colony, see J. David Wood,
"Population Change on the Agricultural Frontier," in Hall, Westfall, and
MacDowell, eds., *Patterns of the Past*, 55–77.

14 McCalla, *Planting the Province*, provides the most comprehensive history
of the economic development of the colony throughout the period.

15 "Mrs Amelia Harris," 113, 116.

16 Peter Russell, "Forest into Farmland: Upper Canadian Clearing Rates,
1822–1839," in Johnson and Wilson, eds., *Historical Essays on Upper Canada*, 131–49, 134. Russell is careful to note, 133, that "there was no univer-
sal clearing rate for the whole colony." The rate depended on a number of
factors, including the skill and number of the choppers and the time that
the farmer could devote to it. He also notes that the high rates perhaps
achieved and necessary in the initial pioneering cycle decreased as the

farms became more productive. See also Cohen, *Women's Work*, 60–1, and McCalla, *Planting the Province*, 13–29, who presents a relatively detailed discussion of what he terms "the loyalist economy."

17 "Mrs Amelia Harris," 143.

18 "But the roads! O, the roads, you need some experience before you could *imagine* what the roads were," Susan Greeley, a loyalist settler remembered: "Susan Burnham Greeley's 'Sketches of the Past'" in *Loyalist Narratives*, 78–108, 101. Time and again, travellers and residents commented on the "intolerable condition" of those few roads that existed. Even those surrounding the principal settlements of the colony were often impassable in spring and fall, and it was not until well into the nineteenth century that a passable trail linked the villages of the upper province. Residents depended largely on water routes to move any distance. Mobility was increased when residents could use sleighs. See for example John Howison, *Sketches of Upper Canada* (1821) (Reprint, Toronto: S.R. Publishers 1965), 21, who noted that the road from Brockville to Kingston was "extremely bad" in 1821. An anonymous "English Farmer" advised prospective immigrants in *A Few Plain Directions for Persons Intending to Proceed as Settlers to His Majesty's Province of Upper Canada* (London, 1820), to travel by durham boat. See also E.C. Guillet, *Pioneer Travel in Upper Canada* (Toronto: Ontario Publishing 1933); McCalla, *Planting the Province*, 132–7.

19 "Mrs Amelia Harris," 116.

20 Ryan, *Cradle of the Middle Class*, 19. See also Tilly and Scott, *Women, Work, and Family.*

21 Catharine Parr Traill, *The Backwoods of Canada* (1836) (Toronto: McClelland and Stewart Ltd. 1966), 113. As Traill noted, "in the most populous and long settled districts," the bee or frolic "is most discontinued."

22 Ryan, *Cradle of the Middle Class*, 20. Within a few years of their arrival the Long Point settlement, where the Ryerses had located, had grown and prospered. "In a half circle of 20 miles," Amelia Harris recalled, "probably there was a population of a Hundred. People had ceased to count the families on their fingers, but no census was taken": "Mrs Amelia Harris," 120.

23 "Mrs Amelia Harris," 145. In 1810, one resident of Kingston proudly commented, "I have seen this wilderness in the course of a few years, converted into fruitful fields and covered with comfortable habitations. I have seen about me thousands, who without any other funds than their personal labour, in possession of extensive and well cultivated farms and abounding in all the substantial comforts of life". "Richard Cartwright,"*Letters of an American Loyalist* (Montreal, 1810), Letter 1.

24 Howison, *Sketches of Upper Canada*, 24, 119.

25 In "Migration, Pioneer Settlement, and the Life Course: The First Families of an Ontario Township," in Johnson and Wilson, eds., *Historical Essays on Upper Canada*, 175–202, 187, Darrell A. Norris considers the movement

into and out of Euphrasia Township in the mid-nineteenth century. He notes specifically that in 1851–52, many of the new arrivals to the area "had previously lived and worked elsewhere in Ontario." In his earlier consideration of "Household and Transiency in a Loyalist Township: The People of Adolphustown, 1784–1822," *Social History* XIII, 26 (November 1980), 399–415, Norris concludes that about half of the first households persisted in the area. In addition, there was a significant movement of individuals who came into and left the area. In his study of "Population Change on an Agricultural Frontier: Upper Canada, 1796 to 1841," in *Patterns of the Past*, 55–77, 63, Wood notes that "the fluidity of the population was a ubiquitous feature of Upper Canada. It occurred from the earliest days of settlement and was still a striking phenomenon in the mid-nineteenth century." See also discussion in Gagan, *Hopeful Travellers*, 6 passim; Katz, *The People of Hamilton, Canada West*; McCalla, *Planting the Province*, 36.

26 See Cowan, *British Emigration to British North America*. The history of immigration to Upper Canada has recently been augmented by a number of very fine studies. See among others Elliott, *Irish Migrants in the Canadas*; McLean, *The People of Glengarry*; Akenson, *The Irish in Ontario*.

27 Traill, *The Backwoods*, 50–2. See Fowler's account, *The Embroidered Tent*, 55–87, for a discussion of the impact this had on Catharine Parr Traill's life in the colony.

28 Traill, *The Backwoods*, 52. For an account of the Strickland's experiences in Upper Canada, see Major C.S. Strickland, in Agnes Strickland, ed., *Twenty Seven Years in Canada West or the Experience of an Early Settler* (London, 1853).

29 E.S. Dunlop, ed., *Our Forest Home, Being Extracts from the Correspondence of the Late Frances Stewart* (Montreal: Gazette Printing and Publishing 1902).

30 Journal of Mrs E.G. O'Brien, 1828–38, Archives of Ontario (AO), MS 199. All further references to Mary O'Brien's papers and correspondence are taken from transcripts of her papers in the Archives of Ontario. Audrey Saunders Miller's edited collection, *The Journals of Mary O'Brien, 1828–1838* (Toronto: MacMillan of Canada 1968) are not as complete, though the annotations do provide useful biographical information.

31 H.H. Langton, ed., *A Gentlewoman in Upper Canada: The Journals of Anne Langton* (Toronto: Clarke, Irwin 1950). The companion volume is W.A. Langton, ed., *Early Days in Upper Canada: Letters of John Langton from the Backwoods of Upper Canada and the Audit Office of the Province of Canada* (Toronto: MacMillan of Canada 1926).

32 Susanna Moodie, *Roughing It in the Bush* (1852) (Toronto: McClelland and Stewart 1970), 68, 117. For some sense of Dunbar Moodie's perceptions of living in Upper Canada, see Carl Ballstadt, Elizabeth Hopkins, and Michael Peterman, eds., *Letters of Love and Duty* (Toronto: University of Toronto Press 1993); Fowler, *The Embroidered Tent*, 93–131.

33 For a general discussion of the experience of immigrant gentlewomen in Upper Canada, see Maas, *Helpmates of Man*.

34 Elizabeth Simcoe had been informed that only Detroit had any "real" society: Innis, *Mrs Simcoe's Diary,* 26 April 1792, 58. See also Anne Powell's experiences there, noted in McKenna, "The Life of Anne Murray Powell," 117–9. McKenna's thesis has been significantly revised for publication as *A Life of Propriety.* As much of the information presented in the thesis does not appear in the book, subsequent references to McKenna's work on Powell are, unless noted, taken from the 1987 thesis.

35 Innis, *Mrs Simcoe's Diary,* 71. There was also a new Anglican church that four years later was described as resembling "a barn more than a church": Liancourt, *Travels,* 76.

For a brief biography of Ann Macaulay see Jane Errington, "Ann Macaulay," in Frances Halpenny, ed., *Dictionary of Canadian Biography,* VII (Toronto: University of Toronto Press 1988), 469. Subsequent references to the *Dictionary* will be to DCB.

36 See Isaac Weld, *Travels Through the States of North America and the Provinces of Upper Canada Lower Canada, During the Years 1795, 1796 and 1797.* 4th ed. (London, 1807), 65, 66. See also J. Ogden, *A Tour Through Upper and Lower Canada* (Litchfield, 1795), 54. There are numerous histories of Kingston. For the early period, see Arthur Lower, "The Character of Kingston," in Tulchinsky, ed., *To Preserve and Defend,* 17–36; Brian S. Osborne and Donald Swainson, *Kingston: Building on the Past* (Westport: Butternut Press 1988); Jane Errington, *Greater Kingston: Historic Past, Progressive Future* (Burlington, Ont: Windsor Publications 1988).

37 Weld, *Travels,* 90. See also Liancourt, *Travels,* 55, 57. Elizabeth Russell Diary, Russell Papers, Metropolitan Toronto Reference Library (MTL). For a brief biography of Elizabeth Russell see Edith Firth, "Elizabeth Russell," *DCB,* VI, 669–70.

38 Weld, *Travels,* 89.

39 See among others, Landon, *Western Ontario*; Hansen and Brebner, *The Mingling of the Canadian and American Peoples*; and Errington, *The Lion, The Eagle and Upper Canada*, Chapter 1.

40 Weld, *Travels,* 88; Liancourt, *Travels,* 61.

41 Heriot, *Travels,* 138–9. For general histories of York, see among others Firth, *The Town of York 1793–1815* and *The Town of York, 1815–1834*; Armstrong, *A City in the Making.*

42 Anna Jameson, *Winter Studies and Summer Rambles* (1838) (Toronto: McClelland and Stewart Ltd. 1965), 35. See also Fowler, *The Embroidered Tent,* 139–75; Thomas, *Love and Work Enough.*

43 Jameson, *Winter Studies,* 35. Traill had similar experiences. She described Cobourg, which before the war had only a few log houses, as being in 1832 "a neatly built and flourishing village, containing many stores, mills, a banking-house and printing office": *Backwoods,* 32–3.

44 S.D. Clark, "The Backwoods Society of Upper Canada," in *The Developing Canadian Community* (Toronto: University of Toronto Press 1962, 1971), 66.
45 Lower, "The Character of Kingston," 23.
46 Jameson, *Winter Studies*, 17.
47 As late as 1821, John Howison remarked that, unlike Kingston or Niagara, York's trade was "very trifling": *Sketches of Upper Canada*, 55. However, between 1815 and 1840, York more than tripled in size, and became the social as well as political capital of the province. Firth, *The Town of York: 1815–1834*, xxiii–xxxv.

Samuel Thompson, arriving in 1833, remembered York as a bustling government and market town. In addition to many wooden stores and numerous taverns, there were also four churches (English, Methodist, Presbyterian, and Roman Catholic) and "a brick and court house ... and Parliament buildings ... of the ugliest architecture": *Reminiscences of a Canadian Pioneer ... An Autobiography* (Toronto, 1884), 39–40. Anna Jameson, wife of the attorney-general, wrote four years later that the growth of Toronto was amazing: *Winter Studies*, 17. See also T. W. Acheson, "The Nature and Structure of York Commerce in the 1820s," in Johnson, ed., *Historical Essays on Upper Canada*, 171–93; Frederick H. Armstrong, "Metropolitanism and Toronto Re-examined, 1825–1850," in Gilbert A. Stetler and Alan F.J. Artibise, eds., *The Canadian City: Essays in Urban and Social History* (Ottawa: Carleton University Press 1984), 57–70.
48 D. McCalla, "Rural Credit and Rural Development in Upper Canada, 1790–1850," in Hall, Westfall, and MacDowell, eds., *Patterns of the Past*, 37–55, 37. As McCalla explains in *Planting the Province*, 9, almost from the beginning of settlement, all Upper Canadians, including those who were farmers, were actively and aggressively involved in the marketplace, "buying and selling, borrowing and lending and creating and dispersing capital."
49 McCalla, "Rural Credit and Rural Development," 45–7, notes that farmers did have some real power in their relations with the storekeeper. They were constantly in search of the best price for their goods, and the best terms of credit.
50 Russell, *Attitudes to Social Structure*, 2.
51 In "Town Fathers and Urban Continuity: The Roots of Community Power and Physical Form in Hamilton Upper Canada in the 1830s" in Johnson and Wilson, eds., *Historical Essays on Upper Canada*, 425–60, Michael Doucet and John C. Weaver propose a basic two-tier structure – "elite" and "non-elite." This would certainly apply throughout the colony. Yet it does not recognize the fine gradations that Upper Canadians assumed existed. In *Attitudes to Social Structure*, 7–9, Russell divides the "perceived social hierarchy of Upper Canada" into five strata – dependent, quasi-dependent, independent, marginal respectable, and respectable. Each is linked

to occupation and to certain income levels. The following discussion will make some reference to these, although it does not adhere strictly to Russell's definitions.

52 Innis, *Mrs Simcoe's Diary,* 86.

53 Shortly after Samuel Ryerse arrived in Niagara in 1794, he apparently made a point of "renewing" his acquaintance with his former comrade-in-arms, now the new lieutenant-governor of the colony, John Graves Simcoe: "Mrs Amelia Harris," 111. In *Becoming Prominent,* Johnson chronicles the various factors that had an impact on the creation of prominence. In particular, he explores the significant social, economic, religious, ethnic, and ideological factors that enhanced or hampered achieving prominence.

54 "Mrs Amelia Harris," 109–27.

55 Gerald E. Boyce, ed., *Hutton of Hastings: The Life and Letters of William Hutton, 1801–1861* (Belleville: Hastings County Council 1972). So did Catharine Parr Traill, Frances Stewart, and Anne Langton.

56 Howard Temperley notes in "Frontierism, Capital and the American Loyalists in Canada," *Journal of American Studies* 13, 1 (1977), 5–27, the importance of half pay toward the injection of capital into the colony and its impact on the status of those who received it. McCalla in *Planting the Province,* 17–19, outlines how other British expenditures, including salaries to colonial administrators and purchases by the British military garrisoned in the colony, had a significant impact on the economic health of the colony.

57 Hamnett Pinhey for example was considered "the squire of Horaceville." See Michael Cross's discussion in "The Age of Gentility: The Formation of an Aristocracy in the Ottawa Valley," in Johnson, ed., *Historical Essays on Upper Canada,* 226–41. Cross's idea of "gentility" and "aristocracy" has been used periodically throughout this work.

58 Traill, *The Backwoods,* 53, 113.

59 See also Needler, *Otonabee Pioneers;* Corbett, ed., *Portraits;* Innis, ed., *The Clear Spirit;* and Morris, *Gentle Pioneers* for a few other accounts of gentlewomen's experiences in early Canada.

60 Gagan, in *Hopeful Times,* 30, estimates that 25 per cent of rural householders were tenants or squatters. See also Glenn J. Lockwood, "Irish Immigrants and the 'Critical Years' in Eastern Ontario: The Case of Montague Township, 1821–1881," in Johnson and Wilson, eds., *Historical Essays on Upper Canada,* 203–36; Russell, *Attitudes to Social Structure,* 19–22.

61 Russell notes in *Attitudes to Social Structure,* 22, that squatters and pioneer farmers, of whom there were a significant number in Upper Canada, were "at the bottom of the farming status hierarchy." Next came the "small-scale farmer." The men and women attached to these three groups regularly "hired out" to earn cash to supplement the produce of their farm.

Only farmers with fifty or more acres cleared did not have the need or the time to hire themselves out, 19–20.

62 See, for example, Pinhey Diary, AO, MS199; Hamnett K. Pinhey Papers, AO, MS732; Benjamin Crawford Diaries, AO, MS796; Diaries of John Thompson, AO, MU846; Diary of George Leith, AO, MS69; Diaries of Captain William Johnson, AO, MS18; Extracts from Diary of Benjamin Smith, AO, MS199. See also McCalla, *Planting the Province*, 134–7.

63 Howison, *Sketches of Upper Canada*, 69, 135–7.

64 Elizabeth Simcoe found Robert Hamilton's home most appealing and comfortable. Innis, *Mrs Simcoe's Diary*, 30 July 1792, 76.

65 Men such as Richard Cartwright, Robert Hamilton, Robert Macaulay, (and after Macaulay's death in 1800 his brother-in-law John Kirby) were among the first members of a burgeoning colonial elite. Cartwright and Hamilton, for example, were the largest civilian employers and creditors in Kingston and Niagara between 1790 and 1810. Daily they and their associates negotiated contracts with agents in Montreal and London, with senior officers at nearby garrisons, and with local artisans, farmers, and labourers. Quarterly, prominent Upper Canadians sat as magistrates and judges of the high court. Annually they led the militia through its training exercises. And periodically, many of these men travelled first to Niagara and then to York to sit on the Legislative or Executive Councils and advise the lieutenant-governor. For further discussion of the composition of the Upper Canadian elite during this period, see Errington, *The Lion, The Eagle and Upper Canada*, Chapter 1; Wilson, *The Enterprises of Robert Hamilton*.

66 See McKenna, "The Union Between Faith and Good Works"; Susan Jill MacMicken, "'To Honour and Serve Him': The Early Life of Harriet Dobbs Cartwright 1808–1843," (MA thesis, Queen's University 1994).

67 As Firth noted, "the majority of the permanent citizens of York belonged to the petty bureaucracy or to the trades and labouring classes": *The Town of York, 1793–1815*, lxxxiv. These Upper Canadians were probably within the stratum Peter Russell termed "dependent" or "quasi-respectable."

68 See Houston, "The Impetus to Reform"; Patricia E. Malcolmson, "The Poor in Kingston, 1815–1815," in Tulchinsky, ed., *To Preserve and Defend*, 281–98; Fingard, *The Dark Side of Life*.

69 Tilly and Scott, *Women, Work, and Family*, 3.

70 Welter, "The Cult of True Womanhood," 151–74. See also Cott, *The Bonds of Womanhood*; Davidoff, *The Best Circles*; Peterson, *Family, Love and Work*; Gorham, *The Victorian Girl*; Burstyn, *Victorian Education*; Errington, "The Softer Sex."

71 "On the Influence of Female Beauty Upon Men," *Gore Gazette*, 17 November 1827. References to manly characteristics were often more indirect in the colonial press.

72 "Traits of Women," *Niagara Herald*, 14 August 1802.

73 "Woman," *Farmers' Journal*, 6 February 1828. See also "Woman," 15 February 1826; "The Happy Match," 19 July 1826; "Mr Editor," *Upper Canada Gazette*, 12 January 1828.

74 "Reckoner," *Kingston Gazette*, 11 August 1812. See also "Matrimony," *Farmers' Journal*, 30 August 1826; "Reckoner," *Kingston Gazette*, 12 May 1812. The "Reckoner" is believed to be John Strachan, in 1812 minister at St George's Church, Kingston. Later that year he moved to York and became increasingly influential in colonial politics. For a more detailed discussion of Upper Canadian attitudes to a woman's "proper" place see Errington, "The Softer Sex" and "Woman ... is a Very Interesting Creature."

75 Davidoff and Hall, *Family Fortunes*, 74. In *Helpmates of Man*, 41–5, Maas discusses the issue of "cultural transference" of such an ideology, particularly from Great Britain to Upper Canada.

76 Davidoff and Hall, *Family Fortunes*. This rests on the assumption that "identity is gendered," 29, and that middle-class women became both creators and the "bearers of status," 30.

77 For a discussion of this as it pertains to a number of middle-class immigrant women in the nineteenth century, see Maas, *Helpmates of Man*, 8.

78 *Kingston Gazette*, 25 September 1810. This volume does not explore the impact that differing ethnicity and religious beliefs had on women and their work. Both did influence women's work and society's expectations of them. To begin to explore the ethnic and religious diversity of Upper Canada, see McLean, *The People of Glengarry*; Marla Waltman, "From Soldiers to Settlers: Patterns of Loyalist Settlement in Upper Canada, 1783–1785" (MA thesis, Queen's University 1981); Landon, *Western Ontario*; Craig, *Upper Canada*; Lita-Rose Betcherman, "The Genesis of an Early Canadian Painter: William Con Moll Berczy" in Johnson, ed., *Historical Essays on Upper Canada*, 286–301; French, *Parsons and Politics*; Stuart Ivison and F. Rosser, *The Baptists in Upper and Lower Canada before 1820* (Toronto: University of Toronto Press 1956); Westfall, *Two Worlds*; Rawlyk, *The Canada Fire*; Grant, *A Profusion of Spires*.

79 Davidoff, *The Best Circles*, 17.

80 Memorandum of Lieutenant-Governor Simcoe to Hon. Henry Dundas, 30 June 1791, in E.A. Cruikshank, ed., *The Correspondence of Lieutenant Governor John Graves Simcoe* (Toronto: Champlain Society 1923–31), Vol. 1, 27. For a discussion of the impact that the colony's proximity to the United States had on political, social, and economic development, and the tension that arose in the colony over Simcoe's proposals, see Errington, *The Lion, The Eagle and Upper Canada*.

81 See discussion in Banfield, "The Well Regulated Family."

82 Both Myres, *Westering Women and the Frontier Experience* and Jeffrey, *Frontier Women*, note the importance of middle-class migrant women in the

American West in helping to recreate the patterns of their former home. Clinton in *The Other Civil War, American Women in the Nineteenth Century,* 7, argues specifically that from the arrival of the first European immigrants to North America in the seventeenth century, "women (native, black and white) were the key to the survival of settlements in North America. They were 'keepers of the culture.' "

83 In her study of *Frontier Women,* xiii, Jeffrey argues that although the conceptions of women's role "seemed far-fetched on the frontier, even counterproductive, they lost little potency." For many women, "they helped women hold on to their sexual identity and offered them hope of an ever-improving life." Myres in *Westering Women,* 239, does not deny that women who trekked west maintained many of their assumptions about separate spheres. She does argue persuasively, however, that as a result of their new environment, they "did enlarge the scope of woman's place." I would argue that the same was true for many middle-class women who arrived in Upper Canada.

84 Carroll Smith-Rosenberg, "The New Women and the New History," *Feminist Studies* 3 (1975), 193, quoted in Maas, *Helpmates of Man,* 2.

PART ONE

1 "Reckoner," *The Kingston Gazette,* 11 August 1812. Paul Banfield in his MA thesis "The Well Regulated Family: John Strachan and the Role of the Family in Early Upper Canada, 1800–1812" (Queen's University 1985) explores in some detail Strachan's attitudes to the family and the connections between the family and society at large. Family history has quite rightly become an important part of our discipline. Peter Laslett's extensive work with the Cambridge Group began an avalanche of studies into the family. See among others Laslett and Wall, eds., *Household and Family;* Gittins, *The Family in Question;* Stone, *The Family, Sex and Marriage;* Anderson, *Approaches to the History of the Western Family;* Ruggles, "The Transformation of the American Family Structure," 103–28; Comacchio, "'Beneath the Sentimental Veil', 279–302; Hareven, "Family History at the Crossroads," ix-xxiii; Hareven, "The History of the Family," 95–124; Bradbury, ed., *Canadian Family History.*

2 "Reckoner", *Kingston Gazette,* 8 January 1811.

3 For a brief examination of the law pertaining to marriage in the colony, see Ward, *Courtship, Love and Marriage,* 35–8; Backhouse, *Petticoats and Prejudice.*

4 "Monitor," *Upper Canada Gazette,* 28 December 1796; "Ladies Department," *Christian Advocate,* 6 January 1827. (Though the *Christian Advocate* was an American paper, it was received particularly by many Methodists in Upper Canada in the 1820s and 1830s. It is not too much to presume

that the views expressed in the *Christian Advocate* were therefore accepted by many Upper Canadians, especially many Methodists).

5 "Marriage," *Farmers' Journal*, 5 September 1827. See also "The Old Bachelor," *Kingston Chronicle*, 4 February 1820; "The Bachelor," 2 August 1826.

6 See for example "For the Gazette," *Kingston Gazette*, 15 July 1814; "The Old Maid's Registry," *York Weekly Register*, 11 March 1824; "Confessions of an Old Maid," *Farmers' Journal*, 21 May 1828. For a brief exploration of attitudes towards single women in Upper Canada and their role in the marketplace see Errington, "Single Pioneering Women in Upper Canada," 5–19. For a discussion of single women in Great Britain and the United States, see John, ed., *Unequal Opportunities*; Vicinus, *Independent Women*.

7 Ulrich, *Good Wives*, 6.

8 Tilly and Scott, *Women, Work, and Family*, Part I. In her ground-breaking study, *Working Families*, 15–16, Bradbury illustrates how this concept of the family economy "is the most useful concept [that] family historians have developed" to understand the contribution all members made to their survival, by both paid and unpaid work.

9 The same expectations were not always made of men. "Man is the creature of interest and ambition," a Washington Irving short story reprinted in a York paper explained. "Love is but the embellishment of his early life, or a song piped in the intervals of the acts." He seeks fame, fortune "and dominion over his fellow man ... A woman's whole life," on the other hand, "was the history of affection. The heart is her world": "The Broken Heart," *The Patriot*, 11 August 1835. See also "Respect for Females," *Gore Gazette*, 3 March 1827.

10 "The Reckoner," *Kingston Gazette*, 8 January 1811.

11 The ideal of the companionate marriage is ably explored in Degler, *At Odds*; Rothman, *Hands and Hearts*; Lebsock, *The Free Women of Petersburg*; Hammerton, *Cruelty and Companionship*; Davidoff and Hall, *Family Fortunes*. For the Canadian context, see Ward, *Courtship, Love and Marriage*; Comacchio, "Beneath the Sentimental Veil," 279–302.

12 "The Ladies," *British American Journal*, 29 July 1834. See also "Domestic Duties," *Christian Guardian*, 17 February 1836.

13 "The Reckoner," *Kingston Gazette*, 11 August 1812.

14 Ulrich, *Good Wives*, 8. See also Ryan, *Womanhood in America*, 1–75, who discusses women in colonial America as "the help mate" or Adam's Rib.

15 Cohen, *Women's Work*; Bradbury, *Working Families*.

16 As Bradbury comments in *Working Families*, 15, because most historians of the working class have "looked closely at skilled workers ... the role of family members in working-class culture and survival are still too often neglected." Indeed, she continues, "little Canadian working-class history explicitly bridges the fields of family, women and labour history."

CHAPTER TWO

1 The Journal of Mrs E.G. O'Brien, 1828–38, Archives of Ontario (AO), MS199, 4 June 1836.

2 Ward, *Courtship, Love and Marriage*, 51. On the basis of selected parish registers and particularly the register from Cornwall, Ward concludes that women married at a younger age than later in the century. Gagan in *Hopeful Travellers*, 87, posits that in the late 1840s and early 1850s the average age of marriage for women was twenty-one. See also Bradbury, *Working Families*, 55–7; Norton, *Liberty's Daughters*, 71–2; Buel and Buel, *The Way of Duty.*

3 "For My Daughter Julia," *Farmers' Journal*, 10 September 1828. This article had originally appeared in "Letter From a Lady to Her Daughter," in the *York Weekly Register*, 24 March 1825. The importance of marriage to a woman's happiness was a frequent topic in the colonial press. See among others, "Matrimony," *Niagara Gleaner*, 2 October 1824; "The Wife," *Farmers' Journal*, 19 December 1827; "Domestic Duties," *Christian Guardian*, 17 February 1836.

4 Ward, *Courtship, Love and Marriage*, 61.

5 Ibid., 102–6. See also Rothman, *Hands and Hearts*, 46–9. It should be noted that in some instances this resulted in very real dilemmas for the young girl. Though "bundling" does not seem to have been prevalent in Upper Canada, there were a number of court cases for breach of promise that suggest that some parents did condone such activities. When the man thereafter refused to marry a pregnant daughter, a few fathers turned to the courts for redress. See *Hogle v. Ham* (1825), Taylor 248 (C.A.). For a discussion of this case, and the implications it had for the rights of both parents and their daughters, see Backhouse, "Seduction," in *Petticoats and Prejudice*, 40–80, and "The Art of Seduction," 45–80; discussion herein Chapter 3.

6 O'Brien Journal, 26 March 1830.

7 Ibid., 27 July 1829.

8 Ibid., 1 January 1830.

9 Ibid., 2 February 1830. In her journal 1 January 1830, Mary noted that she would only accept the proposal if Lucy moved to Upper Canada, and her mother decided she would be happy there.

10 Mary O'Brien's diary includes numerous references to conversations with her relatives. See 29 January 1830; 20 February 1830; 30 March 1830; Journal Entry 32.

11 Ibid., 30 March 1830.

12 Ibid., 29 December 1829.

13 Ibid., 30 March 1830. She also claimed that Edward "would never encourage me to violate obligations which are in his eyes as sacred as mine": 26 March 1830.

14 Ibid., 26 March 1830.

15 Ibid., 19 April 1830.
16 Ibid., 26 March 1830. Davidoff and Hall note in *Family Fortunes*, 325, that such ambivalence was not unusual. Indeed, many middle-class women with "a satisfactory home" and "an assured income … seem to have regarded the seriousness of marriage as a not unmixed blessing." Davidoff and Hall also conclude, however, that a number of women were pressured into marriage by family, friends, and particular financial circumstances, 325–7.
17 O'Brien Journal, 19 April 1830. In *Hands and Hearts*, 115–17, Rothman chronicled many of the anxieties that young middle-class women in the United States experienced on contemplating marriage. She particularly noted the pull of the mother-daughter bond and that between friends. See also Anne Powell's experiences in McKenna, "The Life of Anne Murray Powell"; Carroll Smith-Rosenberg, "The Female World of Love and Ritual," in Smith-Rosenberg, ed., *Disorderly Conduct*, 53–76.
18 Such decisions may have been made somewhat easier for Helen Macaulay and Mary O'Brien because of the fact that they had some family in the vicinity of their new home. Helen had a brother in Montreal and a sister who was married and living in Queenston. Another brother in Scotland was willing to look after their mother. John Macaulay may also have reassured his future wife that she could return to Scotland to visit her mother after their marriage. See Macaulay Papers, AO, MS78. As Barbara Maas has succinctly stated, studies of women's immigration to nineteenth-century Canada are almost "non-existent": *Helpmates of Man*. See Susan Jill MacMicken, "'To Honour and Serve Him': The Early Life of Harriet Dobbs Cartwright 1808–1843" (MA thesis, Queen's University 1994), Chapter 1, for an account of Harriet Dobbs Cartwright's decision to marry.
19 In May 1830, just before her wedding day, Mary was concerned that because mails were slow Edward "will perhaps *be obliged* to be married without receiving the sanction of her [his mother] approval & sympathy under her own hand," even though they assumed he would receive it: O'Brien Journal, 5 May 1830.
20 Errington, "Single Pioneering Women in Upper Canada," 5–20.
21 McKenna, "The Life of Anne Murray Powell," 358. It should be noted that in most cases, though Anne was keen to see her daughters and granddaughters married, in the end she did acquiesce to their decisions. See Davidoff and Hall, *Family Fortunes*, 326–7, for the role British middle-class parents often played in trying to arrange their daughters' marriages.
22 O'Brien Journal, 24 June 1833, 28 June 1833. The two were subsequently married at the O'Briens: 7 July 1833.
23 See Chapter 3 for a discussion of the problems confronted by women who had a child out of wedlock.

24 See Osterud, *Bonds of Community,* Chapter 3 for a discussion of the importance of choosing a partner wisely in rural New York women's lives.

25 "Reckoner", *Kingston Gazette,* 24 March 1812; "Medical Remarks on Marriage," *Colonial Advocate,* 14 February 1828; "Letter to the Editor from T.
Muggins," *Kingston Chronicle,* 3 October 1829. For a general discussion of
the rhetoric of a "good" marriage, see Errington, "Woman ... is a Very Interesting Creature."

26 "For My Daughter Julia," *Farmers' Journal,* 10 September 1828.

27 "The Happy Marriage," *Upper Canada Gazette,* 19 February 1818; "Domestic Love," *United Empire Loyalist,* 7 July 1827.

28 *Farmers' Journal,* 19 July 1826.

29 "Matrimony," *Farmers' Journal,* 3 June 1829. See also *Colonial Advocate,* 16
December 1826.

30 "Reckoner," *Kingston Gazette,* 7 April 1812. See also "The Wedding,"
Farmers' Journal, 14 June 1826; "Married Well," 7 November 1827, where
men were advised to marry not for beauty or money; "The Good Match,"
24 September 1828. See also "Matrimony," *Niagara Gleaner,* 20 July 1833.

31 "Husbands and Wives," *Correspondent and Advocate,* 27 July 1833. See also
"On the Necessity of Domestic Accord," *Niagara Herald,* 18 April
1801; "Married Life," *Farmers' Journal,* 7 November 1832; "The Matrimonial Garden," *The Patriot,* 7 August 1835.

32 "Husbands and Wives," *Correspondent and Advocate,* 27 July 1833. See also
"The Happy Match," *Farmers' Journal,* 19 July 1826; "Rules for Husbands
and Wives," *Christian Guardian,* 5 February 1834.

33 "The Wife," *Upper Canada Herald,* 23 August 1825.

34 "Economy in a Family," *Farmers' Journal,* 3 June 1829. See also "On the Necessity of Domestic Accord," *Niagara Herald,* 18 April 1801; "The Happy
Match," *Farmers'Journal,* 19 July 1826; "A Good Wife," *Hallowell Free Press,*
20 September 1831; "Domestic Duties," *Christian Guardian,* 17 February
1836.

35 "For My Daughter Julia," *Farmers' Journal,* 10 September 1828.

36 See among others "Reckoner," *Kingston Gazette,* 11 August 1812; "Rules
for Husbands and Wives," *Christian Guardian,* 5 February 1834, and following discussion.

37 *Farmers' Journal,* 2 April 1828, reprinted from 11 July 1827.

38 "For My Daughter Julia," *Farmers' Journal,* 10 September 1828.

39 "Advice of a Father to His Only Daughter," *Colonial Advocate,* 12 November 1829; continued 19 November 1829.

40 "Advice to Married Women by Mrs Bennington," *Upper Canada Gazette,* 23
May 1807. See also "Matrimony," *Niagara Gleaner,* 2 October 1824; "Cure
for Anger," *Christian Guardian,* 30 April 1831.

41 "Reckoner," *Kingston Gazette,* 16 April 1811; 21 July 1812.

42 "Code of Instruction for Ladies," *Farmers' Journal,* 30 May 1827; "Matrimonial Maxims," 11 July 1827; "Matrimony," *Niagara Gleaner,* 20 July 1833.

43 Much work still needs to be done on women and religion in Canada in the nineteenth century. Although a woman's faith as well as her ties to organized religion had a very real impact on her life, this exploration of women's work does not discuss the matter, with the exception of women's involvement in benevolent and evangelical organizations. A number of other scholars have begun to tackle the problem, however. See Grant, *A Profusion of Spires*; Rawlyk, *Wrapped Up in God*; Rawlyk, *The Canada Fire*; Morgan, "Gender, Religion and Rural Society"; Albert Schrauwers, *Awaiting the Millennium: The Children of Peace and the Village of Hope 1812–1889*, (Toronto: University of Toronto Press 1993); Johnson, *A Shopkeeper's Millennium*; Ryan, *Cradle of the Middle Class*; Davidoff and Hall, *Family Fortunes*.

44 "On the Difficulties of Ascertaining the Characteristics of Young Women," *Kingston Chronicle*, 19 July 1828; "Wisdom Better Than Beauty," *Christian Guardian*, 24 September 1831. This was particularly stressed in the local Methodist newspapers, which gave considerable attention to the good woman. In addition, obituary notices appearing in the *Christian Guardian* often included lengthy comment on the religious life of the deceased, including her conversion experience.

45 "The Female Character," *Farmers' Journal*, 9 April 1828.

46 *Farmers' Journal*, 16 December 1827; "A Good Wife," *Colonial Advocate*, 10 December 1829. See also "Extract," *Upper Canada Gazette*, 30 August 1800; "Virtue," 19 October 1805; "View of the Comparative Virtue of the Two Sexes," *Niagara Herald*, 12 September 1801; "Advice to Married Women," *Upper Canada Herald*, 23 August 1825; "Married," *Colonial Advocate*, 2 March 1826; "From a Wife to Her Husband in Adversity," 8 November 1827; *Kingston Chronicle*, 16 September 1827; "On the Difficulties," 19 July 1828; "The Mother to Her Child," *Niagara Gleaner*, 7 April 1828; "A Female Teacher's Address to Her Pupils," *Farmers' Journal*, 16 December 1829; "Female Virtue," *Christian Guardian*, 25 July 1832.

47 "Marriage," *Farmers' Journal*, 5 September 1827. See also "Laura," *Upper Canada Gazette*, 5 July 1806; "Young Ladies," *Brockville Gazette*, 21 February 1829; "On Woman," *Cobourg Star*, 15 November 1831.

48 There is considerable work to be done to understand the question of prostitution in Ontario in the first half of the nineteenth century. As Backhouse notes in "Prostitution," *Petticoats and Prejudice*, 228–59, the issue is very complex, "not least because prostitution in nineteenth-century Canada was not a rigidly uniform occupation," 228. Reports in local Upper Canadian newspapers of charges laid and the women involved included *Upper Canada Gazette*, 3 September 1818 (Alice Brayden and Mary Flake, keeping a disorderly house); 21 October 1819 (Mary Losee, keeping a disorderly house); *Kingston Chronicle*, 5 October 1819 (desertion notice of Simon Stedman charging his wife Neoma with "squandering my property" and keeping "a house of ill fame"); 27 September 1822, (Margaret Losee, keep-

ing a disorderly house); *Canadian Freeman*, 22 April 1830 (Mrs Hutchinson, keeping a house of ill fame); *Hallowell Free Press*, 4 September 1832 (William and Mary Ann Granger, keeping a disorderly house); *The Patriot*, 21 January 1840 (noting a fight in a house of ill fame).

For a discussion of prostitution in other communities see Fingard, *Jack in Port*; Fingard, *The Dark Side of Life in Victorian Halifax*; Bradbury, *Working Families*; Stansell, *City of Women*; Mahood, *The Magdalenes*; Carol Smart, "Disruptive Bodies and Unruly Sex: The Regulation of Reproduction and Sexuality in the Nineteenth Century," in Smart, ed., *Regulating Womanhood*.

49 *Colonial Advocate*, 30 July 1829.

50 Some of the most pointed included "The Victim of Innocent Amusements," *Colonial Advocate*, 11 July 1828. "Caution of Females," *Christian Guardian*, 23 April 1831; "Letter to the Editor from Matilda," 13 August 1831. The concern about the deleterious impact of reading novels was apparently evident south of the border. See for example Rothman, *Hands and Hearts*, 39; Kerber, *Women of the Republic*, 233–64; Davidoff and Hall, *Family Fortunes*, 155–92.

51 "Deportment of Females," *Brockville Gazette*, 16 August 1832. See also "Traits of Women," *Niagara Herald*, 14 August 1802; "Diversity," *Kingston Gazette*, 10 December 1811.

52 "Beauty and Genius," *Kingston Chronicle*, 10 October 1829. See also "Sarah," *Niagara Herald*, 7 August 1800; "Letter to the Editor," *Kingston Gazette*, 22 March 1817; "Young Ladies," *Brockville Gazette*, 27 February 1829; "Woman," *Farmers' Journal*, 17 June 1829.

53 "Wisdom Better Than Beauty," *Christian Guardian*, 24 September 1831. See also "Female Virtue," ibid., 25 July 1832; "Observations and Hints," *Upper Canada Gazette*, 3 August 1805; "Diversity," *Kingston Gazette*, 2 July 1811; "The Wedding," *Farmers' Journal*, 14 June 1826; "Woman," *Hallowell Free Press*, 2 October 1831.

54 "Matrimony," *Upper Canada Gazette*, 16 September 1824. See also "The Oracle," *Kingston Chronicle*, 7 May 1819.

55 "Code of Instructions for Ladies," *Farmers' Journal*, 30 May 1827. The problems of women's curiosity and meddling were apparently considered quite acute in Upper Canada. See for example "Female Curiosity," *Upper Canada Gazette*, 19 October 1805; "Advice to Young Ladies, The Story of Amelia," *Kingston Gazette*, 17 December 1811; "The Whole Duty of a Woman," 15 August 1815; "The Happy Match," *Farmers' Journal*, 19 July 1827. An article, "Female Curiosity," *Canadian Correspondent*, 20 July 1833, concluded that sensible, well-educated women could "always find some occupation within the domestic circle;" they also consciously avoided "plunging into the business and affairs of the world, hardening their hearts, polluting their delicate feelings with subjects and details that nei-

ther the senses nor the imagination can become accustomed to contemplate without being tainted with the contagion of crime." In "Rules of Husbands and Wives," *Christian Guardian*, 5 February 1834, it was noted that a good wife "will never interfere in [her husband's] business unless he asks her advice and counsel and will never attempt to control him in the management of it."

56 "Matrimony," *Niagara Gleaner*, 20 July 1833.

57 "Reckoner," *Kingston Gazette*, 11 August 1812.

58 "Matrimony," *Niagara Gleaner*, 20 July 1833. Though the domestic sphere was the wife's domain, she was expected to obey either through "the submission of love" ("Letter to the Editor," *Kingston Gazette*, 21 July 1812) or if necessary at the point of threats and harsh words. See for example a letter to "Reckoner," *Kingston Gazette*, 11 June 1811, where the writer mentioned threatening his wife with the whip. See subsequent discussion on desertions and wife beating.

59 O'Brien Journal, 29 January 1830. When Mary finally accepted his proposal, Edward wrote, 19 April 1830, "I can never be sufficiently thankful to the Almighty for having given me such a monitress and such a companion."

60 See for example, O'Brien Journal, 13 May 1832. William Macaulay wrote to his mother, Macaulay Papers, 22 August 1838, that tomorrow he and Anne were having a special dinner to mark the occasion. See also discussion in Ward, *Courtship, Love and Marriage*, Chapter 7, 148–68; Davidoff and Hall, *Family Fortunes*.

61 McKenna, "The Life of Anne Murray Powell," 358. When Mary O'Brien's sister-in-law was attempting to convince Mary to accept Edward's proposal, she used her own happiness as one of her arguments. O'Brien Journal, 29 December 1829. Mary O'Brien was particularly conscious of the need to be accommodating as she expressed it in her journal, 2 May 1830. She willingly relieved her husband of his work when he periodically came down with the fever. Fanny Hutton both worked beside her husband and made special appeals for financial assistance on the family's behalf to his mother: Gerald E. Boyce, ed., *Hutton of Hastings: The Life and Letters of William Hutton, 1806–1861* (Belleville: Hastings County Council 1972). Certainly, both John and William Macaulay relied a great deal on their wives for advice and help; in their turn, they gave Helen and Anne their support and respect. John and his brother willingly helped nurse their wives through various illnesses and if the situation warranted, took them on trips to speed their recuperation. See for example Macaulay Papers, William to Ann Macaulay, 18 March 1836, where he proposed to take an Atlantic voyage; and a second letter 21 December 1838; John to Ann Macaulay about his intentions to take Helen away after the birth of triplets, 14 May 1840; 17 August 1840; 2 October 1840.

62 Macaulay Papers, William to Ann Macaulay, 15 August 1840. See Ward, *Courtship, Love and Marriage*, Chapter 7.

63 Macaulay Papers, Anne Macaulay to John Macaulay, 27 September 1833.

64 The Playter family was another example of note. Eli Playter's diary, for example, illustrates that with the marriage of each of the Playter children, the family in real terms increased rather than decreased. Parents, children, and grandchildren provided mutual support in times of trouble. They assumed responsibility for each other's well-being and celebrated each other's good fortune. Playter Dairy, AO, MS87. See also H. H. Langton, ed., *A Gentlewoman in Upper Canada: The Journals of Anne Langton* (Toronto: Clarke Irwin 1964); W. A. Langton, ed., *Early Days in Upper Canada: Letters of John Langton* (Toronto: MacMillan Canada 1926).

65 Macaulay Papers. Helen Macaulay visited her brother, John MacPherson (see letter to her husband 11 November 1835) and made an extensive trip to Scotland to see her mother in 1836 and 1837.

66 Ibid. See for example John to Ann Macaulay, 26 July 1839. So too did William Macaulay.

67 Ibid., John to Ann Macaulay, 13 August 1839. See also references in letters to his mother, 4 and 6 August 1839. The O'Briens too were conscious of the importance of family. Edward O'Brien said in a note to Lucy: "Do not make me feel like an intruder on a family party": O'Brien Journal, 19 April 1830. He felt, he wrote, as though he had some acquaintance with Lucy, through Mary's talk of her. He also accepted, apparently without question, that with his marriage to Mary, he became part of her extended family in Upper Canada and assumed some responsibility for their well-being. In particular, he knew that his mother-in-law would live with him and Mary once they were settled in their new home. Moreover, he undertook "to carry her out of the bush when she wishes to escape": 26 April 1830.

For a further discussion of the importance of the extended family in women's lives, see Davidoff and Hall, *Family Fortunes*, 215–22.

68. O'Brien Journal, 4 November 1830.

69 Lebsock, *The Free Women of Petersburg*, 35.

70 On 17 April 1834, the *Colonial Advocate* reprinted an article on "Legal Relations of Husband and Wife" from the *Family Journal*, which specifically laid out the English common law. It ended with the notation that a married woman could only give testimony against her husband when "her personal safety and life" were at stake. For an understanding of the legal position of married women in Upper Canada, see Backhouse, *Petticoats and Prejudice*.

71 In my research I have found only three or four such agreements. For a discussion of the situation in Quebec under the Civil Code, see Bradbury, *Working Families*, 49–52; for the United States, Basch, *In the Eyes of the Law*; for Great Britain, Davidoff and Hall, *Family Fortunes*, 275–9.

72 "Taming the Shrews," *Colonial Advocate*, 12 April 1827.

73 "Beating a Woman," *Colonial Advocate*, 2 April 1829.

74 *Colonial Advocate*, 12 April 1827.

75 This was not particularly unusual. Wife beating was also widely accepted in Great Britain and the United States. See for example Beattie, *Crime and the Courts in England*; Anna Clark, "Humanity or Justice? Wifebeating and the Law in the 18th and 19th Centuries," in Smart, ed., *Regulating Womanhood*; 187–206; Hammerton, *Cruelty and Companionship*; Stansell, *City of Women*; Gordon, *Heroes of Their Own Lives*; Bradbury, *Working Families*, 189–91.

76 Macaulay Papers, Anne Macaulay to Helen Macaulay, 23 September 1839.

77 *Brockville Recorder*, 31 August 1830, report from the Perth Court House.

78 *Kingston Chronicle*, 26 September 1829. See also trial of Mr Avery, *Canadian Correspondence*, 1, 15 June 1833.

79 *Colonial Advocate*, 8 May 1834.

80 *Canadian Emigrant*, 16 February 1832.

81 The Sovereign affair was given considerable coverage in newspapers throughout the colony: *Niagara Gleaner*, 28 January 1832; *Colonial Advocate*, 4 February 1832; *Colonial Spectator*, 8 February 1832; *Brockville Recorder*, 9 February 1832; *Canadian Emigrant*, 16 February 1832; *Christian Guardian*, 22 August 1832; "Sovereign the Murderer," *Brockville Gazette*, 23 August 1832.

82 *United Empire Loyalist*, 13 September 1828. For accounts of other cases, see conviction of Lesslie McCall for murdering his wife, *Colonial Advocate*, 13 September 1827. See also trial and execution of Michael Vincent, *The Loyalist*, 13 September 1828; *Niagara Gleaner*, 18 September 1828; *Niagara Herald*, 18 September 1828; *Canadian Freeman*, 18 September 1828; *Brockville Gazette*, 26 September 1828; *Colonial Advocate*, 27 September 1828; *Farmers' Journal*, 8 October 1828. In 1829, Thomas Easby was convicted and executed for murdering his wife: "Murders," *Brockville Gazette*, 13 February 1829; "Horrid Murder," *Farmers' Journal*, 18 February 1829; 2 September 1829; "The Perth Murder," *Colonial Advocate*, 26 February 1829.

83 See among others *Christian Guardian*, "Terrible Death by Intemperance," 8 May 1830; "Murders," 3 May 1832; "The Murdered Wife," 17 September 1834. See also ibid., 19 December 1829; 27 February 1830; 22 January 1831; 18 June 1831; *Colonial Advocate*, 5 November 1829; *Farmers' Journal*, 23 December 1829.

84 Some newspapers actually condemned the practice. See, for example, *Brockville Gazette*, 24 July 1829; "The Afflicted Wife," *Hallowell Free Press*, 12 May 1834.

85 As Linda Gordon stated in *Heroes of Their Own Lives*, 3, "family violence has been historically constructed." And she explained, "the very definition of what constitutes unacceptable domestic violence, and appropriate responses to it, developed and then varied according to political moods." In Upper Canada, wife battering was "acceptable."

86 Elizabeth Russell Diary, 8 January 1806, quoted in McKenna, "The Life of Anne Murray Powell," 161.

87 Diaries of Isaac Wilson, AO, MS199. The Waites had arrived 7 September 1819, as indicated in a letter between Isaac Wilson and his brother in Ireland.

88 Ibid., Isaac Wilson to his brother, 28 October 1828.

89 Ibid., 26 April 1832; 13 December 1834.

90 Throughout the 1830s there was a general concern about the threat intemperance posed to the life of various family members. In response, the Methodist *Christian Guardian* launched a campaign in 1830 against "the demon rum." See among others, *Christian Guardian*, 27 February 1830; 20 March 1830; 24 July 1834; 12 May 1835; 18 April 1838; 28 August 1839; 11 November 1840. The impetus against alcohol increased throughout the decade and became part of a colonial temperance crusade. See subsequent discussion in Epilogue.

91 McKenna, "The Life of Anne Murray Powell," 361–2. Stuart's subsequent suit for divorce was also considered "shocking in the extreme." McKenna notes that "Elizabeth's sister was implicated in the intrigue" because she had apparently known about her sister's intentions. This meant that even she might be excluded from "polite" society. For further discussion of the Powell/Stuart marriage and the difficulties of obtaining a divorce in Upper Canada, see Johnson, "Friends in High Places: Getting Divorced in Upper Canada."

92 Clara Thomas, "Introduction," to Anna Jameson, *Winter Studies and Summer Rambles* (1838) (Toronto: McClelland and Stewart Ltd. 1965), x.

93 *Kingston Gazette*, 23 September 1817.

94 *Niagara Gleaner*, Michael and Mary O'Connor, 19 May 1827; *The Patriot*, Wellesley and Eliza Richey, 14 June 1833.

95 See among others *Canada Constellation*, Magdeline and David Utter, 6 September 1799; *Upper Canada Gazette*, David Hartman and Catherine Kemp, 26 December 1810; Abel and Mary Conat, 22 April 1812; *Kingston Gazette*, Ebenezer and Sarah Phillip, 23 June 1812; *Niagara Gleaner*, Michael and Mary O'Connor, 19 May 1827; Robert and Mary Cole, 6 April 1833; *Gore Gazette*, Freeman and Rachel Dunham, 24 January 1829; *The Patriot*, Wellsley and Eliza Richey, 14 June 1833; *Correspondent and Advocate*, Jordan and Maria Post, 30 April 1835.

96 *The Patriot*, 16 March 1838.

97 There were at least 17 formal desertion notices in local newspapers between 1800 and 1840.

98 A total of 255 desertion notices were considered. This does not include 17 notices in which no desertion was mentioned, but husbands stated that they would no longer be responsible for their wives' debts. Although this sample canvasses almost all the newspapers in the colony, it is likely that at least some notices were overlooked. Moreover, it should be noted that complete runs of various colonial journals have not survived. Therefore, there were undoubtedly more official "cautions" than are considered here.

99 Notice of Philip Mark, *Correspondent and Advocate*, 14 December 1833.
100 *York Gazette*, 26 August 1811. A number of notices suggest that the wife
    had already left. One notice, from John Smith, *Colonial Advocate*, 12 April
    1825, stated "that for sundry abuses and threats made on my person and
    property by my wife Betsey, I therefore caution the public at large against
    giving her any credit on my account."
101 *Upper Canada Gazette*, George and Mary Crammer, 4 February 1804; *Ni-
    agara Gleaner*, Samuel and Mary Barick, 26 May 1828. See also *Farmers'
    Journal*, George and Martha Harrison, 16 May 1827; Sylvester and Eliza-
    beth Glynn, 23 May 1827. Total of five such notices.
102 *Correspondent and Advocate*, 29 May 1835.
103 *Niagara Gleaner*, 8 May 1830.
104 *Upper Canada Gazette*, Daniel and Deborah Buchore, 14 June 1797; S. and
    Anne Chisham, 23 November 1805; *Kingston Gazette*, John and Elizabeth
    Young, 20 April 1816; *Colonial Advocate*, Sam and Betsy Miller, 8 May
    1828; *Brockville Gazette*, James and Elizabeth Riddle, 14 December 1830;
    The Patriot, Patrick and Margaret McConnachy, 5 June 1840. In the Riddle
    case, Elizabeth was "discarded" because of her "illicit connexion" with a
    married man.
105 *York Gazette*, William and Sarah Thompson, 10 October 1812; *Niagara
    Gleaner*, Thomas and Catharine Bowlby, 24 April 1824.
106 *Upper Canada Gazette*, John and Nancy Anderson, 3 November 1798. See
    also *Farmers' Journal*, Samuel and Sarah Nash, 31 December 1828; George
    Lees' notice, *Brockville Gazette*, 26 February 1830.
107 *Upper Canada Gazette*, 1 March 1800.
108 *Farmers' Journal*, 3 September 1828.
109 Ibid., 12 June 1833. See also *York Gazette*, Abel and Mary Coonet, 18
    March 1812; *Kingston Gazette*, John and Elizabeth Young, 4 May 1816;
    Hallowell Free Press, John and Jemmina Huyck, 13 March 1832.
110 *Upper Canada Gazette*, 3 June 1815. There were other cases. John Young
    claimed that Elizabeth had taken "essential items belonging to me":
    Kingston Gazette, 20 April 1816. Obadiah Rosyell claimed that Sara, his
    wife, had taken "considerable of my property": *Farmers' Journal*, 8 No-
    vember 1826. Benjamin Vannatter claimed that his wife Nancy had taken
    "a long holland law": *Colonial Advocate*, 23 February 1820.
111 For a discussion of this, see Backhouse, *Petticoats and Prejudice*, Chapter
    7; Michael Grossberg, *Governing the Hearth*, Chapter 7. The question of
    custody was clear in this period. Fathers had custody of their children.
112 O'Brien Journal, 13 November 1829. Underlining is mine.
113 *Colonial Advocate*, 29 April 1830.
114 *Farmers' Journal*, Sylvester and Elizabeth Glynn, 23 May 1827.
115 *Upper Canada Herald*, William and Nancy Southand, 13 May 1823; *Niagara
    Gleaner*, Adam and Catharine Beam, 4 September 1830; Nathaniel and Sa-
    rah Wilson, 16 March 1833; *Upper Canada Gazette*, Peter Musselman (the

elder), 10 April 1817; Farewell, concerned about notes taken by his children, 11 August 1825; Leonard and Sally Freeman, 22 December 1825.

116 *Brockville Gazette*, 29 March 1830.

117 *Kingston Gazette*, 20 April 1816. See also, *York Gazette*, Abel and Mary Coonet, 18 March 1812; *Upper Canada Gazette*, 29 July 1815, in which the wife left four small children "to the mercy of strangers"; *The Patriot*, Thomas and Francis Mathews, 6 July 1838; Conrad and Betsey Kaak, 10 March 1840.

An analysis of the "types" of notices indicates that most husbands did not voice their concerns. There were 196 "basic" notices, (77 per cent), and 59 notices with "cause" (23 per cent). These numbers do not include the 17 notices where there is no mention of desertion or the 17 formal separation notices.

118 *Farmers' Journal*, 29 August 1828.

119 *Gore Gazette*, 24 January 1829. See also *Upper Canada Gazette*, Samuel and Backhouse, 12 May 1798; *Canada Constellation*, Magdelaine and David Utter, 6 September 1799; *Niagara Gleaner*, Michael and Mary O'Connor, 19 May 1827; *Colonial Advocate*, 5 August 1830; *Correspondent and Advocate*, David and Disdamay Clock, 22 May 1835.

120 *Canada Constellation*, 21 December 1799. See also *Upper Canada Gazette*, 19 December 1801.

121 *Canadian Freeman*, 30 June 1831. Patrick Molloy's notice indicated that his wife Elizabeth, had left at least twice: *St Catharine's Journal*, 5 May 1836.

122 *Canadian Emigrant*, 3 August 1833. A curious notice appeared in the *Brockville Gazette*, 25 August 1831. R. Wilkinson Whymp bade farewell to his neighbours and informed them that he would no longer be responsible for his wife.

123 *Gore Gazette*, 6 September 1828. The same was true for John Graham, of Catherine, *Kingston Gazette*, 10 April 1830. Isaac Davis waited two months, *Upper Canada Gazette*, 29 March 1821.

124 Mr Chisholm placed notice in *Upper Canada Gazette*, 23 November 1805, his wife, Anne, having left with a man to USA on 1 May 1805; Jacob Nell waited two years and only placed a notice after his wife, Lany, began "committing acts unbecoming of a virtuous married woman," *York Gazette*, 4 February 1812. See also *Upper Canada Gazette*, Catherine and John Smith, 29 July 1815; *Farmers' Journal*, 23 May 1817; David Purdy waited seven years after Abigail left, *Kingston Gazette*, 23 July 1819; Micaih Jon waited two years, 20 December 1822; *St Catharine's Journal*, Elizabeth and Patrick Molloy, 5 May 1836; John Lindsay waited five years after Elizabeth left, *The Patriot*, 28 April 1840.

125 *Gore Gazette*, Elizabeth and P. Livergood, 23 March 1829. The same reason had been given by a Mr Cameron, whose wife, Bethseba, had returned to town after two years absence, *Upper Canada Gazette*, 19 December 1801. She had left 1 January 1799.

126 A statistical analysis of those notices that do exist indicates that, not surprisingly, the total numbers of "desertion" increased over time.

Distribution Over Time

Years	Number	Percentage
1797–1810	25	9.8
1811–1820	37	14.5*
1821–1830	74	29.0
1831–1840	119	46.6
Total	225	

* *Note hiatus in desertion notices mid-1812 to 1815, covering the period of the War of 1812.*

127 Backhouse, *Petticoats and Prejudice*, 168.
128 For a full discussion of this case, and its implications, see ibid., 174–7. The original reporting of the case appeared in the *Kingston Chronicle*, 15 September 1826.
129 Also see Backhouse, "Pure Patriarchy, " 264–312; Stansell, *City of Women*.
130 *Upper Canada Gazette*, 11 May 1811.
131 *Farmers' Journal*, 17 May 1832. See also a notice to the clergy, about Nellie McCarty who was already married, *Kingston Chronicle*, 7 December 1821. There was also a notice from a Mr Bullyea stating that there was a woman calling herself Mrs Bullyea but she was not, *Niagara Herald*, 11 July 1801. It should be noted that women were not the only bigamists: see *The Patriot*, 29 June 1829.
132 *Canada Constellation*, 10 July 1799.
133 *Kingston Gazette*, 21 July 1826.
134 Ibid., 30 July 1811.
135 *Kingston Gazette*, 18 May 1814. Sarah Johnson of York fought to keep her deceased husband's land from his brother Thomas. He placed a notice concerning the land in the *Upper Canada Gazette*, 10 July 1817. A week later she placed a notice stating emphatically that Thomas had no rights.
136 *Canada Constellation*, 14 December 1799.
137 Original notice was placed 31 November 1799; her reply 14 December 1799.
138 *Farmers' Journal*, 4 March 1829. See also notice of Mrs Abbott who stated in the *Correspondent and Advocate*, 20 August 1835, that not only did her husband not own "the bed and board" but he also owed her money. A curious notice was placed by Catharine Tipp, *Upper Canada Gazette*,

15 May 1802, in response to one from William, 1 May 1802. Catharine noted "whereas William Tipp has endeavoured to pass himself up to the public for my husband; and has lately presumed to declare himself such in the *Upper Canada Gazette*, I conceive it a duty which I owe to the welfare of my children and my own future happiness to assure the world that I never was or never will be united in wedlock to that unworthy man."

139 *Niagara Gleaner*, 11 December 1824; original notice appeared 20 November 1824.

140 Original notice appeared *Upper Canada Gazette*, 6 January 1820; her reply 20 January 1820.

141 *Kingston Chronicle*, 10 December 1819; original notice appeared 3 December 1819.

142 Ibid., 17 December 1820.

143 *Brockville Gazette*, 15 September 1831.

144 *Colonial Advocate*, 29 January 1829, reprinted from the *Portsmouth Advertiser*.

145 See Gordon, *Heroes of Their Own Lives*.

CHAPTER THREE

1 See for example, Gagan, *Hopeful Travellers*, 61–94, 90. As Gagan notes, "Domesticity and motherhood were not preoccupations. They were occupations on which the survival of the family depended." See also Katz, *The People of Hamilton, Canada West*, 304; Bradbury, *Working Families*, 107–16; Chad Gaffield, "Canadian Families in a Cultural Context: Hypothesis from the Mid-Nineteenth Century," in Bradbury, ed., *Canadian Family History*, 112–34.

2 "On Education," *Upper Canada Gazette*, 21 August 1802.

3 "Woman," *Farmers' Journal*, 17 June 1829; "Ladies' Department," *Christian Advocate*, 2 December 1826.

4 "On Education," *Upper Canada Gazette*, 21 August 1802; "Female Responsibility," *British American Journal*, 22 July 1834. See also "Maternal Instruction," *Gore Gazette*, 25 January 1828.

5 Ulrich, *Good Wives*, 126. For a general discussion of mothering in the first half of the nineteenth century, see among others Ulrich, *A Midwife's Tale*; Fildes, ed., *Women as Mothers*; Daly, *Inventing Motherhood*.

6 Anne Powell to George Murray, York, 1 April 1818, Powell Papers, Metropolitan Toronto Reference Library (MTL), quoted in McKenna, "The Life of Anne Murray Powell," 144.

7 For a discussion of how this attitude came to affect the medical profession and others throughout the nineteenth century, see Maas, *Helpmates of Man*, 46–56; Mitchinson, *The Nature of Their Bodies*.

8 Historians are now beginning to examine changing attitudes to women's sexuality. As Carol Smart concludes, throughout the nineteenth century, women's bodies were considered "unruly and … a continual source of potential disruption to the social order": "Disruptive Bodies and Unruly Sex: The Regulation of Reproduction and Sexuality in the Nineteenth Century," in Smart, ed., *Regulating Womanhood*, 9–32, 30. See also Stansell, *City of Women*, 20–30; Dubinsky, *Improper Advances*, 126–8; Freedman, *Their Sister's Keepers*, 18–21.

9 See for example "Laura," *Upper Canada Gazette*, 5 July 1806; "Story of Mary Anne" in "Diversity," *Kingston Gazette*, 10 December 1811, *Colonial Advocate*, 4 November 1826; "Grace Neville," by Miss Mary Russell Mitford in *United Empire Loyalist*, 17 March 1827; 5 May 1827; "The Fickle Man," *Hallowell Free Press*, 16 October 1832.

10 "For the Oracle," *Upper Canada Gazette*, 14 February 1801. See also "Legacy for Young Ladies," *Farmers' Journal*, 11 October 1826; "The Lost Heart," 25 November 1829.

11 "For the Oracle," *Upper Canada Gazette*, 14 February 1801.

12 Ward, "Unwed Mothers," 34–56.

13 Quoted in Mitchinson, *The Nature of their Bodies*, 100. Ward notes in "Unwed Mothers" that many unwed mothers were not only tolerated but received into society with little problem.

14 For discussion of the position of unwed mothers in England in seventeenth-century England, see Patricia Crawford, "The Construction and Experience of Maternity," in Fildes, ed., *Women as Mothers*, 3–38; Ursula Vogel, "Whose Property? The Double Standard of Adultery in 19th Century Law," in Smart, ed., *Regulating Womanhood*, 147–65; Carol Smart, "Disruptive Bodies and Unruly Sexuality in the Nineteenth Century," in ibid., 9–32; Thurer, *The Myths of Motherhood*, 178–9, 188.

15 Macaulay Papers, Archives of Ontario (AO), MS 78, Ann to John Macaulay, 26 July 1838, where Ann stated that "I shall be obliged to send Michael away too". To Ann, Michael was clearly as much at fault as Mary. Ann was angered that when he was dismissed, Michael had the timidity to try to get a recommendation from John: Ann to John Macaulay, 8 August 1838. Though still upset with Mary's behaviour, Ann continued to be concerned for her well-being, and was relieved when she was hired as a wet nurse for a local neighbour, Mrs McFarlane: Ann to John Macaulay, 8 August 1838.

16 *Kingston Chronicle*, 6 October 1820. Dubinsky, *Improper Advances*, 64–71, provides a fine discussion on the present state of the Canadian literature on seduction and consensual sex. See also discussion in Backhouse, "The Art of Seduction"; Backhouse, "Seduction," in her *Petticoats and Prejudice*, 40–80; Rothman, *Hands and Hearts*; Palmer, "Discordant Music."

17 *Colonial Advocate*, 5 August 1824.

18 Ibid., 19 August 1824. This practice may not have been unusual. See Ward, "Unwed Mothers"; Ulrich, *Good Wives*, 122–3.

19 Reports included the account in 1825 of a couple convicted of murdering their newborn granddaughter: *Upper Canada Herald*, 30 August 1825. See also reports in "Mr Justice Harding's Address," *Upper Canada Gazette*, 27 July 1805; 21 August 1823; "Supposed Murder," *Farmers' Journal*, 16 February 1829; Dory Caldwell was committed to jail for abandoning her newborn in the yard of an inn: *Brockville Gazette*, 4 September 1829; "Infanticide," 16 October 1829; "The Cruel Mother," *Colonial Advocate*, 29 October 1829. After an inquest into the death of a baby near Bastard, a warrant was issued to apprehend the mother "and another woman" who, it was believed, had helped her: *Hallowell Free Press*, 9 October 1832. Philip Huffman was found guilty of infanticide and incest. He was sentenced to be hung. His daughter, the mother of the child, was also found guilty, and her death sentence was commuted to transportation: *The Patriot*, 19 May 1840.

For a discussion of infanticide, see Backhouse, "Infanticide," in *Petticoats and Prejudice*; Backhouse, "Desperate Women and Compassionate Courts"; Beattie, *Crime and the Courts in England*; R. W. Malcolmson, "Infanticide in the 18th Century," in J. S. Cockburn, ed., *Crime in England* (London: Routledge 1977), 187–209; Fildes, ed., "Maternal Feelings Re-assessed: Child Abandonment and Neglect in London and Westminster 1550–1800," in her *Women as Mothers*, 139–78; Hoffer and Hull, *Murdering Mothers*; Rose, *The Massacre of the Innocents*.

20 *British Whig*, 16 March 1834.

21 *Hallowell Free Press*, 21 July 1834.

22 In 1829, Ann Graham was jailed for the murder of her newborn. She had filled the baby's mouth with dirt: "The Cruel Mother," *Colonial Advocate*, 29 October 1829. At the subsequent trial, however, she was found not guilty: *Brockville Recorder*, 24 August 1830. (This was also a case in which the girl had managed to hide her pregnancy until the birth of the child.) In 1832, Margaret Stewart and her mother Mary were tried for infanticide. "There being no positive testimony of the women's guilt," they were acquitted: *Brockville Gazette*, 13 September 1832. In 1840, Mrs Mary Ekerlinn was charged with infanticide of her granddaughter: *The Patriot*, 7, 27 July 1840. After a lengthy deliberation and although Mrs Ekerlinn had confessed to the deed, the jury found her not guilty. It was determined that the child had been stillborn: *The Patriot*, 30 October 1840.

A few reports included only notice of investigation, and the presumption is that no charges were laid. See for example the case of "a woman named Brady" who was detected "under circumstances which induced the belief that she was about to destroy a fine Male Child": *Brockville*

Chronicle, 10 July 1835. An earlier report, "Supposed Murder," in the *Gore Gazette*, 17 January 1829, noted that a woman had been apprehended after the death of her newborn. Her husband had left her two years before and she was already raising many children. The *Brockville Gazette* reported 6 November 1829 that a father had tried to hide the birth of a stillborn child by throwing the baby into the river.

23 See *Hallowell Free Press*, 22 November 1831 and also "Dreadful to Relate," 3 May 1831, a report from the *Canadian Freeman* that a newborn had been discovered floating in a box in the river, with its skull split open.

24 Reported in the *Colonial Spectator*, 26 February 1834.

25 "Dreadful to Relate," *Hallowell Free Press*, 3 May 1831.

26 *Canadian Freeman*, 21 April 1831. Communities in northern Ontario had a similar attitude in a later part of the century. See Dubinsky, *Improper Advances*, 141–6.

27 Diaries of William Johnson, AO, MS 18, 18 September 1833; 13 September 1835.

28 Anna Jameson noted in *Winter Studies and Summer Rambles in Canada* (1838) (Toronto: McClelland and Stewart 1965), 80, 170, that she had encountered a family of ten or twelve children, and another of five or six. In *Hopeful Travellers*, 86, Gagan estimates that the child-bearing phase of a woman's life in 1851 was on average eighteen years and that during that time, she would have between eight and ten children. Katz notes in *The People of Hamilton*, 33–5, that the size of a family depended on its economic and social status and estimates fertility rates for women aged sixteen to forty-five, with children zero to fifteen years of age at about 2.5. What this indicates is that few adult women were ever entirely free of maternal duties. See also Crawford, "The Construction and Experience of Maternity" in Fildes, ed., *Women as Mothers*; Cohen, *Women's Work*, 72; Norton, *Liberty's Daughters*.

29 The ability of women to determine whether they were pregnant, and their subsequent ability to predict relatively accurately when they could expect to give birth is explored in Crawford, "The Construction and Experience of Maternity," in Fildes, ed., *Women as Mothers*, 3–38, 16–7; Linda A. Pollock, "Embarking on a rough passage: the experience of pregnancy in early modern society," in ibid., 39–67; Leavitt, *Brought to Bed*. Mitchinson notes in *The Nature of Their Bodies* that women often did not realize that they were pregnant until the fetus had "quickened."

30 The Journal of Mrs E.G. O'Brien, 1828–38, AO, MS 199, provides quite good daily accounts of this, particularly Mary O'Brien's experiences. See also Ulrich, *Good Wives*, 135–41; Fildes' bibliography in *Women as Mothers* presents a good overview of the British literature.

31 "From the Desk of Poor Robert the Scribe," *Kingston Gazette*, 18 August 1812.

32 "Medical Remarks on Marriage," *Colonial Advocate*, 14 February 1828.

33 As Mitchinson notes in *The Nature of Their Bodies*, this was not the case in the latter half of the century. Increasingly, as obstetrics and childbirth became a medical problem, doctors freely gave specific advice to their expectant patients. See also Duffin, *Langstaff*.

34 Early in her first pregnancy, Mary O'Brien took advice from a Mrs Munshaw, a local granny: O'Brien Journal, 19 March 1831. For further discussion of midwives during this period, see Ulrich, *A Midwife's Tale*; Leslie Giggs, "The Case of the Missing Midwives: A History of Midwifery in Ontario from 1795 to 1900," *Ontario History* 75 (1983); Scholten, "On the Importance of the Obstetrick Art," 426–45; Mitchinson, *The Nature of Their Bodies*, 162–4; Leavitt, *Brought to Bed*; Donegan, *Women and Men Midwives*.

35 O'Brien Journal, 3 August 1830. See also 9 December 1830.

36 Ibid., 2, 3 January 1829. Mary Southby's pregnancy had been very difficult, accompanied by persistent tiredness and for her last months, physical disability. She had required constant nursing. Mary O'Brien noted her sister-in-law's tiredness, 26 December 1828; her almost "helpless" situation, 15, 29, 31 December 1828.

37 Ibid., 14 January 1829. Mary made daily reports of her sister-in-law's health.

38 Ibid. Recognition of pregnancy came 11 April 1829; her weakness exhibited 20 July 1829. A doctor was suggested 5 August 1829 and she went to York 26 August 1829. Reference to the second miscarriage late in term occurred Journal No. 20, October 1829. See also 2 November 1829.

39 Ibid., 15 March 1830, where Mary Southby was pregnant again for the third time in two years. Her sister-in-law's fears arose from both her general concern about the potential dangers of the pregnancy and the history of Mary Southby's previous pregnancies.

40 Ibid., 28 April 1830; 7, 14 April 1830.

41 Ibid., 10, 13 July 1830.

42 Mary O'Brien noted her general recovery by the third day, ibid., 2 August 1830.

43 Ibid., letter of 16 December 1830.

44 Ibid., 27 February 1831.

45 Ibid., 25 January 1831. See also her comments during her second pregnancy, 6 August 1832.

46 Ibid. Arrangements were made by 27 December 1830. First mention of the birth was 11 April 1831.

47 Ibid., 15 August 1832.

48 Ibid., Entry July 1838.

49 Susanna Moodie, *Roughing It in the Bush* (1852) (Toronto: McClelland and Stewart 1962), 163.

50 As Ulrich concludes in her study of colonial women in New England, the duties of the various attendants during childbirth remain a mystery: *Good*

Wives, 126–7. See also an historiographical essay by Gorham, "Birth and History," 383–94. A number of women such as Mrs Johnson of Georgina appeared to prefer the services of a midwife, even though they could afford a doctor. Certainly the Johnsons relied on midwives during Mrs Johnson's confinements. A doctor attended the family infrequently, to treat illness or injury.

51 O'Brien Journal, 1 February 1830.

52 Ibid. On 26 April 1835, Mary helped a woman at the shanties "whose time had come." In that instance, it was apparently too late in the evening for the doctor to arrive and "none of her immediate neighbours had nerve or experience enough to supply his place." On 9 June 1835 and 29 April 1836, Mary again helped neighbours. In the latter instance the doctor arrived in time to help in the delivery of a dead infant. On 13 July 1838, Mary assisted another "old woman." Though increasingly confident in her ability as a granny, Mary never considered herself a professional and she always welcomed the arrival of professional help.

53 E.S. Dunlop, ed., *Our Forest Home, Being Extracts from the Correspondence of the Late Frances Stewart* (Montreal: Gazette Printing and Publishing Co. 1902), 8 January 1832, 130. Frances Stewart noted that when William was born in 1825, she had "the same old nurse" who could only stay a day: 31 July 1825, 79.

54 *Colonial Advocate*, 8 October 1829.

55 *Kingston Chronicle*, 3 August 1833; *British Whig*, 6 April 1835. Note that Mrs Smith practised for at least two years. See also advertisement of Mrs Bennett, *Colonial Advocate*, 1 May 1828; Mrs Eliza Tooth, 30 April 1829.

56 *Brockville Chronicle*, 18 September 1835, noting the arrival of Mrs Margaret McCaul from York. She stated, her "long experience & good reputation in Toronto" led her to predict that she would be busy in Brockville. See also notice of Mrs Lewis who stated she had ten years experience, and offered testimonials: *The Patriot*, 10 January 1832; Mrs Miller, "A professional mid wife," *Canadian Correspondent*, 3 May 1834.

57 This practice seems to have increased throughout the period. See Giggs, "The Case of the Missing Midwives"; Duffin, *Langstaff*. A growing number of notices began to appear in local newspapers from male doctors offering to attend pregnant and birthing women. See for example, *Farmers' Journal*, Drs Kolf and Marcus Whitman, 29 July 1829; *Colonial Advocate*, Dr Daly and Dr William Ferris, 22 October 1829; *The Patriot*, Dr T. Duggan, 9 August 1833; Dr A.C. Robinson, 10 January 1834 (Dr Robinson also offered free advice to "poor girls"); Dr Dewson, 4 September 1835. This list is by no means complete. Periodically, notices also appeared that other doctors had received licences to practise physic, surgery, and midwifery, licences granted by the lieutenant-governor. For a discussion of the licensing of doctors and the gradual medicalization of childbirth, see Mitchin-

son, *The Nature of Their Bodies*, 16–25. It should be noted, however, that midwifery was still prevalent throughout the Anglo-American world to the end of the century. See Lewis, ed., *The Politics of Motherhood*, 144; Litoff, *American Midwives*.

58 Macaulay Papers, Ann to John Macaulay, [1] December 1838. There had been other references that Helen was poorly, including 23 September 1838. See also Ann to John Macaulay, 26 September 1838; John to Ann Macaulay, 6 December 1838 (nurse), and 3, 6, 10 December 1838 (doctor).

59 Ibid., John to Ann Macaulay, 1 December 1838.

60 Ibid., 23 December 1838.

61 Ibid., John to Ann Macaulay, 26, 28 December 1838; 17 March 1839.

62 Ibid., 30 March 1840. First mention of the pregnancy appeared in a letter Ann Macaulay to Helen Macaulay, 20 January 1840. See also Helen to Ann Macaulay, 23 January 1840. On 30 January 1840 John wrote to his mother, that he wondered if Helen had "miscalculated" her time.

63 Ibid., John to Ann Macaulay, 10 April 1840.

64 Ibid. Report of the first death appeared in John to Ann Macaulay, 13 April 1840; the report of the other two, 17 April 1840. See also John to Ann Macaulay, 20 April 1840.

65 Ibid., Anne Macaulay to Ann Macaulay, 18, 25 April 1840.

66 Ibid., John to Ann Macaulay, 13 April 1840.

67 Ibid., John to Ann Macaulay, 12 May 1840. Helen appears to have recovered quite quickly, despite having problems with her milk (John to Ann Macaulay, 20 April 1840). On 26 April 1840, John wrote to his mother that Helen was at last sleeping well. Reference to Helen's thinness appeared in John to Ann Macaulay, 4 May 1840. Plans for John's trip away with Helen were first announced in a letter to his mother, 18 April 1840. The trip did not happen, however, until well into the fall of that year. It should be noted that Helen's sister in Queenston also turned to a doctor during her confinements. See letter John to Helen, 23 July 1839.

68 Gagan, in *Hopeful Travellers*, 89, estimates that 20 per cent of women did not survive childbearing. See also Pollock, "Embarking on a Rough Passage" in Fildes, ed., *Women as Mothers*, 36–49; Mitchinson, *The Nature of Their Bodies*, 54–5, 127; Duffin, *Langstaff*, 202–3.

69 Macaulay Papers, John to Ann Macaulay, 14 April 1840.

70 Ibid., 20 April 1840. Anne Macaulay also considered it important to provide reports of Helen's progress to their mother-in-law in Kingston. See for example, 25 April 1840.

71 Ibid. In 1838–39, Anne stayed with Helen for at least three weeks. She made reference to finally being at home in Picton in a letter to Helen, 25 February 1839. Even when family and friends left, Helen and also Mary O'Brien continued to have the support of their husbands and staff. Helen

Macaulay also helped her own sister in Niagara during her confinement in 1839.

The Powell family was another example of mothers and sisters helping each other through their confinements. See McKenna, "The Life of Anne Murray Powell," Chapters 9, 10. See also Stansell, *City of Women*, 55; Adrian Wilson, "The Ceremony of Childbirth and its Interpretation," in Fildes, ed., *Women as Mothers*, 68–107. Susanna Moodie was not so fortunate. In *Roughing It*, 164–5, she recounted that following the birth of her son when her husband had recovered, "he was obliged to sow the wheat ... and was, therefore, necessarily absent in the field that greatest part of the day." Susanna, still weak from her confinement, came down with the fever. Though her eldest daughter, Katie, did try to help, at under three years of age there was little she could do. "For hours at a time I had no friendly voice to cheer me, to proffer me a cold drink, or to attend to the poor babe; and worst still, there was no one to help that pale, marble child" Addie. It was not until her brother-in-law heard of Susanna's plight that things began to improve. Though his wife was away tending another sick relative, he sent his maidservant "every day for a couple of hours." Then the twelve-year-old maid's sister arrived to help. Initially, the hired man Jacob had pitched in. After seeing to his sick master, and offering tea or toast to Susanna, "he baked and cooked and churned, milked the cows and made up the butter as well and as carefully as the best female servant could have done." Such a reversal of roles for Jacob had lasted only until Susanna herself, still weak, was able to assume such women's work.

72 "Reckoner", *Kingston Gazette*, 5 March 1811.

73 "To the Reckoner," *Kingston Gazette*, 7 April 1812. Strachan also noted that fathers should find a "most exquisite delight" in their children's presence.

74 "To the Reckoner," *Kingston Gazette*, 12 May 1812.

75 "On Education," *Upper Canada Gazette*, 21 August 1802.

76 "Maternal Love," *Farmers' Journal*, 12 July 1826. This rhetoric of fatherhood echoes that being presented in Great Britain at the time. See Davidoff and Hall, *Family Fortunes*, 329–35, 245–8; Mary Abbott, *Family Ties: English Families 1540–1920* (London: Routledge 1993).

77 "Female Responsibility," *British American Journal*, 22 July 1834. It was also noted that mothers were "the affectionate, the ardent instructress of the children ... training them up to thought and virtue, to meditation and benevolence": "Woman," *Farmers' Journal*, 30 May 1827. See also "Diversity," *Kingston Gazette*, 10 December 1811.

78 "On Education," *Upper Canada Gazette*, 12 August 1802. An article on "Maternal Love," *Farmers' Journal*, 12 July 1826, stated that the relationship of mother and child was "the first, the fondest and the most lasting tie in which affection can bind the heart of man." See also "A Mother,"

Niagara Gleaner, 4 June 1825; "Woman," *Farmers' Journal,* 15 February 1826; "My Mother's Last Prayer," *Christian Guardian,* 7 May 1831.

79 "A Mother," *Niagara Gleaner,* 4 June 1825.

80 *Farmers' Journal,* 6 February 1828. See also *Niagara Herald,* 14 August 1802; *Farmers' Journal,* 15 February 1826; 9 April 1826; 16 July 1826; *Upper Canada Gazette,* 1 January 1828.

81 "On Education," *Upper Canada Gazette,* 21 August 1802. See also "Maternal Instruction," *Gore Gazette,* 25 January 1828.

82 "The Ladies," *British American Journal,* 29 July 1834.

83 "Maternal Instruction," *Gore Gazette,* 25 January 1828. See also "Maternal Love," *Farmers' Journal,* 12 July 1826; "On Education," *Upper Canada Gazette,* 21 August 1802.

84 "Influence of Woman on Society," *Christian Guardian,* 24 September 1834. See also "Maternal Love," *Farmers' Journal,* 12 July 1826; "The Infidel Mother," *Correspondent and Advocate,* 10 May 1834 (which noted that "children [could] be ruined by impious religion by maternal example"); "Women's Influence on Society," *Kingston Chronicle,* 9 April 1836.

85 "Female Responsibility," *British American Journal,* 22 July 1834. The expectations of mothers in the nineteenth-century Anglo-American world are fully explored in the extensive literature on the cult of true womanhood. See particularly Thurer, *The Myths of Motherhood;* Davidoff and Hall, *Family Fortunes;* Kerber, *Women of the Republic.*

86 O'Brien Journal, 4 November 1832. This was a constant refrain for Mary until her journal ended in 1838. See particularly 22 August 1832; Journal 98 (1834).

87 Dunlop, ed., *Our Forest Home,* April 1829, 114.

88 Ibid., 23 May 1827, 103.

89 Mitchinson notes in *The Nature of Their Bodies,* 123–51 that certainly at the end of the period under discussion here, women were using some form of fertility control. Mitchinson also provides a brief but comprehensive discussion of the historiography of birth control. See also Angus McLaren, *Birth Control in Nineteenth-Century England* (London: Croom Helm 1978).

90 Macaulay Papers, Ann to Helen Macaulay, 8 April 1840.

91 O'Brien Journal, 16 January 1832.

92 Ibid., 12 June 1833. Mary first started to wean the baby 29 April 1833. See also 13 June 1833.

93 Ibid., 27 August 1835. Mary noted ten days later, 3 September 1835, that "Baby seemed resigned to her fate."

94 For a general exploration of the use of wet nurses and who provided these services, see Fildes, "Maternal Feelings Re-Assessed: Child Abandonment and Neglect in London and Westminster 1550–1800," in her *Women as Mothers,* 139–78; Thurer, *The Myths of Motherhood,* 173–8; Crawford, "The Construction and Experience of Maternity," in Fildes, ed., *Women as Moth-*

ers, 336–8; Norton, *Liberty's Daughters*, 90–1. Mitchinson explores the premium many colonists placed on breast feeding. *The Nature of Their Bodies*, 199–201.

95 Macaulay Papers. In a letter to John, 26 December 1838, Ann Macaulay reported that Mrs Herschmer, who had a sore breast, and Mrs J. Forsyth, who had no milk, had both hired wet nurses. John Macaulay also hired a wet nurse after the birth of the triplets and in 1842 Helen again had a wet nurse for their latest child: Helen to John Macaulay, 1 September 1842. John Macaulay wrote to his mother 26 July 1839 that Helen's sister, Mrs Hamilton, had been forced to hire a wet nurse for her own child. Although Mary O'Brien noted in her journal that she did not have sufficient milk, she seems to have resorted to a bottle: O'Brien Journal, 2 September 1832. It was probably the practice in most elite households for wet nurses to live in. A notice in the *Kingston Chronicle*, 2 August 1837, specifically called for a woman to move in. In less affluent homes, the child probably moved in with the nurse.

96 *Cobourg Star*, 30 March 1836. See also *Kingston Chronicle*, 23 March 1831; 26 July 1834; 2 January 1835; 5, 16, 30 September 1835; 21 December 1836; 2 August 1837; 2 January 1839; 19 March 1839; 16 November 1839; *Upper Canada Gazette*, 13, 18 August 1821.

97 *Kingston Chronicle*, 26 July 1834. See also ibid., 13 August 1821, 26 March 1831, 16 November 1831, 6 September 1835, 31 December 1836; *The Patriot*, 20 March 1840; 29 May 1840; *Cobourg Star*, 30 March 1836. The few young women offering their services as wet nurses all claimed to have "the most respectful references" and were looking for a "respectable situation": *Kingston Chronicle*, 26 July 1834.

98 Dunlop, ed., *Our Forest Home*, April 1829, 114.

99 See also Amelia Harris, "Historical Memorandum by Mrs Amelia Harris," in J. J. Talman, ed., *Loyalist Narratives From Upper Canada* (Toronto: Champlain Society 1946), 109–48, 119.

100 O'Brien Journal, Journal 118, 1837.

101 Ibid., 19 December 1829. While staying with her grandmother in late 1836 and early 1837, Annie Macaulay "played a pretty trick with the decanter" of wine. On hearing of the news, John advised his mother "to keep the cupboard locked & the key out of her way for the future": Macaulay Papers, John to Ann Macaulay, 20 February 1837.

102 Dunlop, ed., *Our Forest Home*, August 1823, 43–4.

103 Thomas Radcliffe to Reverend Thomas Radcliffe, December 1832, in Thomas Radcliffe, ed., *Authentic Letters From Upper Canada* (Toronto: MacMillan of Canada 1953), 88.

104 O'Brien Journal, 13 May 1832. See also Cott, *The Bonds of Womanhood*; Ulrich, *A Midwife's Tale*. Infant mortality rates for this period are unclear. Evidence suggests that women expected to lose at least one child to acci-

dent or disease before the age of five. See Fiona Newall, "Wet-Nursing and Child Care in Akenham, Hertfordshire, 1595–1716," in Fildes, ed., *Women as Mothers*, 122–38; Davidoff and Hall, *Family Fortunes*, 339–40.

105 O'Brien Journal, 21 December 1831.

106 Ibid., 18 February 1832; Journal 66, March 1832, recorded Mary's attempts to immunize children from disease.

107 References to this are numerous in both the Macaulay Papers and the O'Brien Diaries. In 1837, John Macaulay was relieved to know that Annie was in Kingston. In a letter to his mother, 26 February 1837, he hoped that Annie would escape "the malignant diseases which are now prevailing in the country." On 16 May 1837, he reported to his mother that "a number of children [in York] had been carried off with something very like the influenza." On 18 October 1837, he expressed fear of whooping cough. See also 28 May 1839, noting that Helen and children were in Queenston for the sick season; 6 August 1839, referring to Helen hoping to avoid sickness; fear of measles and scarlet fever, 24 December 1840; 18 February 1841; 7 March 1841. See also Helen to John Macaulay, June 1840, written from Kingston, hoping that baby would benefit from the change of air; Helen to Ann Macaulay, March 1841, noting that she would take the children to Niagara to escape problems in York; John to Ann Macaulay, 31 March 1841, noting that Helen and the children had gone to Queenston "to avoid illness in York." William wrote to John Macaulay, 8 August 1834, advising that their mother leave Kingston to avoid cholera. Other references to cholera include John Kirby to John Macaulay, 21 December 1831; John Macaulay to John Stanton, 31 July 1834; 9 August 1834; Stanton to Macaulay, 1 August 1834.

Mary O'Brien recorded in her diary 4 April 1832, that she was so concerned about measles and scarlet fever that she refused to go to an inn until she was sure there was no illness there. See also O'Brien Journal, Entry 113, October 1836 for reference to Mary's fear of whooping cough.

Of particular concern to all Upper Canadians were the ravages caused by cholera. On 25 July 1832, Mary reported in her journal that cholera had appeared in York. Though Edward did not at that time believe it to be "generally either contagious or infectious," Mary hoped, 19 August 1832, that her mother would come to them to avoid the illness. In 1834, when cholera again appeared, there was considerable alarm.

108 O'Brien Journal, 22 November 1833.

109 Ibid., 10 March 1834.

110 Catharine Parr Traill, *The Backwoods of Upper Canada* (1836) (Toronto: McClelland and Stewart 1966), 107.

111 Macaulay Papers, Ann to John Macaulay, 23 July 1840.

112 William Johnson Diary, 11 July 1832.

113 Amelia Harris remembered that even in the earliest years of settlement although her neighbours lived miles away, "if anyone was ill, they were cared for by neighbours and their wants attended to": "Mrs Amelia Harris," 130.

114 Playter Diary, AO, MS 87.

115 Macaulay Papers, Ann to John Macaulay, 20 July 1840.

116 Ibid., 15 April 1839.

117 The definitive work on changing attitudes to children and child-rearing practices is still Ariès, *Centuries of Childhood*. See also Davidoff and Hall, *Family Fortunes*, 343–5; Norton, *Liberty's Daughters*, Chapter 3; Graff, "Remaking Growing Up," 35–59; Greven, *The Protestant Temperament*. The rhetoric of child-rearing in nineteenth-century Upper Canada seemed to most closely resemble Greven's "genteel" model of child rearing, which emphasized love and the constant attention of parents.

118 "Woman," *Farmers' Journal*, 30 May 1827; "Parental Government," *Christian Guardian*, 14 August 1833. See also "Diversity," *Kingston Gazette*, 10 December 1811.

119 "Family Government," *Niagara Herald*, 6 June 1801; "From the Desk of Poor Robert the Scribe," *Kingston Gazette*, 9 June 1812.

120 See ibid., and "Parental Government", *Christian Guardian*, 14 August 1833. One article on education began by citing John Locke. "Those children who are the most chastised, rarely prove the best men ... punishment, if it be not productive of good will certainly be the cause of much injury": "Education," *Farmers' Journal*, 15 April 1829.

121 "Letter to the Reckoner," *Kingston Gazette*, 17 March 1812. See also "From the Desk of Poor Robert the Scribe," *Kingston Gazette*, 9 June 1812; "Manners and Order," *Farmers' Journal*, 28 November 1827; "Parental Government," *Christian Guardian*, 14 August 1833.

122 John Macaulay's correspondence indicates that he was particularly active in his children's lives. When his youngest daughter, Helen, fell quite ill in July 1840, for example, he fearfully wrote, "It would be a severe blow to me if we should lose this little pet for I have become very fond of her": Macaulay Papers, John to Ann Macaulay, 7 July 1840. See also letter of 24 August 1840. See also Francois Noel, "Research Note – 'My Dear Eliza': The Letters of Robert Hoyle, 1831–1844," *Social History /Histoire Social* XXVI, 51 (May 1993), 115–30; "A Note: Being Letters from Thomas Priestman," *Ontario History* LXXXI, 1 (March 1989), 40–58.

123 Gerald Boyce, ed., *Hutton of Hastings: The Life and Letters of William Hutton, 1801–1861* (Belleville: Hastings County Council 1972), William Hutton to mother, 24 February 1835, 47. In 1833, Catharine Parr Trail wrote to thank her mother for sending clothes for the new baby. "He grows fat and lively, and," she reported, "as you may easily suppose, is at once the

pride and delight of this foolish mother's heart." And Catharine continued, "his father loves him as much as I do": Traill, *The Backwoods*, 2 November 1833, 68. In *Family Fortunes*, 330–2, Davidoff and Hall describe
similar experiences among middle-class fathers in Britain.

124 Macaulay Papers, John to Ann Macaulay, 13 December 1836.

125 Ibid., 11, 17 February 1837. A number of men also hired mother-substitutes if their wife was ill or away for any length of time, or remarried if
their wife died. See Chapters 7 and 9 following.

126 O'Brien Journal, 5 May 1834.

127 Macaulay Papers, Ann to John Macaulay, 14 January 1837; John to Helen
Macaulay, 23 April 1837; John to Ann Macaulay, 16 May 1837.

128 Ibid., Ann to John Macaulay, 20 May 1837.

129 Ibid., William Macaulay reported to Helen Macaulay that Annie was disciplined "when necessary": 3 February 1837.

130 Ibid., John to Ann Macaulay, 6 November 1837.

131 Ibid., 28 January 1840. Ann was reported to have fed the baby a pill.

132 Ibid., 8 February 1838. On 21 December 1838, William reported to his
mother that "Annie was getting a whipping the morning after I arrived.
That will do – that will do, she cried."

133 Ibid., Helen to John Macaulay, 29 August 1839; Helen to John Macaulay,
13 September 1839; Ann to Helen Macaulay, 4 July 1839.

134 "Dreadful Effects of Ardent Spirits," *Christian Guardian*, 26 June 1830.

135 Some testified that he had abused the child for some time: *Canadian Freeman*, 17 November 1831. Instances of children injured after they had
been left by parents unattended also were reported. *Brockville Chronicle*,
30 October 1835, for report of mother's neglect.

136 O'Brien Journal, 22 April 1835. In fact, Mary O'Brien had started teaching Willie his numbers and writing at the age of three: O'Brien Journal,
22 April 1834. For the next few years, Mary assumed responsibility for
teaching all her children their primary lessons by conducting daily lessons in reading and writing.

137 Macaulay Papers, John to Helen Macaulay, 5 March 1837; Ann to John
Macaulay, 14 July 1839.

138 In "Children, Schooling and Family Reproduction," *Canadian Historical
Review*, LXXII, 2 (June 1991), 157–91, Chad Gaffield provides an enticing
review of the literature on schooling in Ontario in the nineteenth century,
and proposes that at least in rural Ontario, literacy was quite high. And
as Houston and Prentice have argued in *Schooling and Scholars*, 84–5, "if
there was an initial falling off in literary skills as a result of heavy [la-
bour] demands ... the decline seems to have been temporary ... The vast
majority of Upper Canadians who grew up after 1830 considered themselves literate." The debate begun by Graff in *The Literacy Myth* contin-

ues, however, for as Gaffield notes, 175, "One major obstacle to a better understanding of rural literacy is the paucity of sources." For a discussion concerning the American situation, see Joel Perlmann and Dennis Shirley, "When Did New England Women Acquire Literacy," *The William and Mary Quarterly* xlviii, 1 (January 1991), 50–67.

139 Dunlop, ed., *Our Forest Home*, April 1829, 116. See also 18 October 1831, 126; 25 January 1827, 105.

140 For a discussion of the importance of the family in education, see Houston and Prentice, *Schooling and Scholars*, Chapter 1; Davidoff and Hall, *Family Fortunes*, 340–1; Bradbury, *Working Families*; Gagan, *Hopeful Travellers*, 84–6; Parr, ed., *Childhood and Family in Canadian History*, numerous articles in Bradbury, ed., *Canadian Family History*, including Bradbury, "Gender at Work at Home: Family Decisions, the Labour Market and Girl's Contributions to the Family Economy," 177–98; John Bullen, "Hidden Workers: Child Labour and the Family Economy in Late Nineteenth-Century Urban Ontario," 199–219; Gaffield, "Canadian Families in a Cultural Context," 135–57.

141 Boyce, ed., *Hutton of Hastings*, William Hutton to his mother 27 March 1836, 56.

142 Ibid., 4 May 1840, 79; 14 February 1841.

143 Dunlop, ed., *Our Forest Home*, March 1832, 128. Frances wrote that the eldest, Anna, "is so careful and steady that I can now leave home with an easy mind; she takes care of everybody and everything."

144 Ibid., 20 April 1834, 131–2; 17 February 1834, 133.

145 Jameson, *Winter Studies*, 80.

146 See following Chapters 6 and 9.

147 Macaulay Papers, John Strachan to Ann Macaulay, 5 July 1803.

148 Ibid., Ann to John Macaulay, 26 January 1808. See also 2 June 1808; 5 July 1808.

149 Ibid., 19 April 1808.

150 Ibid., 25 July 1840. See also Ann to Helen Macaulay, 23 September 1837; Ann to John Macaulay, 19 September 1839; 4 October 1839.

151 Ibid., John to Ann Macaulay, 23, 28 September 1839.

152 Ibid., 12 December 1839. See also 2 March 1840 which reported that the Macaulays had hired Mrs Savigny. See also John to Ann Macaulay, 18 October 1939; 7, 17 August 1840. See also Ann to John Macaulay, 25 July 1840. Further reports of Annie's progress are found in John to Ann Macaulay, 23 November 1840; 5 February 1841. For a more detailed discussion of the increased opportunities for and expectations of formal education in Upper Canada, see Chapter 9.

PART TWO

1 Tilly and Scott, *Women, Work and Family,* 12. Since the publication of this seminal work, a growing number of historians have used the concept of the "family economy." Ryan, *Cradle of the Middle Class,* 19, concluded that on the New York frontier, settlers created a corporate family economy, "a domestic system of production that bound family members together like a single body in a common enterprise of subsistence." See also Cohen, *Women's Work,* Chapter 4; Chad Gaffield, "Canadian Families in Cultural Context: Hypotheses from the Mid-Nineteenth Century," in Bradbury, ed., *Canadian Family History,* 135–57; Bradbury, *Working Families.*

2 Tilly and Scott, *Women, Work and Family,* 21; Tilly and Scott note, 6, 19–20, that "the specific form of the family economy differed" sometimes significantly, depending on where the family lived and the occupation of the male head of the household. One of the most often overlooked but important pioneering studies of women's work in colonial America is Spruill, *Women's Life and Work.*

3 Anna Brownell Jameson, *Winter Studies and Summer Rambles in Canada* (1838) (Toronto: McClelland and Stewart 1965), 171.

4 John Howison, *Sketches of Upper Canada* (London, 1821), 239. See Gagan, *Hopeful Travellers;* Jensen, *Loosening the Bonds;* Osterud, *Bonds of Community.*

5 Catharine Parr Traill, *The Backwoods of Canada* (1836) (Toronto, McClelland and Stewart Limited 1966), 20 November 1832, 54. Soon after her marriage, Mary O'Brien noted that prices for goods and produce were very dear in York, and she wished that she and Edward were well enough established to have a large garden, a number of pigs, and cattle: Journal of Mrs E.G. O'Brien, 1828–38, Archives of Ontario, (AO), MS 199, 1 December 1830. See also comments in Samuel Strickland, *Twenty Seven Years in Canada West,* Vol. 2 (London: Richard Bentley 1853), 291, and discussion in following chapter.

6 Ulrich, *Good Wives,* 9.

7 In *An Economic History of Women in America,* 27, Matthaei asserts that frontier farms were self-sufficient. However, subsequent historians, including McCalla, *Planting the Province,* Ryan, *The Cradle of the Middle Class,* and Jensen, *Loosening the Bonds* have convincingly refuted Mattaei's conclusions.

8 McCalla, *Planting the Province,* 92, notes that a substantial minority of rural households "were not primarily engaged in agriculture." See also Gagan, *Hopeful Travellers,* 37–8.

9 See subsequent discussion, Chapter 8.

10 Cohen, *Women's Work,* 24; Ulrich, *Good Wives,* 67. See previous notes.

11 Cohen, *Women's Work,* 38.

12 Ibid., 41.

13 McCalla, *Planting the Province*, 88. Cohen's premise in *Women's Work* is that the Upper Canadian economy rested primarily on the production of wheat and timber for export and that colonial farmers strove to become part of this. McCalla specifically and successfully challenges this assumption. Cohen's focus is also really on developments in the post-1850 period and often she seems to be reading the record backward.

14 Osterud, *Bonds of Community*, 185.

15 As will be discussed later, Upper Canadians made quite definite distinctions between the "help" and a "servant." See Chapter 5.

CHAPTER FOUR

1 H.H. Langton, ed., *A Gentlewoman in Upper Canada: The Journals of Anne Langton* (Toronto: Clark, Irwin 1950), 4 July 1839, 115. See introduction of *A Gentlewoman* for a brief history of the Langton family's residence in Upper Canada.

2 As her brother anticipated, Anne took over "the whole housekeeping department," and was "Prime Minister of the House." The other two women "each [had] a separate office." John and Anne's mother was "exclusively … left the duties of beautifying the house and garden, no sinecure on a new farm." Aunt Alice, "reign[ed] paramount in the pig stye, poultry yard, etc., and shall be my Master of Wardrobe": Langton, ed., *A Gentlewoman*, John Langton to Thomas Langton (father), 28 July 1834, 5–6.

3 Ulrich notes in *Good Wives*, 9, that a woman in colonial North America was "simultaneously a housewife, a deputy husband, a consort, a mother, a mistress, a neighbour and a Christian." For a discussion of the work American women did in the later period, see Jensen, *Loosening the Bonds*; Osterud, *Bonds of Community*.

4 W.A. Langton, ed., *Early Days in Upper Canada: Letters of John Langton* (Toronto: MacMillan of Canada 1926), John Langton to his brother, 9 January 1834, 64.

5 Edwin Guillet in *Early Life in Upper Canada* (Toronto: Ontario Publishing 1933), 157–8, describes in some detail the construction and appearance of such homes. See also Samuel Strickland, *Twenty Seven Years in Canada West*, Vol.1 (Toronto: Richard Bentley 1853), 165, who recommended that new emigrants build a shanty twenty-four by sixteen feet; Thomas Radcliffe, ed., *Authentic Letters from Upper Canada* (Toronto: MacMillan of Canada 1953), 16–19, noted the cost and method of construction for a shanty sixteen by nineteen feet.

6 Catherine Parr Traill, *The Backwoods of Upper Canada* (1836) (Toronto: McClelland and Stewart 1966), 44–5. See also Robert Sellar, *A Scotsman in Upper Canada: A Narrative of Gordon Sellar* (Toronto: Clarke, Irwin 1969), 62. Before his marriage, Edward O'Brien's home consisted of a "general

apartment including beside … the linen which was hanging from the beams to dry – his dairy, work bench, cellar, pantry, library, larder, drawing room, dining-room & kitchen": Journal of Mrs E.G. O'Brien, 1828–38, Archives of Ontario, (AO), MS 199, 28 January 1830.

7 References are made to this in the Playter Diaries, AO, MS 87; Strickland, *Twenty Seven Years*, Vol. 1, 171; Susanna Moodie, *Roughing It in the Bush* (1852) (Toronto: McClelland and Stewart 1962), 154.

8 William Dunlop, *Statistical Sketches of Upper Canada* (London, 1832), quoted in Guillet, *Early Life*, 168.

9 Langton, ed., *Early Days*, John Langton to his father, 11 February 1837, 185. See also Guillet, *Early Life*, 167–71.

10 Guillet, *Early Life*, 159. See also "Susan Burnham Greeley's Sketches of the Past," in J.J. Talman, ed., *Loyalist Narratives from Upper Canada* (Toronto: Champlain Society 1946), 78–108, 104; Strickland, *Twenty Seven Years*, Vol. 1, 165–71.

11 Traill, *The Backwoods*, 60. Once the house was complete, it was also to have a veranda on two sides "which forms an agreeable addition in the summer, being used as sort of an outer room in which we can dine."

12 Moodie, *Roughing It*, 154.

13 Langton, ed., *Early Days*, John Langton to his mother, 12 September 1833, 25–6.

14 See ibid., John Langton to his brother, 9 January 1834, 64–5. (He noted that he still did not have a table). This was particularly true for earliest arrivals to the colony and for those residents with little or no capital. Among others, see Strickland, *Twenty Seven Years*, Vol. 1, 91–2; O'Brien Journal; E.S. Dunlop, ed., *Our Forest Home: Being Extracts from the Correspondence of the late Frances Stewart* (Montreal: Gazette Printing and Publishing 1902), 8 August 1822, 15; 10 February 1823, 30.

15 Traill, *The Backwoods*, 60.

16 O'Brien Journal, 29 May 1830.

17 In *A Woman's Work is Never Done*, Davidson outlines the impact that available furnishings, home and household size and household technology had on the demands of the houseworker. See also Cowan, *More Work for Mother*; Strasser, *Never Done*.

Carol Shammas in "The Domestic Environment in Early Modern England and America," in Peter Charles Hoffer, ed., *Colonial Women and Domesticity: Selected Articles on Gender in Early America* (New York: Garland Publishing Inc. 1988), 194–215, discusses the changing inventory of colonial homes and the implications this had both for women's work and the choices householders made concerning consumer goods. For further discussion of how size and furnishing affected families' lives, see Demos, *A Little Commonwealth*; Jensen, *Loosening the Bonds*, 48–51; and particularly Ulrich, *Good Wives*.

18 Radcliffe, ed., *Authentic Letters from Upper Canada*, Thomas to William Radcliffe, 10 August 1837, 37.

19 See Guillet, *Early Life*, 159–60.

20 Traill, *The Backwoods*, 60. Wood stoves began to be available in the colony before the War of 1812. It appears that initially they were very expensive. See Guillet, *Early Life*; Cowan, *More Work for Mother*.

21 Langton, ed., *A Gentlewoman*, 70. On 10 October 1838, Anne Langton described in some detail the original cookstove, which they finally supplemented with a "proper" oven

22 Dunlop, ed., *Our Forest Home*, letter of Frances Stewart, 5 November 1823, 48. When the Stewarts first arrived in Upper Canada, they had only one fireplace; which was in the kitchen. Frances frequently noted the problem of the cold: September 1822, 19. See also Playter Diary; Langton, ed., *A Gentlewoman*, 1 January 1839, 87, where she noted that a boy had been hired to bring in wood and keep the fire going.

23 Langton, ed., *A Gentlewoman*, 1 January 1839, 87.

24 The local newspapers often printed advertisements from local candle and soapmakers. In addition, some retailers sold tallow, molds and other equipment needed to manufacture candles at home.

25 O'Brien Journal. Mary O'Brien noted in August 1829 that "I could not write in my journal as we have forgotten to make candles." The next day, 11 August 1829, she recorded that the household now had both wax and tallow candles. See also 18 April 1831. Thomas Ridout also made reference to his mother making candles: letter to George Ridout, 22 December 1815, Ridout Papers, quoted in Firth, *The Town of York, 1793–1815*, 239–40; Strickland, *Twenty Seven Years*, Vol. 2, 291.

26 Langton, ed., *A Gentlewoman*, 4 January 1839, 90. Anne noted that with dipped candles, she could "have one good making and have done for a time than by filling your molds every day". See also 22 December 1839, 137; 10 March 1840, 143; 12 April 1839, 107; 14 May 1841, 183.

27 Langton, ed., *Early Days*, John Langton to his brother, 23 August 1833 (appended to a letter, 2 August 1833), 20.

28 Ibid., April 4 1834, 93–4; letter to his father, 24 May 1834, 115.

29 Langton, ed., *A Gentlewoman*, 13 September 1840, 161. Anne Langton commented, "In England the servants are always crying out for chips. Here, they accumulate in the wood yard to a most inconvenient extent and you cannot get the servants to make use of them."

30 See among others Moodie, *Roughing It*, 202; Radcliffe, ed., *Authentic Letters from Upper Canada*, letters of December 1832, 91; January 1832, 145; Strickland, *Twenty Seven Years*, Vol. 1, 66–80, 173–4; Guillet, *Early Life*.

31 See Cowan, *More Work for Mother*, 20–5, for a description of the basic diet and preparation of food in a pre-industrial American household.

32 O'Brien Journal, 8 December 1830.

33 Langton, ed., *A Gentlewoman*, 10 October 1838, 69–70. See also Ulrich, *Good Wives*, 19–24, for a discussion of the work involved in cooking in colonial American households; Cowan, *More Work for Mother*, 16–39.

34 Moodie, *Roughing It*, 90. See also Gerald Boyce, ed., *Hutton of Hastings: The Life and Letters of William Hutton, 1801–1861* (Belleville: Hastings County Council 1972), 24 February 1835, 43; O'Brien Journal, 11 April 1829.

35 Langton, ed., *A Gentlewoman*, Anne to William Langton, 11 December 1837, 56. Anne Langton took pride in her bread and depending on the ingredients available, made both leaven and unleavened bread, using hops or salt as a rising agent: 10 October 1838, 60–71. So too did Mary O'Brien, who commented, on "a collar of brawn ... which I flatter myself we have now nearly attained perfection": O'Brien Journal, 24 December 1829. In Radcliffe, ed., *Authentic Letters from Upper Canada*, Bridget Lacy sent Mary Thompson a recipe for making Canadian barm and bread: December 1832, 139–40. See also Sellar, *A Scotsman*, 62–3; Dunlop, ed., *Our Forest Home*, 19 August 1827, 103.

36 O' Brien Journal. Mary often noted that her stew had "tipped into the fire": 1, 25 June 1830.

37 Langton, ed., *A Gentlewoman*, 6 April 1846, 227. Langton also noted the problem of acquiring fresh meat throughout the winter, 3 March 1840, 140. Mary O'Brien had similar problems. On 11 February 1832, she bemoaned that "I have been making wonderful contrivances to get a dinner today, having nothing in the house but salt pork & three eggs & fat pork makes me sick & disagrees with Ed'D – now this is a terrible hardship to be sure." She explained that she had not intended to be at home that night and had not killed a chicken. More importantly, she did not want to incur a bill at the butchers. See also 20 May 1829; 30 June 1830; 2 July 1830; 18 May 1832; 14 June 1833; 19 July 1833. Frances Stewart commented, Dunlop, ed., *Our Forest Home*, 5 April 1823, 32, that they "had no great variety in our food as pease soup and boiled pork make our dinner today." Though they did have bread, there were no potatoes or other meat. See also 5 April 1824, 58.

38 Langton, ed., *A Gentlewoman*, 17 October 1838, 77; 25 October 1838, 81. See also O'Brien Journal, Mary's mother butchering pigs, 4, 6, 18 November 1828; Mary killing and butchering pigs, 6, 13 November 1829; 13 November 1830; 28, 30 December 1830; 7 November 1831, Mary cryptically noted "pig killing again"; 4 April 1835; Journal 118, 1837.

39 Anne Langton provided considerable detail on this process. For example she noted, Langton, ed., *A Gentlewoman*, 12 January 1839, 94, "in the first place, we had our shambles meat to take down and examine. The damage was not very considerable but the trouble was ... we also cut up a quarter of beef. John was operator in chief but the saw and cleaver were also wielded by female hands. The kitchen scene would have entertained

some of our English friends and probably shocked others." On 22 March 1840, 147, she again commented "unpacking and re-packing barrels of pork and barrelling pickle made this a busy day and there is more of the same to do tomorrow." See also Boyce, ed., *Hutton of Hastings*, 27 March 1836, 53.

40 Sellar, *A Scotsman*, letter 8 December 1825, 81.

41 O'Brien Journal, 27, 31 November 1828; 16, 18 November 1830. There are also numerous references to this in Langton, ed., *A Gentlewoman*.

42 Langton, ed., *A Gentlewoman*, 3 August 1839, 126–7. See also 22 September 1840, 163. Strickland, *Twenty Seven Years*, Vol. 2, 296–7. Almost all women's correspondence makes references to pickling and preserving.

43 Many housewives also appeared to have made beer and whisky for the family: O'Brien Journal, 28 October 1830; 6 May 1831. See McCalla, *Planting the Province*, 25, 33; Cohen, *Women's Work*, 74–5.

44 Traill, *The Backwoods*, 9 May 1833, 65; Boyce, ed., *Hutton of Hastings*, William to his mother, 24 March 1840, 75. See also O'Brien Journal, 7 March 1829; Radcliff, ed., *Authentic Letters from Upper Canada*, Bridget Lacy to Mary Thompson, December 1832, 138.

45 Traill, *The Backwoods*, 65.

46 See Sellar, *A Scotsman*, 10 March 1826, 90; Moodie, *Roughing It*, 214; Strickland, *Twenty Seven Years*, Vol. 2, 298–311.

47 Moodie, *Roughing It*, 156, 160. See also Radcliffe, *Authentic Letters*, Thomas to Reverend, January 1832, 47. The O'Briens had a bee in July 1832. Mary noted, O'Brien Journal, 25 July 1832, that from her vantage point, this came "at an unlucky moment, seeing that our stock of provisions was getting very low." On 25 September 1833, Mary rather cryptically noted "we have had 15 men to dine in the kitchen today." The men had come to help logging. Strickland, *Twenty Seven Years*, 37, provided a description of a bee supper that Samuel enjoyed soon after his arrival in the colony. See also Dunlop, *Our Forest Home*, 15 July 1841, 172–4.

48 Households also "entertained" and women's and men's correspondence frequently made reference to meals they had either given or taken. Mary O'Brien described one dinner party "where various new bits of smartness were displayed," including silver desert forks: O'Brien Journal, 7 December 1829.

49 Bradbury notes in "Pigs, Cows and Boarders, 13, the importance of such activities in Montreal in the latter half of the nineteenth century. Drawing heavily on data in a manuscript census of 1861 and 1871, she notes that, particularly for the early period, urban families were not solely dependent on wages for subsistence. "Cows grazed in backyards and on street verges. Pigs scrounged in courtyards and alleys and poultry could be seen and heard throughout the city." The same was undoubtedly true in Upper Canadian towns and villages in the first half of the century.

50 Boyce, ed., *Hutton of Hastings*, Fanny Hutton to Mrs Hutton, 2 July 1837, 60.

51 Cowan notes in *More Work for Mother* that the concern for cleanliness was directly related to the tools that women had to sustain this. All colonial women's journals made reference to the problems of cleaning and washing. See comments of Mary O'Brien, Anne Langton, Susanna Moodie, and Frances Stewart. Maas notes in *Helpmates of Man* that a number of British gentlewomen had trouble reconciling their new homes and their amenities with what they had left in Great Britain. See also Osterud, *Bonds of Community*, 169–73; Jensen, *Loosening the Bonds*, 114–28; Strasser, *Never Done*.

52 Langton, ed., *A Gentlewoman*, 25 January 1839, 99.

53 Mary O'Brien's journal makes frequent references to trying to keep a home clean. See among others, 15, 18 December 1828; also Dunlop, ed., *Our Forest Home*, 23 May 1827, 102; 29 April 1829, 114.

54 Langton, ed., *A Gentlewoman*, Anne to her brother, 10 May 1841, 182. O'Brien Journal, Mary O'Brien reported frequently on the problems of the "hibdominal house cleaning, the discomfort of which I must endure": 25 March 1831. Mary apparently used whitewash quite regularly: 21 November 1831. On 22 August 1834, Mary commented on the "radical house cleaning" that she and her maid were about to begin. See Davidson, *A Woman's Work is Never Done*, Chapter 6, for a discussion of the work involved in cleaning British homes.

55 Langton, ed., *A Gentlewoman*, 28 October 1838, 82.

56 Moodie, *Roughing It*, 101.

57 O'Brien Journal, 25 October 1829; Mary Southby, Mary O'Brien's sister-in-law, had a washerwoman.

58 Langton, ed., *A Gentlewoman*, 3 December 1839, 129.

59 Boyce, ed., *Hutton of Hastings*, William to his mother, 17 March 1841, 86.

60 See, for example, Traill, *The Backwoods*, 106, 122; Langton, ed., *A Gentlewoman*, 28 October 1838, 83; O'Brien Journal, 11 February 1829, noting a problem making soap, and 22 July 1831; Strickland, *Twenty Seven Years*, Vol. 2, 295; Cohen, *Women's Work*, 74–5.

61 It was men's work to tan the hides and make and repair shoes. Both Eli Playter, Playter Diaries, and Langton, ed., *Early Days*, discussed making their own clothes and, as McCalla notes, *Planting the Province*, 103–4, tanning quickly became a commercial enterprise in Upper Canada. See also "Testimonial of Roger Bates," in J.J. Talman, ed., *Loyalist Narratives*, 32; "Mrs Amelia Harris," in *Loyalist Narratives*, 109–48, 124; Cohen, *Women's Work*, 76.

62 This was particularly true of British immigrants in the period after the War of 1812. See Boyce, ed., *Hutton of Hastings*; Langton, ed., *A Gentlewoman*; Traill, *The Backwoods*; Dunlop, ed., *Our Forest Home*.

63 "Testimonial of Roger Bates," in J.J. Talman, ed., *Loyalist Narratives*, 37. See also O'Brien Journal, 20 October 1820, for an account of women in the Quaker settlement; Strickland, *Twenty Seven Years*, Vol. 2, 287–97.

64 Cohen, *Women's Work*, 76. Cohen notes that in the early years, cloth making was not a major occupation of colonial women. Once the pioneering stage had passed, it appears that a number of households did engage in spinning, weaving, and knitting, both for themselves and for trade, however. See McCalla, *Planting the Province*, 100–2.

65 "Mrs Amelia Harris," in J.J. Talman, ed., *Loyalist Narratives*, 124. See also the account of Sarah Slaught, in Cohen, *Women's Work*, 77–8.

66 See account of William Nelles, in Cohen, *Women's Work*, 78; McCalla, *Planting the Province*, 101–2.

67 See Sellar, *A Scotsman*, 9 October 1825, 76 where he noted buying ten pounds of raw wool; Strickland, *Twenty Seven Years*, 295.

68 Boyce, ed., *Hutton of Hastings*, 5 December 1834, 44.

69 Ibid., William to his mother, 14 February 1841, 83–4. He noted that "we have about thirty pounds weight."

70 Ibid., 24 October, 1841, 89; 20 October 1842, 102.

71 Catharine Parr Traill described one household where "a large spinning wheel as big as a cart wheel, occupied the centre of the room at which a neatly dressed matron, of lady-like appearance, was engaged spinning yarn, her young little daughters were knitting beside the fire, while the father was engaged in the instruction of two of his sons." All the family was dressed in "a coarse sort of plaid, a mixture of woollen and thread, a produce of the farm and their mother's praiseworthy industry": Traill, *The Backwoods*, 100. For further discussion of the importance of cloth making both for household use and for sale, see Osertud, *Bonds of Community*, 188–90; Jensen, *Loosening the Bonds*, 49–50.

72 Dunlop, ed., *Our Forest Home*, August 1823, 40. Frances continued, "this last I sometimes think I can never get through; a year of wear and tear and no shops from which to procure anything obliges me to plan most carefully." See also July 1824, 60; February 1834, 133; September 1834, 134; 2 September 1834, 138.

73 Langton, ed., *A Gentlewoman*, 5 July 1839, 115.

74 Ibid., 2 April 1839, 103; 3 August 1839, 127. Then see also 4 April 1839, 103; 30 April 1839, 113; 17 July 1839, 120.

75 The O'Brien journal also makes frequent references to sewing, an occupation that had to be fitted into "spare" moments. See for example, 22 October 1828. On 1 June 1830, Mary reported, "I did my usual task of mending a shirt & a pair of stockings before we read our evening portion & went to bed." She also often "refurbished clothes." On 8 September 1834, Mary noted that no talent "has been so useful or given me so much unmixed satisfaction as the rapidity of my needle now does." See discussion Chap-

ter 8, concerning the opportunity available to women to turn an ability to sew into cash.

76 Langton, ed., *A Gentlewoman*, 12 June 1844, 153.

77 Sellar, *A Scotsman*, 22 April 1826, 92.

78 This list is by no means inclusive. For references generally to gardens see Susanna Moodie, *Roughing It*, 215; Boyce, ed., *Hutton of Hastings*, 12 September 1838, 70; Radcliffe, *Authentic Letters*, January 1832, 65; Traill, *The Backwoods*, 28 November 1834, 108.

79 This certainly seems to have been the case for Mary O'Brien, See O'Brien Journal, 24 April 1829; 5 May 1829. Frances Stewart also took considerable solace in her garden: Dunlop, ed., *Our Forest Home*, August 1823, 42; 16 November 1830, 120; February 1831, 125. Barbara Maas concluded in *Helpmates of Man*, 91, that gardens were a way for a number of gentle pioneers to "domesticate" the wilderness.

80 O'Brien Journal, 4 March 1837, Journal 116.

81 See, for example, Boyce, ed., *Hutton of Hastings*, William Hutton's comment that "generally, whatever requires little labour brings the greatest gain": 24 August 1841, 88. See also Langton, ed., *Early Days*, 24 May 1834, 107. On the importance of gardens for the family table, see Jensen, *Loosing the Bonds*; Cohen, *Women's Work*, 74–5; Osterud, *Bonds of Community*; Ulrich, *Good Wives*; McCalla, *Planting the Province*, 222–4.

82 O'Brien Journal, 24 February 1830. Mary O'Brien's mother assumed responsibility for the poultry, the pigs, the fires, and the beds when they first arrived in Upper Canada. Farmers often built hen and poultry houses. The capital outlay in materials was obviously considered worth the long-term gain. Mary Gapper's brother had such a poultry house: O'Brien Journal, 5 May 1829; 5 November 1829. The Langtons found that hens had to be fenced because they either fell prey to predators or scratched up the garden seed so carefully planted in the spring: Langton, ed., *Early Days*, January 1832, 66; Langton, ed., *A Gentlewoman*, 12 April 1839, 106; Traill, *The Backwoods*, 1832, 113.

83 Boyce, ed., *Hutton of Hastings*, 2 July 1837, 61. See also O'Brien Journal. Once established in her new home, Mary O'Brien had 21 turkeys and 70 chickens: 22 July 1831. Poultry was obviously important to farm operations throughout rural North America at this time.

84 Boyce, ed., *Hutton of Hastings*. On 15 June 1835, Hutton noted that he had four cows and calves. See also, Langton, ed., *A Gentlewoman*, 10 June 1840, 151–2; O'Brien Journal, 12 June 1829.

85 Moodie, *Roughing It*, 128–9. Mary O'Brien recounted her first experience trying to milk in her journal, 5 June 1830. The cow kicked the bucket over. She found the attempt tiring and painful. By 1834, Mary was apparently quite an accomplished milker. She still noted, 19 November 1834, that her wrists ached after milking eight cows, however.

86 Cohen, *Women's Work*, 97. Mary O'Brien's sister-in-law sent Mary to make butter, "partly to save herself & partly I believe for the fun of seeing how I should look & how far my patience would hold out through the occupation." After two and a half hours, Mary began to find it tiring. Though she was in the end successful, "if I were not so tired that I can hardly move I should think myself a good dairy woman": O'Brien Journal, 1 March 1830. Mary appears to have become very adept at making butter, however. See also Jensen, *Loosening the Bonds*, Chapters 5, 6 for a discussion of the changing technology of the butter trade and the impact this had on women's work.

87 Boyce, ed., *Hutton of Hastings*, 27 March 1836, 53; 2 July 1837, 59; 6 August 1837, 63; Playter Diary. Mary O'Brien commented, O'Brien Journal, 30 May 1829, that her brother expected his diary to be "profitable."

Cohen argues persuasively that once dairying became a commercial enterprise, women were increasingly excluded from the process. In *Loosening the Bonds*, Jensen finds that this was not the case in the northern United States until at least 1850. In the first half of the nineteenth century, it was farm women in the northern United States who were primarily responsible for the dairy and who sold the surplus. See also McCalla, *Planting the Province*, 77–82, 267–72.

88 Traill, *The Backwoods*, 89.

89 O'Brien Journal, 8 May 1833.

90 Boyce, ed., *Hutton of Hastings*, 15 June 1835, 49. See also "Mrs Amelia Harris," in J.J. Talman, ed., *Loyalist Narratives*, 129. It is clear that farm women turned their hands to anything that needed doing. Both Jensen, *Loosening the Bonds* and Osterud, *Bonds of Community*, 141, discuss this. As Osterud notes, this did not elevate farm women into a position of equality with their husbands. As has already been discussed, gender relations were more "complex and contradictory" than that. But women's work in the fields as well as in the house was of significant value to the farm enterprise.

91 Boyce, ed., *Hutton of Hastings*, William to his mother, 2 July 1837, 61; 12 September, 1838, 70. See also Strickland, *Twenty Seven Years*, 309. The Diary of George Leith, AO, MS69, makes frequent references to Mrs Leith working on the farm, including coping with the dairy and digging potatoes.

92 Moodie, *Roughing It*, 166.

93 *Ibid.*, 202, 222.

94 *Ibid.*, 167.

95 Maas, *Helpmates of Man*, 91–4, 97–9, notes that the problem of transition for some women was quite severe. Certainly Frances Stewart may never have been really reconciled to living in Upper Canada.

96 O'Brien Journal, 26 April 1830. See also 2 December 1830; 3 May 1836. On 23 August 1830, Mary noted that she would rather pick rocks than

cope with housekeeping. Mary O'Brien was quite conscious that her life in Upper Canada was sharply at odds with the rhetoric of the angel in the house. On 7 November 1830 she noted that she was "about to shift my character from cook to gentlewoman."

97 Cohen, *Women's Work*, 73. See also Moodie, *Roughing It*; Traill, *The Backwoods*; Dunlop, ed., *Our Forest Home*; Maas, *Helpmates of Man*, 97–8. For similar problems in colonial America, see Ulrich, *Good Wives*.

98 O'Brien Journal, 11 June 1831. See also 8 October 1830; 20 June 1831; 2 July 1831.

99 Ibid., July entry 1831.

100 Ibid., 2 September 1831.

101 See the Playter Diaries.

102 Cohen, *Women's Work*, 72.

103 Boyce, ed., *Hutton of Hastings*, William to his Mother, 19 April 1842, 97.

104 Langton, ed., *A Gentlewoman*, 13 October 1838, 73. That week, Anne had fed, housed, and looked after a household of ten (six or seven was their usual number), washed clothes, and tackled some upholstery.

105 Boyce, ed., *Hutton of Hastings*, William to his Mother, 20 October 1842, 102. See also Dunlop, ed., *Our Forest Home*. For further discussion of the importance of daughters to farm operations, see Jensen, *Loosening the Bonds*; Osterud, *Bonds of Community.*

CHAPTER FIVE

1 The Journal of Mrs E.G. O'Brien, 1828–38, Archives of Ontario (AO), MS199, 31 January 1831.

2 Ibid., 7 February 1831; 31 January 1831.

3 Ibid., 7, 10 February 1831.

4 Dudden, *Serving Women*, 18. Gagan notes in *Hopeful Travellers*, 63–4, that rural returns indicate that in the post-1851 period, almost 44 per cent of households in Peel County had "live-in extras," which included servants, non-domestic employees and non-family children. Many of these individuals would undoubtedly have been "helps."

5 Basil Hall, *Travels in North America in the Years 1827, 1828 and 1829* (Philadelphia: Carey, Lea and Carey 1829), 156–7, quoted in Cohen, *Women's Work*, 85.

6 The same may well have been true in the colony's towns. Unfortunately, the sources are silent on this matter. Moreover, as will be discussed in Chapter 6, the nature of domestic service was beginning to change in urban areas.

7 O'Brien Journal, 30 October 1837. See also Samuel Thompson's account of a "first rate chopper," quoted in Cohen, *Women's Work*, 70.

8 Tilly and Scott, *Women, Work, and Family,* 13–14, note that women regularly worked in agricultural production in Europe. See also Horn, *The Rural World*; Angela V. John, "Introduction," to her, *Unequal Opportunities,* 1-44.

9 See Diary of George Leith, AO, MS69. Helen Campbell served as dairymaid for George Leith for a number of years, beginning 27 March 1837. When she left, Leith had obvious difficultly replacing her. He noted, 7 September 1841 that there was none to be had.

See Deborah Valenze, "The Art of Women and the Business of Men, Women's Work and the Dairy Industry, c1740–1840," *Past and Present* 130 (February 1991), 142–69, for a discussion of women's role in British dairying and why some farmers wanted dairymaids. As Cohen, *Women's Work,* 95–6, and previous discussion illustrates, often wives acted as dairymaids. As will be seen, so too did general helps.

10 O'Brien Journal, 29 May 1830. Mary O'Brien noted she hired two women to hay, 2 July 1831. In 1832 Edward O'Brien hired a black girl to take up potatoes, 30 October 1832. See also Diaries of John Thompson, AO, MU 846, 31 August 1835, Thompson hired a new servant girl who was reaping; 29 September 1835, girl reaping; 19 December 1837, girl working with the cattle. See also Cohen, *Women's Work,* 85–7; Bitterman, "Farm Households and Wage Labour," 13–45.

11 O'Brien Journal, 30 October 1832. Much more work needs to be done on how race affected women's employment. There are sporadic references to black women and men working on colonial farms and in town, but we know little about how these individuals fared or were regarded and treated by employers and colleagues.

12 O'Brien Journal, 8 July 1830.

13 Cohen, *Women's Work,* 86–7, also notes that availability of field work for women varied from region to region.

14 These included a notice from an English woman who was looking for a place as a housekeeper and who noted specifically that she would "have no objection to take charge of a small family ... either in the city or country": *Christian Guardian,* 15 June 1836. See also notice of young housemaid, *The Patriot,* 24 January 1833. The number of such notices was very small, however.

15 H.H. Langton, ed., *A Gentlewoman in Upper Canada: The Journals of Anne Langton* (Toronto: Clarke, Irwin 1950), 16 October 1838, 76.

16 This is clearly evident in Mary O'Brien's journal: 7 May 1829, she was girl hunting on Yonge Street; 16 October 1829 she went ten miles back into the bush in an unsuccessful search. On 28 April 1830 she noted that she rode to Oakville looking for a girl. See also 22 August 1829; 2, 10, 18 August 1830; 11 February 1831; 16 October 1832; 11 February 1834; 28 October

1834. On 14 December 1828, the family was so desperate they hired men to scrub.

The O'Briens were not the only ones to experience such difficulties. Langton, ed., *A Gentlewoman*, Thomas Langton to his son, 29 November 1837, 51, noted that he had made three trips to Peterborough to find servants.

Thompson Diaries included numerous references to the problem. See among others, 29 March 1834 (unsuccessful); 30 September 1834; 5 October 1835; 25 August 1836 (which included a search of almost two weeks ending 6 September 1836); 8 October 1836.

17 O'Brien Journal, 9 May 1828.

18 Ibid, 8 November 1830. George Leith notes in his diary that he had a similar experience. On 2 October 1837, the girl could not come because her sister was ill.

Frances Stewart noted in 1824 that she was "still without a maid." One of her neighbours had "lent" her her daughter, "but they are all required at home now": E.S. Dunlop, ed., *Our Forest Home: Being Extracts from the Correspondence of the Late Frances Stewart* (Montreal: Gazette Printing and Publishing 1902), May 1824, 57.

19 See *Christian Guardian*, 7 December 1836; 30 September 1840; *Colonial Advocate*, 24 June 1829; *The Patriot*, 15 December 1837.

20 Langton, ed., *A Gentlewoman*, 29 January 1842, 197. The Langtons had been without servants for five weeks. Five years earlier, Thomas Langton had reported to his son William that even after three trips to Peterborough, "and as many to Ops," John had been unable to get a servant. He believed that this was because servants were reluctant to engage so far out of town: 29 November 1837, 51.

21 Ibid., 14 April 1839, 108.

22 O'Brien Journal, 8 October 1833.

23 Langton, ed., *A Gentlewoman*, Thomas Langton to his son, 29 November 1837, 53, noting that he had hired a boy of sixteen; Journal, 16 May 1842, 195; 1 January 1841, 172.

24 O'Brien Journal, 18 August 1829; 20 August 1829. It appears that Edward had problems "managing" his woman.

25 Ibid., 1, 7 June 1830.

26 Lacelle notes in *Urban Domestic Servants*, 26, that, if at all possible, women were hired if there was only one servant in the house.

27 "Historical Memorandum by Mrs Amelia Harris," in J.J. Talman, ed., *Loyalist Narratives from Upper Canada* (Toronto: Champlain Society 1946), 109–48, 127.

28 Ibid., 116, 122.

29 Ibid., 127.

30 O'Brien Journal, 12 August 1830.

31 Jensen, *Loosening the Bonds*, 38, notes that local tenant and artisan families frequently sold their labour when it was not needed at home. Gagan in *Hopeful Travellers*, 100–2, noted that the ability to hire help was a general demarcation between lower- and middle-class residents of Peel County. See also McCalla, *Planting the Province*, 88.

32 O'Brien Journal, 2 November 1830. See also 8 November 1830. In 23 October 1832, Mary noted that she intended to hire "a little girl" whose father was to settle in the neighbourhood.

33 Ibid., 9 June 1835. Dudden notes in *Serving Women*, 5, 27–30, that similar patterns prevailed in rural areas of the United States. See also Jensen, *Loosening the Bonds*, 38–9; Osterud, *Bonds of Community*, 194–5.

34 O'Brien Journal, 17 January 1829.

35 Ibid., 19, 20 January 1829; on 29 January 1829, Mary noted that Betsy was not yet provided for and on 30 January 1829, that she was still trying.

36 Ibid., 10 May 1830.

37 Ibid., 9 June 1835.

38 Langton, ed., *A Gentlewoman*, 11 August 1841, 189.

39 Wages rates for the earliest period are still unclear. And even between 1820 and 1840, although many diaries recorded that a "new girl had come," there is usually no record of her wage. In the period immediately after the War of 1812, Robert Gourlay estimated from the returns he received from his survey that women earned, on average, 5s. 6d. per week: Robert Gourlay, *Statistical Account of Upper Canada* (1822) (Toronto: S.R. Publishers 1966), 621. The reports themselves suggest that the rates varied somewhat throughout the colony – 7s. 6d. in Malden, 282, to a low of 5s. in Landsdown, 504, and Wainfleet, 449. (It should be noted that most Upper Canadians seem to have paid resident help by the month, and not the week.) In his study "Wage Labour Rates," 72–3, Russell estimates that the average rate of pay for female servants decreased from a range of 20s. to 30s. in 1818 to 16s. to 24s. He notes that location obviously made a difference on the scale, and that skill was a "critical factor" for women's wages. These rates are certainly lower that what some farmers were paying their "girl." Two diaries, those of John Thompson and George Leith, illustrate the following rates:
    John Thompson paid maid, 12 December 1836, $3.00/month; 23 February 1838, $4.00/month; "sewer" (Mary Kile), 17 March 1835, $3.00/month. George Leith paid cook, 21 July 1837, $4.00/month; 21 November 1837, $5.00/month; maid, 16 October 1839, $5.00/month; 28 April 1840, $3.00/month; 13 January 1841, $5.00/month. (For exchange rates during this period, see McCalla, *Planting the Province*, Appendix A, 245–7.) The differential in wages does appear to be age and skill or job description. See also Cohen, *Women's Work*, 87–8; McCalla,

Planting the Province, 40–1; Bitterman, "Farm Households and Wage Labour," 13–45.

40 See, for example, references in Gerald Boyce, ed., *Hutton of Hastings: The Life and Letters of William Hutton*, 1801–1860 (Belleville: Hastings County Council 1972), William Hutton to his mother, 14 February 1841, 83; 21 October 1841, 89; 20 October 1842, 102. Hutton stated that wages had not gone down even in 1842, despite the arrival of large numbers of immigrants. He paid his girl 10s./month, a comparatively low wage.

41 Hamnett K. Pinhey Papers, AO, MS732, Accounts.

42 Cohen, *Women's Work*, 87–8.

43 O'Brien Journal, 2 November 1830, Mary noted "I am in treaty for a little girl to come and aid me with house work." See also 27 September 1830.

44 Dudden, *Serving Women*, 24–5, notes both the importance to the prospective mistress of hiring neighbourhood girls, and how the proximity of a help's family also provided the girl with some degree of economic independence. She further notes, 29, that in the United States, at least, girls could "also refer to republican ideology for language and belief with which to defend herself." In rural Upper Canada, girls also appear to have invoked a similar sense of equality with their mistresses.

45 See Diary of Captain William Johnson, AO, MS 18, 1 November 1833, which noted that the mother of Mary Holmes, the help, had come to collect her daughter's wages. See also Pinhey Papers.

46 Mary O'Brien Journal, 16 October, 1828. See also Langton, ed., *A Gentlewoman*, 20 March, 1840, 146.

47 As Jensen concludes in *Loosening the Bonds*, 44, "these women provided an essential workforce for the developing agricultural economy."

48 Dudden, *Serving Women*, 36.

49 Osterud, *Bonds of Community*, 195.

50 Dudden, *Serving Women*, 6. Dudden argues that the term "help" was particularly subject to loose and flexible usage. Helping was an outgrowth of the traditional belief than youth should serve. As a practice, however, helping was transformed in eighteenth- and nineteenth-century America and Upper Canada to meet the needs of the pre-industrial rural and small urban households.

51 O'Brien Journal, 8 June 1835. Mary O'Brien frequently noted in her journal that she was up before six.

52 Langton, ed., *A Gentlewoman*, 1 January 1839, 87. Italics are mine.

53 Ibid., 11 April 1839, 106.

54 Ibid., 14 April 1839, 108.

55 Ibid., 11 August 1841, 189.

56 O'Brien Journal, 18 February 1831. Throughout 1831, Mary made frequent references to Flora's work cleaning and to her exceptional qualities. See for example 24 April 1831; 28 June 1831. Mary's maids regularly cleaned

the floors, 5 November 1829; 8 June 1835. Mary regularly seemed to give her maids and girls "lessons." See also 17 January 1831 where Mary noted that for some time, the girl had been sitting with her book.

57 Ibid., 15 May 1831, where Mary did note that she was sometimes pleased to be without servants. See also 27 June 1831. References to Flora helping with the children are frequent after mid-1831. On 2 September 1831, for example, Flora cleaned the house, cooked breakfast, milked, helped make butter, and looked after the baby. Five days later, Mary noted that after Flora finished her work, she looked after the baby while Mary went to get a recipe for making cider from a neighbour.

58 Ibid. Most references to Flora suggest that the two women split the housework. On 22 August 1831, for example, Flora washed while Mary tackled other tasks.

59 Ibid., 30 December 1831.

60 Ibid., 30 August to 2 September 1832; 3 September 1832. Flora left because of an unhappy love affair with one of the hired men.

61 Ibid., 8 June 1833.

62 See among other things, Langton, ed., *A Gentlewoman*, 1 January 188, referring to Sally Jordan; Boyce, ed., *Hutton of Hastings*, 27 March 1837, 56, William noted that "we must have a girl when milking and churning commence"; 12 September 1838, 69, he commented that though their girl was not good in the house, she was "a good milker and churner." She also helped in the harvest: 24 March 1840, 75.

63 Langton, ed., *A Gentlewoman*, 11 December 1837, 55.

64 O'Brien Journal, 21 August 1831; George Leith Diary, 21 July 1837, hiring of live-in cook at $4.00/month; 21 November 1837; another cook, Phoebe Glass, engaged at $5.00/month. Phoebe Glass also aided in washing and stayed until 6 April 1838.

65 Susanna Moodie, *Roughing It in the Bush* (1852) (Toronto: McClelland and Stewart 1962), 202.

66 O'Brien Journal, 16 October 1837.

67 Ibid., 26 February 1834.

68 John Thompson Diary, 23 October 1833.

69 O'Brien Journal, 21 August 1831.

70 Ibid., 8 June 1833. Shortly after her arrival, Mary O'Brien found herself forced "to make a pye ... to supply the deficiencies of the new girl": 29 May 1829.

71 Langton, ed., *Gentlewoman*, Anne to her brother, 20 March 1840, 146. See also 25 October 1838, 81, when Anne proposed calling in Miss Daniel to assist in a great scrubbing day.

72 O'Brien Journal, March 1835, Journal 99; 12 April 1835. See also previous discussion Chapter 3; subsequent discussion Chapter 9.

73 E.S. Dunlop, ed., *Our Forest Home*, 19 October 1834, 136–7.

74 Ibid., December 1834, 138–9.
75 O'Brien Journal, 21 October 1829.
76 Osterud, *Bonds of Community,* 195.
77 This was particularly the case when the "girl" was the only waged employee in the household and was close in social and economic rank to her employer. See Dudden, *Serving Women,* 36–7. In an interesting twist, Flora, Mary's maid was apparently upset when she had to eat with the family.
78 O'Brien Journal, 29 June 1831. Just before she left the O'Briens, 3 September 1832, Flora was again "obliged to keep her bed" and Mary wrote that "with Amelia's assistance, I have all the work to do." See also Osterud, *Bonds of Community,* 44–5; Dudden, *Serving Women,* 38–9.
79 Dudden, *Serving Women,* 35, 37–8; Osterud, *Bonds of Community,* 194–5. See also Jensen, *Loosening the Bonds,* 37–8.
80 O'Brien Journal, 14 August 1829. Mary noted, 13 October 1829, that the girl had to be scolded to make her work.
81 See Maas, *Helpmates of Man,* 91.
82 O'Brien Journal, 14 August 1829, Mary noted that she had to make two dinners. This seems to have been common practice in relatively affluent farm households. Catharine Parr Traill noted in *The Backwoods of Canada* (1836) (Toronto: McClelland and Stewart 1966), 99, that she and Thomas prided themselves on maintaining that "incontestable proof of our gentility." This, she stated, was in sharp contrast to many of her neighbours. See also Dudden, *Serving Women,* 36–7; Osterud, *Bonds of Community,* 147–8; Maas, *Helpmates of Man,* 98–9.
83 Boyce, ed., *Hutton of Hastings,* 12 September 1838, 69, William complained about his "ignorant, wretched, dirty creature" who had been hired to help Fanny. She "had been living in the back concessions on an equality with her mistress," he explained to his mother, and refused to do certain chores because they were "degrading."
84 Langton, ed., *A Gentlewoman,* 21 April 1839, 110. Similar sentiments were expressed about a new girl, 28 July 1839, 125.
85 O'Brien Journal, 26 June 1829.
86 Dudden, *Serving Women,* 39. She notes that girls could usually order their own days and the manner in which they accomplished their work. This may well have been the case in many households in Upper Canada. In some, however, it appears that the girl, like the farm daughter, was expected to go on to other work when one task was completed.
87 Langton, ed., *A Gentlewoman,* 13 October 1838, 73.
88 O'Brien Journal, 25 January 1829.
89 Ibid., 8 June 1829.
90 Langton, ed., *A Gentlewoman,* 1 January 1839, 87.
91 Ibid., 11 April 1839, 106.

92 O'Brien Journal, 29, 31 October 1830.

93 Ibid., 11, 19 November 1830. See also 15 November 1830, where Mary noted that she hoped the Irish woman would stay at least until the summer; 19 November 1830, where Mary stated that she was willing to put up with her Irish woman's whining "over trifles or supposititious ills" if only she would stay.

94 Ibid., 17 January 1831.

95 Ibid., 11 November 1830; 17 January 1831.

96 Ibid., 7 July 1831. Two months later, 4 September 1831, Mary noted that the wives of her labourers were squabbling.

97 Ibid., 29 December 1835. See also Dudden, *Serving Women*, 33. Cohen notes in *Working Women*, 86, that "the need of girl's labour on family farms would appear to be one explanation for such a severe shortage of female labour."

98 O'Brien Journal, 4 August 1831. See also 28 May 1837, when Mary's maid, Amelia, left to cope with a sick mother; George Leith Diary, 1 October 1837, noted that the maid would not come because her mother was ill.

99 Langton, ed., *A Gentlewoman*, 16 October 1838, 76.

100 O'Brien Journal, 30 December 1831, Flora was away. Mary O'Brien seems to have given her servants time off at least one Sunday a month. See, for example, 25 April 1831; 9 January 1834; 30 November 1834; 1 January 1835; 4 May 1835.

Hamnett Pinhey Diary also noted that maids were away on Sundays. See also John Thompson Diary, 25 December 1833; 1 January 1834, "all away" or "idle and feasting."

101 See among others John Thompson Diary, 20 November 1834, where with the maid away the boys had to assist the cook; 24 August 1836; 21 March 1837, Flora the girl away; William Johnson Diary, 21 October 1832, Mary away; 10 October 1833, Betsy MacDonald away. It is likely that these records helped an employer to work out what he owed the help. It would appear that wages were deducted for time "away."

102 O'Brien Journal, 15 September 1834. On 24 November 1834, Mary had particular problems with a new "page" whom she expected to begin work within a month of the engagement. By the end of December, Journal 98, she was still awaiting his arrival. See also 1 January 1836, servant who had taken a "protracted leave" to attend a family wedding (the maid left, 29 December 1835).

103 Langton, ed., *A Gentlewoman*, 11 April 1839, 106.

104 O'Brien Journal, 4 May 1836, maid left at the age of fifteen to marry one of the labourers; Langton, *A Gentlewoman*, 1 January 1839, Kitty was only fourteen when she arrived. See Dudden, *Serving Women*, 29; Osterud, *Bonds of Community*, 195; Norton, *Liberty's Daughters*, 23.

105 Langton, ed., *A Gentlewoman*, 11 August 1841, 189. See also Thomas Langton to William, 29 November 1837, 53, reference to Mary Scarry who only stayed with the household until her husband came to take up land; 16 October 1838, 76, the maid expected to spend the winter with her mother.

106 Ibid., 16 October 1838, 76. Anne consoled herself that "it is not such a calamity to be left without as it would be at home."

107 O'Brien Journal, 15 October 1829. The maid left, 16 October 1829.

108 John Thompson Diary, 24 August 1836, "the girl was missing." Langton, ed., *A Gentlewoman*, 18 July 1839, 121, a neighbour's girl had left before anyone was up; George Leith Diary, 13 February 1838, Phoebe Glass, the cook, went to an old employer to "dun" him for past wages.

109 See for example, John Thompson Diary, 27 November 1834, Harriet Frith "sent away as unfit"; 14 January 1835; 19 July 1835.

110 Ibid., 25 August 1836.

111 George Leith Diary, 3 March 1838.

112 Langton, ed., *A Gentlewoman*, 3 August 1839, 127.

113 Ibid., 4 March 1840, 141. Both Mary O'Brien's Flora and Anne Langton's Bridgit were unusual in that they stayed for almost a year. O'Brien Journal notes that Flora was hired, 31 January 1831 and left 20 September 1832. See also John Thompson Diary, 31 March 1838, Flora with them for eleven months.

114 Dudden, *Serving Women*, 42–3, 29. See also Osterud, *Bonds of Community*, 194–8.

115 O'Brien Journal, 14 December 1828, unable to find women to wash and therefore hired men; 4 June 1830, Mary received help from a neighbouring Yorkshire woman; George Leith Diary, 26 June 1837, Nancy Benner paid half a dollar for washing one room.

116 Langton, ed., *A Gentlewoman*, 3 December 1838, 129; O'Brien Journal, 24 October 1829, received washing from her old washerwoman; Pinhey Diary, 27 July 1829, Margaret hired as washerwoman. See account in Osterud, *Bonds of Community*, 169–72, concerning the Benton family washing.

117 Langton, ed., *A Gentlewoman*, 25 October 1838, 81. Mrs Daniels' payment may have been Anne Langton teaching her daughter: 16 January 1839, 95.

118 Ibid., 4 March 1840, 141.

119 Ibid., 18 September 1840, 162. First mention of Sally Jordan was made 1 January 1839, 87, when Anne noted that they had "the assistance of one of [their neighbours] Jordan's daughters for 2 or 3 weeks."

120 Ibid., contained in a letter of John to William, 30 November 1840, 184.

121 William Johnson Diary included frequent references to various girls who obviously helped full time. On 12 June 1832, he reported that new maid

Mary Donoghue could neither wash nor milk and he would therefore keep her for only one month. She stayed at least another three months: 21, 23 October 1832.

122 William Johnson Diary, 14 September 1835, received $5.00 for her work; 17 May 1832, Mrs Elwes arrived. She took a day off, 14 June 1832 and received $4.00 toward her wages; 19 July 1832, received an additional $1.00 "for attendance on sick." While Mrs Elwes was ill herself, a Mrs Wheeler came in for four days to help and received $1.00 for her work: 22 May 1832. See also 30 September 1839.

123 See Appendix 1 for a "Patterns of Women's Part Time Employment" in the Johnson household. See Dudden, *Serving Women*, 15–7, for instances of this practice in the United States at a similar time. The Pinheys also hired help for specific needs. Between 1830 and 1838, "Mother Edge" worked off and on in the Pinhey household. In some cases it was only for three or four days; in others, Pinhey's diary noted paying her for twelve to thirteen days' work. Her work included "taters" (probably digging them) and general housework. Often the diary just noted that she had come and left, perhaps with an indication of the number of days. Most of the Pinhey diary notations are brief and give only the first name of the girl hired, and the date she arrived or left, or as in the case of Sarah, was "warned," 6 June 1831. The diary rarely indicates what women were hired to do. One exception was Miss Baker who came 2 June 1835 and was paid 15s. for sewing. Nelly Major came 4 October 1939, apparently to lift "tatoes."

124 O'Brien Journal, 3 June 1830. When Flora was away in August and in December 1831, Mary hired the wife of one of the farm workers to take her place: 4 August 1831; 29 December 1831. Again in 29 December 1835, Mary hired a widow with three children while her girl was away at a wedding.

125 John Thompson Diary, Mrs. Broomsmead arrived, 10 May 1835; left 17 May; returned, 18 May 1835 (her duties now included planting potatoes); left again, 28 June 1835.

126 Ibid. Mrs Thompson's son born 27 July 1837. Mrs Broomsmead arrived, 22 June 1837; left briefly; returned, 12 July 1837; left 4 August 1837, received $14.00 for her services.

127 Potatoes appear to have been a standard crop and many diaries mentioned such work. See, for example, John Thompson Diary, 23 October 1833; Smith children helping with spring planting, 7, 23 May 1834; 2, 3 June 1834; Rick and his wife digging potatoes and piling brush, 21 September 1835; George Leith Diary, labourers' wives working in the fields 11, 13, 14 October 1837.

128 John Thompson Diary, 29 September 1835; 5, 6, 14 October 1835. Both Mrs and Mr Broomsmead worked for the Thompsons. The couple was discharged 6 November 1835.

129 George Leith Diary, 17, 24 August 1836; 31 October 1836. On 15 March 1837, she was paid her wages when John called for her.

130 *Gore Gazette*, 27 September 1828; 30 September 1828. See also *Niagara Herald*, 27 June 1801; *Upper Canada Gazette*, 3 April 1823; *United Empire Loyalist*, 7 June 1828; *Gore Gazette*, 11 October 1828; *Kingston Chronicle*, 9 April 1831. Advertisements included *Colonial Advocate*, 31 July 1828; *British Whig*, 22 September 1835; *Correspondent and Advocate*, 29 October 1835. There were a few couples, however, who preferred to engage with a "gentlemen's family" on a farm: *Upper Canada Gazette*, 8 October 1818; 24 February 1820; *Cobourg Star*, 30 January 1833.

131 John Thompson Diary, 21 July 1835. The Broomsmeads' employment with the Thompsons seems to have begun with Mrs Thompson's confinement. The same may well have been true of John Holland and his wife, employees of George Leith.

132 O'Brien Journal, 31 July 1830 (or 1 August 1830). Mary thought that the couple left, 31 October 1830, because of the woman's bad health and their general dissatisfaction. On 8 November 1830, Mary recorded that the woman was to continue to wash as needed; the man would act as a labourer. Two years later, April 1832, Journal 68, Edward hired another couple who had a child.

133 John Thompson Diary, 16 May 1835, a man usually earned $10.00/month; a couple earned $13.00/month. This practice appears to have been quite widespread. See Jensen, *Loosening the Bonds*, 46; Cohen *Women's Work*, 87.

134 O'Brien Journal, 31 October 1830.

135 Dudden, *Serving Women*, 42.

136 Jensen notes in *Loosening the Bonds*, 44–5, that these women "performed essential types of work." They "were part of a community willing and able to work for their wealthier neighbours." Jensen judges that "we really do not know if there was a stark line between employer and employee." Available evidence suggest that in Upper Canada, this varied from household to household. But in all instances, these women were an integral "part of the ebb and flow of economic and social life." And in many instances in Upper Canada, as it was in New York, "class differences and conflict may also have been an accepted and integral part of this community, merely muffled by the dependence that individuals had on one another." See also Osterud, *Bonds of Community*, 198.

137 See for example the work of Carol Lasser, "Domestic Balance of Power: Relations Between Mistress and Maid in Nineteenth-Century New England," in Kathryn Kish Sklar and Thomas Dublin, eds., *Women and Power in American History: A Reader*, Vol. 1 (Englewood Cliffs, N.J.: Prentice Hall 1991), 130–43, 133.

138 Dudden, *Serving Women*, 72.

PART THREE

1 Elizabeth Russell to Miss Lizzy Kiernan, 1 October 1793. Elizabeth Russell Papers, Metropolitan Toronto Reference Library.
2 Ibid., 18 January 1793.
3 Ibid., 24 February 1794.
4 Ibid., 26 January 1799.
5 See McKenna, *A Life of Propriety.*
6 For discussion of the development of the British and American middle class, their lifestyle and the implications that this had for women's lives, see Davidoff and Hall, *Family Fortunes*; Branca, *Silent Sisterhood*; Peterson, *Family, Love and Work*; Ryan, *Cradle of the Middle Class*; Cott, *The Bonds of Womanhood*.
7 Government offices were not built in York for some time. In a letter to Colonial Secretary Hobart, 19 April 1804, Lieutenant-Governor Hunter requested authority to build legislative buildings. See Firth, *The Town of York: 1793–1815*, 54–6.
8 Gagan, *Hopeful Travellers*, 99–103, 138–41; Katz, *The People of Hamilton, Canada West*, 27, 35–6.
9 Dudden, *Serving Women*, 45. See also Lacelle, *Urban Domestic Servants*; and Stansell, *City of Women*, Chapter 8, for a discussion of who entered domestic service in New York.

CHAPTER SIX

1 Dudden, *Serving Women*, 47.
2 The importance of appearance was not lost on the colony's first lieutenant-governor. When the townsite of the new colonial capital was surveyed in 1796–7, John Graves Simcoe made specific provision that the homes of the colonial elite would reflect their residents' status and influence. Lots "in the front street" of York were to be granted "only on condition that" residents built "a house of not less than forty-seven feet front, two stories high and after a certain order of architecture": Richard Cartwright to Isaac Todd, 14 October 1793, Cartwright Papers, Queen's University Archives. For a discussion of how this plan was received in the colony, see Errington, *The Lion, The Eagle and Upper Canada*, Chapter 2.
3 See Branca, *Silent Sisterhood*, for a discussion of the new work expected of middle-class Victorian women, particularly in the home.
4 See William Jarvis to Rev. Samuel Peters, Newark, n.d., c1792, quoted in McKenna, "The Life of Anne Murray Powell," 128.
5 Elizabeth Russell Papers, Metropolitan Toronto Reference Library (MTL), Elizabeth Russell to Elizabeth Kiernan, 18 January 1973.
6 McKenna, "The Life of Anne Murray Powell," 13.

7 *York Gazette*, 17 August 1811, quoted in Firth, *The Town of York, 1793–1815*, 277. In 1817, in consequence of William's elevation to chief justice of Upper Canada, the Powells added a complete second storey to their house so that they would have room to entertain large numbers downstairs.

8 In *The Refinement of America*, 100, Bushman traces how changes in American housing reflected their residents' aspirations of gentility. He particularly notes that the new houses of the late eighteenth and early nineteenth century "were part of a broad transformation of upper-middle class" desires and needs that had emerged in both Great Britain and the United States. See also Davidoff and Hall, *Family Fortunes*, 357–64; Davidoff, *The Best Circles*, 86–7.

9 Manuscript evidence in the Russell, Powell, and Macaulay Papers indicates that it was the master of the house who organized accommodation. This was undoubtedly part of that new sense of masculinity that was emerging among the British middle class. See Davidoff and Hall, *Family Fortunes*, 357–66.

10 Macaulay Papers, Archives of Ontario (AO), MS 78, John to Helen Macaulay, 27 May 1834.

11 Ibid., 22 March 1837.

12 Ibid., John to Ann Macaulay, 7, 9 March 1837.

13 Edith Firth, *The Town of York*, lxxvi.

14 Russell Papers, Elizabeth Russell to Edward Wiley, 23 August 1795.

15 Powell autobiography, quoted in McKenna, "The Life of Anne Murray Powell," 157.

16 Anne Powell to George Murray, 16 April 1816, quoted in ibid., 180.

17 Macaulay Papers, John to Ann Macaulay, 9 January 1837.

18 Ibid., John to Helen Macaulay, 2 January 1837; John to Ann Macaulay, 26 August 1837.

19 Ibid., John to Ann Macaulay, 26 August 1837.

20 Ibid., John to Helen Macaulay, 4 September 1837. He also noted in a letter to his mother, 26 August 1837, that the grounds of the Powell house would require much less upkeep.

21 Ibid., John to Helen Macaulay, 11 September 1837.

22 Ibid., and 30 October 1837.

23 Ibid., John to Ann Macaulay, 31 May 1837; 26 August 1837; John to Helen Macaulay, 6 September 1837 noting orders from Montreal; John to Ann Macaulay, 22 September 1837, noting plans for new curtains; John to Ann Macaulay, 9 October 1837 noting orders for a drawing-room and cook-stoves. Just after they moved into their home, John was surprised when he estimated the value of his household goods in excess of £2000. John to Ann Macaulay, 29 November 1837. See also John to Ann Macaulay, 18 October 1837.

24 Ibid., John to Ann Macaulay, 3 November 1837.

25 Davidoff and Hall, *Family Fortunes*, 360, explicitly state that "women were mainly responsible for creating and maintaining the house, its contents and the human constituents." The Macaulays expected to live in some confusion until the New Year, for, among other things, they could not "find a carpet to please them": Macaulay Papers, John to Ann Macaulay, 29 November 1837.

26 Macaulay Papers, John to Helen Macaulay, 22 July 1837. Correspondence of other Upper Canadians suggests that men hired men who were responsible and attached to the master of the house. See, for example, comments by William Jarvis about his servant, Richard, quoted in McKenna, "The Life of Anne Murray Powell," 138.

27 Macaulay Papers, John to Ann Macaulay, 22 September 1837; John to Helen Macaulay, 28 September 1837; 7 October 1837. Even when Helen was away from home, she apparently continued to supervise the hiring of staff by mail: Helen to John Macaulay, 29 August 1839; John to Ann Macaulay, 6, 23 December 1838; 28 April 1839.

28 Ibid., John Macaulay reported to his mother, 9 March 1837, that families in York kept "several [servants] of both sexes and never think of attempting the washing at home." Lacelle notes, in *Urban Domestic Servants*, 33, that multi-servant households in Montreal and Quebec had "a cook, a female servant who did housework and a manservant who drove the carriage, looked after the outside work … and also handled the task of waiting on table." Larger households might well have had a housekeeper or a head servant.

29 There were a number of advertisements in local newspapers of employers looking for laundry women, for example. See among others, *Kingston Chronicle*, 13 April 1821; *Upper Canada Gazette*, 9 January 1823; 21 August 1823; 5 September 1833. See Chapter 8 for further discussion of part-time domestic workers in Upper Canadian towns.

30 Powell Papers, MTL, Anne Powell to George Murray, 26 January 1816. Upper-class Upper Canadians certainly believed that the number of servants they had was a reflection of their status and rank. See McKenna, "The Life of Anne Murray Powell," 139–40; Dudden, *Serving Women*, 108–14; Gagan, *Hopeful Travellers*, 103–5.

31 Mary Quayle Innis, *Mrs Simcoe's Diary* (Toronto: University of Toronto Press 1965), letter to Mrs Hunt, February, 1793, 87.

32 Russell Papers, Elizabeth Russell to Lizzy Kiernan, 18 January 1793.

33 Ibid., 27 November 1793.

34 Ibid., 24 February 1794. Five years later, Elizabeth Russell was frustrated by her search for reliable help and the high cost that even "a common charwoman" could demand: Elizabeth Russell to Lizzy Kiernan, 26 January 1799.

35 Russell Diary, MTL. Our understanding of the lives of slave and "free" black women in Upper Canada is still woefully incomplete, particularly for this very early period. Certainly it seems that black women and men did face some discrimination from both their employers/owners and their white colleagues. See McKenna, *A Life of Propriety,* 81. Much more work needs to be done on this subject. It is likely that race was a major determinant both in the work the colonial women did, and how society viewed them and their accomplishments.

36 Comment of Hannah Jarvis, quoted in McKenna, "The Life of Anne Murray Powell," 139.

37 Ann Macaulay twice took in boys as her servants for specified periods of time. In 1814, Thomas Dogherty (with the blessing of his mother) committed himself to five and a half years service in exchange for his bed, board, clothes, and instruction in English. He was also to receive £40 in wages to be paid at the end of the term (agreement dated 19 December 1814, Macaulay Papers). Ann entered into a similar quasi-indenture in 1818 with Leonore Smith and her son James Anderson Smith (agreement dated 9 December 1818, Macaulay Papers). I have not discovered many indenture contracts for this period, definitely not the wealth that Claudette Lacelle was able to use in *Urban Domestic Servants.* On the basis of the runaway notices, both young men and women did enter indentured service. For another example of a contract see "The Apprenticeship of Mary Ann Thompson," 1825, quoted in Light and Prentice, eds. *Pioneer and Gentlewomen,* 18–9.

38 Hannah Jarvis to Rev. Samuel Peters, 25 September 1793, quoted in McKenna, "The Life of Anne Murray Powell," 139.

39 After Elizabeth Russell and her brother moved to York, John Denison and his family, recent immigrants and friends of Elizabeth, came to manage the farm and additional staff were engaged to help in the house. See Firth, *The Town of York, 1793–1815,* 232; Russell Papers. Anne Powell too was able to maintain more servants on a permanent basis as the colony matured. See Anne Powell to George Murray, 29 July 1809, quoted in McKenna, "The Life of Anne Murray Powell," 141.

40 Anna Jameson, *Winter Studies and Summer Rambles in Canada* (1838) (Toronto: McClelland and Stewart 1965), 71. These sentiments were obviously echoed in New York City about this time: Stansell, *City of Women,* 156–7.

41 Macaulay Papers, Ann to John Macaulay, 3 December 1836. This advice was frequently given to British gentlewomen. See Branca, *Silent Sisterhood,* 31; Davidoff and Hall, *Family Fortunes,* 389.

42 Macaulay Papers, Ann to John Macaulay, 23 January 1837, noting that she had just hired a new man. She was clearly satisfied with him: 26 February 1837.

43 Ibid., 4 October 1839,

44 Ibid., John to Ann Macaulay, 18 October 1839. Helen Macaulay seemed to have a constant problem keeping a cook: Helen to Ann Macaulay, 13 March 1839, noting that the present cook wanted more wages; Helen to John Macaulay, 25 May 1841; 16, 23 June 1841; 7 July 1841, all letters noting the impossibility of getting a good cook.

45 Ibid., 4 May 1840, John again reported to his mother that both the Macaulay's new cook and housemaid would require "a little training." Not all upper class mistresses had the time or inclination to train a new servant. In 1837, believing that she and her husband were living beyond their means, Anne Macaulay of Picton decided to decrease the size of her household. She reported to her sister-in-law, Helen, that as a result she had a great deal to do before Caroline, her girl, left. "I would like to keep her instead of Mary as she is not Roman Catholic and is now a decent well behaved girl but she cannot do the washing & She cannot iron but when she has been a little longer in service to learn I may get her back again": Anne Macaulay to Helen Macaulay, 9 October 1837.

46 Anne Powell to George Murray, 17 March 1811, quoted in McKenna, "The Life of Anne Murray Powell," 141.

47 Macaulay Papers, Helen to Ann Macaulay, 5 February 1838.

48 Ibid., John to Ann Macaulay, 22 September 1837; 17 October 1837; 18 October 1839.

49 It was only after considerable searching in Kingston, Picton, and finally Toronto, that William sent a young girl, Margaret MacBride, to his mother with a note recommending her as "an excellent servant – a thorough worker & trusting": Macaulay Papers, William to Ann Macaulay, 15 September 1838. William had noted a month earlier, 22 August 1838, that he had been unable to find a maid in Kingston or in Picton. On 11 April 1839, John Macaulay in York inquired of his mother if she knew anyone who could replace his manservant Roach. John was willing to pay a servant $12.00/month. See also 16 November 1837.

50 Ibid., Helen to Ann Macaulay, 23 January 1840.

51 Ibid., John to Ann Macaulay, 28 September 1839, Eliza had gone to Mrs Strachan's for a higher salary.

52 Dudden, *Serving Women*, 72–4.

53 *Upper Canada Gazette*, 11 December 1823.

54 Notice by Patrick McGan of an agency run out of his auction store, *Upper Canada Gazette*, 29 March 1828. Patrick McGan's fees included 1s. 3d. for a master's registry and the same for each merchant and servant who registered. This notice continued until 17 May 1828. Other agencies included R. Langer, minister of the Church of England at Brantford, *Upper Canada Gazette*, 22 March 1828; *Gore Gazette* office, *Gore Gazette*, 5 July 1828; Peter Ramberger's Inn, registering for farming and housework, *Colonial Advo-*

cate, 24 June 1830; *Cobourg Star* office, *Cobourg Star*, 1 March 1831; 27 July 1835; York Emigration Society, *Christian Guardian*, 25 April 1832; The Emigration Society of the Midland District, *The Patriot*, 5 June 1832; Travellers Inn, *Hallowell Free Press*, 8 January 1833; York Dairy, House Agent, *The Patriot*, 1 March 1833.

55 Immigrants were especially urged to register "their names, ages and professions" and the position they sought: *Niagara Gleaner*, 6 November 1824. This notice continued until the end of 1825.

56 Most advertisements appear to have been placed by households looking for an "active" clever girl who would be the only domestic employee. See for example *Upper Canada Gazette*, 2 May 1822; *Colonial Advocate*, 26 May 1831. Much more work has yet to be done analysing the "help-wanted" and "looking for a situation" notices in colonial newspapers. The following provides only a cursory glance of the state of the market.

57 *Upper Canada Gazette*, 2 May 1822.

58 *Niagara Herald*, 28 November 1801. A girl's character was mentioned in, among others, *Upper Canada Gazette*, 9 January 1817; *Upper Canada Herald*, 7 June 1825; *Colonial Advocate*, 8 September 1831.

59 See *Colonial Advocate*, 23 January 1824; 10 June 1824; 23 January 1827; 25 March 1830; 8 September 1831. Those advertisements not mentioning experience at all included *Niagara Herald*, 28 November 1801; *Kingston Chronicle*, 4 August 1818; *Upper Canada Gazette*, 1 June 1820; *Colonial Advocate*, 10 June 1824; 29 May 1828; *Gore Gazette*, 1 September 1827; *Cobourg Star*, 17 June 1835; 27 July 1836; *The Patriot*, 27 March 1838. Advertisements mentioning specific experience included *Kingston Gazette*, 15 September 1818; *Upper Canada Gazette*, 2 May 1822; *Colonial Advocate*, 29 July 1824; 25 March 1830; 26 May 1831; *The Patriot*, 3 July 1832; 24 August 1838; *Cobourg Star*, 4 April 1832; 6 May 1835; *Kingston Chronicle*, 20 December 1834; 22 April 1835.

60 *Niagara Herald*, 14 November 1801; *Upper Canada Gazette*, 27 August 1818; 13 December 1828; *The Patriot* 7 March 1835; *Kingston Gazette*, 25 January 1817. See also *Upper Canada Gazette*, 6 June 1822; *United Empire Loyalist*, 13 December 1828; *Kingston Chronicle*, 25 January 1834; *The Patriot* 20 February 1825; 24 August 1838.

61 One household advertised, *Kingston Chronicle*, 8 March 1834, "Wanted – a respectable woman, to keep house and nurse an infant. A person of good character and not burthened with a family, may obtain a comfortable situation where there is little work to be done, a liberal compensation to be given." See also *Canadian Freeman*, 14 July 1831.

62 *Niagara Herald*, 14 November 1801 (looking for a housekeeper with a husband); *Upper Canada Gazette*, 4 September 1817 (he as a gardener); 20 March 1823; 7 June 1828; *Kingston Gazette*, 15 September 1818; *The Patriot*, 31 July 1828 (coachman and cook); 27 February 1835 (coachman and cook); *Kingston Chronicle*, 11 July 1829.

63 These included *Kingston Gazette*, 20 November 1810; 15 September 1818; *United Empire Loyalist*, 1 June 1820; 6 June 1822; 14 July 1826; 19 January 1828; 5 September 1833; *Colonial Advocate*, 27 April 1824; *Kingston Chronicle*, 27 November 1830; 23 November 1833; *Niagara Gleaner*, 29 June 1833; *The Patriot*, 1 November 1833; 21 October 1834; 27 February 1835; 29 December 1835; 27 March 1838; 7 January 1840; *Cobourg Star*, 16 December 1835. Some of these ads for cooks also asked for honesty and sobriety: *Kingston Gazette*, 15 September 1818; *United Empire Loyalist*, 1 June 1820; 6 June 1822. A number of cooks were wanted for Upper Canadian hotels. See *Kingston Chronicle*, 29 April 1815; 11 March 1835; *Upper Canada Gazette*, 15 December 1822; *Colonial Advocate*, 13 April 1826; 11 August 1831; *The Patriot*, 29 May 1835. There were only a few advertisements that solicited young women "accustomed to the care of young children": *Gore Gazette*, 13 September 1828; *United Empire Loyalist*, 13 September 1828; *Kingston Chronicle*, 7 May 1831; *Cobourg Star*, 28 Mary 1834. A nursemaid, with a respectable character and some specific skills who was willing to help in the kitchen or was skilled with a needle was in much greater demand: *Cobourg Star*, 26 November 1834. Advertisements for governess, see *Cobourg Star*, 4 February 1834; *The Patriot*, 25 February 1834; 28 August 1836; 19 June 1838; 28 August 1838; *Christian Guardian*, 29 November 1837. For further discussion of the role of the governess in upper-class households, see Chapter 9.

64 *Colonial Advocate*, 21 July 1831; *Canadian Correspondent*, 4 May 1833; *Niagara Gleaner*, 10 August 1833; *The Patriot*, 8 June 1838.

65 *The Patriot*, 7 March 1834, also offering to be a laundry maid; 21 August 1838, someone hoping to return to England. *The Patriot*, 14 February 1840, read "A young person who has a plain education wishes to engage herself in a respectable family as a NURSERY GOVERNESS". See also *Colonial Advocate*, 21 July 1831; *Niagara Gleaner*, 10 August 1833; *The Patriot*, 8 June 1838; *Christian Guardian*, 11 March 1840.

66 Edward Higgs, "Domestic Service and Household Production," in John, ed., *Unequal Opportunities*, 125–51, 137. Katz estimates in *The People of Hamilton*, 27–8, that in the 1850s, 90 per cent of domestic servants were female and 95 per cent of these were unmarried; 75 per cent of them were under twenty-five years old. Lacelle, *Urban Domestic Servants*, 18–19, found that on the basis of contracts in Montreal and Quebec, the servant population was almost equally divided between men and women and that, on average, they were somewhat older than in Hamilton. These statistics do not, of course include what were likely hundreds of servants who did not enter into formal and relatively long-term contracts with their employers. See also Bradbury, *Working Families*, 140–1; Dudden, *Serving Women*, 44–6.

67 For example, in 1831, four young English sisters, aged sixteen, eighteen, nineteen, and twenty-three were looking for work who had come to Up-

per Canada "from the neighbourhood of York, England": *Patriot*, 30 June 1831.

68 As cook, *Upper Canada Gazette*, 16 April 1818; *Colonial Advocate*, 24 January 1828; *Kingston Chronicle*, 5 March 1831; 12 April 1834. Housekeeper: *Upper Canada Gazette*, 29 October 1929; *Colonial Advocate*, 11 October 1832; *Canadian Correspondent and Advocate*, 30 November 1833; *The Patriot*, 17 October 1834; 20 September 1836; 11 August 1837; 13 October 1837. There was one "elderly woman of respectability" who wanted a situation "in any capacity except cook," *Upper Canada Gazette*, 18 November 1829. There were some young women looking for a position as a cook: *Colonial Advocate*; 21 July 1831, cook or housemaid; *The Patriot*, 15 November 1836; 8 June 1838, cook or nurse.

   For governess, see *Colonial Advocate*, 20 January 1825; *Gore Gazette*, 13 October 1827; *Upper Canada Gazette*, 20 October 1827; *The Patriot*, 23 January 1835; 9 May 1837; 9 June 1837; 8 December 1837; 20 March 1838.

69 This was particularly true of women who were looking for situations as governesses. Though many women stated that they had a "plain education," *The Patriot*, 14 February 1840; *Christian Guardian*, 11 March 1840, a number of women offered the qualification of being a "lady": *Canadian Correspondent*, 17 August 1833; *Colonial Advocate*, 10 October 1833. The term "lady" was probably consciously used; certainly not all notices claimed to be from "ladies."

70 *Kingston Chronicle*, 12 April 1834. See also *The Patriot*, 20 March 1838, notice from a Lady from England which ended, "Salary not so much an object as a comfortable home." Other women stated that if the applicant "could be treated as a companion … A smaller salary than usual would be required": *The Patriot*, 22 August 1837. See also 11 October 1833. Another curious advertisement placed by "the Friends of a young lady" concluded "she is most respectably connected and Salary is less an object with her friends than seeing her established in a family where she will see Kindness and protection": *The Patriot*, 3 October 1834. Though many of these women were widows, a few were as young as twenty: *The Patriot*, 11 October 1833; *Christian Guardian*, 11 March 1840.

71 The notice concluded, "Enquire for Mrs Lyon, at Mr Drury's New Market Lane. York, October 10, 1832": *Colonial Advocate*, 11 October 1832. For similar notices, see *The Patriot*, 11 October 1833; *Cobourg Star*, 5 October 1836.

72 *The Patriot*, 14 February 1834.

73 *Colonial Advocate*, 15 September 1831; *The Patriot*, 20 March 1838; 8 April 1836; 8 December 1837; 16 October 1840. Older women who were seeking positions as a governess were often in a somewhat anomalous position. As M. Jeanne Peterson notes, "The Victorian Governess," in Vicinus, ed., *Suffer and Be Still*, 3–19, many of them were gentlewomen who had fallen on hard times. Their employment as a governess "was a contradiction of

the very values she was hired to fulfil," however. And "the result was a situation of conflict and incongruity for both the governess and the family," 5. See also Vicinus, *Independent Women*, and Chapter 9 following.

74 *Patriot*, 20 March 1838. See also *Colonial Advocate*, 15 September 1831; *The Patriot*, 23 January 1835; 8 April 1836.

75 *The Patriot*, 28 August 1838. See also 25 February 1834. These qualifications are drawn from various advertisements in local newspapers. Among others, see *Cobourg Star*, 4 February 1834; *The Patriot*, 28 August 1836; 8 December 1837; 28 August 1838 and following footnotes.

76 *The Patriot*, 23 January 1835; 20 March 1838; *Colonial Advocate*, 20 January 1825; *Gore Gazette*, 13 October 1827; *Upper Canada Gazette*, 20 October 1827; *Cobourg Star*, 5 October 1836; *The Patriot*, 8 April 1836; 9 May 1837; 9 June 1837; 8 December 1837; *United Empire Loyalist*, 3 June 1826.

77 Dudden notes in *Serving Women*, 79, that ads alone "could not canvass the supply of servants." She also posits that many prospective servants were probably illiterate and some may not have had a residence in which to see potential employers. See Lacelle, *Urban Domestic Servants*, 29–31, for recruitment practices in Montreal and Quebec.

78 Dudden, *Serving Women*, 78. See also Branca, *Silent Sisterhood*, 29–31; Davidoff and Hall, *Family Fortunes*, 388–9.

79 See Katz, *The People of Hamilton*, 123–30; Gagan, *Hopeful Travellers*, 114–20.

80 See Dudden, *Serving Women*, 44–55, for a discussion of hiring practices in the United States. She notes, 79, that many American mistresses also resented having to use employment agencies. Davidoff and Hall, *Family Fortunes*, 389–90, conclude that members of the British middle class experienced similar problems with recruitment. They also confronted the contradiction of having servants who became part of their households but who were engaged through impersonal market relations.

81 Davidoff and Hall, *Family Fortunes*, 395.

82 Macaulay Papers, Anne Macaulay to John Macaulay, 5 December, 1838.

83 See for example Lydia Marie Child, *The American Frugal Housewife* (Boston, 1829). Branca, *Silent Sisterhood*, discusses in some detail the household guides available and widely used in Britain at this time. It is known that many of these were also available in Upper Canada.

84 *The Patriot*, 25 November 1836.

85 See for example an article in the *Kingston Gazette*, "To the Reckoner," 10 March 1812. See also Dudden, *Serving Women*, 156–63; Branca, *Silent Sisterhood*, 30–2.

86 "The English Housekeeper," *The Patriot*, 25 November 1836.

87 Davidoff and Hall, *Family Fortunes*, 390–3, discuss the importance of maintaining discipline within the house and the problems some women had doing this. One Upper Canadian newspaper did give advice to servants. They were encouraged to be attentive to their mistresses' demands.

In addition, "Be careful of your master's property, for wastefulness is sin." Servants should "rise early for it is difficult to recover lost time." And most importantly, "The servant that often changes his place works only to be poor," a brief article on "Useful Rules for Servants" stated emphatically: *Brockville Gazette*, 12 June 1829.

88 When she first arrived in the colony, Elizabeth Russell was clearly upset that she had no accommodation for a female servant and this may have had some influence on her inability to hire one. On accommodation generally provided to servants, see Lacelle, *Urban Domestic Servants*, 43–4.

89 Macaulay Papers, Ann to John Macaulay, 10 July 1837. As Stansell notes in *City of Women*, 160–1, the "separation of work and leisure between downstairs and upstairs advertised both the social distance between the two sets of residents and the power of one set to make the other climb stairs."

90 Ibid., John to Ann John Macaulay, 22 July 1837.

91 Dudden, *Serving Women*, 47. Lacelle, *Urban Domestic Servants*, 46, notes a similar practice.

92 Journal of Mrs E.G. O'Brien, 1828–38, Archives of Ontario (AO), MS 199, 26 January 1830.

93 As Lacelle notes in *Urban Domestic Servants*, 48, we know surprisingly little about servants' actual conditions of work. Lacelle suggests that many servants were in "ordinary dress." But fragmentary evidence suggests that in Upper Canada's most prominent households, servants were expected to be in uniform.

94 As upper-class daughters began to attend schools and be trained to be a "good" woman and wife, their contribution to the housekeeping in many instances decreased. See Chapter 9; Peterson, *Family Life and Work*, Chapter 2; Gorham, *The Victorian Girl*, 125–52.

95 Macaulay Papers, Helen to Ann Macaulay, 21 January 1840. In this letter Helen noted that she considered adding another servant to relieve Sarah of the burden. Lacelle notes, *Urban Domestic Servants*, 41, that in Lower Canada, the workday was fifteen or sixteen hours.

96 The growing specialization of urban domestic servants contrasts sharply with the generalized work of a "help." One essential difference was that many urban servants worked to time and not to task and they were expected always to be busy when "on duty": Dudden, *Serving Women*, 179. See also Lacelle, *Urban Domestic Servants*, 33; Stansell, *City of Women*, 158; Davidoff, *The Best Circles*, 87–8.

97 Dudden, *Serving Women*, 137. See Dudden, Chapter 4, for a discussion of the impact of the new domestic ideology on expectations of how a home should be kept. See also Stansell, *City of Women*, 161; Norton, *Liberty's Daughters*, 26–9, which describes plantation households that at times resembled Upper Canadian elite households in their domestic organization.

98 Dudden, *Serving Women*, 115–7.

99 Powell Papers, Anne Powell to George Murray, 26 January 1818. Anne continued that "much superintendence falls on me." Helen Macaulay was able to advise her mother-in-law a decade later not to go out in the winter. "You have servants that have been long with you now; and they surely ought to know how to please you & they are respectable so that your mind must be easy": Macaulay Papers, Helen Macaulay to Ann Macaulay, 20 November 1840. Anne Macaulay of Picton too seems to have been well served by her servants. After visits to York and Kingston, Anne often returned to Picton to find her home and gardens in good order.

100 Macaulay Papers, Ann to John Macaulay makes a number of references, periodically and sporadically, to having to pay the servants. See for example, 14 April 1841, 3 April 1841, in which she specifically noted she had to pay the staff, as she had not done so since December. See Lacelle, *Urban Domestic Servants*, 38, for rates of pay and days off. Dudden, *Serving Women*, 51–2, suggests that servants were paid more than household help. There is even less information on rates of pay in colonial towns than there is for rural communities. It does appear that wages were dependent on skill.

101 The Jarvises were willing to double wages for a good servant, noted in McKenna, "The Life of Anne Murray Powell," 138–9. Macaulay Papers, Ann Macaulay informed her son, 4 October 1839, that though she "ought to lessen her establishment," she decided to keep one of the girls on, because she was trustworthy, "a good sewer," and cost only $2.50/month.

102 It was this complaint that prompted Helen to appeal to her mother-in-law for Flora.

103 Ironically, Elizabeth noted that Mary "had broken the nasty habit" just before she died: Russell Papers, Elizabeth Russell to Lizzy Kiernan, 1 January 1795; 25 November 1795. See also 1 October 1793 for first mention of this; 26 February 1797; 19 July 1797, further reference to her loss.

104 Macaulay Papers, Helen to John Macaulay, 15 June 1841.

105 Ibid., Helen to Ann Macaulay, 23 January 1840; John to Ann Macaulay, 18 July 1837. On 17 August 1840, John again wrote to his mother praising Elinore; he had noted two days earlier that he intended to leave Elinore in charge of the house while he and Helen did some travelling.

106 This was done at considerable inconvenience to the family. There were other examples of such concern. William Macaulay wrote to his mother, 5 January 1838, that their servant was somewhat better, but they had been under considerable inconvenience as they had not been able to replace her. In 1841 Helen Macaulay refused to let her maid Bertha, who was ill, go home. "It is better for her to stay here," she concluded: Macaulay Papers, Helen to John Macaulay, 25 May 1841. For further discussion of the claim that servants could make on their employers, see

Davidoff and Hall, *Family Fortunes*, 389; Lacelle, *Urban Domestic Servants*, 39–40; Branca, *Silent Sisterhood*, 33–4.

107 Jarvis-Peters Papers, National Archives, Hannah to William Jarvis, Newark, 26 September 1793, as quoted in McKenna, "The Life of Anne Murray Powell," 139. Ann Macaulay reported to her son a generation later that she had "a very poor servant woman, who cannot even make a bit of toast." As a result, Ann felt unable to invite anyone, even for tea, except her immediate relations. Macaulay Papers, Ann to John Macaulay, 11 February 1838.

108 Russell Diary, 18 January 1806.

109 Ibid.

110 Ibid., 25 January 1806.

111 Ibid., 21 January 1806. Ironically in 1801 the Russells had attempted to get rid of their slave, Peggy, by sale. However the sale was not successful: Peter Russell to Captain Matthew Elliott, 19 September 1801, as quoted in Firth, *The Town of York: 1793–1815*, 243.

112 Russell Diary, 18 March 1806. Helen Macaulay too was willing to put up with a bad-tempered servant and was disappointed when he decided to leave the family "as he was good": Macaulay Papers, Helen to Ann Macaulay, 5 February 1838. Servants' bad temperedness or insolence created problems for many mistresses. See Davidoff and Hall, *Family Fortunes*, 388–9; Dudden, *Serving Women*, 53–4; Norton, *Liberty's Daughters*, 22–3. Rollins in *Between Women*, 36, argues that the potential for conflict between mistress and maid was higher in the United States than it was in Great Britain at this time, because American servants had quite different expectations of their work. In the Canadian colonial context, at least, it may be that because so many servants were probably recent immigrants, the differences were less evident. Much more work needs to be done on how ethnicity affected women's expectations and actions.

113 Macaulay Papers, Anne Macaulay to mother-in-law Ann Macaulay, 25 April 1840.

114 Ibid., William to Ann Macaulay, 30 April 1840.

115 Ibid., John to Ann Macaulay, 4 May, 1840.

116 Ibid., 7 May 1840.

117 Ibid., 26 February 1841.

118 For example, Ann Macaulay wrote to her son, John, that she regretted having to discharge one of her servant girls "though I shall miss her." Ann explained, "I think there is too great an expense to keep three servants especially as I have been laying out so much money this year." Ibid., Ann to John Macaulay, 4 November 1839. Dudden argues, *Serving Women*, 56–7, that servants were frequently dismissed for "cause" or because they did not suit. The same does not seem to have been the case in Upper Canada.

119 "To the Reckoner," *Kingston Gazette*, 9 June 1812.

120 Ibid.

121 Dudden, *Serving Women*, 123.

122 Stansell notes in *City of Women*, 165–6, that servants in New York were willing and able to exert their independence.

123 Macaulay Papers, Helen to Ann Macaulay, 25 January 1840.

124 Helen Macaulay's coachman, Roach, left because he thought his mistress did not trust him: Macaulay Papers, 5 February 1838.

125 Ibid., John to Ann Macaulay, 26 January 1837. A similar problem occurred, 5 March 1837. See also 31 August 1838, a report that the maid, Ann, had left to marry; William to John Macaulay, 27 April 1840; 21 May 1840; McKenna, "The Life of Anne Murray Powell," 136; Norton, *Liberty's Daughters*, 22–3; Dudden, *Serving Women*, 54, 175–83; Davidoff and Hall, *Family Fortunes*, 389.

126 Russell Diary, 3 April 1807.

127 Macaulay Papers, John to Ann Macaulay, 26 October 1837.

128 See Bradbury, *Working Families*, 140–1.

129 Macaulay Papers, John to Ann Macaulay, 19 November 1839, in which he noted that his manservant, Roach, had left to set up a boarding house.

130 See for example *Niagara Herald*, 12 September 1801; *Farmers' Journal*, 3 December 1828; *Gore Gazette*, 7 February 1829, a notice by Conrad Knoll, noting that Vasty Post had run away; 9 March 1929, a notice from Wm. D. Dutton, noting that Maria Post had run away; *Brockville Gazette*, 14 December 1830; *Farmers' Journal*, 17 May 1832; *British Whig*, 14 November 1834. The whole question of indenturing in early Upper Canada needs considerably more attention.

131 See Dudden, *Serving Women*, 175–6; Davidoff and Hall, *Family Fortunes*, 390.

132 Macaulay Papers, William to Ann Macaulay, 30 April 1840.

133 Ibid. Ann to Helen Macaulay, 11 July 1833, reporting her return home and the conditions there; William Macaulay to his mother, 21 May 1840. Ann Macaulay, who kept at least two or three maids, also seems to have helped with the housework. In her letters to her son, Ann Macaulay made frequent references to household affairs, including to members of her staff: see, for example 30 March 1840, 15 May 1840.

134 Dudden, *Serving Women* argues that the difference between helps and servants was primarily one of locale. Helps worked on the farm; servants worked in towns. However, as Davidoff and Hall, *Family Fortunes*, 388–9, note, of greater significance was the number of domestic servants in a household. When there was only one girl, the relationship seemed to be one of "helping." When families could afford two or more domestic employees, these women tended to be viewed as servants. See also Norton, *Liberty's Daughters*, 22–33.

CHAPTER SEVEN

1 Anna Jameson, *Winter Studies and Summer Rambles* (1838) (Toronto: Mc-Clelland and Stewart 1965), 17 February 1838, 48–9.
2 Ibid., 49. Charles Stuart commented in his immigrant guide, *Emigrants Guide to Upper Canada* (London, 1822), 120–1, that "the state of society in Upper Canada ... is not attractive." He continued, "the Canadian society has rather roughness than simplicity of manners; and scarcely presents a trace of that truly refined, that nobly cultivated and that spiritually improved tone of conversation and deportment which, even in the most highly polished circles and amidst all the inflations of real or imagined superiority, is rarely to be found." Not all agreed. James Strachan, brother of the Archdeacon of York, an influential member of the elite, judged that provincial "society ... both as it respects the ladies and the gentlemen" was "superior in such as few towns in England can furnish": *A Visit to the Province of Upper Canada in 1819* (1822) (Toronto: S.R. Publishers 1968), 198–9. Strachan described this society, which in the second generation resided in York, as "the judges, the crown officers, the heads of different departments, several professional gentlemen, merchants and officers of half-pay, all living with their families in the greatest harmony."
3 Clara Thomas, ed., "Introduction" to Jameson, *Winter Studies*, x.
4 Jameson, *Winter Studies*, 28 April 1838, 69.
5 McKenna, "The Life of Anne Murray Powell," 127–30.
6 These rituals reflected those that were practised in Great Britain in the late eighteenth and throughout the nineteenth century. See Davidoff, *The Best Circles*; Gorham, *The Victorian Girl*, 101–24.
7 Jameson, *Winter Studies*, 22.
8 Julia to David R. Lambert, 27 August 1821 as quoted in McKenna, "The Life of Anne Murray Powell," 132.
9 Reported in Angus, "A Gentlewoman," 73–85, 75.
10 The same was true for Miss Lambert: McKenna, "The Life of Anne Murray Powell," 132. The question of social precedent practised in Upper Canada was reminiscent of that which prevailed in London at this time. See, Davidoff, *The Best Circles*, 41–9; Davidoff and Hall, *Family Fortunes*, 21.
11 McKenna, "The Life of Anne Murray Powell," 123.
12 Macaulay Papers, Archives of Ontario (AO), MS 78, John to Helen Macaulay, 12 February 1837.
13 Ibid., John to Ann Macaulay, 17 February 1837.
14 Ibid., 12 March 1837. See also 16 March 1837.
15 Ibid., 27 November 1837.
16 Quoted in Angus, "A Gentlewoman," 76.

17 Elizabeth Russell Papers, Diary, Metropolitan Toronto Reference Library (MTL), 7 January 1808.

18 "Powell Papers," MTL, Anne Powell to George Murray, 2 February 1818.

19 McKenna makes this point very clear in "The Life of Anne Murray Powell." For Anne, social conventions helped her cope with the conditions of life in Upper Canada, and with the problems she confronted in the years prior to the War of 1812 establishing and maintaining her place in society. This was undoubtedly true of other British women immigrants to the colony. See Davidoff, *The Best Circles*; Peterson, *Family, Love, and Work*, 120–2.

20 Christopher Hagerman informed his friend John Macaulay that his wife was angry because he had not yet subscribed to a ball in 1823, even though they would be unable to attend: Macaulay Papers, Christopher Hagerman to John Macaulay, December 1823. On 27 January 1839, John Macaulay wrote to his mother that he and Helen expected to go to a ball. A week later, however, 8 February 1839, he noted that Helen would be unable to go because of ill health. This was only two months after her confinement and the premature birth of her second daughter.

21 Mary Quayle Innis, *Mrs Simcoe's Diary* (Toronto: University of Toronto Press 1965), 151, Elizabeth Simcoe to Mrs Hunt, February 1793.

22 Quoted in McKenna, "The Life of Anne Murray Powell," 130.

23 Mrs Anne Powell to George Murray, 19 January 1806, quoted in Edith Firth, *The Town of York, 1793–1815*, 270–1.

24 McKenna, "The Life of Anne Murray Powell," 158–63, details this dispute.

25 For a brief discussion of the political chronology and ramifications of the Thorpe affair, see Errington, *The Lion, The Eagle and Upper Canada*, 48–51, 64–5.

26 McKenna, "The Life of Anne Murray Powell," 168.

27 Ibid., 162–6.

28 Ibid., 170.

29 Jameson, *Winter Studies*, 24–5.

30 Quoted in Angus, "A Gentlewoman," 77.

31 Macaulay Papers, John to Helen Macaulay, 9 December 1833.

32 Ibid., John to Ann Macaulay, 13 February 1839.

33 Ibid., Anne Macaulay to Ann Macaulay, 31 January 1839.

34 McKenna, "The Life of Anne Murray Powell," 180.

35 John Elmsley to Mrs Mary Elmsley, 10 December 1827, quoted in Firth, *The Town of York, 1815–1833*, 318–19.

36 Macaulay Papers, John to Ann Macaulay, 27 November 1837.

37 Ibid., 30 January 1840.

38 Ibid., 6 January 1840. The importance of formal, but private, dinner parties is explained in Davidoff, *The Best Circles*, 46–9.

39 Russell Papers, Elizabeth Russell to Lizzy Kiernan, 18 January 1793. The same was also true of Anne Powell's household and probably most others of the upper class: McKenna, "The Life of Anne Murray Powell."
40 See Davidoff and Hall, *Family Fortunes*, 195.
41 *Brockville Gazette*, 13 September 1832.
42 See Jane Errington, "Ann Kirby Macaulay," *DCB*, Vol. VII, 469.
43 See McKenna, "The Life of Anne Murray Powell," 466. See also George Sheppard, *Plunder, Profit and Paroles: A Social History of the War of 1812 in Upper Canada* (Montreal & Kingston: McGill- Queen's University Press 1994), 66–8.
44 Anne Powell to W.D. Powell, York, 10 May 1813, quoted in McKenna, "The Life of Anne Murray Powell," 466. This is reminiscent of the work some women did during the American Revolutionary War. See Norton, *Liberty's Daughters*, 195–227; Potter-MacKinnon, *While the Women Only Wept*, 31–62.
45 "Letter to the Editor," *Kingston Gazette*, 17 March 1818.
46 For a general discussion of the rise of organized reform in Great Britain and the United States and varying interpretations on how women's involvement in these activities affected their lives, see Davidoff and Hall, *Family Fortunes*, 419–36; Lebsock, *The Free Women of Petersburg*, 195–236; Ryan, *Cradle of the Middle Class*, 105–44; Cott, *The Bonds of Womanhood*; F.K. Prochaska, *Women and Philanthropy*; Melder, "Ladies Bountiful," 231–54; Hewitt, *Women's Activism*.
47 Ulrich, *Good Wives*, 9. One of the aspects of reform that has attracted most controversy is the question of the motivation of the reformers. Davidoff and Hall, *Family Fortunes*, 419–45, 421, argue that it was a combination of sincere religious impulse coupled with the perceived needs of the rising middle class to defend its vision of the world. In short, "it was both Christian and expedient to improve the labouring poor, morally and physically." Others, including Rothman, *The Discovery of the Asylum*, have argued that the reform impulse was a thinly disguised attempt at social control. As Lebsock has stated in *The Free Women of Petersburg*, 302 n10, "this latter thesis is difficult to prove or disprove." In Upper Canada, motivation of the women involved in various philanthropic and religious organizations differed, depending on whom one is discussing.
48 Davidoff and Hall, *Family Fortunes*, 430–4; Hewitt, *Women's Activism*, 54.
49 See Davidoff and Hall, *Family Fortunes*, 430–4. As Lebsock concludes in *The Free Women of Petersburg*, 233, there is some irony in this. "Once the basic tenets of true womanhood were established, they could be, and were, used in diametrically opposite ways." Certainly, "the true woman's claim to superior virtue and piety could be [and was] used to justify the creation of new spheres of activity outside the home." It could be and was also used "to repel some new female incursion on male prerogative," such as political activities. Much more work needs to be done in the Upper Cana-

dian context to judge whether and how the new social ideology became a double-edged sword for women's public activities.

50 More work is also required to determine whether benevolent and reform organizations in Upper Canada actually united women in common cause and created what some have suggested was a "women's culture." Hewitt, *Women's Activism*, argues that in Rochester, there were at least two and sometimes three distinct networks of women – Evangelical, Moral Crusaders, and Ultraists – who formed different organizations for different purposes. Davidoff and Hall, *Family Fortunes*, indicate that reform activities were led largely by the middle-class men and women who believed that the lower classes and the unconverted needed to be reformed. Cott, *Bonds of Womanhood*, argues strongly that reform organizations and their activities provided an opportunity for women across the classes to unite in common cause.

Only rather fragmentary evidence exists for this early period in Upper Canada. It would appear, however, that there were two broadly based impulses in Upper Canada after 1815 – Evangelical and Benevolent. Up to about 1825, most reform activities were organized and supported primarily by men and women of the upper and upper-middle classes who shared a desire to meet the needs of the "lower orders" and the unfortunate immigrant. By the mid-1830s, however, a number of evangelical women had become involved in religious and benevolent reform and they had begun their own organizations.

51 Daily prayers and even Sunday services were conducted by the many families in their homes. Often servants and labourers joined their employers in an affirmation of their faith. In the O'Brien household, when Edward O'Brien was away, Mary led prayers. Through April 1832, Mary, now settled in her new home, noted "we shall return to our accustomed habits of daily family prayer." See also Journal of Mrs E.G. O'Brien, 1828–38 AO, MS 199, 4 August 1829.

52 *Kingston Gazette*, 11 November 1817.

53 Reported in ibid., 11 January 1817.

54 The Kingston Association was formed on 25 January 1817 as reported in *Kingston Gazette*, 5 February 1817. A report about the formation of the Niagara group appeared, 7 December 1816. The establishment of a third society for all the Midland District was announced 8 March 1817.

55 "Address," printed in the *Upper Canada Gazette*, 12 December 1816.

56 Ibid. See also *Kingston Gazette*, 11 January 1817.

57 *Upper Canada Gazette*, 12 December 1816. It should be noted that there was dissent, particularly from some Methodists, to the founding of this society. See for example *Kingston Gazette*, 1, 8, 15 February 1817. In many cases these residents preferred the Niagara Society, which did not note the Common Prayer Book aspect of it.

58 See list of contributors in *Kingston Gazette*, 11 January 1817. The presence
of women was not as evident in the Kingston organization. A report of the
Kingston Association in the *Kingston Gazette*, 27 January 1818 included
only Mrs Foster as one of the subscribers. This continued to be the case a
year later: *Kingston Chronicle*, 22 January 1819.

59 Hewitt notes in *Women's Activism*, 50, that for some women, turning affluence into contributions to the poor was one sign of their membership in
the local elite.

60 See John Strachan to Hamilton, 5 January 1820, quoted in McKenna, "The
Life of Anne Murray Powell," 467.

61 One of the first references to a Sunday school appeared in a letter to the
editor from Obadiah, *Kingston Gazette*, 9 March 1816. In a letter to the editor, 29 July 1817, *Kingston Gazette*, an anonymous contributor noted the
need for Sunday schools. See Alan Greer, "The Sunday Schools of Upper
Canada," *Ontario History* LXVII, 83 (September 1975), 169–83.

62 "To the Citizens of the Flourishing Village of Hallowell, from A Friend of
Youth," *Upper Canada Herald*, 5 July 1825.

63 *Kingston Chronicle*, 29 July 1817. See also 22 September 1820.

64 See, for example, "For the Herald," from Scongal, *Upper Canada Herald*, 25
May 1825, which reported that there were four schools in Kingston. The
Colonial Advocate printed a Sunday School Union Report, 30 December
1824, commenting on the situation in York. The *Kingston Chronicle*, 9 No-
vember 1821, noted the formation of a Sunday School Union there. *The
Observer*, 9 December 1822, commented favourably on the part that Thad-
deus Osgood had played in the formation of the London Society in Great
Britain. The *Farmers' Journal*, 3 December 1828, noted the formation of a
Sunday school society under the direction of Osgood.

For a discussion of Sunday School formation in Great Britain, see
Davidoff and Hall, *Family Fortunes*, 420, who characterize this as the first
category of philanthropic society, which also included establishing infant
schools and charity schools to teach the poor. (Category two was organizations formed to meet the cultural needs of the middle class themselves; three was business and property associations; four was political
organizations.)

65 See for example the Report of the Sunday School Society of Kingston,
Kingston Chronicle, 5 November 1824. See also *Weekly Register*, 11 December 1823 for Canadian Sunday School Society.

66 See for example the Annual Report of St George's Sunday School, *Upper
Canada Herald*, 6 March 1825.

67 Reference is made to this in a letter from John Strachan to Hamilton, 5 January 1820, Strachan Letter Books, quoted in McKenna, "The Life of Anne
Murray Powell," 467. See also William Bell, *Hints to Emigrants* (Edinburgh: Waugh and Innes 1824), 197.

68 McKenna, "The Life of Anne Murray Powell," 467.

69 O'Brien Journal, 2, 16 August 1829. For references to other aspects of Mary's Sunday school teaching career see 9, 25 August 1829; 13 September 1829; 18, 25 October 1829; 5 December 1829. Throughout the months of December 1829 and January, February, April, May, and August 1830 Mary's diary makes regular mention of her teaching at the local Sunday school. On 18 February 1834, at her new home, Mary noted that there was a need for "a regular system of Sunday Schools."

70 See, for example, "Report," *Upper Canada Herald*, 29 March 1825.

71 See the Report of the Union Church Sabbath School, *Upper Canada Herald*, 29 March 1825. See also Davidoff and Hall, *Family Fortunes*, 431–2, 435–6.

72 McKenna, "The Life of Anne Murray Powell," 468.

73 Consideration of the lot of single women in the nineteenth century is increasing. McKenna, *A Life of Propriety*, 229–39, discusses Eliza Powell's experiences within the context of the "Limitations of Women's Sphere." Vinicus, *Independent Women, Work, and Community* looks at how single women in Great Britain coped with their "situation" by forming residential institutions. See also Errington, "Single Pioneering Women," 5–19.

74 *Kingston Gazette*, 8 March 1817.

75 The first announcement for the British Methodist Missionary Society for Kingston appeared in the *Kingston Chronicle*, 22 September 1820.

76 Most of the various reports of individual Methodist missionary societies that appeared in the *Christian Guardian* specifically listed contributions made to missionary boxes or collected by individual or pairs of women.

77 *Christian Guardian*, 14 August 1830; 16 January 1833.

78 Also listed amongst contributors were the Misses McCord, who ran a prominent girls' school and Miss Bliss who had opened an infants' school. In addition to being personally committed to the aims of the Bible Society, the Misses McCords and Miss Bliss may have felt that their contributions might be well received by the "ladies" of York. See Hewitt, *Women's Activism*, 50.

79 *Upper Canada Herald*, 12 April 1825. In the *Kingston Chronicle*, 27 November 1830 it was also noted that the Kingston Dorcas Society was serving meals and holding a sewing meeting.

80 *Kingston Chronicle*, 31 October 1829.

81 "Missionary," *Christian Guardian*, 16 April 1831. This article also made references to similar societies at other mission stations.

82 The Methodists were not alone in their concern for the state of native Upper Canadian souls. In 1830, the "good" citizens of York formed the Society for Converting and Civilizing the Indians and Propagating the Gospel among Destitute Settlers in Upper Canada: *Christian Guardian*, 6 November 1830. Other references to this organization appear in "A Sermon in Aid of the Poor and Destitute of Upper Canada," *Patriot*, 23 February 1838; see also 20 January 1837.

83 *Christian Guardian*, 10 September 1831.

84 See, for example, the formation of the Female Missionary Society of York, which was associated with the Missionary Society of the Methodist Episcopal Church: *Colonial Advocate*, 9 October 1828. Soon a St Catharines' branch was started: *Farmers' Journal*, 4 February 1829. The *Christian Guardian*, 20 February 1830, reported donations made to the Canada Conference Missionary Society from the York Female Missionary Society, the Hope Female Missionary Society, the Burford Female Missionary Society, and the St Catharines Missionary Society. A report in the *Christian Guardian*, 3 September 1834, noted the formation of the Matilda Missionary Society.

A number of women also formed various tract and Bible societies. See, for example, formation of the Cramahe and Haldimand Female Tract Society, *Christian Guardian*, 28 May 1831; *Christian Guardian*, 16 January 1833; Brantford Tract Society, 10 September 1834; Toronto Ladies' Society, *Kingston Chronicle*, 31 May 1837. In the *Upper Canada Gazette*, 4 February 1830, a notice appeared of the meeting of the York Bible Society, calling for both men and women to attend.

85 See, for example, Report in the *Christian Guardian*, 1 April 1835; 29 March 1837.

86 *Kingston Gazette*, 11 November 1817.

87 See for example references to this and loud calls for aid by Joseph Scott, surgeon in *Kingston Gazette*, 17 March 1818. See also Houston, "The Impetus to Reform"; Patricia E. Malcolmson, "The Poor in Kingston 1815–1850," in Tulchinsky, ed., *To Preserve and Defend*, 281–97; Rainer Baehre, "Paupers and Poor Relief in Upper Canada," in Johnson and Wilson, eds., *Historical Essays on Upper Canada*, 305–40. Women and men in Great Britain and the United States had similar fears. See Stansell, *City of Women*, 32; Lebsock, *The Free Women of Petersburg*, 203, 214–5; Ryan, *Cradle of the Middle Class*, 111–12; Hewitt, *Women's Activism*, 24–37.

88 *Upper Canada Gazette*, 30 October 1817, a report of the meeting five days earlier.

89 *Kingston Gazette*, 9 December 1817.

90 Ibid., 16 December 1817. See also for example *Kingston Gazette*, 9 December 1817; "Reports of the Annual Meeting," *Upper Canada Gazette*, 2 December 1819; 13 April 1820; 7 December 1820; 11 December 1823; 13 December 1828, and various references throughout the 1820s, including *Upper Canada Gazette*, a report of the Kingston Compassionate Society, 27 January 1820. An Ernestown Auxiliary of the Kingston Compassionate Society was formed in 1819; see for example *Kingston Gazette*, 23 June 1818; *Kingston Chronicle*, 22 January 1819.

91 Reported in the *Upper Canada Gazette*, 27 January 1820.

92 Ibid., 7 December 1820.

93 *Colonial Advocate*, 28 December 1826.

94 "Report," in ibid., 11 December 1828.

95 *Canadian Freeman*, 26 April 1832.

96 *Kingston Gazette*, 9 December 1817. See also ibid., 16, 30 December 1817, all to contributions from Mrs Cartwright and Mrs Hagerman. See also Stansell, *City of Women*, 34–6, for work of New York women.

97 *Upper Canada Gazette*, 4 December 1817. See also McKenna, "The Life of Anne Murray Powell," 466.

98 Report of the Annual Meeting, in ibid., 3 December 1818.

99 The Kingston branch was formed a month later, *Kingston Chronicle*, 4 January 1827. The importance of women's work, "behind the scenes" is ably discussed in Davidoff and Hall, *Family Fortunes*, 432–3.

100 "First Annual Report," *Upper Canada Gazette*, 22 November 1821.

101 Eliza Powell was involved in this society. See McKenna, "The Life of Anne Murray Powell," 467.

102 *Christian Guardian*, 17 September 1834. See also "Report," 30 January 1833.

103 A good deal of funding for the organization also came from local churches: *The Patriot*, 31 December 1833.

104 See, for example, *Kingston Chronicle*, 23 April 1819; Report of the Kingston Compassionate Society, *Upper Canada Gazette*, 27 January 1820. The need for medical services was first highlighted in a letter to the editor from H. McGee, Surgeon, in the *Kingston Gazette*, 7 April 1818.

105 A pamphlet-broadsheet appears in the Macaulay Papers which is edited in Ann Macaulay's handwriting.

106 *Kingston Chronicle*, 4 May 1827.

107 Ibid., 14 January 1825.

108 McKenna, " 'The Union Between Faith and Good Works'," 2. See also Susan Jill MacMicken, " 'To Honour and Serve Him': The Early Life of Harriet Dobbs Cartwright 1808–1843" (MA thesis, Queen's University 1994).

109 McKenna, "The Union Between Faith and God," 29–30.

110 Ibid., 28.

111 Ibid., 25.

112 *Colonial Advocate*, 15 April 1830; *Christian Guardian*, 17 April 1830; *Canadian Freeman*, 22 April 1830.

113 *Christian Guardian*, 15 May 1830

114 *Brockville Gazette*, 21 May 1830.

115 *Christian Guardian*, 15 May 1830.

116 Ibid., 28 May 1831, noted that £236.0.3 had been raised. In 1832, the *Canadian Correspondent*, 26 August 1832 noted that £315.17.1 was raised and the following year, 26 June 1833, £330.0.7. A second bazaar in 1833 raised £210.11.4, *The Patriot*, 25 October 1833.

117 *The Patriot*, 6 July 1838; 5 March 1840. For formation of the House of Industry, see *Christian Guardian*, 11 January 1838.

118 *Brockville Recorder*, 17 May 1831, noted that a bazaar was to be held in Kingston in June 1831. *The Hallowell Free Press*, 19 May 1834 noted that the ladies of Brockville had held a bazaar to raise money for a local infant school. *The Upper Canada Herald*, 27 November 1827 reported that the Kingston Benevolent Society had hosted a bazaar.

119 *Upper Canada Gazette*, 24 February 1835, Mr and Mrs Pemberton held a concert; *Colonial Advocate*, 19 January 1826, notice of Mrs Smith Benefit; *Upper Canada Gazette*, 7 June 1828, notice of Mrs Bennet Benefit.

120 Stansell, *City of Women*, 33–6, argues that in New York, "the early charities developed a set of assumptions about the depraved character of the labouring poor that were to influence class relations for the entire antebellum period ... these charities also exercised power within a field intensifying class conflicts." Too little research has been done on the reform tradition in early Upper Canada to determine if similar sentiments and results developed there. And we know next to nothing on how the efforts of Helen Cartwright or Anne Powell were viewed by the recipients.

PART FOUR

1 George Walton, *York Commercial Directory and Street Guide and Register, 1833–34* (York: Thomas Dalton 1834).

2 *The Patriot*, 8 December 1833; *British American Journal*, 25 February 1834; *The Patriot*, 24 April 1840.

3 *The Patriot*, 2 August 1833. This establishment was also listed in the *Directory*.

4 Ulrich, *Good Wives*, 36.

5 Ibid., 49. As Tilly and Scott note in *Women, Work, and Family*, 48, a woman in a pre-industrial society "was her husband's indispensable partner." See also the work of Cohen, *Women's Work, Markets, and Economic Development*; Ryan, *The Cradle of the Middle Class*, particularly her discussion of frontier women; Stansell, *City of Women*; Norton, *Liberty's Daughters*; Rule, *The Labouring Classes*; for the later period, Bradbury, *Working Families*.

6 Tilly and Scott, *Women, Work and Family*, 48. See also Sally Alexander, "Women's Work in Nineteenth-Century London," in Mitchell and Oakely, eds., *The Rights and Wrongs of Women*, 59–111, 64–5.

7 Ulrich, *Good Wives*, 50, 37, 47. This, of course, was most graphically illustrated during the American Revolution. See Norton, *Liberty's Daughters*, Chapter 7; Potter-MacKinnon, *While the Women Only Wept*.

8 Tilly and Scott, *Women, Work, and Family*, 19. See also Bradbury, *Working Families*, Chapter 5.

9 Ulrich, *Good Wives*, 37–8.

10 Stansell, *City of Women*, 12. See also Alexander, "Women's Work," 97–9.

11 See John's "Introduction" to *Unequal Opportunities*.

12 In the pre-industrial world of Upper Canada, as in Montreal in a later period, no one assumed that the male head of the household would, or perhaps indeed even should be able to support his family on one wage: Bradbury, *Working Families*, 13–16. The assumption that the head of the household should be the sole "breadwinner" is quite modern. And although it is to some degree a product of the nineteenth-century middle-class ideology that has been examined so eloquently by Davidoff and Hall, *Family Fortunes* as in so many aspects of this, the rhetoric enunciated by the few did not, nor was it expected to be lived by the many.

13 Tilly and Scott, *Women, Work and Family*, 51, 53, 47.

14 Hammerton, *Emigrant Women*.

15 Ulrich, *Good Wives*, 48.

16 Alexander, "Women's Work," 77.

17 Ulrich, *Good Wives*, 48.

18 Rule, *The Labouring Classes*, 13. See also McCalla, *Planting the Province*, 113, who notes that though women were involved in considerable "productive" work, it "was not captured by standard statistics." Alexander, "Women's Work," 72, found a similar situation in London, England during this period.

CHAPTER EIGHT

1 *Upper Canada Gazette*, 7 May 1808.

2 Thomas Fuller, *The Holy and the Profane State*, 1642, quoted in Ulrich, *Good Wives*, 36.

3 In Upper Canada, women who advertised themselves as milliners seem to have been engaged in a number of activities based on general sewing and selling sewing supplies. Most certainly made clothes; as will be discussed, some may have made hats.

4 *Hallowell Free Press*, 31 July 1832.

5 See Stansell, *City of Women*, 13; Bradbury, *Working Families*, 175. Katz, *The People of Hamilton, Canada West*, 230–2, notes that boarding was particularly important for young people looking for work.

6 *Canadian Correspondent*, 9 November 1833, Mrs Parsons; *The Patriot*, 8 February 1833, Mrs Oliver. There were many other tradesmen and professionals whose advertisements included their address. *Upper Canada Gazette*, 9 February 1828, D. Davidson of York had a room at Mrs Stebbins' and obviously saw patients there. Abel Cole, a tailor, informed the people of Brockville, *Brockville Recorder*, 22 March 1832, that he was operating out of Mrs Seaman's boarding-house. Miss Barker, a seamstress, saw clients in her residence at John Jones' boarding-house, *Hallowell Free Press*, 8 September 1834. The Baynons of Kingston advertised only once in the 1830s:

Kingston Chronicle, 13 February 1830. There were, however, numerous references to their boarding-house in advertisements of their tenants: *Kingston Chronicle*, advertisement of Mr and Mrs Cook, portrait painters, 17 May 1834; an unnamed doctor maintained his surgery from his room, 26 July 1834. Report of fire damage in 1833 and again in 1837, *Canadian Correspondent*, 9 November 1833; 22 March 1837.

7 The first boarding-house advertisement appeared in the *Upper Canada Gazette*, 15 January 1810, which informed the residents of York that a "Boarding House" had been established in the premises previously occupied by the Widow Hull.

8 *Christian Guardian*, 13 November 1833. See also *The Patriot*, 5 December 1834.

9 *Kingston Chronicle*, 27 June 1835. See also 27 September 1834.

10 *The Patriot*, 19 October 1838. This advertisement was placed by a land agent, James Henderson, which suggests that the family was concerned to keep their anonymity and wanted a buffer between themselves and potential clients.

11 Ibid., 15 May 1840.

12 *Niagara Gleaner*, 19 January 1929.

13 *Colonial Advocate*, 11 December 1834. See also advertisement of Mrs Little in the *Cobourg Star*, 20 December 1831. "She takes this opportunity of expressing her obligations to her former boarders, and respectfully solicits a continuance of those favours so liberally bestowed and begs leave to inform her friends she has still a vacancy for a few genteel boarders."

14 *Niagara Gleaner*, 24 November 1832; 19 January 1829, Mrs Fitzgibbons. See also *Kingston Chronicle*, 21 December 1833, Mrs Parson; *Correspondence and Advocate*, 11 December 1834, Mrs Handy.

15 Almost all histories of women and work confirm this. See among others, Norton, *Liberty's Daughters*, 144–5; Bradbury, *Working Families*, 175–9; Sally Alexander, "Women's Work in Nineteenth-Century London," in Mitchell and Oakley, eds., *The Rights and Wrongs of Women*, 59–111, 73.

16 *York, Upper Canada Commercial Directory 1833*, AO, B70, Series D-5, Reel 2, listed nine boarding-house keepers, eight of whom can definitely be identified as widows; *City of Toronto and Home District Commercial Directory and Registry, 1837*, listed only three boarding-house keepers. I suspect that both of these statistics underrepresent the number of households in York who took in boarders. Both registers list a number of widowed women with no visible means of support. Moreover, as Katz notes in *The People of Hamilton West*, 220–31, boarding was common in colonial towns. See also Bradbury, *Working Families*, 175–9, for a discussion of how women used boarding to make money.

17 One advertisement in the *Cobourg Star*, 12 November 1834, for example, was directed specifically at immigrants. Stressing the superiority of their

situation, it was noted that "families arriving at our village will find this a desirable temporary retreat from the bustle of the tavern."

18 Margaret McBurney and Mary Byers, *Tavern in the Town: Early Inns and Taverns in Ontario*, (Toronto: University of Toronto Press 1987), 4. "Mrs Amelia Harris," in J. J. Talman, ed., *Loyalist Narratives from Upper Canada* (Toronto: The Champlain Society 1946), 109–48, 118–19, noted "all were made welcome," and "the meals, victuals, and a night's lodging were freely given" to passing travellers or newly arrived settlers.

19 "Mrs Amelia Harris," 118–19. See also John Maude, *Visit to the Falls of Niagara* (London, 1826), 117, concerning an inn near Fort Niagara.

20 John Howison, *Sketches of Upper Canada* (1821) (Reprint, Toronto: S.R. Publishers 1965), 32, commenting about Kingston inns. See also Patrick Campbell, *Travels in the Interior Inhabited Part of North America in the Years 1791 and 1792* (1793). (Reprint, Toronto: Champlain Society 1937), 123, who also commented about Kingston's inns.

21 "Regulations for Inns and Taverns in Niagara," *Farmers' Journal*, 14 May 1828. See also "Regulations of Innkeepers, 1818," in Edwin C. Guillet, ed., *The Valley of the Trent* (Toronto: Champlain Society 1957), 293. In 1816, an inhabitant of Kingston noted that "Kingston is filled with dram shops, not taverns." By that, he meant that these establishments had no accommodation for travellers and had no "household furniture in the house." Taverns, he continued, "are intended for the accommodation of travellers": *Kingston Gazette*, 23 March 1816. In the 1820 and 1830s, the difference between the two appears to have been that an inn had to have someone who was responsible for looking after travellers' horses. It appears that it may have been more prestigious to own an inn than a tavern. *Kingston Gazette*, 18 December 1810. See also Edwin C. Guillet, *Pioneer Inns and Taverns* (Toronto: Ontario Publishing 1963).

22 Howison, *Sketches*, 29; Robert Sutcliffe, *Travels in Some Parts of North America in the Years 1804, 1805 and 1806* (London, 1815), 167. See also references by J.M. Duncan, *Travels through Parts of the United States* (London, 1823), 32, to an inn in Kingston; D'Arcy Boulton noted in *Sketch of His Majesty's Province of Upper Canada* (London, 1805), 48, that at the head of Lake Ontario, there was a very good inn. It was noted that there was a good inn in Johnston: *Canadian Letters – A Description of a Tour through the Province of Lower and Upper Canada in the Course of the Years 1792 and '93*. Reprint. *Canadian Antiquarian Journal* 9, nos 3, 4 (1912), 116.

23 Howison, *Sketches*, 27, mentioned that this was even the case if the ballroom was used only once a year.

24 When the Traills arrived in Peterborough in 1832, the hostess of the only inn in town gave up her "sleeping room and bed" to accommodate them. The room was, Catharine reported, clean and the hospitality generous: *The Backwoods of Upper Canada* (1838) (Toronto: McClelland and Stewart

1966), 41. Traill reported, 31, receiving "good treatment" at all the various inns in which she and her husband stayed.

25 Isaac Weld, *Travels Through North America and the Provinces of Canada* (1907) (New York: Augusta Kelly 1970), 293. Note that Weld is speaking of northern New York. Given the similarity of settlement patterns and people, the same division of labour probably prevailed in many taverns, inns, and boarding-houses in Upper Canada.

26 Howison, *Sketches*, 118–19. See also Maude, *Visit to the Falls*, 117, concerning an inn near Fort Niagara.

27 Mrs Davis of Cobourg had obviously been running the Amherst Hotel for some time before her husband John died in 1831. In the call for outstanding accounts against her husband's estate, John Davis was identified as a tailor: *Cobourg Star*, 17 June 1831. The importance of a wife to an innkeeper was perhaps amply expressed in the obituary notice for Mrs Anna Sandford, wife of Thomas D. Sandford. "Mrs Sandford was for many years the esteemed hostess of the Union Hall Inn in Cramahe, and her loss will be long and severely felt in that neighbourhood," the notice concluded: *Cobourg Star*, 15 February 1831.

28 See for example, advertisements in the *Kingston Gazette*, 29 April 1815; *Upper Canada Gazette*, 5 December 1822; *Colonial Advocate*, 13 April 1826; 11 August 1831; *The Patriot*, 3 July 1832; 29 May 1835. An article in the *Cobourg Star*, 6 December 1833, noted that two maidservants had barely escaped a fire in one of the hotels in Kingston.

29 *The Patriot*, 8 November 1833.

30 Ibid., 5 December 1834. See also ibid., 8 November 1833, Mr William Miller having set up a boarding-house. The editor of *The Patriot*, 25 August 1837, commented on a boarding-house in Ancaster run by John Tidy, his wife, and daughter which the editor considered was very good because, in his view, it had the finest food, liquor, and accommodation.

31 *Kingston Chronicle*, 13 February 1830.

32 *The Patriot*, 23 December 1834. The Griegs charged $6.00/week for weekly residents; $5.00/week for monthly residents; $4.50/week for yearly tenants.

33 Tilly and Scott, *Women, Work, and Family.* 53.

34 Ulrich, *Good Wives*, 50.

35 This may well have been the case of one inn visited in 1797, by Isaac Weld, *Travels*, 140–1. "The habitation was the property of an old woman, who in her younger days had followed the drum and now made her livelihood by accommodating, to the best of her power ... travellers." The inn was a small, one-room log house. "A sorry habitation it was," Weld commented. The door was off its hinges, the windows were without glass, and "as we lay folded in our skins on the floor the rain beat in upon us, and the wind whistled about our ears." This was not the worst, however. "There

seemed to be a great scarcity of provisions," Isaac Weld and his companions discovered and they left "old Mother Palmer's" before "they should be famished."

36 *Kingston Chronicle*, 6 September 1828.

37 *Correspondence and Advocate*, 13 September 1832. There were also a number of other references to married or widowed women running inns, with no mention of their husbands. See for example reference to the Widow Osterhout's tavern in *Niagara Spectator*, 13 February 1817; Mrs Pointer's tavern at Kingston, *Niagara Spectator*, 12 March 1820; Mrs Nelson's tavern, *Kingston Chronicle*, 21 November 1829; Widow Brown's Tavern Stand, *Cobourg Star*, 17 May 1832; Mrs Cadner's tavern, *Cobourg Star*, 30 March 1836.

38 Mrs Bell's last advertisement appeared in the *Canadian Freeman*, 10 October 1832. By 27 December 1837, Robert Horsley was apparently running and probably owned the Half Moon Inn. Mrs Scantlebury sold the hotel to George Millward, *Kingston Chronicle*, 31 October 1829. Mrs Scantlebury seems to have got back into the hotel business in 1832: there was a notice in the *Canadian Correspondent* of fire damage to her hotel, 21 December 1833.

39 *Canadian Freeman*, 11 October 1832. The Commercial Hotel was described as being "commodious," *Kingston Chronicle*, 6 September 1828.

40 *Colonial Advocate*, 23 August 1832. The newspapers included a number of notices of widows offering their taverns for let or sale. See for example, *Niagara Spectator*, 14 February 1817, notice of widow Edith Osterhout looking to let her tavern; *Niagara Spectator*, 12 March 1812, Mrs Pointer looking to let her tavern; Mrs Nelson looking to let her tavern in Kingston, 21 November 1829; Mrs Hadner, looking to let her big house which had been a tavern in Colborne, *Cobourg Star*, 30 March 1836.

41 *Cobourg Star*, 17 June 1831.

42 Sarah Moore, who intended to continue the Mansion House, *Kingston Chronicle*, 17 November 1826; Elizabeth Reid, *Gore Gazette*, 7 February 1829; Jane Marion, to continue as draper and innkeeper, *Upper Canada Gazette*, 7 May 1808. There were many women in similar circumstances. Jane Erskine informed the "good" people of York in 1840 that she intended to continue on her husband's pleasure grounds and confectionary, *The Patriot*, 16 June 1840.

43 See for example *Kingston Chronicle*, 6 April 1821, where Widow Thibodos opened a tavern. Her notice offered "WINES and LIQUORS of the best quality and the greatest attention paid to those who may honour her with their company."

44 Catherine Stebbins and Lea Flannigan were only two women amongst twenty-one men who received tavern licences in the York area in 1817; *Upper Canada Gazette*, 21 August 1817. In the Gore district in 1827, only three women, Rachel Babcock, Margaret Terriberry, and Mary Price com-

pared with twenty-eight men received liquor licences: *Gore Gazette*, 2 June 1827. On 15 May 1834, *Colonial Advocate*, Mary Copper and Elizabeth Trigg were listed as tavern-keepers in York. *The Patriot*, 18 February 1840 reported that three women, Margaret Lesley, Margaret MacLean, and Mary Ramage had tavern licences for the Home District. In Kingston in the early years, Christina Ferris also had a tavern licence: Adam Shortt, *Early Court of Ontario, being Extracts from the Records of the Court of Quarter Sessions in the District of Mecklenburg* (Kingston, 1900), 25 April 1809, 56.

45 In addition to the foregoing, Mrs Bowen of Bath Road advertised that she ran a ship's tavern that accommodated travellers: *British Whig*, 4 November 1834. Mrs Patterson of Port Robinson appeared to offer the same service: *Niagara Gleaner*, 19 May 1832.

46 Notice from an engineer, *Niagara Gleaner*, 31 May 1831; J. Lane, a tailor worked from Mrs Darley's inn in Kingston, *Kingston Chronicle*, 8 November 1822. Mrs Patrick's inn in Kingston was a local point of reference for businesses, *Kingston Chronicle*, 8 December 1818. So too was Mrs Haddin's Inn of Niagara, *Niagara Gleaner*, 4 August 1827; and the Widow Gore's Inn in Brockville, *Brockville Recorder*, 31 August 1830.

47 *Kingston Chronicle*, 26 March 1831. The Township of Pittsburgh met at Mrs Franklin's, *Kingston Chronicle*, 21 December 1833.

48 *Cobourg Star*, 18 September 1833; *Kingston Chronicle*, 21 October 1833; *Brockville Chronicle*, 24 April 1835. Auctions were also held at Mrs Shaw's in Clark, *Cobourg Star*, 1 November 1831.

49 *Niagara Gleaner*, 11 January 1823; 24 September 1825. Mrs Hawke's hotel in York was the site of a public dinner: *The Patriot*, 14 April 1837.

50 *A Few Plain Directions for Persons Intending to Proceed as Settlers to His Majesty's Province of Upper Canada* by an "English Farmer" (London, 1820), 51. This anonymous author also recommended Mrs Campbell's inn at Lachine, 47.

51 *Upper Canada Gazette*, 1 October 1821.

52 *Colonial Advocate*, 11 July 1827, dentist's advertisement; 2 August 1828, Mr Stennett; 23 August 1828, Mrs Gibson, milliner; *United Empire Loyalist*, 23 August 1828. The York Hotel was also referred to in advertisements as Mrs Jordan's tavern.

53 *Colonial Advocate*, 9 July 1829.

54 Ibid., 10 June 1830.

55 In 1833, she was looking for "5 or 6 persons to board": *Christian Guardian*, 26 June 1833. On 24 April 1840, a small notice in *The Patriot* informed the residents of the capital that "A LARGE SPACIOUS AND COMMODIOUS HOUSE TO LET, formally known by the name of 'York Hotel' with Big house and Outhouses, Stabling and Gardens. Possession may be had immediately. Enquire of Mrs Jane Jordan."

56 This may have been the case with Mary Barnet who opened a "Genteel Boarding House" in Kingston, *Kingston Chronicle*, 15 October 1819. In addition to providing travellers and gentlemen with accommodation, she offered warm soups and coffee, ready made.

57 See Lorna McLean, "Single Again: Widow's Work in the Urban Family Economy, Ottawa, 1871,"*Ontario History* LXXXIII, 2, (June 1991), 127–50, for a discussion of the position in which widows often found themselves in the later period.

58 Tilly and Scott, *Women, Work, and Family,* 51–2.

59 Mrs Field, *Niagara Spectator*, 2 March 1820.

60 *Hallowell Free Press*, 16 August 1831, Nancy Robert advertised bricks for sale of "superior" quality. She also noted "other brick makers have but two qualities, best and second best, whereas I have five ... any who wish to purchase are directed to call at my office at the sign of the Water Poplar, #1, Juggling Street." Four years later, in Grantham, Elizabeth Parnall, together with William Harrison also advertised bricks for sale, *British American Journal*, 23 July 1835. It appears that Elizabeth Parnall did not make bricks; she merely had some extras.

61 *Christian Guardian*, 6 August 1831. The notice of her husband's death appeared in the *Canadian Freeman*, 14 July 1831 and her intentions to carry on the business appeared 4 August 1831. These notices continued until December of 1832. Alexander noted in "Women's Work," 89–91, that book binding was one of the crafts traditionally open to women.

62 The *York Directory,* 1833 listed twelve women who kept grocery or provision shops; ten of them were definitely widows; one of them also apparently took in lodgers. The *Toronto Directory,* 1837 listed eleven similar businesses. Stansell notes in *City of Women,* 14, that building a small stand to sell refreshments, maintaining a stall in a local market, or opening a grocery was quite common for women in New York at this time. Bradbury concludes in *Working Families,* 198–9, that most businesses run by women in Montreal were small and precarious and women frequently could not depend on this alone for their subsistence. See also Alexander, "Women's Work," 100–2.

63 Jane McLeod, *Kingston Chronicle*, 6 October 1826. Mrs Elizabeth Thompson noted in *Niagara Herald*, 28 February 1801, that she would accept payment in wheat. There is no indication however what business Elizabeth Thompson was in. See also Mrs Tolkien, *Cobourg Star*, 6 November 1833; *Canadian Correspondent*, 9 November 1833, which included a full report of the fire. Mary Ann Reid did not advertise in the *Kingston Chronicle*, but notice of her business appears in a brief "Information Wanted" when she mysteriously disappeared: *Kingston Chronicle*, 21 March 1835.

64 First mention of Mary Miller is an advertisement for her shop in the *Niagara Gleaner*, 21 January 1828. On 8 June 1833 she placed a notice in the pa-

per looking for information about her parents. See also notice of Mrs Parmentier in the *Kingston Chronicle*, 2 April 1831, who had plant and fruit trees for sale.

65 See, for example, *Upper Canada Gazette*, 25 March 1812, a notice that Catharine Chesney of York would carry on her deceased husband's saddlery business.

66 *Hallowell Free Press*, 23 July 1833. The partnership expired that month, 30 July 1833, and a David Barker, perhaps Mary's son or husband commenced business on his own: *Hallowell Free Press*, 5 August 1833. I have argued elsewhere that Ann Macaulay of Kingston ran the family business until her sons were old enough to take over: "Ann Kirby Macaulay," *DCB*, Vol. VII, 469.

67 *Niagara Gleaner*, 23 May 1835.

68 See previous discussion, Chapter 5.

69 *Upper Canada Gazette*, 21 December 1808.

70 Ibid., 19 December 1810. She moved her shop, *Upper Canada Gazette*, 9 October 1811. There was a new advertisement in the *Upper Canada Gazette*, 9 September 1815, and she engaged an apprentice, *Upper Canada Gazette*, 28 January 1811. See also Alexander, "Working Women," 84; Stansell, *City of Women*, 105–7.

71 *Kingston Chronicle*, 28 September 1816; 17 May 1817; 6 October 1818.

72 Ibid., 27 July 1818. There was also a Miss Reil who opened a shop, and notified residents that she was going to Montreal to buy "the most fashionable spring articles."

73 *Niagara Spectator*, 9 April 1818.

74 Ibid., 2 November 1820.

75 *Upper Canada Gazette*, 11 September 1817; 10 February 1820; *Kingston Gazette*, 14 December 1816.

76 *Niagara Spectator*, 7 February 1817.

77 *Upper Canada Gazette*, 30 December 1826. A notice appeared in the *Niagara Spectator*, 7 February 1817, from a Miss Leigh, who may have been Miss Lewis.

78 *Upper Canada Herald*, 18 June 1825. Mrs Metzler noted that she only intended to be in town for three or four days; *Upper Canada Gazette*, 7 July 1825, staying there for a week.

79 *Colonial Advocate*, 24 January 1828; *Upper Canada Gazette*, 30 August, 1828. Mrs Metzner may well have been touring the whole colony annually, or at least as business warranted, in the intervening years.

80 There were a few other women who arrived in the 1830s. Mrs Searight of Montreal came to Kingston, *Kingston Chronicle*, 27 September 1834, and took orders for dresses, apparently to be delivered later. Four years earlier, 13 February 1830, a Mrs Gregory had advertised in Kingston that she was in town for a few days and had fancy articles for sale, including children's clothes.

81 Advertisements in local newspapers in the post-1815 period suggest that most milliners, dressmakers, and hatmakers gravitated to the largest communities in Upper Canada. A breakdown of establishments by community indicates that, between 1815 and 1840, of the 71 businesses that had at least one notice in a newspaper, 56 per cent (40) were located in York or the immediate vicinity; 25 per cent (18) in Kingston; 7 per cent in Niagara, and the rest were scattered in other towns and villages.

82 Marie de Dieman, *Upper Canada Gazette*, 21 December 1808; Francis Murray, *Upper Canada Gazette*, 19 December 1810; Mrs Ritter and Miss Culver, *Niagara Spectator*, 9 April 1818; E. Turquand and M. Carey, *Upper Canada Gazette*, 10 February 1820; Mrs Ferguson, *Niagara Spectator*, 2 November 1820; Stroughton and Dayton, *Upper Canada Herald*, 15 March 1825; Mrs Bachus, *British Whig*, 25 April 1834; Miss McBratney, *Brockville Recorder*, 2 May 1833; Mrs Cooper, *Cobourg Star*, 6 August 1834.

83 *Christian Guardian*, 19 August 1840. This latter claim was made by a number of milliners. See for example Misses S. and R. Parsons, *Niagara Gleaner*, 29 April 1826.

84 See for example Stroughton and Dayton, *Upper Canada Herald*, 15 March 1825; Miss Shelton, *Gore Gazette*, 25 August 1827; Mrs McAuliffe had apparently arrived from New York with fresh supplies of the latest fashions, *Brockville Gazette*, 16 April 1830; Miss Currice, *Cobourg Star*, 22 November 1831; Miss Sewers, *The Patriot*, 26 November 1833; Mrs Bachus of Kingston noted that she had contacts in York, *Kingston Chronicle*, 28 December 1833; Miss Laing, *Cobourg Star*, 21 May 1834; Miss Lane, *Christian Guardian*, 21 May 1834; Mrs Conrey and Miss Donlevy, *Canadian Freeman*, 24 May 1834; Mrs Cochrane, *British American Journal*, 12 August 1834; Mrs Hall, *The Patriot*, 13 December 1836; 13 June 1837; Mrs Price, *Christian Guardian*, 19 July 1837; M. McCord, *The Patriot*, 27 April 1838.

85 *British Whig*, 14 February 1834.

86 *Upper Canada Herald*, 28 May 1839; 4 November 1840. See also Miss Shelton, *Gore Gazette*, 25 January 1827; Mrs Smith, *Canadian Freeman*, 25 November 1830, who sold needles, threads etc.

87 See for example Misses Ritter and Culver, *Niagara Spectator*, 9 April 1818; Mrs Jones and Miss Rose Anne Osbourne, *United Empire Loyalist*, 7 June 1828; Miss Parsons, *Christian Guardian*, 29 May 1833 and *Correspondent and Advocate*, 27 November 1834; Misses Rankin and Chestnut, *Christian Guardian*, 12 October 1836; Miss Madden, 22 March 1837; Mrs Porter and Miss King, 9 October 1839; Mrs George and Co., *The Patriot*, 5 June 1840. There was also an anonymous ad in *The Patriot*, 15 December 1837.

88 Mrs Norris, *Upper Canada Herald*, 12 April 1825; Miss Shelton, *Gore Gazette*, 1 September 1827; Mrs Carpenter, *Colonial Advocate*, 16 September 1830; Mrs Coleman and Miss Boucher, who also engaged in cleaning leghorns, *Canadian Freeman*, 24 March 1831; M. Haldenby, *Kingston Chronicle*, 6 August 1831; Mrs Dickson, *The Patriot*, 15 December 1834. See also

Mrs Miller, *The Patriot*, 27 April 1838, who also offered to make and clean hats to the clients' instructions.

89 *Christian Guardian*, 4 October 1837.

90 *Gore Gazette*, 25 August 1827.

91 *Upper Canada Gazette*, 10 February 1820.

92 *Brockville Recorder*, 21 July 1834.

93 *The Patriot*, 26 October 1838. There were a few other staymakers in the province in this period. Miss Stillman advertised in *The Patriot*, 12 September 1837.

94 Of a total of 71 millinery, hatmaking and dressmaking businesses that placed notices in local colonial newspapers between 1815–40, almost 75 per cent were from women who appeared to work alone (53/71). It is difficult to tell how many of these women were wives working part time and how many were women trying to make this a career.

95 *Brockville Recorder*, 2 November 1830. *York Directory* 1833 and 1837 illustrates that a significant proportion of milliners were married and sharing premises with their husbands. It is more difficult to determine if a woman who was registered in business apparently on her own was a widow, or maintained a shop separate from that of her husband. The category below, "widow/single" includes all women registered as sole operators.

Women Listed as Sole Operators, *York Directory*, 1833 and 1837

Year	Total No.	Married	Single/Widowed
1833	21	8	12 (1 definitely widow)
1837	16	6	8*

* *Includes four establishments operated by related women, and one by two unrelated women. See also Appendix II, Marital Status of Women in the Needle Trades in York, Upper Canada.*

96 *Christian Guardian*, 7 May 1834.

97 Her husband advertised separately: *Brockville Recorder*, 26 July 1832.

98 *Kingston Chronicle*, 11 January 1827. Mrs Shaw advertised in *Colonial Advocate*, 4 September 1834. Her husband was also a watchmaker.

99 *Kingston Chronicle*, 24 December 1831. So too would S. Mayhew, whose husband ran a drygoods store in York: *Christian Guardian*, 17 October 1838; 11 September 1839.

100 *Christian Guardian*, 25 March 1835. Both businesses continued until at least 1840, *Christian Guardian*, 23 December 1840.

101 *Christian Guardian*, 29 May 1833. The shop moved and they continued to share premises, *Canadian Correspondent*, 27 November 1834.

102 Stansell notes in *City of Women*, 107, that before 1812, tailors "would not touch women's work" which included making shirts, dresses, children's clothes, and mending. Women would, however, do plain sewing and therefore, would help their tailor husbands. See also Alexander, "Women's Work," 105–7.

103 *Christian Guardian*, 23 December 1840. The business was first advertised 25 March 1835.

104 *Brockville Recorder*, 22 March 1832; 16 May 1833.

105 See for example Mrs Cooper of Cobourg who noted in the *Cobourg Star*, 6 August 1834, that she had moved next to her husband's shop (he was in an unnamed trade) at the request of her clients. She had ready-made clothes and also made bonnets. The first announcement of her business appeared in the *Brockville Recorder*, 22 March 1832. Mrs Laing and Miss Langley opened a shop in Toronto in 1834, *The Patriot*, 8 August 1834. Mrs Laing's husband was a drawing instructor.

106 *Colonial Advocate*, 15 November 1832.

107 *The Patriot*, 2 August 1833. Throughout, Mrs Claris noted that she "kept in touch" with fashion developments in Paris and London. See for example *Correspondent and Advocate*, 5 January 1833.

108 They were selling groceries, wines, haberdasheries, hosiery, and fruit: *The Patriot*, 2 August 1833.

109 Ibid., 31 December 1833.

110 Ibid., 21 January 1834; 4 February 1834. In *The Patriot*, 12 September 1834, creditors began to receive eight shillings on the pound. There had been two previous calls for creditors, 14, 18 March 1834.

111 On 31 January 1833, *The Patriot*, Mrs Claris "wanted immediately five or six respectable Girls" as apprentices. Two months later she was advertising for several indoor or outdoor apprentices: *Correspondent and Advocate*, 30 March 1833. See also 4 May 1833; 24 August 1833; 14 September 1833; *The Patriot*, 2 August 1833; 6 September 1833.

112 *York Directory*, 1833, 99. Interestingly enough, in the *City of Toronto and the Home District Commercial Directory*, 1837, 38, Mr and Mrs Robinson are listed separately, Mrs Robinson as "straw bonnet manufacturer." This may have been a reflection of the increased viability of Mrs Robinson's business. It may also, of course, be a consequence of how the information was gathered.

113 *United Empire Loyalist*, 24 May 1828.

114 Mrs Scott, *Cobourg Star*, 24 August 1836; Miss Stillman, *The Patriot*, 12 September 1837; M. McCord, *The Patriot*, 27 April 1838. From the old country see among others, the Misses Rubergall, *Colonial Advocate*, 21 January 1830; the Misses S. and J. Ross of Brockville, *Brockville Recorder*, 28 July 1831.

115 Jane McBradney, *Brockville Recorder*, 21 July 1831. Miss Wilson of Kingston stated that she had become an independent dressmaker and milliner

only after she had had five years training under Mrs Kennedy: *Kingston Chronicle*, 22 November 1834. See also Jane Arnold, *Brockville Recorder*, 6 August 1830; Mrs Jones and Miss Rose Anne Osborne, *United Empire Loyalist*, 24 May 1828; Misses S. and J. Ross, *Brockville Recorder*, 28 July 1831; Mrs Steward, *Colonial Advocate*, 6 June 1834. See Alexander, "Women's Work," 84–5; Stansell, *City of Women*, 117–8.

116 Mrs Cochrane, *Canadian Freeman*, 12 August 1830; E. Butler, *The Patriot*, 19 November 1833. Miss Barker probably only made dresses. In her advertisement in the *Hallowell Free Press*, 4 August 1837, she noted that she was working from her room in John Jones' boarding-house. See also Mrs Kurtschalts, *Kingston Chronicle*, 21 July 1818.

117 *Niagara Gleaner*, 29 April 1826. The Parsons sisters had apparently had a shop before, for the notice refers to having "again" commenced. In 1828, the sisters acquired a new machine to clean leghorn, *Niagara Gleaner*, 26 May 1828. The Rosses: *Brockville Recorder*, 28 July 1831; The Warrens: 17 July 1832.

118 *Upper Canada Herald*, 15 March 1825.

119 Ibid., 29 March 1825; 1 November 1825.

120 The partnership was first opened, *The Patriot*, 8 August 1834. Notice of Miss Langley's death appeared 3 October 1834. Advertisements in newspapers indicate that there were at least eighteen joint proprietorships formed in Upper Canada between 1820 and 1835. Of these, six were definitely partnerships that were familial, mother-daughter or sister combinations. Of the other twelve, five were partnerships between two apparently unrelated single women; seven were partnerships between a married or widowed woman and a single woman.

121 The *York Directory*, 1833 and the *City of Toronto and the Home District Commercial Directory*, 1837 both include women milliners, hatmakers and seamstresses who do not seem to have advertised their businesses.

122 *Colonial Advocate*, 1 August 1833; *The Patriot*, 9 August 1833; *Colonial Advocate*, 19 September 1833.

123 Ibid., 31 May 1834, looking for two needlewomen. Mrs Scott wanted six or seven girls: *Christian Guardian*, 24 August 1836. An anonymous ad in *The Patriot*, 17 January 1840, asked for a "clever" assistant in millinery and dressmaking.

124 *Christian Guardian*, 16 March 1836.

125 *Upper Canada Gazette*, 9 October 1811.

126 *British American Journal*, 12 August 1834. See also *Kingston Chronicle*, 7 March 1823 (looking for two apprentices); Mrs O'Farrell, *Upper Canada Herald*, 1 March 1825 (three apprentices); Mrs Chapman, *Niagara Spectator*, 10 August 1833 (wanting two apprentices); Mrs Claris, *Canadian Correspondent*, 30 March 1833 (looking for a few); 7 September 1833; Mrs Morse, *Brockville Recorder*, 16 May 1833; Mrs and Miss Stonehouse, *Colo-*

nial Advocate, 1 August 1833 (wanted several); Mrs Cochrane, *British American Journal*, 12 August 1834 (wanted one, located in St. Catharines); an anonymous notice, *The Patriot*, 25 November 1834 (looking for "respectable girls"); *The Patriot*, 17, 31 January 1840.

127 Misses Conrey and Donlevy, *Canadian Freeman*, 24 May 1832; Mrs Claris, *Colonial Advocate*, 31 January 1833. This was in addition to "a young woman who well understands" the business: *Canadian Correspondent*, 1 May 1833. S. Mayhew, *Christian Guardian*, 17 October 1838; 11 September 1839. It appears that the Mayhews' business probably also included a drygoods shop. In "Sweated Labour," 105–36, McIntosh discusses the emergence of women's sweated labour in the industry. He notes that the traditional clothing trade, which had developed in Upper Canada in the first half of the century, depended on apprenticeships. See also Stansell, *City of Women*, 106–19; Bradbury, *Working Families*, 136–9; Alexander, *Women's Work*, 104- 7.

128 This girl noted that she was willing to accept a position as a nursemaid. *Colonial Advocate*, 1 December 1831. See also *Correspondent and Advocate*, 20 August 1835.

129 *Kingston Chronicle*, 20 August 1836.

130 Ulrich, *Good Wives*, 50.

131 See for example Miss Steward, a seamstress who arrived in the colony in 1834 and promised prospective clients to execute "any order with which [they were] entrusted with neatness, taste of according to the latest fashions": *Colonial Advocate*, 6 June 1834. See also Mrs Page, *Upper Canada Gazette*, 11 September 1817; Misses Rubergall, *Colonial Advocate*, 28 January 1830; Miss Sewerts, *The Patriot*, 26 November 1830; Misses S. & J. Ross, *Brockville Recorder*, 28 July 1831; M. Haldenby, *Kingston Chronicle*, 6 August 1831; probably Misses M. and P. Warren, *Brockville Recorder*, 19 July 1832.

CHAPTER NINE

1 *Cobourg Star*, 4 February 1834. This advertisement also ran in *Kingston Chronicle, Dundas Post, Hamilton Free Press, Niagara Reporter and London True Patriot* and originally in *Canadian Courier*, 22 January 1834. Some of the material discussed in this Chapter first appeared in Errington, "Ladies and Schoolmistresses: Educating Women in Early Nineteenth-Century Upper Canada," *Historical Studies in Education* 6, 1 (Spring 1994): 71–96.

2 *The Patriot*, 6 September 1833; 25 February 1834.

3 See for example Ulrich, *Good Wives*; Cott, *The Bonds of Womanhood*, 105–23; Kerber, *Women of the Republic*, 204; Peterson, *Family, Love, and Work*, 123. Gardner notes in *The Lost Elementary Education*, 111, teaching "of-

fered a source of independent remunerative employment for the woman who was progressively denied an outlet for her labour other than through its complete constriction into 'housework.'" For Canadian examples, see Prentice and Theobald, eds., *Women Who Taught*; Heap and Prentice, eds., *Gender and Education*; Gidney and Millar, *Inventing Secondary Education*; Houston and Prentice, *Schooling and Scholars*.

4 Alison Prentice, "From Household to School House: The Emergence of the Teacher as Servant of the State," in Heap and Prentice, eds., *Gender and Education*, 25–50, 43.

5 The history of schooling in Upper Canada is ably discussed in Gidney and Millar, *Inventing Secondary Education*; Houston and Prentice, *Schooling and Scholars*.

6 H.H. Langton, ed., *A Gentlewoman in Upper Canada* (Toronto: Clarke, Irwin 1950), 2 January 1839, 89.

7 Ibid., 30 July 1841, 186–7. Anne made numerous references to her students in her diary. See for example 16 January 1839, 95, noting that the little Daniels girl had started to come; 1 April 1839, 102–3, when she noted the arrival of two more pupils; 9 July 1839, 117; 21 February 1841, 179; 3 May 1841, 181–2.

8 Ibid. See 19 December 1839, 134–5; 22 February 1841, 179.

9 Ibid., 19 December 1841, 134; 9 July 1839, 117. See also 19 December 1838, 134–5.

10 The Journal of Mrs E.G. O'Brien 1828–38, Archives of Ontario (AO), MS 199, 5–11, 31 May 1835.

11 Interestingly, the boys and the girls were often taught separately. In part this may have been because the boys, who were Mary's sons, were often with their father in the fields: O'Brien Journal, 8 June 1835. Over the next two years, she did take in a "damsel" to learn English for a month. The girl received one dollar less in wages for the month: ibid., 12 September 1836. That winter, Mary also exchanged a girl's help for teaching her: Journal 114, January 1837.

12 *Colonial Advocate*, "Report," 12 March 1829. This report commenced 26 February 1829, and continued 5 March 1829.

13 *British American Journal*, "Education of Farmers' Sons and Daughters," 19 March 1835.

14 *Kingston Gazette*, 3 December 1811. The domestic arts were important, for among other things, it was asserted that this taught a girl the advantages of hard work and discipline. As one matron noted, it also prevented the nation's daughters "from forming improper attachments" as youths: *Kingston Gazette*, 3 December 1811. See also *Upper Canada Gazette*, 19 October 1805.

15 *Kingston Gazette*, 3 December 1811. See also 18 August 1812; *Upper Canada Gazette*, 3 August 1805; *Farmers' Journal*, 26 September 1827.

16 *Kingston Gazette*, "From the Desk of Poor Robert the Scribe," 18 August 1812.
17 Ibid., 12 May 1812. This view was also reflected in "Letter to the Reckoner," 16 April 1811; *Gore Gazette*, 17 November 1827. For further discussion of this, see Errington, "The Softer Sex."
18 *Kingston Gazette*, "Letter to the Reckoner," 12 May 1812.
19 Ibid., 18 February 1812. See also 16 April 1811. An extract from Ledyard's "Celebrated Eulogy on the Talents and Disposition of the Fair Sex" noted that there was "no deficiency in the female mind." And it continued "if the delicacy of their constitution and other physical causes allow the female sex a smaller share of some mental powers, they posses others in superior degree": *Upper Canada Gazette*, 23 August 1828. See also *Farmers' Journal*, "Respect for Females," 14 March 1827.
20 McKenna, "The Life of Anne Murray Powell," 331–4; Anne Powell to George Murray, 9 July 1816, quoted in ibid., 336.
21 *Farmers' Journal*, "On Female Education," 9 April 1828.
22 *Upper Canada Gazette*, 25 November 1797.
23 *Farmers' Journal*, "The Female Character," 9 April 1828. See also *Kingston Gazette*, "Desk of Poor Robert the Scribe," 18 August 1812.
24 *Farmer's Journal*, "On Female Education," 9 April 1828.
25 *Upper Canada Gazette*, "On Female Education," 25 November 1797. See also *Farmers' Journal*, "The Female Character," 9 April 1828; *Kingston Chronicle*, "Why Should Females Have a Good Education," 14 September 1833.
26 *Farmers' Journal*, "A Women Teacher's Address to Her Pupils," 16 December 1829. See also "On the Education of Young Ladies," 26 September 1827; "Influence of Education by a Young Lady," 13 March 1830; *Christian Guardian*, "From Brief Hints to Parents on the Subject of Education," 5 February 1831.
27 An article in the *Kingston Chronicle*, 9 April 1836, noted specifically the importance of educated women as mothers. See also *Colonial Advocate*, "Female Education," 28 May 1828; "Ladies Department," 22 October 1831.
   These sentiments echoed what was being said in Great Britain and the United States at this time. See among others Cott, *The Bonds of Womanhood*, 103–25; Kerber, *Women of the Republic*, 185–232; Lebsock, *The Free Women of Petersburgh*, 172–6; Norton, *Liberty's Daughters*, 256–94; Gorham, *The Victorian Girl*, 101–20; Pederson, *Family Love and Work*, 34–57; Davidoff and Hall, *Family Fortunes*, 289–97.
28 Marjorie R. Theobald, "'Mere Accomplishments'?: Melbourne's Early Ladies Schools Reconsidered," in Prentice and Theobald, eds., *Women Who Taught*, 71–92, 73. See also Theobald, "The Sin of Laura," 257–72. Theobald has written extensively on the question of education for middle-class girls in the nineteenth century. In "Mere Accomplishments" she convinc-

ingly argues that historians have consistently misunderstood what was meant by the accomplishments and have down-played the academic rigour which accompanied girls' education. See also Gidney and Millar, *Inventing Secondary Education*, 13–19; Houston and Prentice, *Schooling and Scholars*, 77–9.

29 Kerber in *Women of the Republic*, 200–3, argues that the perceived need in the new republic for educated and responsible mothers also helped to propel American parents into supporting formal education for their daughters. This did not mean, however, that women were in any way "liberated." Rather, Kerber argues, women's education was essentially "anti-intellectual" because leading Americans believed that its essential purpose was to train good wives and mothers. Norton, on the other hand, concludes in *Liberty's Daughters*, 287, that, despite all attempts to restrict curriculum in American girls' schools, "an academic education had unanticipated consequences ... some of the graduates of schools showed in their adulthood a desire to go beyond the standard roles of wife and mother and to widen the boundaries of the feminine sphere."

30 *Upper Canada Gazette*, 11 August 1827. See also advertisement of Mrs Scott of Colborne, *Cobourg Star*, 9 July 1834, who opened an "infant school" for children between the ages of two and a half and seven. The Misses Savigny of Toronto offered, *The Patriot*, 13 November 1840, to teach young ladies until the age of twelve.

31 *The Patriot*, 10 November 1835.

32 Joyce Senders Pedersen, "Schoolmistresses and Headmistresses: Elites and Education in Nineteenth Century England," in Prentice and Theobald, eds., *Women Who Taught*, 37–70, 39, discusses the plight of "poor ladies obliged to work for pay."

33 See Gardner, *The Lost Elementary Schools*, 20; J.H. Higginson, "Dame Schools," *British Journal of Educational Studies* 22, 2 (1974); Houston and Prentice, *Schooling and Scholars*, 33–5; Monaghan, "Literacy Instruction," 18–41.

34 The *York Directory*, 1833 listed what seems to have been seven such schools in the capital. Three were operated by married women; one by a widow, and three by women whose status it is impossible to determine, though they were either widowed or single.

35 A total of 105 girls' schools – academies, seminaries, boarding and day schools, or schools that had a separate ladies' department – have been identified from local newspapers. This undoubtedly under-represents the number of schools in the colony, particularly in the later period. It is nevertheless evident that the number of such schools dramatically increased in the 1830s: 1800–20, 14 schools, (13.3 per cent); 1821–30, 20 schools, (19.2 per cent); 1831–30, 72 schools, (67.5 per cent).

36 *Niagara Herald*, 13 February 1802.

37 Ibid. Houston and Prentice, *Schooling and Scholars*, 67–8, note that a number of women carried on what was effectively three careers, wife/mother, teacher, and another trade.

38 *Kingston Gazette*, 1 October 1814 (Pringle); 10 May 1817 (Woolf); *Upper Canada Gazette*, 19 June 1817 (Roberts). See also schools run by Mrs MacIntosh, who started an academy with the Reverend R. Fletcher in Ernestown, *Kingston Chronicle*, 8 October 1818; Mr and Mrs Andrews who opened a school in York, *Upper Canada Gazette*, 9 April 1824; and Mrs Spilsbury, who opened a school "under the conduct of Mr Leech" at Colborne, *Cobourg Star*, 31 May 1831.

39 *Christian Guardian*, 10 October 1832 (Maitland). See also 23 January 1833. Of a total of 105 schools (sample taken from notices in local newspapers) that were established in Upper Canada between 1790 and 1840 that were either just for girls or those with a "Ladies' Department," nine were begun by couples that expressly stated that it was a "family" school (for example, Mr and Mrs Maitland). Given that all schools did not advertise in local newspapers, it is likely that there were a number of others, however. *York Directory*, 1833, listed two couples who had opened schools who do not appear to have advertised in local newspapers: Richard and Mrs Foster had a boys' and girls' school; Miss Hamilton and James Hamilton (a brother or father) had a boys' and ladies' school.

40 *Kingston Chronicle*, 8 September 1826, Mr and Mrs Twiggs' school. The same may also have been the case for the Roberts. After Mr Roberts' death in 1819, Mrs Roberts continued to teach: *Niagara Spectator*, 2 March 1820.

41 *Brockville Recorder*, 11 April 1833. See also *Hallowell Free Press*, 30 June 1834, an expanded advertisement.

42 This was specifically referred to in the case of the Tylers and Maitlands: *Gore Gazette*, 10 October 1832. See also advertisement of Mr Johnson, opening a Lancasterian School, *Kingston Gazette*, 22 September 1818, who noted that his wife would teach needlework, and superintend the "Ladies Department"; W. Ward, 28 March 1831, *Christian Guardian*, who noted that his wife would teach needlework. A "MARRIED MAN" looking for a position in a "respectable neighbourhood in the country" noted specifically, *The Patriot*, 31 March 1835, that he would "be assisted by his wife in the female department if necessary." Parents in Ancaster in 1837 advertised, *The Patriot*, 30 May 1837, for a married couple to teach at a boys' and girls' school. The wife was to teach in the girls' school and would also look after a few boarders. See also Houston and Prentice, *Schooling and Scholars*, 68–9.

43 A cursory search of local newspapers between 1815 and 1840 indicates that of the 105 schools identified 71 (67.61 per cent) were begun by women; 49 (69 per cent) of these were by sole proprietors. Much more work needs to be done, however, to determine the actual demographic profile of colonial schoolmistresses during this period.

44 *Colonial Advocate*, 23 September 1830. Mrs Crombie and her daughters could depend, to some degree at least, on Mr Crombie, schoolmaster of a local district school: *The Patriot*, 3 January 1840. The 1833 *York Directory*, 80, included three schools that were obviously run by married women. Their husbands were labourers.

45 *York Directory*, 1833, 80. The *Directory* also listed Mrs Drury school for children; her husband, Thomas, ran a small grocery. Mrs Flay had a children's school; her husband was a carpenter. Hannah Hepburn had a hat school; David was a tailor. Mrs Ross ran a girls' and boys' day school; Mr Ross was a carpenter. See Davidoff and Hall, *Family Fortunes*, 293–9, for a discussion of women as teachers in Great Britain at this time.

46 *Hallowell Free Press*, 9 October 1832.

47 *The Patriot*, 5 September 1834. Another mother-daughter pair were the Savignys, who announced in *The Patriot*, 13 November 1840, that they would take boarders under the age of twelve years. See also Mrs Crombie and daughters, *The Patriot*, 3 January 1840; the Misses Wellstead, *Upper Canada Gazette*, 9 June 1825. See subsequent discussion.

48 See for example, Mrs Haines of Kingston who was assisted by Mrs and Miss Johnson in 1818, *Kingston Gazette*, 15 September 1818; Mrs O'Brien's school in Prescott, which had an assistant, *Niagara Gleaner*, 21 January 1831; Misses Purcell and Rose, *Colonial Advocate*, 28 August 1826; Mrs Roy and Mrs Driscoll jointly announced the opening of their school in Toronto, *The Patriot*, 11 January 1839. Approximately 30 per cent of girls' schools run by women were owned and operated by two or three women together.

49 *Cobourg Star*, 13 March 1833; 12 November 1834. A second school in Cobourg was run by the Butchers, 12 December 1832 and it was still going 20 November 1833.

50 *Canadian Freeman*, 29 November 1834; *Canadian Emigrant*, 13 December 1834; 28 March 1835. The Misses Wellstead, *Upper Canada Gazette*, 9 June 1825, may have been more successful.

51 Mrs Weatherstone, *Kingston Chronicle*, 26 July 1834. They were still advertising 31 December 1836. Mrs Marshall and Mrs Davidson, *Cobourg Star*, 6 August 1834.

52 *Cobourg Star*, 2 January 1833. *Niagara Gleaner*, 30 July 1833; 9 July 1834. Another mother-daughter pair were the Savignys, who announced in *The Patriot* 13 November 1840 that they would take boarders under the age of twelve years. Gidney and Millar in *Inventing Secondary Education*, 48–9, also note the case of the Skirvings. After the death of Mr Skirving, one of the daughters became a governess, and Mrs Skirving and her other daughter tried to establish a girl's school. After two unsuccessful attempts, they finally settled in York in 1840 and the school prospered until Mrs Skirving died in 1846.

53 The proliferation of girls' schools was also evident in Great Britain and the United States. Indeed, it is likely that Upper Canadians' attraction to the ladies' academies was, in part at least, an attempt to emulate what they considered was suitable for a "civilized" state. See Kerber, *Women of the Republic*, 199; Norton, *Liberty's Daughters*, 273; Lebsock, *The Free Women of Petersburg*, 172–3; Davidoff and Hall, *Family Fortunes*, 293–4.

54 *Kingston Chronicle*, 25 February 1820.

55 *Cobourg Star*, 20 July 1834. The importance of location was also emphasized by Mrs Bickerton, who noted the scenery around Picton, *Hallowell Free Press*, 8 November 1831 (her school continued until at least 14 May 1833) and by Miss Savigny, *The Patriot*, 13 November 1840. Mrs Marshall and Miss Davidson "recommended" their comfortable and "commodious" home in its "elevated and pleasant situation": *Cobourg Star*, 6 August 1834.

56 For example, the Streets, Ancaster Boarding School: *Niagara Gleaner*, 30 July 1833; 9 July 1834.

57 *Upper Canada Gazette*, 13 August 1829. See also announcement of Mrs Bullock, *Cobourg Star*, 18 December 1833, of Mrs Marshall and Mrs Davidson, *Cobourg Star*, 6 August 1834; much of this was also made by Mrs Holland, 7 January 1831; by Mrs Gibson, *Hallowell Free Press*, 14 April 1834.

58 *Upper Canada Gazette*, 29 May 1816. See also notice from Mrs Lancaster, 10 November 1815 whose school, though exclusively for girls, appears to have been a dame school.

59 From notice of Mrs Fraser's school, *The Patriot*, 4 September 1835.

60 *Brockville Gazette*, 4 August 1831; 27 October 1831.

61 See for example Prentice, "From Household to School House," 25–50. Both Houston and Prentice, *Schooling and Scholars*, 76, and Gidney and Millar, *Inventing Secondary Education*, note the difficulty of obtaining textbooks in Upper Canada at the time.

62 *Brockville Gazette*, 27 October 1831.

63 See among others, ibid. and the Paris Female Seminary, *Christian Guardian*, 7 October 1840.

64 Miss Acland, *Brockville Recorder*, 9 January 1931; Miss Mossier, *Niagara Gleaner*, 9 March 1833; Mrs Scott, *Canadian Emigrant*, 27 December 1834; Mrs Fraser, *The Patriot*, 16 August 1836. Even at many of the larger schools such as Upper Canada Academy, students were expected to bring linen and towels: *Christian Guardian*, 29 August 1838.

65 Mrs Wynne certainly had servants, *The Patriot*, 27 June 1834.

66 *Cobourg Star*, 6 August 1834. The Montjoy School, *Hallowell Free Press*, 9 October 1832, only took fifteen students. See also advertisement of Mrs Black, *Upper Canada Gazette*, 13 August 1829.

67 *The Patriot*, 16 August 1836. Similar sentiments were expressed by Mrs Acland of Perth, *Brockville Recorder*, 1 September 1831 and Mrs Hamilton, *The Patriot*, 7 January 1840.

68 See for example, Mrs Hill's School in Kingston, *Kingston Gazette*, 22 September 1818. For neighbouring families: Miss R.A.Charlton, who ran the Paris Female Seminary, *Christian Guardian*, 7 October 1840. See also Mrs Black, *Farmer's Journal*, 17 August 1829; Misses Kile in the *Brockville Recorder*, 18 October 1832; Miss Leah in Kingston, *Kingston Chronicle*, 17 August 1833; Miss Currier, in Peterborough, *Cobourg Star*, 13 November 1833, whose school took in a few "parlour boarders" and had just extended its facilities for out-of-town students; Miss Mary McNeighton, *British Whig*, 10 January 1834; Mrs Haines, *Kingston Chronicle*, 25 July 1835; Mrs Hamilton who announced in *The Patriot*, 7 January 1840 that she provided "the advantages of public school ... combined with private education"; Miss Crombie, 11 August 1840.

69 See among others Miss Greenland, *Kingston Chronicle*, 10 June 1825; Miss Parsons, 9 June 1832; Miss Dennison, 14 March 1833; Miss Farrand, who ran the Brockville Seminary, *Brockville Gazette*, 27 October 1831; the Misses Skirving, *The Patriot*, 22 September 1840. For school attendance, see, for example, Mrs Acland, of Perth, *Brockville Recorder*, 9 June 1831 and Mrs Scott of Sandwich, *Canadian Emigrant*, 29 November 1834, who both required students to register, and pay fees, for at least a quarter and provide a month's notice before leaving.

70 The women who ran French schools included Miss Merrill, *Kingston Gazette*, 3 August 1816; Mrs Goodman, *Upper Canada Gazette*, 24 December 1818; Mrs Kingman, *Niagara Spectator*, 29 January 1819; Mrs Harris, *United Empire Loyalist*, 9 September 1826. Monaghan notes in "Literacy Instruction and Gender in Colonial New England," 24, that in the early colonial period, women taught reading and men taught penmanship. "Writing," she notes "was considered a craft" and "was largely a male domain." Similar attitudes appear to have prevailed in Upper Canada 150 years later.

71 *Upper Canada Gazette*, 9 September 1826; *United Empire Loyalist*, 30 August 1828. Madam Harris, like many dancing masters, was also engaged to teach dancing at one of the local ladies academies, Misses Purcell and Rose. She appears to have been replaced by Mr Whale: *Colonial Advocate*, 10 December 1829.

72 Miss Williams, *Brockville Recorder*, 28 June 1833; Mrs Butler, *Niagara Gleaner*, 5 October 1833; Miss Taylor, *Cobourg Star*, 29 October 1834; Mrs Bickerton, (also landscape painting) *Kingston Chronicle*, 24 May 1834; Madam Walther, *The Patriot*, 29 July 1836; an anonymous lady from England, *The Patriot*, 8 December 1840; 22 May 1838. There were about a dozen schools run by men in the province, some of which, like Mr Hill's "A Young Ladies Singing School," *Kingston Gazette*, 21 December 1816, taught both boys and girls, or like Mr Colton, had a female assistant, *Kingston Chronicle*, 5 July 1834.

73 McKenna notes in "The Life of Anne Murray Powell," 423, 432–3, that though Anne Powell senior was pleased that her daughter Anne took an active part in educating her nieces, William Dummer Powell refused to permit his daughter to establish a school of her own. Apparently he claimed that she was not sufficiently educated to be a school-teacher, and suggested that teaching was not suited to a woman of her status. See also, Theobald, "The Sin of Laura." One group of women who did display such skills publicly were actors and performers on the Upper Canadian stage. Colonial attitudes to these women varied considerably. Most residents seem to have accepted, however, that no self-respecting "lady" engaged in such activity. Much more work needs to be done on women in such public professions.

74 Gidney and Millar, *Inventing Secondary Education*, 1, 19–20. They note that coeducation posed moral dangers as well as problems with the curriculum. See also Houston and Prentice, *Schooling and Scholars*, 77–8.

75 The use of the term "professional" is quite deliberate. Though there was no "professional" training available to women during this period, these women did have specific expertise and experience in the classroom and, I would argue, would have considered themselves professional teachers. This issue has generated considerable debate. Norton in *Liberty's Daughters*, 273–87, argues that just after the revolution, although many schools for girls continued to be small, a growing number of ladies' academies with permanent buildings, staff, and a standard curriculum emerged in response to parental demands. Norton would not go so far as to suggest that the women who opened these establishments had any special qualifications, however. Lebsock in *The Free Women of Petersburg*, 173–4, found, on the other hand, that the best schools in the city were "rigorous" and their mistresses were "versatile and learned." Theobald's work on women teachers in Australia made similar conclusions, findings which also apply to a growing number of schools in Upper Canada. See Theobald, "Mere Accomplishments?"; "The Sin of Laura"; Errington, "Ladies and Schoolmistresses."

76 *Upper Canada Gazette*, 14 October 1824; *Niagara Gleaner*, 6 November 1824; *Kingston Chronicle*, 19 November 1824; *Upper Canada Herald*, 22 February 1825. A similar notice had appeared two years earlier in the *Kingston Chronicle*, 4 January 1822.

77 *Kingston Chronicle*, 18 March 1825.

78 Mrs Hamilton noted that in Britain she had taught at "the principal school in the City of Limerick and afterwards one at Ambleside": *The Patriot*, 7 January 1840; Mrs Bickerton, *Hallowell Free Press*, 1 November 1831; Mrs Weatherstone, *Kingston Chronicle*, 26 July 1834 to at least 9 April 1836; Mrs Crookshank, *Christian Guardian*, 30 November 1836. See also reference of Mrs Croan of York, *Colonial Advocate*, 2 April 1829 to 6 January 1831, and

Mrs Brega, whose mother who helped her in the school had previous experience, *Christian Guardian*, 15 October 1834.

79 *The Patriot*, 2 January 1838.

80 *Farmers' Journal*, 6 May 1829.

81 *British American Journal*, 13 May 1834. See also the Streets, *Cobourg Star*, 2 January 1833; Mrs Butler, *Niagara Gleaner*, 17 August 1833.

82 Although few women explicitly made a point of their nationality, their advertisements often indicated that they were "recently arrived from England," or were "British." Whether parents considered nationality or a school mistress' religion important needs more exploration. See Hammerton, *Emigrant Gentlewomen*, for an exploration of career women who migrated to Australia.

83 *Upper Canada Gazette*, 4 September 1817. Mrs Goodman had previously run a school in Montreal: *Upper Canada Gazette*, 20 January 1820. Mr Tobias gave dancing lessons: ibid., 30 March 1820. See Gidney and Millar, *Inventing Secondary Education*, 48; McKenna, "The Life of Anne Murray Powell," 58.

84 Ibid., 30 May 1822.

85 Gidney and Millar, *Inventing Secondary Education*, 28.

86 *The Patriot*, 21 July 1835.

87 Ibid., 23 August 1836.

88 *Upper Canada Gazette*, 26 August 1826.

89 Madam Harris arrived to teach French, *Upper Canada Gazette*, 30 August 1828. A music master was engaged, *Colonial Advocate*, 12 August 1830.

90 *Upper Canada Gazette*, 11 June 1829.

91 *Canadian Freeman*, 5 September 1833. The last announcement for Mrs Beynon appeared in July 1834.

92 *Christian Guardian*, 16 June 1831. These Misses McCords may also be the milliners who advertised their work at about the same time.

93 Ibid., 12 August 1835. There was a notice in *The Patriot*, 25 August 1840, to reopen the school.

94 *The Patriot*, 10 June 1834; 29 December 1840.

95 School opening, *Kingston Chronicle*, 27 August 1831; an announcement by brother, *Cobourg Star*, 4 October 1831.

96 *Farmers' Journal*, 18 March 1829; *Christian Guardian*, 27 February 1833; Announcements of examinations appeared in the *Niagara Herald*, 21 January 1830; *Niagara Gleaner*, 17 December 1831. *Niagara Gleaner*, 12 February 1831, a Miss Fraser was hired as an assistant.

97 *Niagara Gleaner*, 17 August 1833; 23 May 1835.

98 Ibid., 28 June 1823; 3 July 1823.

99 *Brockville Gazette*, 17 July 1829.

100 *Brockville Gazette*, 24 July 1829; *Kingston Chronicle*, 8 August 1829; 9 January 1830.

101 *Cobourg Star*, 24 May 1831.
102 Gidney and Millar, *Inventing Secondary Education*, 65–6. For a more detailed examination of the ephemeral nature of Upper Canadian schools, see Gidney and Millar, "From Voluntarism to State School," 443–73. Houston and Prentice, *Schooling and Scholars*, 67–8, quite rightly question Gidney and Millar's conclusion. Given the nature of the Upper Canadian economy and of those women who taught, it is very likely that many proprietors, like milliners, did not advertise in local newspapers, but rather relied on word of mouth and their reputation within the community to gain pupils.
103 *Farmers' Journal*, 1 April 1829.
104 Ibid., 5 August 1829. At this time, boarding was arranged with families in the area.
105 Ibid., 11 November 1830; 3 January 1831.
106 Ibid., 16 November 1831. For a time, it appears the school was financially solvent and thus the salary of its teachers assured. On 20 May 1834, the *British American Journal* announced, however, that Grantham Academy was closing due to overwhelming financial difficulties. After failing to obtain a grant from the provincial government, trustees were forced, *The Patriot*, 5 August 1834, to auction off the school building and pay off their creditors. See also *British American Journal*, 5 August 1834. The various public notices about the college suggest there were more than financial difficulties. In its first four-year history, there were four different principals and a number of male assistants. The school was revived, due largely to the efforts of William Merritt. In the 1840s, it became the St Catharines Grammar School. See Gidney and Millar, *Inventing Secondary Education*, 23, 70–1.
107 *Farmers' Journal*, 1 April 1829.
108 *Christian Guardian*, 1 October 1831.
109 *Farmers' Journal*, 3 January 1831; 10 November 1830.
110 Commercial and Classical Academy, *Christian Guardian*, 14 August 1833. A notice informed residents of York that eighty students were already enrolled. For at least the next three years, young men and women took a variety of classical and standard subjects from "qualified masters and mistresses." For Bay Street Academy, see notice of its first public examination, *The Patriot*, 30 August 1833. Notice of other examinations appeared 30 December 1834; 5 January 1836. Toronto Academy, ibid., 14 November 1837.
111 *Christian Guardian*, "Concerning the Commercial and Classical School," 14 August 1833. See also *Colonial Advocate*, 15 August 1833.
112 *Christian Guardian*, 20 June 1832. See also 29 September 1830; 31 July 1839.
113 Ibid., 7 August 1833.

114 Ibid., 6 May 1840.

115 Ibid., 23 September 1840.

116 Ibid., 27 December 1832. It was also noted that it was automatic grounds for expulsion if male students entered the girls' section of the school.

117 Ibid., 2 May 1838.

118 *Farmers' Journal*, 1 April 1829.

119 *British Colonial Argus*, "Communications," 6 August 1833.

120 *Christian Guardian*, 19 February 1840; 29 April 1840. Miss Barnes opened her own school with Mrs Van Norman, ibid., 4 May 1842. There were a few other women of similar circumstances. A Mrs Hulbert who was preceptress at Upper Canada Academy for a number of years, ibid., also started her own school a year later.

121 *Farmers' Journal*, 26 September 1827. See also *Christian Guardian*, 5 February 1831; *British American Journal*, 19 March 1835.

122 Theobald, "Mere Accomplishments," 73.

CHAPTER TEN

1 Although this work does not consider the matter, they also came from different racial backgrounds.

2 Cott, *The Bonds of Womanhood*, argues that American women during this period were part of a women's culture. I would argue that a women's "culture" per se did not exist in Upper Canada. And others have argued that it did not really exist in the United States. See Ryan, *Cradle of the Middle Class*; Lebsock, *The Free Women of Petersburg*.

3 "An Address Upon the Effects of Ardent Spirits" *Farmers' Journal*, 30 April 1828. This address obviously taken from a US newspaper, was continued 7, 14 May 1828. See also *Upper Canada Gazette*, 10 September 1818.

4 "On Intemperance," *Farmers' Journal*, 22 February 1826.

5 "An Address," *Farmers' Journal*, 30 April 1828.

6 *Ibid*. See also "Intemperance by Mephaliotes," *Farmers' Journal*, 23 December 1829.

7 "Intemperance," *Farmers' Journal*, 23 December 1829.

8 *British American Journal*, 20 August 1833.

9 In 1831, for example, the members of the Belleville Temperance Society resolved that "the influence of females in this cause was considered beneficial, and that they kindly solicited to become members of this society": *Christian Guardian*, 19 March 1831. Similar sentiments were expressed in Prince Edward County and in Toronto in 1834: *British American Journal*, 12 August 1834.

10 McKenna, "The Union Between Faith and Good Works," 31.

11 This is not to suggest that men were not involved. Despite arguments of other historians that ante-bellum reform in the United States was largely

a women's movement, it is clear that in Canada at the time, men were actively involved. But women did seem to find a special place for themselves. Much more work needs to be done exploring who became involved in the temperance crusade and why.

Bibliography

This bibliography is a guide to some of those secondary works that either directly contributed to my understanding of women's experiences in Upper Canada or had some considerable influence on how I interpreted their lives. It includes collections of articles and many general works on both Upper Canada and on women's history. This bibliography is by no means complete, however. The foregoing notes provide detailed references to the primary sources consulted for this study and complete references of other secondary works considered.

Acton, Janice, Penny Goldsmith, and Bonnie Shepard, eds. *Women at Work, 1850–1930.* Toronto: Canadian Women's Educational Press 1974.

Akenson, Donald Harman. *The Irish in Ontario: A Study in Rural History.* Montreal & Kingston: McGill-Queen's University Press 1984.

Alexander, Sally. *Women's Work in Nineteenth-Century London: A Study of the Years 1820–1850.* London: Journeyman Press and London History Workshop Centre 1983 (1976).

Anderson, Michael. *Approaches to the History of the Western Family, 1500–1914.* London: MacMillan 1980.

Angus, Margaret. "A Gentlewoman in Early Kingston." *Historic Kingston* 24 (1975): 73–85.

Ariès, Philippe. *Centuries of Childhood: A Social History of Family Life.* Translated by Robert Baldick. New York: Random House 1960, 1962.

Armstrong, Frederick H. *A City in the Making: Progress, People and Perils in Victorian Toronto.* Toronto: Dundurn Press 1988.

Backhouse, Constance. "The Art of Seduction: Fathers and Daughters in Nineteenth Century Canada." *Dalhousie Law Journal* 10 (1986): 45–80.

– "Desperate Women and Compassionate Courts: Infanticide in Nineteenth-Century Canada." *University of Toronto Law Journal* 34 (1984): 447–78.

– *Petticoats and Prejudice: Women and Law in Nineteenth-Century Canada.* Toronto: Osgoode Society 1991.

– "'Pure Patriarchy': Nineteenth-Century Canadian Marriage." *McGill Law Journal* 31 (1986): 264–312.

Banfield, Paul. "The Well Regulated Family: John Strachan and the Role of the Family in Early Upper Canada 1800–1812." MA thesis, Queen's University 1985.

Basch, Norma. *In the Eyes of the Law: Women, Marriage, and Property in Nineteenth-Century New York.* Ithaca: Cornell University Press 1982.

Beattie, J.M. *Crime and the Courts in England, 1660–1800.* Princeton, N.J.: Princeton University Press 1986.

Bitterman, Rusty. "Farm Households and Wage Labour in the Northeastern Maritimes in the Early 19th Century." *Labour/Le Travail* 31 (1993): 13–45.

Bradbury, Bettina, ed. *Canadian Family History: Selected Readings.* Toronto: Copp Clark Pitman 1992.

– "Pigs, Cows and Boarders: Non-Wage Forms of Survival among Montreal Families, 1861–91." *Labour/Le Travail* 14, (1984): 9–48.

– *Working Families: Age, Gender, and Daily Survival in Industrializing Montreal.* Toronto: McClelland and Stewart 1993.

Branca, Patricia. *Silent Sisterhood: Middle Class Women in the Victorian Home.* Pittsburgh: Carnegie-Mellon University Press 1975.

Buel, Joy Day, and Richard Buel Jr. *The Way of Duty: A Woman and Her Family in Revolutionary America.* New York: W.W. Norton 1984.

Burstyn, Joan N. *Victorian Education and the Ideal of Womanhood.* London: Croom Helm 1980.

Bushman, Richard. L.*The Refinement of America: Persons, Houses, Cities.* New York: Knopf 1992.

Clinton, Catherine. *The Other Civil War, American Women in the Nineteenth Century.* New York: Hill and Wang 1984.

Cohen, Marjorie Griffin. *Women's Work, Markets, and Economic Development in Nineteenth-Century Ontario.* Toronto: University of Toronto Press 1988.

Comacchio, Cynthia R. "'Beneath the Sentimental Veil': Families and Family History in Canada." Review essay, *Labour/le Travail* 33 (1994): 279–302.

Corbett, Gail, ed. *Portraits: Peterborough Area Women Past and Present.* Peterborough Ont.: Portraits Group 1975.

Cott, Nancy F. *The Bonds of Womanhood: 'Woman's Sphere' in New England, 1780–1835.* New Haven: Yale University Press 1977.

– and Elizabeth H. Pleck, eds. *A Heritage of Her Own: Toward a New Social History of American Women.* New York: Simon and Schuster 1979.

Cowan, Helen I. *British Emigration to British North America: The First Hundred Years*. Toronto: University of Toronto Press 1961.

Cowan, Ruth Schwartz. *More Work for Mother: The Ironies of Household Technology from the Open Hearth to the Microwave*. New York: Basic Books 1983.

Craig, Gerald. *Upper Canada: The Formative Years, 1784–1841*. Toronto: McClelland and Stewart 1963.

Cuthbert Brandt, Gail. "Postmodern Patchwork: Some Recent Trends in the Writing of Women's History in Canada." *Canadian Historical Review* 72, 4 (1991), 441–70.

Dally, Ann. *Inventing Motherhood: The Consequences of an Ideal*. London: Burnett Books 1982.

Davidoff, Leonore. *The Best Circles: Society, Etiquette and the Season*. London: Croom Helm 1986 (1973).

– and Catherine Hall. *Family Fortunes: Men and Women of the English Middle Class, 1780–1850*. Chicago: University of Chicago Press 1987.

Davidson, Caroline. *A Woman's Work is Never Done: A History of Housework in the British Isles, 1650–1950*. London: Chatto & Winders 1982.

Degler, Carl N. *At Odds: Women and the Family in America, from the Revolution to the Present*. New York: Oxford University Press 1980.

Demos, John. *A Little Commonwealth: Family Life in Plymouth Colony*. New York: Oxford University Press 1970.

Donegan, Jane. *Women and Men Midwives: Medicine, Morality, and Misogyny in Early America*. Westport, Conn: Greenwood Press 1978.

Douglas, Ann. *The Feminization of American Culture*. New York: Anchor Press/Doubleday 1988.

Dubinsky, Karen. *Improper Advances: Rape and Heterosexual Conflict in Ontario, 1880–1929*. Chicago: University of Chicago Press 1993.

Dudden, Faye E. *Serving Women: Household Service in Nineteenth-Century America*. Middletown, Conn.: Wesleyan University Press 1983.

Duffin, Jacalyn. *Langstaff: A Nineteenth-Century Medical Life*. Toronto: University of Toronto Press 1993.

Elliott, Bruce S. *Irish Migrants in the Canadas: A New Approach*. Kingston & Montreal: McGill-Queen's University Press 1988.

Errington, Jane. *The Lion, The Eagle and Upper Canada*. Montreal & Kingston: McGill-Queen's University Press 1987.

– "Ladies and Schoolmistresses: Educating Women in early Nineteenth-Century Upper Canada," *Historical Studies in Education* 6, 1 (Spring 1994), 71–96.

– "Single Pioneering Women in Upper Canada." *Families* 31, 1 (1992): 5–20.

– "The Softer Sex: A Preliminary Probe into the Reality and the Rhetoric of Women's Experiences in Upper Canada, 1793–1830." Paper presented to the Canadian Historical Association Annual Meeting 1988.

- "'Woman … is a Very Interesting Creature'": Some Women's Experiences in Early Upper Canada. *Historic Kingston* 30 (1990): 16–35.

Fildes, Valerie, ed. *Women as Mothers in Pre-Industrial England*. London, New York: Routledge 1990.

Fingard, Judith. *The Dark Side of Life in Victorian Halifax*. Porters Lake, N.S.: Pottersfield Press 1989.

- *Jack in Port: Sailortowns of Eastern Canada*. Toronto: University of Toronto Press 1982.

Firth, Edith. *The Town of York, 1793–1815*. Toronto: Champlain Society 1962.

- *The Town of York, 1815–1834*. Toronto: Champlain Society 1966.

Fowler, Marian. *The Embroidered Tent: Five Gentlewomen in Early Canada*. Toronto: Anansi 1982.

Freedman, Estelle. *Their Sisters' Keepers: Women's Prison Reform in America 1830–1930*. Ann Arbor: University of Michigan Press 1981.

French, Goldwin. *Parsons and Politics*. Toronto: Ryerson Press 1962.

Fryer, Mary Beacock. *Elizabeth Postuma Simcoe, 1762–1850: A Biography*. Toronto: Dundurn Press 1989.

Gaffield, Chad. "Children, Schooling and Family Reproduction." *Canadian Historical Review* 72, 2 (1991): 157–91.

Gagan, David. *Hopeful Travellers: Families, Land, and Social Change in Mid-Victorian Peel County, Canada West*. Toronto: University of Toronto Press 1981.

Gardner, Philip W. *The Lost Elementary Education of Victorian England: The People's Education*. London: Croom Helm 1984.

Gidney, R.D., and W.P.J. Millar. "From Voluntarism to State School: The Creation of the Public School System in Ontario." *Canadian Historical Review* 66, 4 (1985): 443–73.

- *Inventing Secondary Education: The Rise of the High School in Nineteenth-Century Ontario*. Montreal & Kingston: McGill-Queen's University Press 1990.

Gillis, John. *For Better, For Worse: British Marriages, 1600 to the Present*. New York: Oxford University Press 1985.

Gittins, Diana. *The Family in Question: Changing Households and Familiar Ideologies*. New Jersey: Handmills, Basingstoke, Hampshire: MacMillan 1985.

Gordon, Linda. *Heroes of Their Own Lives: The Politics and History of Family Violence: Boston 1880–1960*. New York: Penguin Books 1989.

Gorham, Deborah. "Birth and History." *Histoire Sociale/Social History* xvii, 34 (1984): 383–94.

- *The Victorian Girl and the Feminine Ideal*. Bloomington: Indianna University Press 1982.

Graff, Harvey J. *The Literacy Myth: Literacy and Social Structure in the Nineteenth-Century City*. New York: Academic Press 1979.

– "Remaking Growing Up: Nineteenth-Century America." *Histoire Sociale/
Social History* XXXIV, 47 (1991): 35–59.

Grant, John Webster. *A Profusion of Spires: Religion in Nineteenth-Century
Ontario.* Toronto: University of Toronto Press 1988.

Greven, Philip. *The Protestant Temperament: Patterns of Child-Rearing, Religious
Experience, and the Self in Early America.* New York: Knopf 1977.

Griffiths, Naomi. *Penelope's Web: Some Perceptions of Women in European and
Canadian History.* Toronto: Oxford University Press 1976.

Hall, Catherine. *White, Male and Middle Class: Explorations in Feminism and
History.* Cambridge: Polity Press 1988.

Hall, Roger, William Westfall, and Laurel Sefton, eds. *Patterns of the Past:
Interpreting Ontario's History.* Toronto: Dundurn Press 1988.

Halpenny, Frances, ed. *Dictionary of Canadian Biography,* Vols IV-VIII. Toronto:
University of Toronto Press 1979, 1983, 1987, 1988, 1989.

Hammerton, A. James. *Cruelty and Companionship: Conflict in Nineteenth-
Century Married Life.* London: Routledge 1992.

– *Emigrant Gentlewomen: Genteel Poverty and Female Emigration, 1830–1914.*
Canberra: Australian National University Press 1979.

Hansen, Marcus L., and J.B. Brebner. *The Mingling of the Canadian and
American Peoples.* New York: Russell and Russell 1940.

Hareven, Tamara. "Family History at the Crossroads." *Journal of Family
History* 12 (1987): ix-xxiii.

– "The History of the Family and the Complexity of Social Change."
American Historical Review 96, 1 (1991): 95–124.

Heap, Ruby, and Alison Prentice, eds. *Gender and Education in Ontario.*
Toronto: Canadian Scholars' Press 1991.

Hewitt, Nancy. *Women's Activism and Social Change: Rochester, New York, 1822–
1872.* Ithaca: Cornell University Press 1984.

Hoffer, Peter C., and N.E.H. Hull. *Murdering Mothers: Infanticide in England
and New England, 1558–1803.* New York: New York University Press 1981.

Horn, Pamela. *The Rural World 1700–1850: Social Change in the English
Countryside.* New York: Hutchison 1980.

Houston, Susan. "The Impetus to Reform: Urban Crime, Poverty and
Ignorance in Ontario, 1850–1875." PHD. thesis, University of Toronto
1974.

– and Alison Prentice. *Schooling and Scholars in Nineteenth-Century Ontario.*
Toronto: University of Toronto Press 1988.

Innis, Mary Quayle, ed. *The Clear Spirit: Twenty Canadian Women and their
Times.* Toronto: University Press 1966.

Isaac, Rhys. *The Transformation of Virginia, 1740–1970.* Chapel Hill: University
of North Carolina Press 1982.

Jeffrey, Julie. *Frontier Women: The Trans Mississippi West, 1840–1880.* New York:
Hill and Wang 1979.

Jensen, Joan. *Loosening the Bonds: Mid-Atlantic Farm Women, 1750–1850*. New Haven: Yale University Press 1986.

John, Angela, ed. *Unequal Opportunities: Women's Employment in England, 1800–1918*. Oxford: Basil Blackwell 1986.

Johnson, J. K. *Becoming Prominent: Regional Leadership in Upper Canada, 1791–1841*. Kingston: McGill-Queen's University Press 1989.

– "Friends in High Places: Getting Divorced in Upper Canada," *Ontario History* LXXXVI, 3 (September 1994), 201–18.

– ed., *Historical Essays On Upper Canada*. Toronto: McClelland and Stewart 1975.

– , and Bruce G. Wilson, eds. *Historical Essays on Upper Canada: New Perspectives*. Ottawa: Carleton University Press 1989.

Johnson, Paul E. *A Shopkeeper's Millenium: Society and Revivals in Rochester, New York, 1815–1837*. New York: Hill and Wang 1978.

Katz, Michael. *The People of Hamilton, Canada West: Family and Class in a Mid-Nineteenth-Century City*. Cambridge, Mass: Harvard University Press 1975.

Kelly, Joan. *Women, History and Theory*. Chicago: University of Chicago Press 1984.

Kerber, Linda K. "Separate Spheres, Female Worlds and Woman's Place: The Rhetoric of Women's History" *Journal of American History* 75, 1 (1988).

– *Women of the Republic: Intellect and Ideology in Revolutionary America*. New York: W. W. Norton and Co. 1986.

Lacelle, Claudette. *Urban Domestic Servants in 19th Century Canada*. Ottawa: Ministry of Supply and Services Canada 1987.

Landon, Fred. *Western Ontario and the American Frontier*, (1941). Toronto: McClelland and Stewart 1967.

Laslett, Peter. *The World We Have Lost* (1965). London: Methuen 1971.

– and R. Wall, eds. *Household and Family in Past Time: Comparative Studies in the Size and Structure of the Domestic Group*. London: Cambridge University Press 1972.

Leavitt, Judith Walzar. *Brought to Bed: Birthing Women and their Physicians in America, 1750–1950*. New York: Oxford University Press 1986.

Lebsock, Suzanne. *The Free Women of Petersburg: Status and Culture in a Southern Town, 1784–1860*. New York: W.W. Norton 1984.

Lerner, Gerda. *The Creation of Patriarchy*. Toronto: Oxford University Press 1986.

Lewis, Jane, ed. *The Politics of Motherhood: Child and Maternal Welfare in England, 1900–1939*. London: Croom Helm 1980.

Light, Beth, and Alison Prentice, eds. *Pioneer and Gentlewomen of British North America, 1713–1867*. Toronto: New Hogtown Press 1980.

Litoff, Judith. *American Midwives, 1860 to the Present*. Westport, Conn: Greenwood Press 1978.

Luxton, Meg. *More Than a Labour of Love: Three Generations of Women's Work in the Home*. Toronto: Women's Press 1980.

Maas, Barbara. *Helpmates of Man: Middle-Class Women and Gender Ideology in Nineteenth-Century Ontario*. Bochum: N. Brockmeyer 1990.

Mahood, Linda. *The Magdalenes: Prostitution in the Nineteenth Century.* London: Routledge 1990.

Malcolmson, R. W. "Infanticide in the 18th Century." In *Crime in England, 1550–1800*, edited by J. S. Cockburn, 187–209. London: Routledge 1977.

Matthaei, Julie A. *An Economic History of Women in America: Women's Work, the Sexual Division of Labor, and the Development of Capitalism*. New York: Schocken Books 1982.

Matthews, Glenna. *"Just a Housewife": The Rise and Fall of Domesticity in America*. New York: Oxford University Press 1987.

McCalla, Douglas. *Planting the Province: The Economic History of Upper Canada, 1784–1870*. Toronto: University of Toronto Press 1993.

McIntosh, Robert. "Sweated Labour: Female Needleworkers in Industrializing Canada." *Labour/le Travail* 32 (1993): 105–36.

McKenna, Katherine Mary Jean. "The Life of Anne Murray Powell, 1755–1849: A 'Case Study' of the Position of Women in Early Upper Canadian Elite Society." PHD thesis, Queen's University 1987.

– "'The Union Between Faith and Good Works: The Life of Harriet Dobbs Cartwright 1808–1887." Paper presented to the Canadian Historical Association Annual Meeting 1991.

– *A Life of Propriety: Anne Murray Powell and Her Family, 1755–1849*. Kingston & Montreal: McGill-Queen's University Press 1994.

McLaren, Angus. *Birth Control in Nineteenth-Century England*. London: Croom Helm 1978.

McLean, Marianne. *The People of Glengarry: Highlanders in Transition, 1745–1820*. Montreal & Kingston: McGill-Queen's University Press 1991.

Melder, Keith. "Ladies Bountiful: Organized Women's Benevolence in Early Nineteenth Century America." *New York History* 48, (1964): 231–54.

Mitchell, Juliet, and Ann Oakely, eds. *The Rights and Wrongs of Women*. New York: Penguin Books 1976.

Mitchinson, Wendy. *The Nature of Their Bodies: Women and Their Doctors in Victorian Canada*. Toronto: University of Toronto Press 1991.

Monaghan, E. Jennifer. "Literacy Instruction and Gender in Colonial New England." *American Quarterly* 40 (1988): 18–41.

Morgan, Cecilia. "Gender, Religion and Rural Society: Quaker Women in Norwich, Ontario, 1820–1880." *Ontario History* LXXXII, 4 (1990): 273–88.

Morris, Audrey Y. *Gentle Pioneers: Five Nineteenth-Century Canadians*. Don Mills, Ont.: Paperjacks 1973.

Myres, Sandra. *Westering Women and the Frontier Experience, 1800–1915*. Albuquerque: University of New Mexico Press 1982.

Needler, G. H. *Otonabee Pioneers: The Story of the Stewarts, the Stricklands, the Traills and the Moodies*. Toronto: Burns & MacEachern 1953.

Newton, Judith L., Mary P. Ryan and Judith R. Walkowitz, eds. *Sex and Class in Women's History.* London: Routledge & Kegan Paul 1983.

Norton, Mary Beth. *Liberty's Daughters: The Revolutionary Experience of American Women 1750–1800.* Boston: Little, Brown 1980.

Osterud, Nancy Grey. *Bonds of Community: The Lives of Farm Women in Nineteenth-Century New York.* Ithaca: Cornell University Press 1991.

Palmer, Bryan. "Discordant Music: Charivaris and Whitecapping in Nineteenth Century North America." *Labour/Le Travailleur* 3 (1978): 5–62.

Parr, Joy, ed. *Childhood and Family in Canadian History.* Toronto: McClelland and Stewart 1982.

– *The Gender of Breadwinners: Women, Men, and Change in Two Industrial Towns, 1880–1950.* Toronto: University of Toronto Press 1990.

Peiss, Kathy, and Christina Simmons, eds. *Passion and Power: Sexuality in History.* Philadelphia: Temple University Press 1989.

Peterson, M. Jeanne. *Family, Love, and Work in the Lives of Victorian Gentlewomen.* Bloomington: Indiana University Press 1989.

Pierson, Ruth Roach. "Experience, Difference and Dominance and Voice in the Writing of Canadian Women's History." In *Writing Women's History: International Perspectives,* edited by Karen Offen, et. al., 79–106. London: MacMillan 1991.

Potter-MacKinnon, Janice. *While the Women Only Wept: Loyalist Refugee Women in Eastern Ontario.* Montreal & Kingston: McGill-Queen's University Press 1993.

Prentice, Alison, Paula Bourne, Gail Cuthbert Brandt, Beth Light, Wendy Mitchinson, and Naomi Black, eds. *Canadian Women: A History.* Toronto: Harcourt Brace Janovich 1988.

Prentice, Alison, and Marjorie Theobald, eds. *Women Who Taught: Perspectives on the History of Women and Teaching.* Toronto: University of Toronto Press 1991.

Prochaska, F. K. *Women and Philanthropy in Nineteenth-Century England.* Oxford: Clarendon Press 1980.

Rawlyk, G. A. *The Canada Fire: Radical Evangelicalism in British North America 1775–1812.* Montreal & Kingston: McGill-Queen's University Press 1994.

– *Wrapped Up in God: A Study of Several Canadian Revivals and Revivalists.* Montreal & Kingston: McGill-Queen's University Press 1988.

Rollins, Judith. *Between Women: Domestics and Their Employers.* Philadephia: Temple University Press 1985.

Rose, Lionel. *The Massacre of the Innocents: Infanticide in Britain, 1800–1939.* London: Routledge & Kegan Paul 1986.

Rothman, David J. *The Discovery of the Asylum: Social Order and Disorder in the New Republic.* Boston: Little, Brown 1971.

Rothman, Ellen K. *Hands and Hearts: A History of Courtship in America.* Cambridge, Mass.: Harvard University Press 1987.

Ruggles, Steven. "The Transformation of the American Family Structure." *American Historical Review* 99, 1 (1994): 103–28.

Rule, John. *The Labouring Classes in Early Industrial England, 1750–1850*. London: Longman 1986.

Russell, Peter. *Attitudes to Social Structure and Mobility in Upper Canada, 1815–1840*. Lewiston, N.Y.: Edwin Mellen Press 1990.

– "Wage Labour Rates in Upper Canada, 1818–1840," *Social History* XVI, 31 (1983): 61–80.

Ryan, Mary. *Cradle of the Middle Class: The Family in Oneida County, New York, 1790–1865*. New York: Cambridge University Press 1988 (1981).

– *Womanhood in America: From Colonial Times to the Present*. New York: Viewpoints 1975.

Scholten, Catherine M. "On the Importance of the Obstetrick Art: Changing Customs of Childbirth in America, 1760 to 1825." *William and Mary Quarterly* 34 (1977): 426–45.

Scott, Anne Firor. *Making the Invisible Woman Visible*. Urbana and Chicago, University of Illinois Press 1984.

Scott, Joan Wallach. *Gender and the Politics of History*. New York: Columbia University Press 1988.

Shammas, Carol. "The Domestic Environment in Early Modern England and America." In *Colonial Women and Domesticity: Selected Articles on Gender in Early America*, edited by Peter Charles Hoffer, 194–215. New York: Garland Publishing Inc. 1988.

Sklar, Kathryn Kish. *Catharine Beecher: A Study in American Domesticity*, (1973). New York: W.W. Norton & Company 1978.

Smart, Carol, ed. *Regulating Womanhood: Historical Essays on Marriage, Motherhood and Sexuality*. New York: Routledge 1992.

Smith-Rosenberg, Carroll. *Disorderly Conduct: Visions of Gender in Victorian America*. New York: Oxford University Press 1986.

Spruill, Julie Cherry. *Women's Life and Work in the Southern Colonies* (1938). New York: W.W. Norton 1972.

Stansell, Christine. *City of Women: Sex and Class in New York, 1789–1860*. Urbana: University of Illinois Press 1987.

Stone, Lawrence. *The Family, Sex and Marriage in England, 1500–1800*. London: Wiedenfeld and Nicolson 1977.

Strasser, Susan. *Never Done: A History of American Housework*. New York: Random House 1982.

Strong-Boag, Veronica, and Anita Clair Fellman, eds. *Rethinking Canada: The Promise of Women's History* (1986). 2d ed. Toronto: Copp Clark Pitman 1991.

Theobald, Marjorie R. "The Sin of Laura: A Pre-History of Women's Tertiary Education in Colonial Melbourne." *Journal of the Canadian Historical Association* 1 (1990): 257–72.

Thomas, Clara. *Love and Work Enough: The Life of Anna Jameson*. Toronto: University of Toronto Press 1967.

Thurer, Shari. *The Myths of Motherhood: How Culture Reinvents the Good Mother.* Boston: Houghton Mifflin 1994.

Tilly, Louise A., and Joan W. Scott. *Women, Work, and Family.* New York: Routledge 1989.

Trofimenkoff, Susan Mann, and Alison Prentice, eds. *The Neglected Majority: Essays in Canadian Women's History.* Vols 1 and 2. Toronto: McClelland and Stewart 1977, 1985.

Tulchinsky, Gerald, ed. *To Preserve and Defend: Essays on Kingston in the Nineteenth Century.* Montreal: McGill-Queen's University Press 1976.

Ulrich, Laurel Thatcher. *Good Wives: Image and Reality in the Lives of Women in Northern New England, 1650–1750* (1981). New York: Vintage Books 1991.

– *A Midwife's Tale: The Life of Martha Ballard, Based on Her Diary, 1785–1812* (1990). New York: Random House 1991.

Valenze, Deborah. "The Art of Women and the Business of Men Women's Work and the Dairy Industry, c1740–1840." *Past and Present* 130 (1991): 142–69.

Vicinus, Martha. *Independent Women: Work and Community for Single Women, 1850–1920.* Chicago: University of Chicago Press 1985.

– ed. *Suffer and Be Still: Women in the Victorian Age.* Bloomington: Indiana University Press 1973.

Ward, Peter. *Courtship, Love and Marriage in Nineteenth-Century English Canada.* Montreal & Kingston: McGill-Queen's University Press 1990.

– "Unwed Mothers in Nineteenth-Century English Canada." *CHA Papers,* 1981: 34–56.

Welter, Barbara. "The Cult of True Womanhood." *American Quarterly* 18 (1966):151–74.

Westfall, William. *Two Worlds: The Protestant Culture of Nineteenth Century Ontario.* Montreal & Kingston: McGill-Queen's University Press 1989.

Wilson, Bruce. *The Enterprises of Robert Hamilton.* Ottawa: Carleton University Press 1984.

Index

194; for wages, 77, 91,
108, 111, 116
Claris, Mrs (milliner, dressmaker), 185, 201, 203–4;
hiring apprentices, 206,
207
Class and status, 15–16,
18–19, 23, 175, 256n51,
257n61; impact on
women's lives, xvi, 5, 6,
15, 182, 238, 239. See also
Artisan/urban house-
holds; Elite; Farm/
artisan households;
"Ordinary" women; Ru-
ral communities; Urban
communities
Cohen, Marjorie, 83, 102,
104, 113–14
Colborne, Lady: "at
home," 166–7; bazaar,
180–1; patroness of la-
dies' academy, 220; pa-
troness of missionary
societies, 173–4; philan-
thropic work, 182, 239
Colborne, Lieutenant-Gov-
ernor, 177
Committee for the Relief of
the Poor and the Desti-
tute, 181, 182
Community of women: in
elite households, 134–5,
137, 182; among elite
women, 132–3, 157–8,
170, 182–3, 236; as
helps, 70–2, 106, 127,
129; interdependence of,
xvi, 233–5, 237–9, 241;
and motherhood, 54, 59,
62, 65–6, 72, 79; in rural
communities, 71, 83–4,
86, 99, 100, 104, 129,
308n136; urban artisan
women, 183, 208
Companionate marriages,
26, 37–8, 39, 51, 78,
267n61
Confinement, 58, 64, 70, 71,
126–7. See also Mother-
hood; Mothers
Corsetmakers, 200. See also

Milliners; Staymakers
Cott, Nancy, 235
Courtship, 29, 30–1
Craftswomen, 188, 200,
205. See also Female
trades; Milliners
Cult of true womanhood.
See True womanhood

Dairy, 92, 102, 105, 118,
297n86; dairy maid, 109,
117, 122, 142, 145, 299n9,
303n62; and the market,
83, 102, 297n97
Daughters, xii
– education: formal
schooling, 210, 213, 215–
16; training, 76–7, 213.
See also Schools
– and work: in family, 21,
76–7, 97, 103, 106, 116,
119, 193–4, on the farm,
15, 76–7, 86, 99–101
passim, 103; waged,
108, 111–12, 114, 125,
126, 129
Davidoff, Leonore, 22, 148
Denison, Mrs John, 156;
John, 153, 312n39
Deserted wife, 23, 49–50,
147
Desertion, 44–51; survey of
notices, 51, 270n98;
272n117, 273n126
Detroit, 3, 11
Dictates of domesticity. See
True womanhood
Divorce, 42–3, 270n91
Doctors, 55, 60, 62, 63–4,
71, 179, 278n33, 279n57
Domestic work: definition
of xvi, 79. See also Farm
women; Elite women;
Helps; Servants
Dorcas society, 174–5
Dressmakers. See Milliners
Dudden, Faye, 115, 150

Education: boys and girls
taught separately, 76–7,
215, 344n11, 351n74; im-
portance of, 76–8, 211,

212–13; interrupted by
children's work, 76–7;
necessary for girls, 76,
77, 188, 213–15, 217,
231–2, 346n29. See also
Schools
Elinore (Helen Macaulay's
children's maid), 150–1,
152
Elite: aristocracy, 18, 133;
definition of, 15–16, 18,
132–3, 256n51, 258n65;
households, xii, xvi, 77,
100, 134, 157–8
Elite women: symbols of
status, xi–xv, 4, 14, 23,
157, 159, 161, 167, 182,
236, 240–1
– in family: as household
managers, 141–3, 148,
150–2, 157–8, 182–3,
239, 311n26; pregnancy
and childbirth, 59, 62–6;
work of, 3–4, 18–19,
132–3, 150, 161
– and servants: "bad" servants, 152–4, 156;
"good" servants, 142–5,
151, 156; hiring prac-
tices, 140, 142–5, 147,
153, 313n49, 317n80;
need for, 134, 137, 140–
1, 143, 156, 157; training
of, 136, 143, 148–9, 151,
154, 313n45
– as society matrons: be-
nevolent work, 133, 157,
168, 182, 237, 238,
324n49; social responsi-
bilities of, 133, 136, 157,
159, 162–8, 293n48.
See also Ann Macaulay;
Anna Jameson; Anne
Powell; Helen
Macaulay; Housing; Ser-
vants
Elwes, Mrs (help in
Johnson household):
as midwife, 58, 70–1;
as midwife/nurse, 127
Emigrant aid organiza-
tions, 144, 176–8